Designing Distributed and Cooperative Information Systems

Roger Tagg
and
Chris Freyberg

Department of Information Systems
Massey University
New Zealand

INTERNATIONAL THOMSON COMPUTER PRESS
I(T)P™ An International Thomson Publishing Company

London • Bonn • Boston • Johannesburg • Madrid • Melbourne • Mexico City • New York • Paris
Singapore • Tokyo • Toronto • Albany, NY • Belmont, CA • Cincinnati, OH • Detroit, MI

Designing Distributed and Cooperative Information Systems

Copyright © 1997 International Thomson Computer Press

I(T)P   A division of International Thomson Publishing Inc.
The ITP logo is a trademark under licence.

For more information, contact:

International Thomson Computer Press	International Thomson Computer Press
Berkshire House	20 Park Plaza
168-173 High Holborn	Suite 1001
London WC1V 7AA	Boston, MA 02116
UK	USA

Imprints of International Thomson Publishing

International Thomson Publishing GmbH	International Thomson Publishing Asia
Königswinterer Straße 418	60 Albert Street #15-01
53227 Bonn	Albert Complex
Germany	Singapore 189969
Thomas Nelson Australia	International Thomson Publishing Japan
102 Dodds Street	Hirakawacho Kyowa Building, 3F
South Melbourne, 3205	2-2-1 Hirakawacho
Victoria	Chiyoda-ku, 102 Tokyo
Australia	Japan
Nelson Canada	International Thomson Editores
1120 Birchmount Road	Seneca, 53
Scarborough, Ontario	Colonia Polanco
Canada M1K 5G4	11560 Mexico D. F. Mexico
International Thomson Publishing South Africa	International Thomson Publishing France
PO Box 2459	Tours Maine-Montparnasse
Halfway House	33 avenue du Maine
1685 South Africa	75755 Paris Cedex 15
	France

British Library Cataloguing-in-Publication Data
A catalogue record for this book is available from the British Library

Library of Congress Cataloging-in-Publication Data
A catalog record for this book is available from the Library of Congress

First Printed 1997

ISBN 1-85032-165-5

Cover Designed by Button Eventures
Printed in the UK by Cambridge University Press, Cambridge

Designing Distributed and Cooperative Information Systems

Contents

Preface

This book arose out of a need for a suitable text to support a final-year undergraduate paper in Distributed Systems for students majoring in Information Systems (IS). It unashamedly takes a demand-side, business-oriented stance, attempting to answer the question 'what are the modern organization's needs, and how do we design systems to support them?' – rather than adopting a supply-side approach and answering the question 'what communications technology is available and what can we do with it?'.

The title of the book, naturally enough, reflects this stance. We consider the principal activity to be learnt is 'designing', rather than 'describing', 'analyzing' or 'constructing'. What is to be designed is the 'Information System', with all the connotations that this term implies. This means that we should address the design of all aspects of any system, rather than just one specific artifact such as a 'database' or a 'network'. Concentrating on Design also means that we dwell only very briefly on Analysis, Implementation and other development stages.

In addressing 'Distributed and Cooperative' information systems we recognize that the business needs of modern – often geographically dispersed – organizations are likely to be supported by a wide spectrum of computing styles. Some of these styles are generated by top-down design, but in others, systems arise out of federations and voluntary cooperation agreements.

'Distributed' implies a conscious decision to divide a given set of Information Processing and Storage tasks between a number of processors, often on a geographical basis, but possibly also on a functional or even a parallel processing basis.

'Cooperative' implies, in contrast, a collaboration between existing processors, or between processors that are designed primarily for autonomous organization units or individual users. Such collaboration may be formally 'federal' – or it may be based on relatively loose, casual interaction. Often, the end result does not appear much different from a Distributed information system.

The term 'Client/Server' has been deliberately omitted from the title as it appears to have so many different interpretations, and has suffered from being overworked as a marketing buzzword. However, the concept will be examined in some detail in the text.

Distributed and Cooperative computing have come to be regarded today as the norm for new IS development, rather than the exception. Yet development methodologies have lagged behind this trend, often being still oriented to centralized computing or a limited view of Client/Server. Furthermore, most of the methodologies exhibit two biases as follows.

- The Design is essentially concerned with structuring Data and Procedure, either separately or embedded together in Objects. In practice there are, and always have been, other design **dimensions**, e.g. the **location** of the human or robotic participants. With Distributed and Cooperative computing these other dimensions assume greater relative importance.

- The Conceptual or Logical Design always precedes Physical Design. This is desirable for Database Design, but is less relevant to other Design areas, where considerations of feasibility in the **engineering** sense are often more important.

It has not been easy to find suitable texts to go with our teaching program. Plenty of good books cover Data Communications, but they tend to be too heavy on technical detail for most of our students, and are almost all 'supply-driven'. 'Distributed Systems' has appeared in the title of a number of texts, but these show a very wide range of different meanings of the term 'Distributed', some being almost entirely concerned with multi-processor computer architectures. There has also been a recent rash of books on Client/Server approaches, but again, these are more narrowly focused than we feel suits the needs of our students.

Our own curriculum is geared to the potential career paths of our graduates. We do not aim to prepare students for specialist technical (IT) careers, and certainly not as Data Communications Experts. What we envisage – and to some extent observe already – is that our graduates will work for user organizations or consultancies, but will be able, because of their background, to act as an interface with technical experts and suppliers.

Because it is aimed at this wider group of students, the book does not aim to be highly academic or to introduce original research ideas. There are already many good tools available which other authors and companies have developed, and our preference has been to bring together the best design ideas we could find from these various sources.

Part One gives a background to the trends in both Business and Computing which have resulted in the current state of the art, and introduces a set of Case Examples for illustrative use throughout the book.

Part Two provides a basic compendium of Data Communications knowledge required to understand later sections of the book. It is not intended to replace the need for fuller technical texts, a number of which are highlighted in the reading lists. Our treatment is different in that Business Needs are considered first, followed by discussion of the alternative technologies available to meet those needs.

Part Three describes a number of different styles that have developed in Distributed and Cooperative sytems, and introduces four key 'themes', namely Distributed Transaction Processing, Client/Server, Distributed Databases and Message Passing.

Part Four introduces an composite methodology for designing Distributed and Cooperative systems. Particular techniques are introduced to address key design decisions. The topic of working with experts and suppliers is included as the final chapter, in line with our view of the nature of Information Systems graduate careers.

The Glossary provides brief definitions of the main technical terms and acronyms with which the topic abounds. The Bibliography contains an alphabetic list by author of literature referred to in the text, or of useful additional reading. Some of these references are duplicated as further reading that is applicable to each chapter.

The material included in this book has been assembled over a period of four years (1992–95) of teaching experience. Part of the material formerly appeared as the Data Communications module in a second-year paper on Application of IS, the remainder in a third-year Database paper. These papers have been recently regrouped so that there is now a single semester-length paper on Distributed Systems. There is consequently a significant Database thread in our approach. We have persisted with this because we feel Database and Data Communications meet a common objective, namely the sharing of data between all the players that need to cooperate in today's business environment. To make an analogy of Marshall McLuhan's famous quote 'the Medium is the Message', our motto is that 'the Network is the Database'.

We acknowledge the help of many colleagues and friends for their ideas and comments. Roger especially acknowledges the work of his former colleagues at Scicon (now part of EDS) and at TI Information Engineering (formerly James Martin Associates). Particular mention should be made of the ideas contributed by Ian Macdonald, Ed Tozer and the late Ian Palmer. Experience in using the ideas also owes much to the cooperation, during consultancy work, of staff in such organizations as British Petroleum, Shell, ICI Pharmaceuticals, Scottish Health Services, UFB Humberclyde and CERES.

Certain of the existing textbooks, which we have used or referenced in our teaching, have also provided tools for our design toolkit, which we also acknowledge. In this respect we would particularly mention William Stallings, Jerry Fitzgerald, John Burch, Tom Gilb, James Martin, David Bell, Jane Grimson and Messrs Whitten, Bentley and Barlow.

Massey University
Palmerston North, New Zealand
October 1995

Information Systems Engineering Series Foreword

The ITP Information Systems Engineering Series represents a vision. That vision is to provide a set of books that give readers what they need for their work and learning environment. This appears simple in theory, but is very difficult in practice. The theme is the application of the best theory from computer science to the engineering of systems to support applications in commerce and industry. The guiding principles have been quality, relevance to the information problems of today and a style that is easy to read (for learning about a subject) while being also easy to use for reference.

The target audience is:

a. Information Systems professionals in commerce and industry: IT Directors, DP managers, analysts, programmers and others;

b. Academics, both for teaching and for research;

c. Final year undergraduate students specialising in Information Systems and postgraduates researching the area.

The authors have been chosen carefully for their ability to explain clearly the relevant theory and demonstrate the application of the theoretical principles in real-world systems. As series editor I would like to record my pleasure in working with these talented people to bring the individual books of this series to the marketplace. The ITP staff have worked closely with both the authors and myself; I would like to acknowledge particularly the work of Samantha Whittaker who was brave enough to share the vision and demonstrated the professionalism to make it happen.

Keith G Jeffery
Series Editor

Head, Systems Engineering Division
Computing and Information Systems Department
Rutherford Appleton Laboratory
UK

PART ONE
BACKGROUND AND
CASE STUDIES

Part One provides an introduction to the rest of the book, and contains just two chapters.

Chapter 1 gives a background to the trends in computing which have resulted in the current state of the art. It also discusses the possible direction in which information systems may develop in future.

Chapter 2 introduces a set of case examples. These are primarily for student exercise and assignment purposes. At the end of almost all subsequent chapters, a selection of comments is offered, indicating how the ideas in that chapter could apply to each case. The exercises in each chapter include some questions specific to the case studies. It is recommended for assignment work that students choose one case study at the outset and develop the outputs from each chapter using their chosen case study.

1 Business needs and information system trends

1.1 INTRODUCTION

For most of the six decades that electronic computers have been with us, they have forced an unnatural model of information upon their users. This model regarded information as something which needs to be brought together in one place and mass-processed by a big, expensive machine to achieve economies of scale. Suddenly, with the cost/performance revolution of single-chip processors, this has all changed. Now, not only are the central monoliths of yesterday being broken up and replaced with smaller, scattered systems; but at the same time more and more of these autonomous systems are being interlinked to support cooperation amongst their owners.

The purpose of this first chapter is to set the scene for the rest of the book, in terms of trends: firstly, trends in business needs and thinking, and secondly in the technologies and methods which support information systems (IS). We also set a further theme for the book by addressing the question of the **value** of the IS to the organizations and humans which use them.

1.1.1   *Basic definitions*

For the purpose of this book, 'distributed information systems' means IS which are operated within a single scope of control, but in which not all the data, and/or not all the processing, takes place on a single processor. Some people use a stricter definition, where 'distributed' implies that there is some geographical distance between these processors, but in this book we allow the wider view.

'Cooperative' is defined as an agreed pattern of voluntary sharing and exchanging of data and/or procedures between autonomous IS. Other authors have used the term 'cooperative' to indicate a system split between processors, which are not necessarily geographically dispersed, primarily for efficiency purposes. Again, we prefer to use the term 'cooperative' in the first, wider sense.

An 'information system' is taken as meaning any established pattern of processing of data which is geared to supporting some user activity. This allows not only IS that are formally designed, but also those that have evolved or 'just grown'. IS can include non-computer processing, but we do not regard all computer processing as 'information systems'. We tend to pay less attention in this book to control systems completely 'embedded' in devices which automate a process, and where the only action the user takes is to install the devices and turn the system on and off.

'Distributed' and 'cooperative' IS may differ little in computer architecture terms. The distinction is one of purpose, management control and evolution. Distributed implies a move from centralized processing in order to be more cost-effective, but within a single scope of management control. Cooperative, on the other hand, implies a federal style of control, arising from a wish of autonomous users – often with PCs (personal computers) – to cooperate.

1.1.2   *What could be included as distributed or cooperative*

Even within the dual nature of our subject topic, there are several varieties of distributed and cooperative IS. Some of the main **flavours** are:

- geographically distributed (different sites hold and process the data relevant to each geographical area)

- functionally distributed (different sites hold and process the data on different aspects of the whole application)
- client/server (different computers, not necessarily remote, specialize in the types of processing they do)
- federal (different computers, doing similar – or different – things, collaborate in an agreed way in order to interchange data and service requests)
- replicated (different sites hold and process copies of the same data, for speed or security purposes)
- casual (different computers have no formal cooperation agreement, but they pass messages among themselves, using industry standard protocols which are described later).

These different styles are not discussed further here. A fuller treatment is provided in Chapter 8.

1.2 TRENDS IN MANAGEMENT AND ITS INFORMATION NEEDS

In this book, our principle is that IS must reflect the needs and the styles of the management functions which they are there to support. In other words, our whole philosophy is 'demand-driven' rather than 'supply-driven'. So it is essential at the outset to understand the current trends, not only in technology, but also in management.

We also regard IS as constituting part of the communication subsystem in any business or organization.

1.2.1 *Centralization versus decentralization*

Business management fashions, like political ideas, are subject to the swings of the pendulum. The swing between large centralized combines, arguing economies of scale, and groups with autonomous profit units and independent collaborators, arguing individual motivation and responsibility, is a good example. We have seen an era in which de-mergers are as common as mergers, and in which flatter management structures (Figure 1.1), with a greater number of autonomous profit and cost centres, have been introduced. This swing to decentralization has, as a by-product, caused a change in recent years from monolithic centralized computer information systems to distributed and cooperative ones.

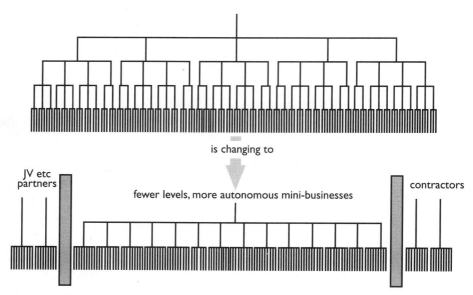

Figure 1.1 Flatter management structures.

1.2.2   *The 'inquisition' of BPR*

The recession in many nations in the late 1980s and early 1990s has put tighter financial constraints on the operation of many organizations. In particular, the burgeoning overheads (e.g. massive bureaucratic structures, including information technology (IT)) of the 1970s and 1980s have had to be trimmed back. Business process re-engineering (BPR) has been employed by many organizations in an attempt to return to a concentration on the essentials of their business. In many cases the results of this have been drastic reductions in administrative staff and middle management headcounts – so that the acronym could justifiably be reinterpreted as 'big personnel reductions'.

1.2.3   *Mushrooming complexity*

At the same time, the complexity and scope of what organizations and their personnel have to cope with, both internally and externally, has grown. Examples are worldwide markets, government and international regulations, environmental, social and sponsorship pressure, and more intense competition. As well as becoming more complex, much of business activity has also become more immediate – partly as a by-product of communications improvements. Not only are there slimmer workforces in organizations in the 1990s, but also the level of empowerment of individual staff is an order of magnitude higher than in the 1960s, and IS have to match this.

1.2.4 *Business reinterpreted as cooperative work*

Part of the i'ncrease in complexity has arisen through a trend towards more work that is cooperative, both in consortia among organizations, and in interdisciplinary, problem-oriented task-groups both within and between organizations (Figure 1.2). As neat organizational boundaries break down, so does the

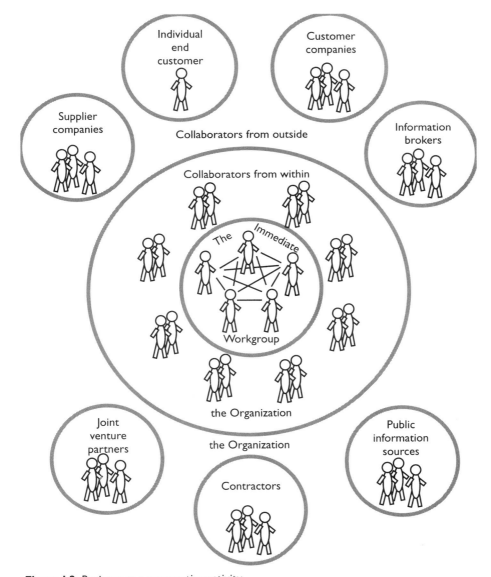

Figure 1.2 Business as a cooperative activity.

adequacy of tightly aligned IS. Much of the information an organization needs to operate successfully these days lies outside its own scope of management control.

1.2.5 *Information as a business in itself*

Information has for some time been recognized as a commodity, and so people wishing to retrieve information will pay money to its owner or custodian. This recognition ranges from the traditional examples like newspapers, through to operations like database providers or information brokers. Even a travel agent or insurance broker is trading primarily in information. In all these types of business, the only competitive edge is through offering clients a better information service – which has to be achieved largely through the quality of the IS.

It is interesting to note recent moves in which leading players in the traditional information business, e.g. the *New York Times,* Reuters, cable TV companies, are buying into, or forming joint ventures in, the next generation of electronic information services. ABC and Disney have formed 'the biggest merger ever' in this area.

1.3 TRENDS IN IS DEVELOPMENT METHODS

1.3.1 *The structured (process-oriented) approach*

In many early applications of computers, the scarcest resource was computer processor power. Examples involving heavy number-crunching included nuclear reactor simulation, linear programming (LP) models, or solving complex sets of equations by successive approximation. The **program**, with its essential algorithms, was the center of much of the design effort. The same approach continued with early commercial data processing systems such as accounting systems, which involved the storage of data on files external to the computer's main memory.

As applications became more complex, programs had to be broken down into smaller units, and the prevailing methodology for this process, the so-called structured approach, still holds sway in many organizations today. In data flow diagramming, the major analysis and design technique in this approach, data is treated as the inputs and outputs of each functional unit (Figure 1.3).

Top Level (Context Diagram)

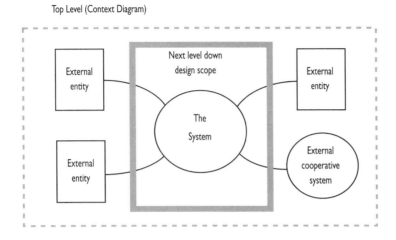

Lower level - System or Process

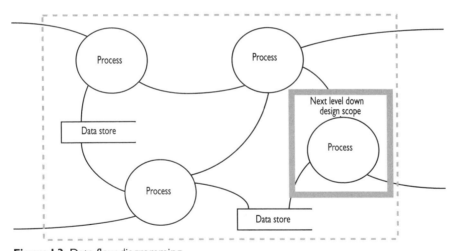

Figure I.3 Data flow diagramming.

1.3.2 *The database (data-oriented) approach*

The above treatment of data in analysis and design was soon seen as too weak for developing effective commercial systems where the data is shared between many purposes. The database approach to analysis and design starts with building a model of data structures. Original methods were based on Bachman diagrams and the early database management systems (DBMS). These also

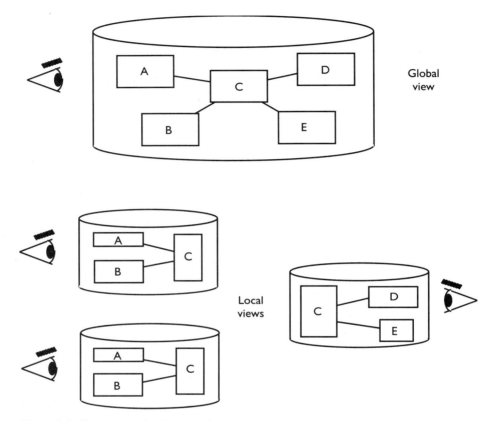

Figure I.4 Global versus local views of data.

distinguished a **global** view of shared data from the view required by individual programs (Figure 1.4).

In time, a whole set of methodologies, built around **data** rather than programs and processes, held sway in the commercial-applications development arenas. Phrases such as 'data is a corporate resource' were quoted like a religious mantra.

But these methods had major liabilities, one of which was that they addressed only a limited number of types of application. Also the commercial DBMS packages (in recent times, mainly of the relational variety) do not always provide good support for new kinds of data, e.g. computer-aided design (CAD), multimedia, full text and time-dependent.

For example, to a librarian or 'information professional', a 'database' is not a structure representing a range of information on different business entities, but a single indexed file of bibliographic references. The 'database market' is not so much about which DBMS to buy, but rather the competing collections of data that are commercially available on host computers or CD-ROMs.

To a home-based networker, a 'database' is likely to mean any service that can be dialled into and which supplies information, e.g. a bulletin board, electronic conference, stock market prices or information broking services etc. (Figure 1.5).

Many businesses have already recognized that much of the data they need is external. The in-house IT installation no longer has the monopoly on an

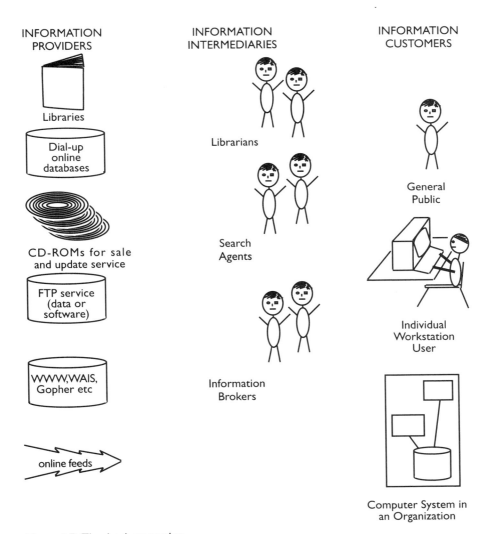

Figure 1.5 The database market.

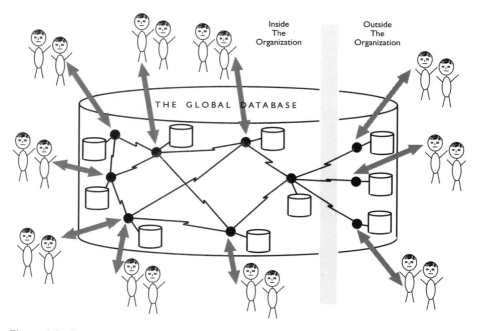

Figure I.6 '*The network is the database*'.

organization's information. The external market for data – and knowledge – already exists. The 'corporate database', i.e. the resource which provides the major support for the sharing of data in the organization, now really lies in the network itself. To paraphrase Marshall McLuhan, '*the network is the database*' (Figure 1.6).

Finally, the database approach over-emphasized the role of central control, typified by the much advocated – but rarely implemented – post of corporate data administrator. Spheres of control are not wide enough in practice to enable anyone to have control over a very wide range of data. Rather, in the modern paradigm, data is owned by autonomous groups and is traded as part of cooperative activity.

1.3.3   *Object oriented approaches*

We have a skeptical reserve about endorsing anything which has gained as much 'fashion' momentum as object orientation (OO). But the principles behind it seem irrefutable, and it models quite accurately the cooperative management environment on which our ideas in this book are based.

Using a totally unofficial definition, the OO approach appears to be about building systems out of components that communicate through defined interfaces. A useful parallel can be drawn with automobile design. If we are designing a new car model, we look at the various existing components and produce better versions, sometimes at a low level, sometimes at higher levels of assembly. We are most unlikely to start from scratch – in spite of what some advertisements claim.

However, we feel that OO may be a valid and advantageous discipline in certain environments, but not all. Furthermore, most existing, or 'legacy', code is not object oriented. It is littered with inter-process calls and 'free' procedure code. If we are to take an evolutionary view of development, we need to both incorporate this legacy code and have a policy on phasing it out. The equivalent in car design would be a policy of gradually introducing small replacement components with standard interfaces (Figure 1.7).

From Spaghetti approach:

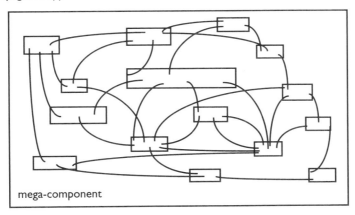

mega-component

To Component approach:

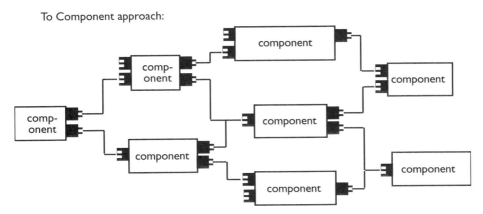

Figure 1.7 Replacing spaghetti code by components.

1.3.4 *More flexible development approaches*

The mainstream of IS development has in the past tended to follow a rather deterministic pattern. The model has been 'you want this output, you need this input, here's how you have to do it'. For some years it has been recognized that this is inadequate, and that users are often dissatisfied with the IS solutions they are given. Three trends have emerged which help to reduce this problem.

Contingency planning involves giving greater weight to what should happen when things do not go as the information system decrees. An air traffic control system is a good example – 90% of the logic is there to handle the exceptions. Many contingency procedures will involve human intervention.

Prototyping is an approach which has become popular because users cannot wait for the many months it takes to develop most computer systems – the environment is often changing so quickly that the system will be out-of-date before it starts operation. Prototyping involves creating a partial solution quickly. This can either be used to test the design and then be thrown away, or implemented for real use and gradually improved by adding in extra functions. Most PC-based systems develop in this way, going through revisions in which functionality is added.

Soft systems methodology involves placing greater importance on what the users' real needs and objectives are, instead of forcing on them the need to accept or reject specifications of a 'mechanical' system.

1.4 TRENDS IN DATA COMMUNICATIONS

Communications is a field very much characterized by spiralling supply and demand. An improvement in communications capability (increased supply) can take many forms, from a reduction in the time to transfer a single message from one place to another, or a reduction in the cost of transferring that message, to an increase in the accuracy of messages received, or an increase in the number of locations available for sending and receiving messages.

But communication is an essential part of both business and social human activity. As the supply of communication capability is improved new possibilities open up, especially for business, generating new forms of business activity which depend on the improved capability. That is, new demand is generated. Increasing demand, in its turn, encourages the development of improved supply. This has resulted in a remarkable upward spiral in which, over just a short 150 years since the invention of the telegraph, data transmission capacities over a single cable have risen from a few bits per second to more than 100 million times that initial figure.

1.4.1 *A view of data communications history*

The invention of the telegraph by Samuel Morse in 1837 allowed nearly instantaneous terrestrial communication over long distances using copper wires. The system out-performed the fastest transfer of the written word, which was then by train, but was limited both because of the small number of locations serviced by the wires and because a specialist operator was needed at each end.

The invention of the telephone by Alexander Graham Bell in 1876, just 40 years later, dispensed with the need for a specialist operator at each end and sparked a remarkable period of growth. Suddenly, social and business activity could be carried out at a distance without the delay of passing the written word to and fro. Within a few brief years, telephone exchanges and public telephones had appeared, and engineering improvements saw the distance over which a telephone conversation could take place rapidly extend. By 1915, telephone conversations could span continents and oceans. The same electrical circuits used for telephone conversations could also be used for sending messages between electromechanical teleprinters, but only over short distances. With the advent of, first, large-scale commercial data processing in the 1960s, and then the multi-user systems of the 1970s, pressure was created to locate input and output devices nearer to points of need, such as outlying branch offices.

The development of the modem, a device which allows computing devices to communicate over nearly any distance using standard telephone circuits, enabled the revolution of on-line processing where a central computer can be accessed from any point touched by the telephone network. Although line capacities were initially only just 150 bits per second, engineering improvements have seen this limit creep steadily up to over 28 000 bits per second at the time of writing, and as the telephone network made use of satellites and mobile cellular radio systems, computer communications followed (Figure 1.8).

Public networks for purely computer communication, that is public digital networks, emerged in the 1980s – mostly using a new paradigm called packet-switching. These initially offered capacities of up to 64 000 bits per second to the subscriber, which was then an order of magnitude greater that those available through the public telephone system. Advances in engineering have seen capacities rise steadily over the last 15 years to 10 megabits per second or more.

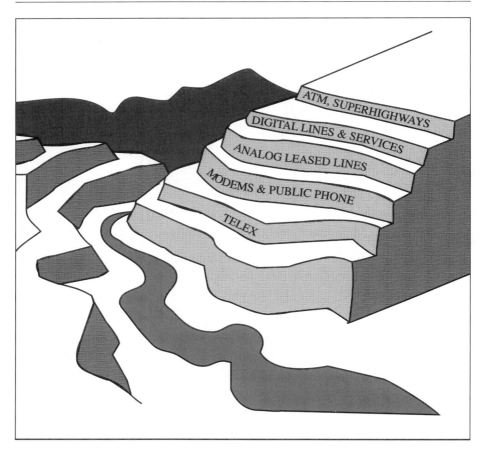

Figure I.8 Plateaux and slopes in data communications technology.

1.4.2 *Convergence*

Authors and commentators on the strategic implications of information systems often refer to technological convergence. They describe this phenomenon as a merging of all forms of communication, voice, video and data, concurrently with different user interfaces and transmission mechanisms, towards an integrated multimedia user interface with an integrated transmission mechanism. At present, much of this is well in evidence. Established private data networking systems, such as the Internet, transport multimedia data in support of the World Wide Web. The established public voice network of the telephone system is converting to digital encoding, for trunk or inter-city transmission systems, for telephone exchanges, and for the local subscriber loops, partly in anticipation of integrated systems such as ISDN (see later).

Fax, global live TV programming, cable TV, mobile communications via satellite and cellular radio, and multimedia presentation systems all raise consumer expectations about individual mobility and choice. The expectation is building that individuals will be able to communicate by means up to and including full-motion images whenever and wherever they choose. An example might be selecting the movie of your choice, from all those that have ever been produced, from your armchair at home and at the time you have chosen for that leisure activity. Another example might be an individual video-phone call home to your partner from a commercial airline flight.

These expectations of greater individual choice in selection of entertainment programs, especially video, have created a demand for increased communications capacity to the consumer at their place of work or leisure. Some of this demand is being met by cable TV systems. However, very high capacity local loop systems, using optical fiber as the transmission medium, are under trial in a number of countries, and at least one nation, Japan, is committed to delivering this technology to all homes and to all places of work.

1.4.3 *Emergence of high-level protocols*

Just as data communication between computing devices has been common-place for the last 20 years, so the engineering for reliable transport of streams of bytes or bits has been in place for nearly as long. Advances in this basic level of engineering still continue, but the underlying stability of the base technology – and the steady increase in capacity – have seen the range of potential functions achievable over a distance blossom. Examples are electronic mail, distributed file systems, distributed databases, and distributed Hypertext. Although the software implementation of these high-level functions on a single processor had been well developed, distance-related effects and other factors create new problems when these functions are implemented on distributed processors. New, high-level communications engineering (in software) has steadily developed under the generic label of 'protocols' (Figure 1.9).

These high-level protocols are stacked layer upon layer, with different organizations sometimes developing competing protocols (not all compatible) for the same basic function. Of particular interest to users of databases is the development of remote data access protocols – these include the use of the 'structured query language' (SQL) data language.

- Which language are we going
  to communicate in?
    eg English, French, Chinese
    eg COBOL, SQL

- Are we going to scramble the
  messages?
    if so, using what system?

- How will we know if the
  other person got the whole
  message?

- How will the message be
  routed through the
  network?

- How will we indicate when
  blocks of transmission start
  and finish?

- What sort of connection will
  we be using?
    eg wires/waves/telecoms
       service

Figure 1.9 The concept of protocols.

1.5 APPLICATIONS WHICH DEPEND ON THE USE OF DISTRIBUTED SYSTEMS

Distributed applications can be classified by the nature of the underlying processing pattern, which in turn supports the requirements of the business or social process.

The first group involves summary and analysis of events recorded at remote sites, where the data has to be combined to give a global picture. Examples are central accounts, sales recording and management.

Similar to the above, but with more emphasis on timeliness, are 'control systems' which involve rapid reaction to remote events, which is often not possible without fast data communications. Examples are space probe guidance, airline/hotel reservation, air traffic control and site security.

Networked computing can also be introduced to support more efficient trading between an organization and its customers, suppliers or other partners. Examples are home banking or shopping, telephone insurance broking, EFTPOS (electronic funds transfer at point of sale) and EDI (electronic data interchange).

Another use of distributed systems is simply to allow the same IS to be processed at a cheaper overall information processing cost. Examples are the use of parallel cheap computers, or client/server techniques.

The next group supports fast access to a wide range of available information, very often external as well as internal. The concept is one of the 'global library' or 'cyberspace'. Examples are bibliographic information retrieval, credit reference checking, Teletext and Videotex, and 'surfing' the Internet.

The final group enables a dispersed team of people to work cooperatively. Examples include the well-known messaging applications such as electronic mail, bulletin boards and conferencing, fax, voice mail, video conferencing. Other applications could include automatic translation (protocols, codes, spoken languages), group decision support and other 'groupware'.

1.6 VALUE FROM THE MANAGEMENT PERSPECTIVE

The value to organizations of distributed and cooperative systems lies in their ability to add to the organization's performance, both by improving efficiency and by enabling new business opportunities. This can be considered at four levels.

1.6.1 *Strategic organizational advantage*

The primary strategic advantage of distributed and cooperative IS is that they enable an organization to operate more effectively over a wider geographical spread. Examples are: to enable new markets or products involving joint ventures with new business partners; to offer superior service to customers; and to provide greater protection against business risks and 'acts of God' – a problem of great recent concern to banks and finance houses.

1.6.2 *Tactical effectiveness*

Distributed IS help at the tactical level by supporting cooperative decision making processes. Example benefits are to distribute expertise effectively; to enable comparisons between information from different sources; to bypass intermediaries and lock in customers and suppliers; and to reduce costs tied up in inventory at different sites.

1.6.3   *Operational efficiency*

Distributed and cooperative IS help at the operational level by bringing together data from remote sources to allow on-line control of the operation, and, if necessary, to provide an up-to-the-second state of the business. Example benefits are in just-in-time (JIT) manufacturing, automatic process control, and financial or commodity dealing.

1.6.4   *Cost and benefit*

It is easy for an organization to get sucked into spiralling costs of networks and distributed systems. Upgrading can either be regarded as a painful necessity to match competitors, or a pro-active move, not without risk, to steal a march on them (albeit usually only temporary). Cost is not simply that of the IT elements – there are also many organizational and human factors.

Many of the benefits are indirect, in the form of the 'better management' advantages listed above. A potential cost saving that is often quoted is a reduction in staff travel to remote sites when the job could be done using a cooperative system or data communications technology. This saving is both in staff time saved for useful work and in direct travel costs. The ultimate benefit is the growth – or survival – of the organization itself.

1.7   THE USER PERSPECTIVE

1.7.1   *The enabling of cooperative work*

The biggest difference that distributed and cooperative systems make to the user is that they are beginning to change the way teams may be composed, permitting teamwork across site boundaries.

Such systems also tend to reduce the need for intermediary information experts within teams – each end user is enabled to get the information he or she needs. Intermediaries are not, however, redundant – they are still present as librarians (in the wider electronic sense) and as information brokers who are almost universally contractors.

1.7.2   *Problems with the technology marketplace*

Users faced with having to make, and justify, decisions to invest money in distributed systems, have their task made harder by the rapid rate of development and obsolescence of technologies, especially in telecommunications. The 'plateaux' referred to earlier seem to be very narrow ones. There is a difficult balancing act in trying to keep compatible with standards and avoid too many periods of change.

There is also a danger of becoming obsessed by the technology itself, and demanding more technology than is really necessary for the business purpose. Marketing techniques everywhere espouse the 'wine buff syndrome' in which products – which are of only marginally more value to the user – are given nicer labels and a much higher price. The same technique is also applied against the 'computer buff' – with just as much success.

With so many people in western countries having to make a living out of the information industry, there is a very high 'fog' factor in trying to appreciate all the concepts and subtle differences between both different techniques and different suppliers' offerings. Data communications experts, in particular, are the 'high priests' who can name their price and who could become as anti-social as the fictional James Bond's antagonist Ernst Stavro Blofeld (Fleming, 1960), who brokered information to both the Allies and Axis and then went into the extortion business.

1.8 THE INDIVIDUAL AND SOCIETY PERSPECTIVE

Individuals in organizations may benefit from distributed systems, as employees, contractors or private individuals, by being more productive and better informed, and saving time on routine tasks. This must be set against a risk of turning entrepreneurial human-oriented people into 'screen slaves', with associated 'information overload'. For more on this, see Clifford Stoll's entertaining book *Silicon Snake Oil* (Stoll, 1995).

The quality of leisure may (or may not!) improve with home shopping, private Email/fax, 'video on demand', etc. Lonely people may, if they can afford to connect, gain an additional social lifeline – recently a UK businessman used Email to communicate with his deaf mother. Society in general will gain something by having more of its members aware of a wider range of experience.

The most immediate danger is of further polarization between the information 'haves' and the information 'have nots'. We already have growing differences between rich and poor nations, and between those in work and those out of work, and we will soon have a gulf between those who are network-connected and those who are not. The 'global village' (McLuhan again) is only a reality for the 'haves'.

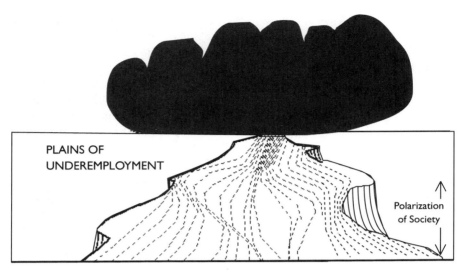

PLAINS OF
UNDEREMPLOYMENT

Polarization
of Society

HIGH-TECH PLATEAU

Figure I.I0 The lemming effect.

This may produce a 'lemming effect', where the few who remain in full-time work get fewer and have to work faster, until they eventually drop off the cliff of what society as a whole can afford (Figure 1.10).

Unlimited growth and development of networks, as with most organisms, is not sustainable for ever. In many other technologies, good plateaux have been reached: examples are the telephone, jet airplanes, cars and bicycles. Although there is an ever-present urge to improve products in these areas, the basic concepts – or at least their user interfaces – have been stable for a number of years. Distributed IS, however, have yet to reach this steady state. Perhaps there are more pressing needs in the world – or other commercial opportunities – that could provide a better outlet for the energies of our progress-crazed technocrats!

Further reading

Keen, P. (1988) *Competing in Time: Using Telecommunications for Competitive Advantage*, Ballinger, Cambridge, MA.

Kling, R. (1991) *Multivalent Social Relationships in Computer Supported Workplaces*, Communications of the Association for Computing Machinery.

Lewis, E. (1994) Where is computing headed? *IEEE Journal* Aug.

Roche, E. (1991) *Telecommunications and Business Strategy*, Dryden, Orlando, FL.

Spurr, K. (1994) *Computer Support for Cooperative Work*, Wiley, Chichester, UK.

Stoll, C. (1995) *Silicon Snake Oil*, Doubleday, New York.

Tagg, R. (1994) *The Network IS the Database*, Massey University, New Zealand.

2 Case studies illustrating the issues in different styles of organization

This chapter differs from the rest of the book. Its sole purpose is to introduce a set of examples which will be used throughout the rest of the book. Rather than introduce the details piecemeal in each chapter, we describe at the outset all the basic business and IS background for each of the example organizations.

MODE OF USE

The illustrative discussions and exercises which appear at the end of each chapter are, for the most part, aligned to these example organizations. If this book is being used as a student text, then assignments could make use of these imaginary organizations. However, real organizations which are known personally to students or lecturers, and where individual contact persons are prepared to answer students' questions, are preferable if available.

The seven case studies below are chosen to illustrate a range of distributed or cooperative IS problems, covering small, medium and large users, and both private businesses and public services.

Numbers 1 and 2 are deliberately small-scale, and are included to provide simple backgrounds against which the principles can be grasped, but they are less well suited as examples for student assignments in using the design techniques.

The next four, numbers 3 to 6, are the most suited to student exercises and assignments, and resolution of the design issues – after a brief discussion of the main points – is left to the reader or student.

Number 7, on the other hand, is included for use as a standard thread of illustration in Part Four of this book. A large proportion of the examples of completed analyses and designs are in terms of this case.

All of these example organizations are based loosely on real situations, but this is no guarantee that the problems and solutions discussed in this book are appropriate to any particular real-world case!

The details that are given for each case are arranged under the following headings:

- background description of the line of business
- business partners – the other parties with which business is done
- current mode of operation – the process flows on the main value chain
- key issues – the things of most concern to the chief executive
- future directions – in the business, and with information in particular
- volumes – the numbers or frequencies of entities and transactions
- IS situation – the systems that currently exist, or are planned
- location model – user groups, location types and geography.

The location model diagrams shown at the end of each case aim to provide easy, natural models of the types and locations of the potential IS users. We are using a convention which is an enhanced version of that proposed in Whitten, Bentley and Barlow (1994). Further explanation is given with the first diagram in section 2.1.8 below.

2.1 A ONE-PERSON (AND FAMILY) BUSINESS

2.1.1 Background description

Mr A has started up in business from his home in the UK, supplying building materials which provide special heat, damp and sound insulation properties for home, office, industrial and agricultural premises.

2.1.2 Business partners

His customers are mainly in the European Union, but many suppliers are in the USA. He is also dependent for information on libraries and other public or commercial information sources. He employs a clerical assistant and a contract accountant. Other 'business partners' are the Inland Revenue (IR) and Customs.

2.1.3 Current mode of operation

Mr A basically operates from his home using the telephone and fax, and also runs a home computer. However, he has to spend a lot of time away from his home base, e.g. at clients' premises, trade shows, at various other meetings, and at public and specialist libraries.

His main information flows are with his suppliers and customers. Suppliers send catalogues, price lists, agent briefing notes, technical reports, glossy brochures and of course invoices and statements of account. Mr A sends them payments, orders, returns and customer complaints. Most suppliers send price lists, agent briefing notes and answers to complaints by fax. Mr A sends some key provisional orders and urgent complaints by fax, but the rest by post. However, virtually all the information that is sent in either direction originates from a computer system.

Data exchanged with customers includes his own price list, brochures, invoices and letters, with mailed payments coming in. The telephone is more heavily used than with suppliers. Few customers (small builders, home owners, farmers, etc.) are on PCs or fax yet, but this is changing. Again, nearly all the information he sends out, except product brochures, originates from his computer.

The research data he gets from libraries, mainly using an on-line bibliographic search terminal which he uses on his visits there. He also has a friend in a local university, Prof. N, who researches into insulation materials, and who sometimes involves Mr A in laboratory tests of new materials.

Internally, he prepares monthly accounts, and he sends quarterly returns to his accountant for both IR and VAT (value-added tax) tax purposes.

2.1.4   *Key issues*

Because part of his strategy is to be at the front of the technology, he has to give a high priority to keeping abreast of new scientific developments, new supplier products and news about building regulations and safety and environmental questions.

He also has to be efficient in general operation, to impress customers and partners favourably, and to keep costs competitive. At the same time he must free himself as much as possible from administrative tasks so that he has plenty of time to work at his main business.

2.1.5   *Future directions*

He would like his business to grow, ideally doubling his turnover in five years. He would also like to open an office with a colleague, or colleagues, working in the same or related areas. He would like to raise his profile in the area by doing more technical research, for example by publishing joint research papers with Prof. N, or getting involved in Internet conferences and mailing lists.

2.1.6   *Volumes*

He has, at present, 18 active clients, each purchasing on average 20 product lines with two or three orders per year. He receives up to 100 trade enquiries per month, sometimes ten or more per day. He is away from home about 50% of the time.

2.1.7   *IS situation*

Mr A has a home computer on which he keeps client and prospect details, a product list with supplier details, and his accounts including debtors, creditors and invoices. He has also acquired a portable 'notebook' computer so that he can capture data immediately while he is on the move.

His beat-up second-hand fax machine is rather over-utilized and subject to breakdowns, but looking at the information that flows into – and out of – his business, he realizes that much of it either originates or finishes up in someone else's computer system. He wonders, for each type of information he exchanges with the outside world, what might be the cost-benefit of transmitting it directly from computer to computer.

The bibliographic databases that he uses most, namely Materials abstracts and Materials databank, are now available either on CD-ROM or by dialling in from a PC to a central computer. It would save Mr A a lot of time if he could review new articles and books, or ask *ad hoc* questions about certain materials, while sitting at his computer. Access from his portable PC, while he is holed up in a distant motel, would be even better!

Prof. N at the local university has told him that there is now a news group called **sci.materials.insulation** in the international Usenet News system available over the Internet. Prof. N is on the Internet himself and communicates quite often with fellow researchers in the insulation materials field. Mr A would like to have access to some of this data in order to keep abreast of the technology.

To help ease the backlog of administrative work, Mrs A has started working as an assistant, using the home PC. While Mr A is away on sales trips, he often needs to send to her, from the motel where he is staying, **remote corrections** to offer letters and other documents, so that she can edit them and post them off without having to wait for his return. While the telephone is adequate for dictating small volume corrections, commercial fax charges are high, and electronic mail could be worth considering.

Finally, since he keeps all his **tax return** data on file, and the Inland Revenue are now accepting tax returns on computer files, he wonders if it would be possible or worthwhile to submit his tax returns electronically.

2.1.8 *Location model*

The user groups, location types and geographical locations relevant to Mr A's business are summarized in Figure 2.1. These three aspects of location, which will be discussed in more detail later in the book, are each covered by one layer of the diagram.

The icons on the top layer represent user groups of a particular type, e.g. salesmen, accounts clerks, top managers. The organization may have several groups of one type, possibly in different geographical locations. If groups outside the organization's management scope are to be considered as part of the information system(s), then they should also be shown – a vertical barrier is used to separate them. User-group types may form hierarchies, e.g. accounts payable clerks and accounts receivable clerks are both subtypes of account clerk. The icons are not standard and depend on the user's choice of clip art or graphic object.

The User Groups are associated with generic location types, e.g. warehouse, office, accounts department area. The user group icons are joined by lines to the circles on the second layer which represent the location types. Location types may form hierarchies, for example 'accounts department area' may lie within 'office'. Location types for external user groups should also be shown, though they may be

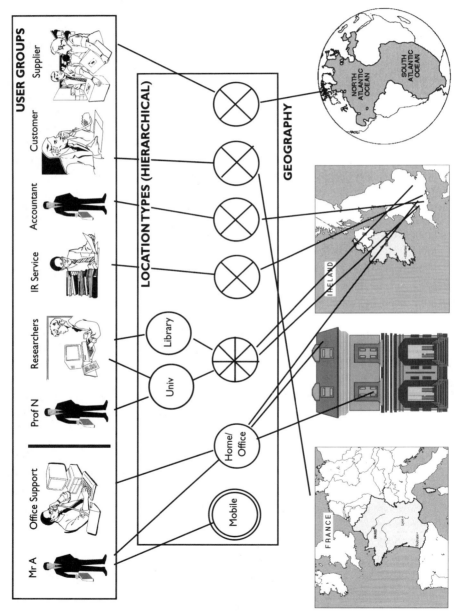

Figure 2.1 Location model for Mr A.

merged to simplify the diagram. The convention for the type of circle follows that of Whitten, Bentley and Barlow (1994):

- Maltese cross for a location type that has sub-locations
- plain for an atomic location type
- double perimeter for mobile (i.e. user groups on the move)
- Saltire (diagonal) cross for external.

Location types are linked in turn to a variable number of icons representing geographical extents. Some of these may be maps (e.g. one state, the USA, Europe, the whole world), and if there are not too many occurrences, the location type circle can be linked to dots on the map representing actual locations, e.g. Chicago, Mexico City. Other examples of geographical extent icons are office buildings, factories and so on, depending on the available 'clip art'. The lines to these icons represent the fact that locations of a type are located geographically within the Extent. It is useful to annotate a diameter measure to each geographical extent, showing the maximum distance apart of two locations in this extent.

Typical organizations require an A3 sheet to show a reasonable amount of detail, so the examples here are somewhat simplified.

2.2   A SMALL BUSINESS

2.2.1   *Background description*

The Bay Organic Produce Cooperative (BOPC) buys certain types of agricultural produce, all organically grown, from 2000 + farmers in a region of New Zealand, and attempts to get the best prices over the medium term. It also retains some produce warehousing capacity.

2.2.2   *Business partners*

The main business partners are Farmers, Food Processing Factories, Produce Market Operators, Distributors who supply supermarkets and specialist shops, Marketing Boards and Major Overseas Buyers. The cooperative also has relationships with a number of Agricultural Consultants, and must also report to Regulatory Bodies. There are also the usual ancillaries such as Accountants, Lawyers, etc., and Staff can also be considered.

2.2.3   *Current mode of operation*

Ten full-time staff and a similar number of part-timers operate from one office servicing local (up to 200 km) farmers, with whom contact is by meetings at markets, visit or phone. Because some staff are part-timers, phone calls from a particular farmer or buyer may be dealt with by different staff on different occasions. Some of the full-time staff specialize in either the supply, selling or warehousing side.

2.2.4 *Key issues*

The operation is oriented to creating a niche market, with quality and product appearance being used to command a price differential over conventional produce, by trading on the district's 'Clean Green' image. However the cooperative has to offer a service that makes it worthwhile farmers using them as an intermediary. This means that it must operate efficiently to keep up margins.

2.2.5 *Future directions*

BOPC's governing body is keen that the cooperative should be active in encouraging the successful marketing of organically grown produce, and one staff member is taking responsibility for developing this side of the business.

Both traditional and new food processing and packing firms are getting in on the organic act, and as the Bay area has had many successful organic farms, the market is likely to grow significantly.

2.2.6 *Volumes*

The cooperative currently deals with 2250 farmers, who deliver an average of 20 lots of produce each per week (typically four products daily). There are three major food-processing factories who do packing, freezing, canning, etc., and 25 smaller firms who simply pack fresh products. Produce does not tend to remain in the warehouse for more than a few hours, except for some root crops and fruit which can be kept for a few days or weeks. Produce which fails inspections or is too old, which accounts for around 10% by volume, is sold to any of 50 pig farmers.

2.2.7 *IS situation*

Data on farmers, buyers and on lots bought/sold has up until now been kept in a large revolving manual filing system located in the centre of the large office where most of the staff work. Apart from time wasted in retrieving the file when someone rings, the files are getting so full and messy that without a computer system, a new manual filing system would be imperative. Unfortunately, however,

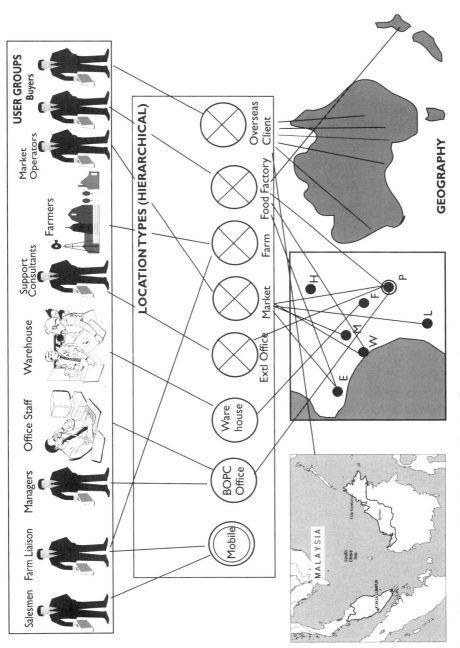

Figure 2.2 Location model for Bay Organic Produce Cooperative.

the Cooperative has decided that it cannot afford the centralized computer system that has been proposed. It therefore plans to give each desk an inexpensive PC to improve service and productivity when dealing with phone transactions, and to provide shared access to the data on farmers, supply, customers, sales and storage. At the same time the cooperative wants the staff to be able to share a laser printer in order to improve the quality of contract notes, letters, etc.

2.2.8 Location model

The user groups, location types and geographical locations relevant to BOPC's business are summarized in Figure 2.2.

2.3 A MEDIUM-SIZED PRODUCER

2.3.1 Background description

Detox Pharmaceuticals is a producer of generic drugs. It has set up operations fairly recently in Gdansk, Poland, with the intention of competing with the major multinationals whose prices have become unaffordable for Eastern European customers. The factory is adjacent to a coastal oil refinery, whose operating company owns a part share of Detox. The location allows access to the refinery's wharves, which Detox uses for incoming raw materials.

2.3.2 Business partners

The major partners are Health Authorities, Hospital Trusts, Pharmacies (chains as well as private chemists), Raw Material Suppliers, Departments in the Refinery, Maintenance Contractors and Detox's own Staff.

2.3.3 Current mode of operation

Market research determines the total market for generic drugs of each type by sales area. Detox's market share is forecast using trend and causal analyses. Current stock levels are considered before the future production plan (firm for one month, provisional for the next two months, then notional for budgeting purposes) is set. Production plans are reviewed each month.

Storage life of products is quite variable. Some are limited to one or two years before use, while others can be stored indefinitely until they are either obsolete or withdrawn.

Disposal of obsolete or withdrawn medicines has recently become subject to strict environmental controls and each disposal has to be recorded.

While Detox does not research new drugs, it still has to comply with government drug testing regulations, so sampling and laboratory analysis is routine at the plant.

A considerable amount of Process Control equipment has been installed at the site, and flows of materials which feed straight from the refinery are also monitored, as is tank ullage.

Warehouses with Sales and General offices are maintained in each of the main population centres nationally, eg Warsaw, Poznan, Bydygoscz, Lodz, Wroclaw, Katowice and Krakow.

2.3.4 *Key issues*

Detox is essentially in a 'commodity' market. Its success is tied to keeping a good market share by having competitive prices. Locality of manufacture is a help, but it has to keep fully up to date with its manufacturing machinery, which is continually being upgraded.

Business has been good so far, but is coming under pressure from two different directions. On the one side, government is regularly introducing new testing requirements; on the other, the multinational competitors are starting to cut costs and are threatening market share.

Since Detox's products are mainly generic and do not have market brand names, it must present its up-to-date product and price information frequently to health boards and family doctors.

2.3.5 *Future directions*

Detox wants to improve its market share through three main strategies:

- to widen the range of drugs produced
- to improve market share by making it easy for pharmacies and hospitals to do business with them, by setting up computer links so that customers can tap into Detox's systems to place orders
- to improve cost competitiveness by integrating its production control systems with the production plan.

2.3.6 *Volumes*

The most recent survey found that Detox has six process groups, 500 product lines, 200 processes, 7500 process control sensors or switches, 1500 customers, 300 orders per week (each with an average of 20 products) and 180 staff.

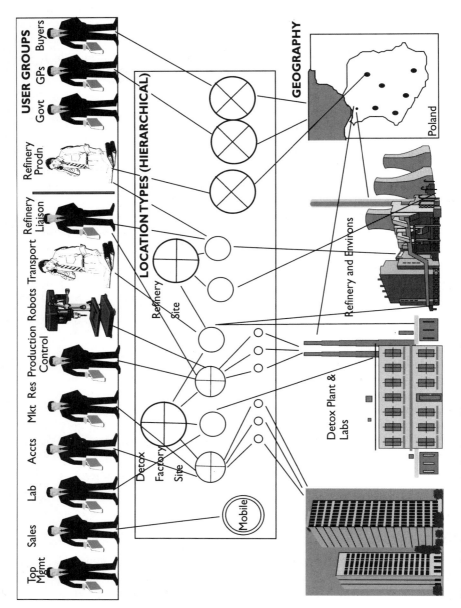

Figure 2.3 Location model for Detox Pharmaceuticals.

2.3.7 *IS situation*

The Process Control systems, each controlling a particular group of processes, are currently stand-alone special-purpose computers. However, engineering staff have succeeded in interfacing PCs as a first step to replacing manual data logging functions in the control rooms.

Routine data processing is done on an IBM AS/400 using RPG-based software. Warehouses and Sales Offices are connected to this machine using IBM 3270 terminals or PCs emulating mainframe terminals.

There are both PCs and Apple Macintosh machines (Macs) on staff desks, some of which are networked in workgroups, but access to the IBM is still generally through separate terminals.

Electronic Data Interchange (EDI) is considered a possibility, both with customers and with raw material suppliers. A leased telephone line to the refinery is currently used for exchanging data with the neighbouring refinery's systems.

2.3.8 *Location model*

The user groups, location types and geographical locations relevant to Detox's business are summarized in Figure 2.3.

2.4 A NATIONWIDE BUSINESS WITH INTERNATIONAL PLANS

2.4.1 *Background description*

Electric House is a US-wide electrical appliance and fittings retail chain, based in Oakland, California. It has stores in most centers of population, with several new superstores in out-of-town malls in the main conurbations. It also acts as a wholesaler, with products packaged to a house style, for independent retail outlets in smaller centers.

2.4.2 *Business partners*

Apart from the Buying Public, the main partners are Suppliers, Wholesale Customers, Transport Contractors, Store Development Contractors and Advertising Agencies – with Staff (both in offices and stores) being especially vital.

2.4.3 *Current mode of operation*

The company uses bulk contracts with a range of suppliers, largely in the Asia Pacific region, to manufacture products to a specification, which includes the standard Electric House packaging style. Sales trends and market research are used to determine the plan for the coming 12 months. Supply orders are generated from this plan, though occasional urgent replenishment orders are also made.

Supplies are delivered to a number of strategically located warehouses (often adjoining the new superstores). A perpetual inventory count is kept, with rolling physical stock checks to control inaccuracies and pilferage.

Stores use point of sales (POS) terminals to record movements of all product lines. EFTPOS and Credit Cards are also catered for. Nightly processing generates replenishment orders to be delivered from warehouse to stores. Bulk transfers from warehouse to warehouse are also sometimes scheduled.

2.4.4 *Key issues*

There is a high degree of rivalry in the market, with frequent attempts to undercut competitors, to find even cheaper manufacturers and to attract competitors' customers with high-profile advertising campaigns and offers. Up-to-date intelligence on competitor activities is absolutely vital.

Another key factor is the reduction of replenishment times for both stores and warehouses.

2.4.5 *Future directions*

The company is involved in merger discussions with a similar chain in Mexico which is appropriately named 'Casa Electrica', and which also has subsidiaries in a number of Latin American countries.

Electric House would also like to get into Home Shopping using computer networks, and is commissioning a feasibility study.

2.4.6 *Volumes*

Electric House has just under 200 stores. A typical store expects to make 1000 sales transactions each per day. Each transaction includes, on average, 1.5 different product items. There are 7500 products currently marketed. There are potentially 500 suppliers, but 80% of the volume is supplied from the top 50 suppliers, 30 of whom are in the Far East.

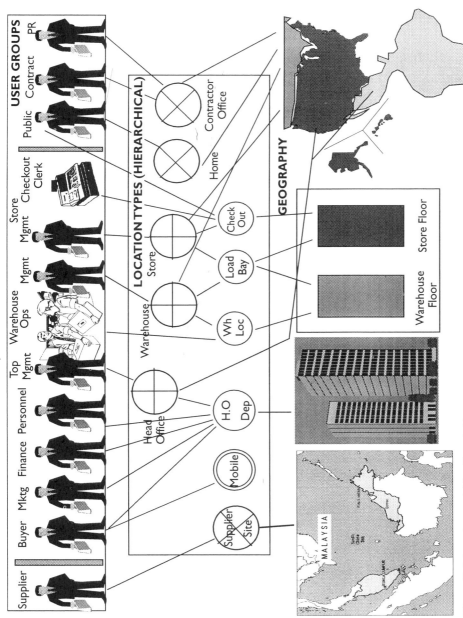

Figure 2.4 Location model for Electric House.

2.4.7 *IS situation*

Electric House has a centralized data processing operation in its Head Office. Larger stores have a number of PCs and POS terminals, but these are not systematically integrated for Management Information purposes. Warehouses have minicomputer-based inventory tracking systems.

Planned improvements being considered at this time are:

- Access for PC users to the Head Office mainframe
- Linking of other staff onto the organization's network
- EDI with Suppliers and Large Volume Clients
- Transport fleet management.

A firm of consultants, who are advising Electric House on the prospective merger, report that the prospective partner's IS are several years old. If the new group is to compete successfully, a new wave of IS, including more immediate and detailed data capture at point of sale, will be required.

2.4.8 *Location model*

The user groups, location types and geographical locations relevant to Electric House's business are summarized in Figure 2.4.

2.5 AN EDUCATIONAL ESTABLISHMENT

2.5.1 *Background description*

The Commonweath Open Polytechnic (COP) is a new foundation, partly funded by the Australian Government but also by a consortium of major Australian corporations, which is geared to offering tertiary educational opportunities in key technical and social areas with a more practical orientation and a more convenient mode for working students than is offered by the Universities and local Technical Colleges (TAFEs). The COP intends to maximize its use of modern learning techniques including CBT (computer-based training), multi-media, CD-ROMs and remote tutoring.

2.5.2 *Business partners*

The main parties that the COP 'does business with' are Students, Staff, Funding Agencies, Libraries and Contractors. Contractors include academics who produce teaching materials and provide tutoring, but may also include providers of more general services. Also involved with COP, but of lesser importance, are Suppliers and other Academic Institutions.

2.5.3   *Current mode of operation*

The COP operates from a small central campus just outside Broken Hill, NSW. There is also a network of regional centers where on-campus teaching and tutoring takes place. Students are primarily home-based and they are required to have a PC selected from an approved list. Teaching is done through a cycle of 'short fat' courses, when students meet at their nearest site for 3–4 weeks. The remainder of the year they are involved in reading, writing and practical assignments which are tutored remotely using electronic mail. To assist student learning, COP has produced a range of CD-ROMs which can be borrowed from libraries.

2.5.4   *Key issues*

In this early growth phase, it is vital for COP to have good information on the market. This means building links with potential students, and closely monitoring the quality of services delivered through student comments, peer evaluations, etc. The product must also be seen to be differentiated from alternatives offered by existing institutions.

At the same time, the COP is expected to be financially solvent and produce a reasonable – but not excessive – return on the capital invested.

2.5.5   *Future directions*

The COP would like to extend its coverage beyond national boundaries, offer a wider range of courses, develop the quality of remote tutoring, and introduce more interactive discussions between tutors and students.

2.5.6   *Volumes*

The forecast is that in two years time, there will be 10 000 students enrolled. Each student is expected to take 1.3 courses per year. A student will stay enrolled for an average of four years. Potential students, to whom mailings are sent, already number 50 000.

There are 100 permanent staff, but 2000 contractors. 500 different courses are planned to be available.

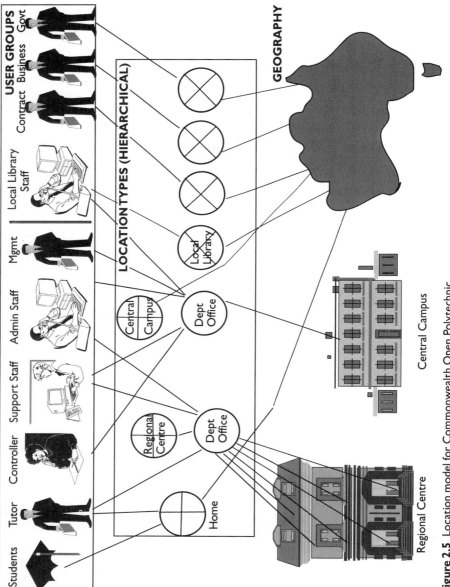

Figure 2.5 Location model for Commonwealth Open Polytechnic.

2.5.7 *IS situation*

Current applications are fairly limited at present. Operational systems are:

- Library – remote bibliographic query, CD-ROMs at local centers
- Timetabling – lecturers, facilities at regional centers
- Registration – students, courses, papers, locations
- Accounting, including student fees.

Future requirements that have been recognized are:

- Remote log-in facilities for students to access regional computer labs
- Student access to the Internet
- Automation of the COP's Prospectus and other reports and publications
- A database of potential students and alumni
- Distribution of multimedia interactive teaching videos
- Videoconferencing for remote discussions and tutorials.

2.5.8 *Location model*

The user groups, location types and geographical locations relevant to the COP's business are summarized in Figure 2.5.

2.6 A GOVERNMENT WATCHDOG

2.6.1 *Background description*

The National Environmental Protection Board (NEPB) is a new Quango entrusted with the task of monitoring the implementation of a South East Asian country's newly introduced environmental legislation. Its officers' tasks include:

- keeping abreast of international research in environmental hazards and protection
- collecting statistics on environmental measurements
- gathering on-the-spot reports from vulnerable areas
- issuing and analyzing questionnaires for companies and public
- reviewing environmental legislation both internally and abroad.

2.6.2 *Business partners*

The primary 'business partners' are the Organizations which have to be monitored, Testing Contractors known as 'compliance agents', and the Board's own Staff. Other groups the NEPB must work with are Government Departments, Political Representatives and the Press, as well as Libraries, Universities, Research Institutions and Members of the Public.

2.6.3 Current mode of operation

Depending on the regulation being monitored, rolling schedules are prepared for the issue of questionnaires or scheduling of inspection visits. Where possible, inspections are combined to cut down the number of visits and the disruption factor for companies.

The Statistics Section analyzes results and trends, both on a routine basis for regular reports (whether published or unpublished) and on an *ad hoc* basis for answers to Parliamentary Questions and enquiries from interested parties.

The Research Department's job is keeping abreast of international research in environmental hazards and protection, and also in methods of testing and inspection. They have access to public technical libraries.

2.6.4 Key issues

The main critical success factor is deemed to be efficient team working, through making sure that everyone who needs to know information does so immediately and fully.

Management has also endorsed the aims of openness, fairness, keeping costs down and quick processing of reports.

The NEPB needs to be continuously able to expand its activities to cover a fast-increasing range of environmental legislation without adding to the costs of its service to the taxpayer.

2.6.5 Future directions

As a new organization, the first priority is to get 'up and running' as quickly as possible, and to set up good systems which will keep costs down. Later on, the Board will attempt to get into a position where it can take a more pro-active role in advising both Government and Organizations.

2.6.6 Volumes

There are estimated to be 20 000 organizations subject to current environmental Acts, each of which should be inspected once every two years. Each organization is required to complete returns every quarter on emissions and internal controls. Currently there are five different Acts to be monitored, each with an average of eight separate headings. The number of Acts is expected to double within the next five years, with the number of subject organizations rising to 50 000.

There are currently 250 inspectors working out of six local offices, and just over 100 head office staff.

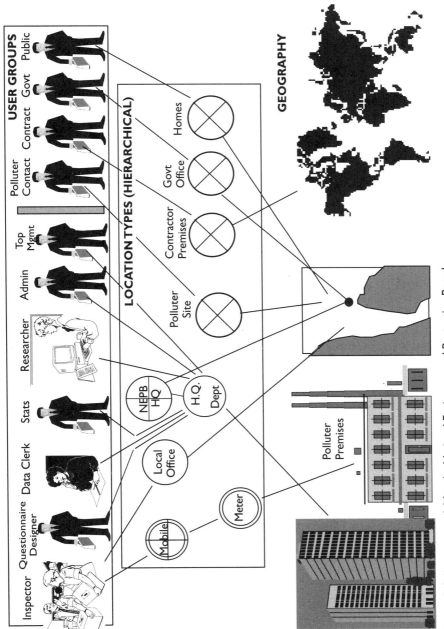

Figure 2.6 Location model for the National Environmental Protection Board.

2.6.7 *IS situation*

An integrated IS architecture has not yet been settled, and PCs are currently being used in an *ad hoc* manner. More formal IS support is envisaged for:

- scientific research – technical papers, statistics and surveys
- in-house statistical databases and analysis
- local office administration
- communication with compliance agents who are traveling or are at an external site
- data interchange with subject organizations
- supply of standard monitoring devices at subject organizations
- cooperative authoring and desk-top publishing of reports.

The main aim is never to get into the paper mountains experienced by other Quangos. 'Paperless from day 1' is the newly-appointed Chairman's optimistic motto!

2.6.8 *Location model*

The user groups, location types and geographical locations relevant to NEPB's operations are summarized in Figure 2.6.

2.7 A SOFTWARE HOUSE

N.B. This case study is used as the basis of many completed diagrams in Part Four, and should not be used for student assignments.

2.7.1 *Background description*

ABC Software Company is a large software house based in Auckland, New Zealand, and is geared to serving clients in Australasia. Its mission is to develop application software for Client/Server architectures (see Chapter 10). ABC's approach is to build what it calls 'Tailorable Blueprint Applications' or TBAs. It uses CASE (see Glossary for description) tools for the Server software and Application Generators for Windows, Mac and XTerminal clients.

2.7.2 *Business partners*

Existing and potential Customers are ABC's vital business partners. Special among these are two sub-groups, namely 'Beta Test Sites' and 'Vertical Market Clients'. The latter are those organizations which buy several of ABC's products for different aspects of their businesses.

Staff also are vital, and ABC is very sensitive to the slightest hint of discontent, threats of resignations or defections to competitors.

2.7.3 *Current mode of operation*

The company is largely driven by a group of marketing-oriented entrepreneurs who started the company. They identify potential Product Groups, plan Research, organize Public Relations and look after the Vertical Markets.

Another group conceives individual Products, and when the designers have built the products, this group packages them and sets sales targets.

Teams of salespeople, based in Regional Sales Offices in all the main centers of population, identify prospects, gain commitment, negotiate sales, assess credit and arrange contracts. A central pricing section carries out research into competitive pricing and sets target prices for sales.

The design team is located in a Research Laboratory in Palmerston North, NZ, although some design staff are seconded to work for a period at beta-test sites. Their main function is to develop the physical software product.

Other staff in Auckland look after purchasing and human communications. An administration director looks after personnel, legal and office administration.

2.7.4 *Key issues*

The key objectives are to hold on to ABC's current 30% market share in new application software sales, and to maintain 15% return on capital. The strategies to achieve this are to keep up a competitive range of product developments, and to concentrate on the vertical markets. Competition is getting very tight, and competitors are continuously trying to 'leap-frog' each others' offerings.

Critical to success are good reports from beta test sites, favorable publicity and availability of competent and committed staff.

2.7.5 *Future directions*

ABC wants to bring out a whole new range of 'Object-Oriented Application Components', in order to ride the new wave of technological development, and to take advantage of recent standards for distributed object interfacing.

It is also considering a move into Chinese language versions of the current product range.

2.7.6 *Volumes*

In a staggering growth period over the last few years, ABC have sold their products to 800 organizations at 2 000 sites. Of these organizations, 200 are

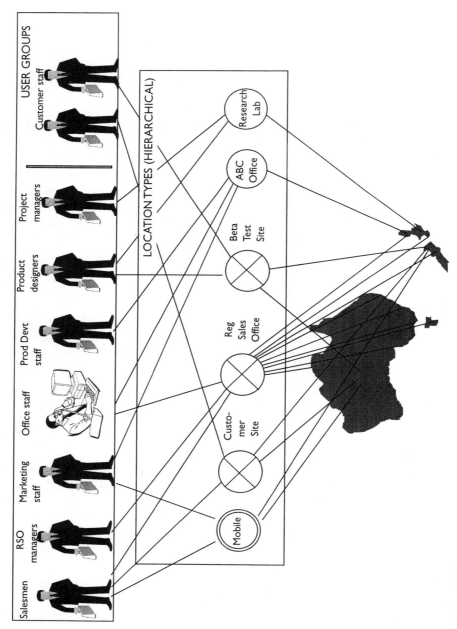

Figure 2.7 Location model for ABC Software Company.

currently 'vertical market', and there are 25 beta-test sites. There are six product groups at present, and each has on average five individual products. A customer buys on average three products.

ABC has 170 staff, 70 at Auckland, 50 developers at Palmerston North and 50 regional salesmen. Salesmen each contact on average about 20 new potential customers per month.

2.7.7 *IS situation*

·Proving the saying that 'the cobbler's children are the worst shod', ABC has currently only very patchy IS coverage. An old minicomputer is used for accounting. Sales prospect data is collected centrally for PR mailings. Sales activity is also processed for management control. Some of the salespeople have their own notebook PCs.

The designers at the lab. use CASE tools, but they are short of workstations and there is no formal sharing of design repositories. Files are passed on disk between designers and, frequently, to and fro between the lab. and the beta test sites. A PC package is used for development project control.

The Board has now decided that it should review its own internal IS Strategy.

2.7.8 *Location model*

The user groups, location types and geographical locations relevant to ABC's operations are summarized in Figure 2.7.

The following extra information is supplied to help explain the significance of the entries in the matrices in Chapters 14 and 15.

2.7.9 *High-level process hierarchy*

ABC marketing and product development

Marketing
    Plan Research
    Manage Product Group
    Manage Public Relations
    Manage Vertical Market

Product Management
    Conceive Product
    Implement Product
    Establish Sales Target

Selling
 Assess Credit
 Gain Commitment
 Negotiate Sale
 Amend Contract

Designing
 Develop Specification
 Develop Product
 Track Design
 Identify Needs

Pricing
 Analyse Research
 Set Prices

Purchasing

Communicate

2.7.10 *Major entity types*

Advertising Medium
 A route for advertising ABC or its products, e.g. a magazine, a radio/TV channel, etc.

Commitment
 A contract made with a Customer to supply ABC Products. A Commitment may also involve the reselling of tools acquired from a Supplier.

Competitor
 Another vendor of Application Software.

Competitor Product
 A Product offered for sale by a Competitor.

Customer
 A company, organization or individual to whom ABC sells its Products.

Customer Survey
 An exercise to determine the needs and current practices of a group of Customers.

Design Project
 A project to design and build a new Product or a new version of an existing Product.

Financial Transaction
Any event that changes the state of ABC's financial records, ledgers, etc.

Geographical Zone
A geographical area defined by ABC for dividing up business responsibilities.

Market
A division of potential Customers.

Market Need
A common thread of Customer requirement recognized from surveys and other contacts, as a possible opportunity for selling ABC Products.

Market Research
A unit of intelligence about a Market, Market Needs, and market shares.

Portfolio Strategy
A planned development of a Product Group for a Market.

Product
A separate software package produced by ABC.

Product Application
A type of business or organizational process to which Products are addressed.

Product Group
A grouping of Products for management purposes.

Product Price
A set of conditions (including time, Customer type, etc.) for which a particular price is charged for a particular Product.

Purchase Order
A specific order for tools, materials or services from a Supplier.

Sales Target
A set of target sales achievements for a Product Group in a Market, Geographical Zone or Time Period.

Supplier
A company or individual from which tools, materials or services are purchased.

Supplier Product
A particular type of tool, material or service purchased from a Supplier.

FURTHER READING

Whitten, J. *et al.* (1994) *Systems Analysis and Design Methods*, Irwin, Burr Ridge, IL.

PART TWO
DATA
COMMUNICATIONS

This part is intended to provide a designer of a distributed information system with a background to data communications. There are two objectives:

- first, to give a designer enough knowledge about the technology to make sensible design decisions at the overall information system level;
- secondly, to give the designer confidence in dealing with data communications engineers, both in conveying requirements to them and in evaluating the suitability of their proposed solutions.

We do not attempt to traverse much of the engineering detail which underlies data communications, as it has little or no direct impact on design decisions. Moreover, this part of the book would be far too large and bewildering, and there are several excellent books (to which we often refer) which take a supply-side view. Instead, we concentrate on fundamental concepts as they directly impact design and, in the process of exploring these, introduce significant terminology.

Chapter 3 Data communications: principles and fundamentals first places data communications in context, as a sub-system which provides services to a (distributed) information system. It then spells out the nature of the sub-system and critical success factors for the service. Five fundamental principles affecting design are introduced, and these are further developed in the succeeding chapters.

Chapter 4 Efficiency: capacity and performance explores the means that are used to ensure that a data communications service delivers data in a timely fashion at an appropriate cost.

Chapter 5 Effectiveness: reliability, accuracy and security explores the issues and design decisions which affect the accuracy of data delivery, the security of confidential data, and the counter-measures which need to be incorporated during design.

Chapter 6 Implementation: layers and standards introduces the concept of a multi-layer structure for data communications facilities, the most commonly used frameworks or architectures for this multi-layer structure, and the standards which apply at the individual layers.

Chapter 7 LANs and WANs highlights particular techniques, including software, which are used when data communications are either confined to a small geographic region or spread over larger geographical distances. It also discusses the practice of 'internetworking'.

Illustrative examples from the first six Case Studies in Chapter 2 are introduced from Chapter 4 onwards: Chapter 3 is not treated in this way as its function is to introduce basic material and concepts.

3 Data communications: principles and fundamentals

3.1 INTRODUCTION

We have seen that there is a business need for distributed and cooperative IS – the demand side of the issue. Just as businesses which are naturally dispersed use information systems, telephony and unit carrier systems (mail, courier) to 'glue' the business process together, so also at the IT infrastructural level the components of distributed information systems themselves must cooperate through the use of some communication mechanism. The active components of

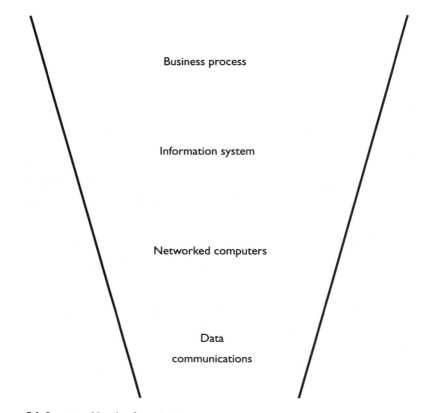

Business process

Information system

Networked computers

Data

communications

Figure 3.1 Structural levels of processing.

the information system are, in general, 'programmed' computer systems, each of which is an autonomous sub-system of the distributed information system. The means by which these components communicate is generally referred to as **data communications** (DC) (Figure 3.1).

Within the information system, communication between components is for two purposes.

The first of these is control, which can be defined as transfer of details about the sender's state between a sender and another component. Control information is generally not visible to the users of the information system – it is contained within the information system proper, passing between sub-systems so that they work together, in consort as it were, to execute the overall grand design of the system. It is significant only to the builders and maintainers of the information system.

The second is data itself, since the IS primary design objective is to receive, store, process, and distribute the product called 'information'. Data is the stuff of which information is made, and formatted data is the product which the computer components receive, store, process and distribute, both among themselves and to and from users.

The data communications sub-system (of the information system), the **network**, services the IS in which it is embedded, just as the IS service business processes and procedures. For a network to be successful in meeting the needs of the information system it must:

- transport the product – data – in a timely fashion
- keep data accurate, both uncorrupted and without loss
- be secure against theft and malicious interference
- do these things at reasonable cost.

There are five simple principles which the designer of a distributed system can use for guidance in bridging the gap between supply and demand. These are developed here as themes, and are then discussed further in the next few chapters.

- Standards are paramount
- Cost is proportional to Volume over Time
- Value resides in data
- Timing is of the essence
- There are many means

3.2 STANDARDS ARE PARAMOUNT

In order to understand the paramount importance of standards in data communications, we need first to explore the nature of those standards, and then look at their impact on design.

3.2.1 *The nature of a communications standard*

Consider the most basic communication between two independent, intelligent parties. What does the sender need to do to communicate with the other party, the recipient?

First, pick a mode

What is a mode? For person to person communications we can use many different modes, depending on the circumstances. If we are close enough we can talk directly – verbal mode. If we are further apart, we might talk over the telephone (which is not nearly as simple as it might first appear). We can use touch (but this might not work very well as it can be ambiguous). We can use a visual mode, signing with hands, or holding up a message written on cardboard. There are several others, see for example Liebenau and Backhouse (1990).

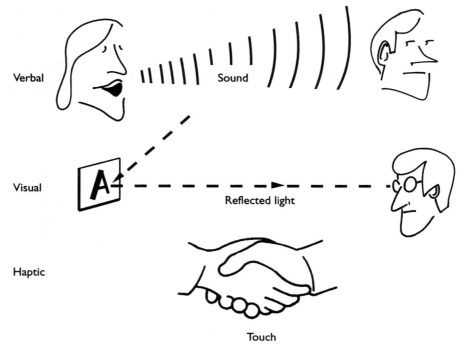

Figure 3.2 Modes.

A mode consists of a matched quartet (Figure 3.2):

- Transmitter
- Channel
- Medium
- Receiver.

In this person to person context, the above three modes, verbal visual haptic, have the following quartets of transmitter – channel – medium – receiver:

Transmitter	Channel	Medium	Receiver
voice	sound	the atmosphere	ear
sign	visible reflected light	free space	eye
hands	'touch'	nil	feeling of pressure

Note that in each case, the channel and the medium must be common to and be accessible by both parties. In essence, it must be agreed on (Figure 3.3).

Figure 3.3 Channels.

You may find it useful to think of the channel as a path through the medium between two end-points, the transmitter and receiver. There can be many channels, many paths, through a single medium (Figure 3.3). For example, broadcast entertainment programs such as radio shows come to you each using a separate channel (i.e. a different waveband) but the same medium (the ether).

For reasons which will become more apparent later, data communications makes use of **media** (plural of medium) through which electromagnetic radiation (e.g. radio waves, microwaves, light) will propagate. Common data communications media include telephone cables (sometimes termed 'twisted-pair'), coaxial cables, fiber-optic cables and the atmosphere or free space.

Clearly, the party wishing to begin communication will expect that the mode chosen will be effective, that is, it will work.

Secondly, gain their attention

The sender also needs to attract the attention of the other party by creating an appropriate disturbance. This is not as easy as it might first appear. Often channels are noisy – you might be trying to communicate across a crowded room where a party is going on; often the other party's receiver is switched off or busy – try waving to someone whose back is turned! People are generally very adept at detecting, amongst everyday background noise, significant disturbances designed to attract their attention and are also adept at trying alternative modes when one fails. Unfortunately, computer systems are not so adaptable.

In any case, the sender has to find a 'disturbance' that will be recognized by the other party as being appropriate to them. Sometimes, the most effective attention-getting disturbance will be a symbol which is, in effect, the recipient's name. For example, yelling 'Joe' might be more effective than 'rhubarb'.

Thirdly, agree on symbols

The sender, assured that a connection is established to the other party, now begins to send **symbols**, and these symbols must be such that both sender and recipient understand them; that is, they share a common experience of them. In the audio example, they will be phonemes, and in the visual example, hand-signs or letters of the alphabet. An agreed collection of symbols is called, naturally enough, an **alphabet**.

In data communications, the basic alphabet often used is a binary one – just a symbol for '1' and a symbol for '0', the conventional two values of a 'bit'. The actual symbols used, voltage levels or sound waves of particular frequency, will vary from mode to mode but there will be only two symbols nevertheless. However, most alphabets have many more than two symbols, and, if the channel will permit it, this will make communications faster. You can see that this would be so in the case of data communications by recognizing that each symbol could stand for a sequence of two or more bits – the 26 letter Roman alphabet could effectively represent all possible sequences of four bits, 16 in all, and still have some 'redundant' symbols. Most modern modems (see section 6.5.2) use complex alphabets (Figure 3.4).

Fourth, agree on syntax

A symbol on its own is often not readily useful in communications. Generally symbols are combined into larger groups which form the basic unit of exchange. In the case of person to person communications, if we were brought up in a western society, these would be words and sentences. In the case of data communications, names such as **character**, **frame** and **message** are often used. As in sentence construction, the construction of frames and messages has a fair degree of variability within certain basic rules. As before, agreement between sender and recipient on the rules of syntax, on the form of a frame or message, is essential to effective communication.

And so on

There are many other things that also have to be agreed on. Some of the more obvious are:

- names and addresses
- how to behave if something goes wrong
- how to detect that something has gone wrong
- how to decide who is going to talk next.

Binary

Traffic Lights

Roman

Sign Language

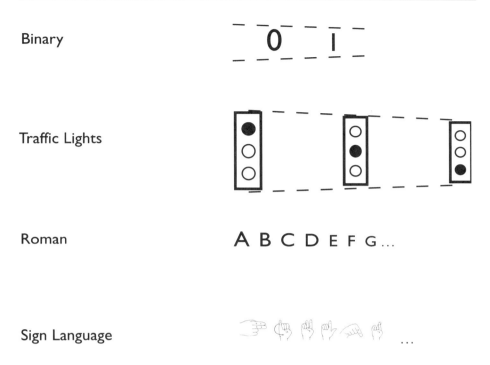

Figure 3.4 Symbol systems.

Standards are necessary

You can see that, for effective communication, the two parties must agree tacitly (through common experience) or explicitly on a number of things. Agreement on all these things must precede an attempted communication – without the agreement communication just cannot work.

In data communications, agreements are embodied in **standards**. There are hundreds of standards in use in data communications and the vast majority will describe that which is necessary for two (or more) components to be linked together. It will describe the common interface and the nature of the agreement. It will generally **not** describe **how** to make a component conform to the agreement; or how to construct a component. This is perhaps the single most commonly misunderstood point in data communications!

Some standards have special names. A standard which describes an alphabet is called a **code**: ASCII is an acronym for American Standard Code for Information Interchange. A standard which describes valid sequences of events is called a **protocol**.

3.2.3 *Implications for design*

The essential points are:

- the very nature of communication requires agreements and common standards
- data communication standards primarily describe the **interface** between two or more components.

Once clearly defined, standards become a tool for the systems designer. Components manufactured by suppliers will conform to some commonly accepted standards and not to others. The designer will need to be assured that two components that need to communicate with one another will share a common communication standard. This is generally accomplished by a designer declaring a suite of standards that the system will use in its data communications, as part of defining an **architecture.** Subsequently, components will be purchased or developed which conform to the architecture and, in consequence, the declared standards.

3.3 COST IS PROPORTIONAL TO VOLUME OVER TIME

The goal of the network designer is to create a data communications sub-system which has the desired level of functionality and performance at minimal cost. As we shall see in Chapter 4, there are a number of problems in expressing the desired level of performance but, for the present, we will assume that this has been done. This means that the nature of the demand for data traffic between any two processor/storage nodes has been declared and that we can now plan the supply side.

3.3.1 *Cost factors*

As a general rule, the cost of a data communications link increases, first, as the distance to be spanned increases and, secondly, as the maximum data rate – or capacity – of the link increases. This situation is probably a consequence of two things:

- a greater distance to cover means more materials (more wire, more fiber) or more power (you talk louder when someone is further away) or both
- a general pressure on supply means that you have to pay more to get more (capacity) – the bigger the pipe the more you pay.

So:

$$\text{Cost} \propto \text{distance} \times \text{capacity}.$$

When a network is being planned, the designer has little or no control over the distances involved. These are determined by factors external to the system being designed. Thus distance is an environmental constraint and the designer can set it aside for the time being, and so the calculation above becomes:

$$\text{Cost} \propto \text{capacity}.$$

Thus the most critical factor (as far as the designer is concerned) in determining the cost of a data communications link is the capacity required. A first-order approximation can be arrived at by estimating how much data needs to be moved across the link and how long we can take to do it. 'How much' means the volume of data, in bits, while 'how long' means the time available (Figure 3.5). So the calculation becomes:

$$\text{Cost} \propto \text{Volume over Time}.$$

Even a cursory analysis of this simple statement will show that it is, in reality, not so simple at all. The time period over which the volume estimate is made is critical (Figure 3.5). Should it be a year, a week, a day, an hour, a minute or even a few seconds? Demand patterns vary – if this were a system associated with retailing then we know demand varies with time of day and time of year, and there will likely be a demand peak during a certain hour of a certain shopping day just before Christmas. This area is explored in greater detail in Chapters 4 and 16.

3.3.2 *Implications for the designer*

The essential points are that:

- cost of data communications will be reduced if the volume of data movement is minimized at the design stage
- accurate estimates of demand are needed to minimize cost.

Clearly, when a distributed system is being designed there will be trade-offs between volumes of data movement and a number of other factors. One major factor is the cost of maintaining (or not maintaining) replicated data in several locations. Consider, for example, file sharing between office workers. If both office workers regularly use a file then there are two alternatives. First, have one file which they share; secondly, have two files (master and replicate), one for each worker. Some considerations are as follows:

- If they share, what will be the cost of one worker waiting while the other uses the file?
- If they share what will be the cost of accessing the data, in terms of data movement?
- Otherwise, what will be the cost of having two copies in terms of duplicated storage space?
- What will be the cost of keeping the additional copy up-to-date?

	bits	Low quality telephone line 2K4	High quality telephone line 19K2	ISDN Basic Rate (B Channel) 64K	Apple's Localtalk 230K	ISDN primary rate 2M048	Ethernet / IEEE 802.3 10M	Broadcast TV Satellite 45M	FDDI IEEE 802.6 100M	Optical Fibre 2G
Credit Check	1K	0.4	0.1	0.0	0.0	0.0	0.0	0.0	0.0	0.0
Electronic Mail (A4)	10K	4.2	0.5	0.2	0.0	0.0	0.0	0.0	0.0	0.0
Second of digitised voice	56K	23.3	2.9	0.9	0.2	0.0	0.0	0.0	0.0	0.0
Facsimile page	100K	41.7	5.2	1.6	0.4	0.0	0.0	0.0 *Acceptable*	0.0	0.0
Second of slow-scan video	128K	53.3	6.7	2.0	0.6	0.1	0.0	0.0	0.0	0.0
Second of full-motion video	10,000K	4,167	521 *Unacceptable*	156	43.5	4.9	1.0	0.2	0.1	0.0
Application binary	150,000K	62,500	7,813	2,344	652	73.2	15.0	3.3	1.5	0.1

Transmission time in seconds

Figure 3.5 How much in how long?

Cases can easily be found in which the cost of data movement in maintaining replicates of a file at several locations exceeds the cost of data movement in accessing a single copy of the file at one location.

Thus one major implication for designers is that data movement volumes must be estimated at the design stage. Another factor is that a considerable amount of painstaking work may be needed to estimate demand patterns – good recording of historical demand is an important management task.

3.4 VALUE RESIDES IN DATA

3.4.1 *Business value*

There is a temptation amongst data communications specialists to see value in the data communications infrastructure itself, typically in how modern the technology is, or in its capacity. This may be human nature, but in reality nothing could be further from the truth! One of our favourite aphorisms is 'It's what is in the truck that counts, not the truck and not the road!'. The analogy is excellent – the road is a data communications channel, the truck a message, and what is in the truck is data. It is the data that has business value, not the data communications infrastructure (Figure 3.6). If anything, the data communications infrastructure is a liability in that it has a high operating cost but little return on assets, and it has the potential, if unreliable or poorly designed, to have a severe negative impact on business procedures and processes.

The effectiveness of a data communications network is how well it answers its purpose; and its purpose is to make information available at a distance, which it

Figure 3.6 Where value resides.

does by transporting data in a manner which is:

- reliable
- accurate
- secure.

3.4.2 *Reliability*

A data communications network must be reliable. That is, it must transport data from end-point to end-point in an appropriate timeframe. This must continue to be true for large volumes of data and for long time periods. A network with long or frequent outages will almost always negatively impact on business activity. In a network, there are many potential sources of corruption, destruction and delay as we shall see.

3.4.3 *Accuracy*

A data communications network must also be accurate. A network which allows data to be lost is of little use, and one which allows corrupted data to be presented to the user is worse than useless. Very large volumes of data may have to be transported for seemingly simple 'click-of-the-button' operations such as starting up an application package on a PC when the executable file for the package is stored on another system. Any corrupted or missing data may render the package unusable. There is almost no latitude for error!

3.4.4 *Security*

Generally, a data communications network must also be secure against malicious human activity. Both intrusive and non-intrusive behavior must be guarded against, and protection must extend beyond just the obvious matter of data in transit to the functioning of the network itself and the systems connected to it.

Non-intrusive malicious activity includes both eavesdropping on passing data (which might result in the loss of confidential information) and monitoring patterns of use (which might result in a disclosure of confidential facts about, for example, levels of corporate activity).

There are a raft of possibilities for intrusive malicious activity. The simplest might be denial of service, by cutting a cable, or inserting a computer virus or worm, which might result in a loss of regular business or a business opportunity. A less straightforward action might see data in transit modified by inserting, deleting or altering bits, possibly resulting in a benefit to the guilty party. Probably the most common such activity is masquerading, where the guilty party pretends to be an authorized user (which might result in them being able to illegitimately access a database) or inserts what appears to be a transaction from a trusted device (which might result in a transfer of credit from someone else's account to their own).

3.4.5 *Implications for the designer*

For the designer, the implication is that, once the appropriate capacity is assured, engineering for effective data movement is paramount. Failure of the network to deliver data error-free and on-time may bring the entire information system, the business procedures that depend on it, and even whole business processes into disrepute.

The prudent network designer will pay close attention to both potential sources of problems (threats) and the techniques (controls and countermeasures) that can be used to deal with them.

In general, counter-measures involve the addition of redundancy. This redundancy can involve additional bits of data, additional components or additional procedures (both operational and software). Typically, there will be some redundancy in all these areas with the most common being additional data and additional software procedures.

A cost is incurred in any redundancy. For additional components, the cost is obvious. For additional data, the cost is in lower throughput for a given transmission capacity. The designer will need to weigh these costs against the potential losses.

3.5 TIMING IS OF THE ESSENCE

One of the most fundamental influences on the design of communication systems, especially data communications, is **time**. There are two reasons:

- it takes time to move something from one place to another
- each party in a communication operates in their own time.

We are not talking about the General Theory of Relativity here, but making allowance for time pervades many aspects of data communications.

3.5.1 *Timing issues at four levels*

At the most basic level, in order to identify a stream of bits on a channel, the receiver has to know when to 'read' each bit. It has to know both when to read the first bit of a stream and, since bits are sent at regular intervals, it also has to know how long to wait between readings. Imagine someone taking in a continuous stream of sound – we unconsciously use the short gaps between words and sentences to help our recognition of words; to synchronize our communication 'clocks'.

At a higher level, if a channel is shared amongst a number of stations then there will be confusion when more than one station starts transmitting at the same time, and possibly inequities in which stations gain the greatest share of the channel for their business. Imagine a big meeting without a chairperson! Note that this problem cannot be solved simply by expecting each station, once a clash has been detected, to wait a fixed length of time before trying again – they may simply collide again.

Yet higher, at the level of updating of a database which is spread over several geographical locations, events which we would like to believe occur simultaneously are, in reality, spread out over considerable periods of time. How long does it take after one person's telephone number is changed before everybody's own telephone directory is updated?

These problems, and many others in data communications, are simply a consequence of the fact that parties to data communication operate independently, not sharing a common clock, taking different amounts of time to accomplish identical tasks and having other things to do than sit and wait; and, of course, moving data from one place to another consumes time. We will now briefly examine some of the common schemes, and terminology, used by data communications designers in dealing with questions of time.

3.5.2 *Synchronous and asynchronous*

Two processors communicate in a **synchronized** manner if they share a common sense of time, otherwise we say that the communication is **unsynchronized** or **asynchronous**. In synchronized communications each party knows what the other is doing (or should be doing) at any given time, and data is passed to and fro in a regimented manner according to the common clock.

At the most basic level, sending streams of bits to one another, we have seen that it is necessary to establish this common sense of time, to synchronize the clocks, at the beginning of the stream and then to maintain that synchronization for the duration of the stream. Any scheme for doing this will involve sending some signal, other than the data itself, along with the data. This signal 'costs', in the sense that it consumes channel capacity – the trick is to keep the cost as low as possible.

An old scheme used for low-speed data communications, originally to electromechanical devices, is called **asynchronous transmission**. In this scheme, each character (byte) is treated as an independent stream of eight to ten bits. The beginning of the stream is 'flagged' by a significant change on the channel for one bit time, which allows the receiver to synchronize their clock and count off the 'reading' time for the bits that follow. Each stream is of fixed length, so the receiver knows when to stop reading the bits, and it is assumed that the receiver's clock can keep accurate time for that short period. At the end of the stream, the channel has to be placed in a predetermined state for one bit time, so that a new 'flag' can be created for the following character. The 'cost' is the wasted bit time at the beginning and the end of the bit stream – for eight-bit characters, 20% of the capacity of the channel is wasted.

A slightly more modern scheme, called **synchronous transmission**, uses a special pattern for eight or more bit times (a 'sync' character) at the beginning of a longer stream of bits to flag the beginning of the stream. This allows a more precise synchronization of the receiver's clock at the beginning of the stream, which in turn permits longer streams of bits to be received reliably. Wastage is reduced with this scheme – probably less than 10% of channel capacity (depending on the average length of the bit streams).

More modern schemes, while still needing to flag the beginning of bit streams in some way, maintain synchronization by representing the bits in such a way that a clock 'tick' is evident with each bit. In some schemes, the clock 'ticks' are recognizable by the receiver regardless of whether there is valid data present – they are associated with the **carrier** signal. This helps in detection of lost connections and in trying to prevent collisions between competing messages.

The point to note here is that, while a communication may be synchronized at one level (e.g. the basic 'bit' level) it may not be synchronized at some higher level (e.g. for whole messages).

3.5.3 *Control and contention*

When it comes to sharing channels, a related problem arises (as we have seen earlier). Here there is competition for a shared resource amongst a collection of stations, each operating more or less independently. There are four basic schemes for coping with this situation.

The first scheme is to designate one station as the 'master', the chairperson of the meeting, and have them control the sequence of events in such a way that few collisions occur and the channel is shared equitably. In effect, events are synchronized by the dominant station. This scheme is especially suitable to situations where most communication goes to and from a single station, as we might expect would happen between host and terminals in transaction processing systems. The most common example is the line control method called **poll-select** or **polling**.

If there is no naturally dominant station, then another scheme is to employ a token which is passed from one station to another in a circular fashion – the token acts as the clock. Of course, there are problems if a station loses the token – the clock stops and nothing happens for a while. The most common example of this scheme is in **token-passing** rings. Note that there is still a very clear sense here in which communications are synchronized.

We can also have schemes in which there is a 'free for all' – there is no attempt at synchronization. Each station makes a grab for the resources when it needs them, and we expect that there will be times when two or more stations all grab at once. Such schemes are not inherently fair, in the sense that some stations can dominate use of the resource.

If we want to totally prevent collision, then we can put in place a locking scheme. Each lock is so arranged that only one station can open it at a time – generally by locating it on a processor capable of resolving conflicts. A station first opens the lock, possibly not at the first attempt, then uses the resource, then releases the lock for the next station. Locking schemes are used most often at the application program level of distributed systems. Distributing locks is a tricky business – if you stretch your imagination a bit you will see that token-passing is a scheme where the lock circulates, and there are unfortunate consequences when the lock becomes inaccessible!

Lastly, if collisions are allowed then the scheme is called a **contention** scheme. A contention scheme requires good mechanisms to detect and recover from collisions. These include strategies such as each station waiting a random length of time after a collision before a second attempt. A common use of contention is in the CSMA/CD method of media access control which is used by the Ethernet and IEEE 802.3 local area network standards (see Chapter 6).

Note that the greater the emphasis put on synchronization, the greater the consumption of channel capacity (and processing power). One way of looking at it is that contention schemes are quick and dirty, whereas synchronized schemes such as poll-select are slow but reliable and fair. Another view is that asynchronous schemes are for optimists, synchronized schemes are for pessimists. Optimistic schemes, such as contention, are best suited to times of low utilization and where demand comes in short bursts.

3.5.4 *Connections and connectionless*

At higher levels, two communicating processes may need to maintain 'synchronization' so that they can conduct an exchange either of a substantial volume of data or maintain the connection over an extended period of time. Common problems in these cases involve lost chunks of data or 'data over-run' (where the receiving station cannot process data as fast as it is being sent). Synchronization of this type involves sharing more than just a common notion of time. For example, it may involve implicit recognition of access rights (as, for example, would be established in a login session on a time-sharing system).

If each chunk of data being transferred stands virtually on its own, the scheme used for transporting it between the processes can be **connectionless**. Connectionless schemes effectively mean that the relationship between the processes is asynchronous – the sending process leaves the receiving process to process the data 'in its own time'.

If, on the other hand, there is some close relationship between chunks of data being exchanged, then the scheme used would be a **connection-oriented** one. A single use of a connection-oriented scheme is sometimes referred to as a **session**. Connection-oriented schemes often maintain sequence numbering systems to control the flow of data and to detect lost chunks. In essence, a scheme is connection-oriented if some history is carried forward from one transmission to the next.

3.5.5 *Valid time and transaction time*

Ideally, the data recorded in an Information System should exactly match the state of the 'real world' at any given moment. In practice, communication and processing delays in a distributed Information System inevitably result in its state lagging behind that of the real world. The time at which the real-world event occurs is sometimes called **valid time**, while the time at which a copy of the corresponding stored data is updated is called **transaction time**.

3.6 THERE ARE MANY MEANS

Once the basic demand constraints, such as the geographical locations of components and approximate channel capacities, have been determined, the network designer will select an appropriate network architecture from those available. It is possible, of course, that this will be dictated by other considerations, such as choice of supplier for some major information system component such as computer processors, terminal units or even software.

More often than not, however, the network designer is faced with a choice, not only of architecture but also of individual components in the data communications sub-system. In other words, there are many means of achieving the same goal and of supporting the same requirement (Figure 3.7).

3.6.1 *Implications for the designer*

For the novice, and sometimes even the experienced designer, a plethora of possible architectures makes the choice difficult. Often, the situation is confused by the promise of a 'sunrise' technology, one which is just around the corner. Often too, the situation is confused by an independent potential application which, some time out, would demand more capacity than that necessary for the system under consideration. Many factors should be considered.

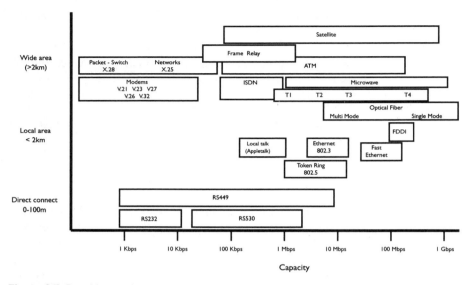

Figure 3.7 Bewildering choices.

- Can the architecture meet existing demand constraints?
- Is it likely that the architecture will meet future demand over its lifetime?
- Are the standards involved stable?
- Is the major supplier committed to the architecture?
- What is the general level of support for the architecture in the IS community?

3.7 EXERCISES

(The Case Studies are not used in this chapter as the material covered is limited to basic principles and an introduction to some of the major concepts.)

1. Describe the two basic purposes behind communication between computer systems.

2. Identify four criteria for a successful data communications network.

3. Describe the relationship between channel and medium.

4. Identify four common media.

5. What is the name given to a collection of symbols?

6. Discuss the statement 'Most standards in data communications describe the interface between two components'.

7. Discuss the statement 'The most critical factor in determining the cost of a data communications link is the capacity required'.

8. What are the implications of the previous statement for the network designer?

9. Why is it important for the designer to recognize that business value resides in data?

10. In what sense do security counter-measures involve the introduction of redundancy?

11. What is masquerading?

12. What is the difference between asynchronous and synchronous styles of data communication?

13. When would a contention approach be justified over an approach with greater control and prevention of collisions?

14. In what circumstances would a connection-oriented scheme be required, rather than a connectionless one?

15. How might a designer choose between two technologies of similar cost and capacity?

FURTHER READING

Hammer, M. and Mangurian, G. (1987) The Changing Value of Communications Technology. *Sloan Management Review* 28(21), 65–71.
Liebenau, J. and Backhouse, J. (1990) *Understanding Information*, Macmillan, London.

Efficiency: capacity and performance

4.1 INTRODUCTION

In Chapter 3, we showed that the cost of data communications, which forms a significant part of the cost of an information system, was related to a significant factor under control of the designer, i.e. traffic volumes. In this chapter we discuss tactics which are used to improve cost efficiency in a network once demand has been characterized. Because the best tactics for making links cost-efficient often depend on the patterns of traffic placed on those links, we commence with a discussion of demand.

4.2 PATTERNS OF DEMAND

4.2.1 *Effects of failure to meet demand*

In business, one of the more certain things is that failure to meet client demand brings on disaster. The same tenet can also apply to the data communications sub-system, for two reasons.

First, in the service and retail sectors particularly, a customer transaction may directly involve data communications activity. Examples are checking out at a supermarket using an EFTPOS card or booking an airplane flight. A failure of the network to meet the demand of a transaction may cause the transaction to fail and the customer may either walk away or go to a rival supplier next time.

Secondly, the communications sub-system is supplying a service to the computer applications which make up the corporate information system. Sometimes these applications are intolerant and may fail if communication delays occur. In this context, a special term is used for tolerant applications; they are said to be **network aware**.

It is thus vitally important that a network is designed in such a way that the capacity of each of its data communication links exceeds any reasonable demand placed upon them. However, the estimation of demand, in appropriate units, is often not as simple as it first appears. In many cases, it will become a job for a professional communications engineer.

4.2.2 *Estimating demand*

Let us assume that each station uses the network as a direct result of some event. Examples might be:

- an EFTPOS transaction from a cash register at a supermarket outlet
- the starting up of an application program stored on a shared file server
- the reporting of the status of some piece of manufacturing plant.

An obvious requirement is to estimate the volume of data being transported as a result of each event. However, in order to produce an effective estimate of demand on links in a network, we also typically have to look at the time-oriented behavior of each station on the network in terms of the way it generates demand. There are three major factors which influence this behavior, on their own but often in combination.

Predictable events

Events may occur on a predictable basis. This can be characteristic of systems involved in basic operational or production procedures. In this case, the demand generated by a station can also be predicted with certainty. If this is true for all stations using a channel then, in theory at least, a concrete model can be built which will predict the demand, over time, on that channel. The maximum demand on a channel can be derived with some certainty. In the unlikely case that the activity of each station is uniform over time, then a model can be built which will predict the steady level of demand on each link.

People-driven events

More commonly, the traffic generated at a station will be linked to a pattern of client (or other human) behavior. Activity will vary with time of day, day of week and week of year, so the demand generated by a station will not be uniform over time. Similarly, for any given moment, the activity of a particular station may not be able to be predicted with certainty – a station may be active in bursts at infrequent and unpredictable intervals. A network design which provides for all stations being continuously active will, in all likelihood, be very wasteful of expenditure. Consequently, network designers have to work with probabilistic models of station activity. If, as is generally the case, links in the network are shared, then cost efficiencies can be achieved – but at the expense of the time taken to transfer individual messages. In other words, there will be queuing for the use of a link. This, in turn, may violate other constraints, such as the maximum time allowed for an individual message to cross the network (as in, say, an EFTPOS transaction).

Growth

In estimating demand, the prudent designer will also consider growth in use of an information system over its life. There are several reasons for this. First, a successful system may well alter work practices to the extent that use of the system exceeds original design levels – system designers often under-estimate the long-term effects of a new system being introduced. Secondly, the life of a system is usually sufficiently long for its usage levels to be influenced by demographic (i.e. population growth) or other effects external to the business. This growth has to be planned for by designing for future traffic volumes as well as current ones. This is discussed again in Chapter 16.

4.3 DEDICATED CHANNELS

The simplest communication system is just two active nodes connected by some medium through which they can communicate. An example might be two computers connected by a **twisted pair**, i.e. a single pair of wires, twisted together as we would find in telephone cabling.

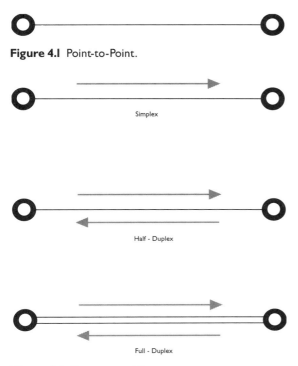

Figure 4.1 Point-to-Point.

Figure 4.2 One-way and Two-way.

In data-communication terms, we say that the two nodes are connected **point-to-point**, or that they share a **dedicated line** or **dedicated circuit**. Point-to-point (Figure 4.1) describes the **topology**, or how active components are physically arranged. This can be shown using a 'ball and string' diagram (Figure 4.2). The terms 'dedicated line' or 'dedicated circuit', which are somewhat dated, refer to the fact that cable is used only for communication between two nodes, so that it is 'dedicated' to that purpose. The terms **line** and **circuit** hark back to the days when copper wires between transmitter and receiver were commonplace for telephone lines – like true electrical circuits. Nowadays, these terms are used more loosely and encompass logical as well as physical 'circuits', and the term **channel** is preferred for a physical data path.

4.3.1 *Half-duplex and full-duplex*

A line or circuit can be employed to send data only in one direction, in which case we say that we employ it in **simplex** operation or that it is a **simplex channel**. Most radio and television broadcasting are simplex operations. However, most modern data communication is bi-directional. This can be accomplished by sending data first in one direction and then the other, with a short wait in between, which is called **half-duplex** or two-way-alternate operation. Alternatively, data can be sent in both directions simultaneously, if required, which is called **full-duplex** or two-way simultaneous operation. Full-duplex offers the greatest flexibility and consequently is the most common nowadays for point-to-point communications.

You might think that full-duplex would require two circuits (two twisted-pairs), one for each direction. Indeed, this is often how full-duplex is implemented, especially for short distances. However, a full-duplex channel can be regarded as just two simplex channels – this can be implemented using a single circuit and medium, provided that the signals on the two channels do not interfere with one another as they pass through the medium. This type of engineering solution is quite common, as we will see under **multiplexing** below.

4.3.2 Point-to-point topologies

Given a number of stations that need to be linked together with dedicated lines, we have some choice in the physical arrangement, or topology, of the multiple lines. There are basically two approaches, mesh and star – all the others require some lines to be shared.

Mesh topology

The most obvious way to physically interconnect a number of stations using point-to-point, dedicated lines is the **mesh** or clique topology (Figure 4.3). In this, each component is connected to each other by a single line. Because the number of lines (and hence cost) increases rapidly with the number of components, this topology is seldom used in practice. Often, however, a network covering a wide area will form a partial mesh because of the deliberate addition of redundant lines (e.g. to allow alternative paths in case of failure).

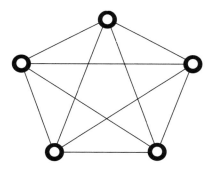

Figure 4.3 Mesh Topology.

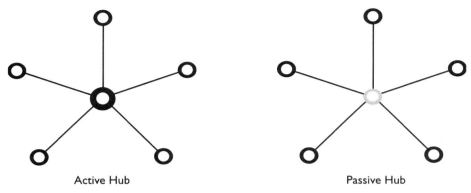

Active Hub   Passive Hub

Figure 4.4 Star Topology.

Star topology

In a **star** topology, all the active components but one are connected by dedicated lines to the last, a shared central **hub** (Figure 4.4). There are two cases to consider. The hub might be in some sense dominant, for example a central mainframe with outlying terminals, or the hub might be just a passive repeater of messages between outlying components; as in a small network of PCs. Star topologies are quite common, especially using twisted-pair cabling. This is because, in buildings, data cabling is often laid in conjunction with telephone cabling, which has traditionally been organized in star arrangements.

4.4 MAKING THE MOST OF DEDICATED CHANNELS

When we lease a dedicated channel from a commercial company, or install our own channels according to some standard, we fix (in effect, purchase) a certain channel capacity. The designer's task is then to use that capacity in an efficient way.

4.4.1 *The Shannon–Hartley law*

Once a physical communications path – the **channel** – has been established, the physical characteristics of that channel determine a theoretical upper limit on the **channel capacity**. The channel capacity is the maximum rate at which data can be sent through the channel, and is generally expressed in **bits per second** or **bps**. Sometimes the channel capacity is called the **data rate**.

The theoretical capacity of a data communications channel is given by the Shannon–Hartley Law:

$$C = W \log_2(1 + S/N)$$

where C is the capacity in bps, W is the bandwidth (i.e. range of frequencies carried) measured in Hertz, and S/N is the **signal-to-noise** ratio.

All this may seem unduly technical, but two valuable lessons can be taken from it.

- First, every channel technology has a capacity limit, which is determined in part by the bandwidth available. Bandwidth is as much a property of the transmitter and receiver as it is a property of the medium. This carries the implication that, as our overall demands to transmit data grow, we will need to replace current technologies by newer and faster ones.
- Second, noise affects capacity. You need to talk louder in a noisy room, or go somewhere quieter. Some environments, such as around heavy machinery lifts or even fluorescent lights, have more background electromagnetic noise. Some technologies are more noise-immune than others. We can expect that sometimes what seems to be the simplest cheapest solution will not work because of the environment.

The actual capacity of a channel is generally well below the theoretical capacity as given by the Shannon–Hartley law. For example, using a standard telephone system as the channel, we can calculate a theoretical maximum capacity of about 31 000 bps, which is above that currently available in practice.

The reader should never confuse the data capacity of a channel in bits per second with the speed at which a disturbance travels through the medium. Speed of propagation between transmitter and receiver is determined by the laws of nature – the spoken voice travels at the speed of sound in air, while electromagnetic disturbances, such as those used to carry telephonic and digital messages, travel at close to the speed of light.

4.4.2 Repeaters

The further a signal has to travel through a medium, the less distinguishable it will become. It will get weaker (attenuation), more noise will appear, and there are several other negative effects as well. Channels, both media and transceivers, are carefully designed to minimize these effects but, even then, the distance that can be covered by a channel of a particular type is effectively constrained. Money can be spent on reviving signals when the distance gets too great for reliability – components that do this are called **repeaters**. A repeater will not only attempt to boost the desired signal, but will also attempt to filter out, or eliminate, undesirable activity such as noise. In effect, repeaters allow the designer to extend the effective distance covered by 'chaining' pieces of channel together. Many repeaters connect to multiple channels simultaneously, repeating any signal received on one channel to all of the others. Such components are called **multi-port repeaters**, and are common in local-area networks.

4.4.3 *Data compression*

Often, a block of data to be sent has a high level of **redundancy**, by which we mean that some of it is not significant to the receiver. One example is the white space on a typewritten page. Getting rid of insignificant parts of a block of data before sending it, but in such a way that the original form of the whole block can be recreated at the other end of the channel, is called **compression**.

Compression reduces the number of bits to be sent through the channel for a given block of data (Figure 4.5). This reduces the length of time it takes to move the block through the channel. This in turn increases the number of blocks which can be sent inside a given capacity, which gives the appearance of a greatly increased channel capacity – something for nothing, almost!

Compression carries a cost in terms of processing time, both for sender and receiver (Figure 4.5). Although apparent speed gains can be made of 20 times for formatted files or ten times for fax or video, it sometimes produces little or no gain if there is a lot of variation in the original data. Clearly, compression requires agreement between sender and receiver and consequently is defined by standards. The V42bis and MNP5 standards for modems (see Chapter 6) are common examples.

Two basic ideas underlie most compression techniques.

Adaptive

The first of these identifies, on the fly, repeated patterns in the data and abbreviates them after the first occurrence; much as we use pronouns in conversation after we have identified the person by name. This can be a very powerful technique. For example, a television image is sent and displayed on your screen 50 or 60 times every second. This allows smooth movement of parts of the image, such as an arm. When transmitting digitized video, as in videoconferencing for example, the fact that very little of the background changes in a 50th of a second can be recognized and can be abbreviated to a code indicating 'this chunk is the same as last time'.

Frequency-based

The second technique uses prior knowledge of the relative frequency of symbols in an alphabet, or in groups of symbols, words, and recodes the alphabet so that

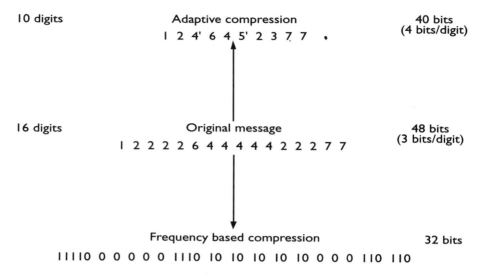

Figure 4.5 Compression Schemes.

few bits are used for common letters and more bits for infrequent ones. Morse code uses this technique, with the most commonly used letters E and T (in English at least) represented by a single bit (dot or dash), while uncommon ones are represented by three or four bits. The most widely used schemes make use of some form of what is known as **Huffman encoding**.

4.5 SHARING CHANNELS

Often there are a number of stations in close proximity to one another and, **providing a given channel or line has sufficient capacity to meet the aggregate of their traffic demands**, components can share them. As a consequence, there could be a reduction in overall cost. The traffic demands of the stations might all be directed to a common service point as in, for example, a number of POS terminals in a store connected to a central mini- or mainframe, or the demands may be directed at a variety of shared service points, e.g. a number of PCs needing to access shared files, mail and the World Wide Web.

There are number of different designs which permit shared lines or channels, and a designer choosing amongst these will be constrained primarily by patterns of demand. Topological constraints, such as the structure of a building or the layout of a site, or geographic position of sites, will also need to be considered.

4.5.1 *Circuit switching*

The simplest way in which a line can be shared is where each station uses the line in a dedicated manner for a certain time – which could be from a few seconds to several minutes – and then relinquishes it. Each station is connected by a dedicated line to a special node which is capable of connecting the station to the shared line. This special node is called a **switch** and the shared line is referred to as a **trunk** or **switched circuit**.

Conceptually, this is very similar to the public telephone system, where each telephone handset is a station and the local telephone exchange the switch. However, two problems arise:

- it takes a significant amount of time to create a connection through a switched circuit
- a connection, once created, can be held indefinitely and block other stations from using the line.

Thus this approach should not be used if stations are active more or less continuously. It is more suited to a demand pattern where each station can generate a short burst of a few seconds worth of data transmission with long quiet periods. An example is the traffic generated by EFTPOS or credit-card transactions at a retail counter. Generally, circuit switching is found only in low-speed applications with a wide geographic spread of sites. If the required peak capacity is low enough, the public telephone system can be used to do the switching (see 4.6.1 below).

With today's higher volumes and speeds, more sophisticated switching approaches are required. We describe these schemes in 4.6.2 below.

4.5.2 *Multiplexing*

Often, the patterns of demand from nearby stations which might share a line are not sufficiently intermittent to use circuit switching. Multiplexing is an approach where a line is shared, but no station appears to have its communication blocked for more than a small fraction of a second. Figure 4.6 shows how a multiplexing scheme can keep communications on a shared line separate. **Multiplexors** are stand-alone hardware devices which allow as many as 24 stations to share a line, and they generally operate in matched pairs, one at each end of the shared line.

Figure 4.6 Multiplexing.

Frequency division multiplexing (FDM)

This, the most simple scheme, divides up the total bandwidth of a channel into a number of smaller bands, i.e. ranges of frequencies. Each of these sub-bands can then carry a sub-channel of proportionately smaller capacity. The sum of the capacities of the sub-channels cannot exceed the theoretical capacity of the main channel. The sub-channels are independent of each other, which has the advantage that no station will have its communication blocked by another for even so much as the time it takes to transmit a single bit. A disadvantage is that unused capacity on one sub-channel cannot be dynamically redeployed to assist another, overloaded sub-channel.

FDM has found significant use in two areas. The first is in sharing of expensive trunk circuits, especially those leased from utility companies, amongst dissimilar traffic types. Some multiplexors can mix digital traffic with analog traffic including voice. The second area is in sharing of coaxial cable in local area networks and for cable TV.

Time division multiplexing (TDM)

A TDM multiplexor gives a short fixed time interval to each station in turn for it to communicate on the shared line. These time intervals, called slots, are the time needed to send a fixed number of bits or bytes. If ten stations use TDM multiplexors to share a line, then they get to use one tenth of the capacity of the shared line. As with FDM, the proportion of overall capacity allocated to each station is fixed, with the same advantages and disadvantages.

Statistical multiplexing (STDM or StatMux)

Statistical multiplexing overcomes this last major disadvantage of FDM and TDM, by dynamically reallocating unused capacity from one station to another.

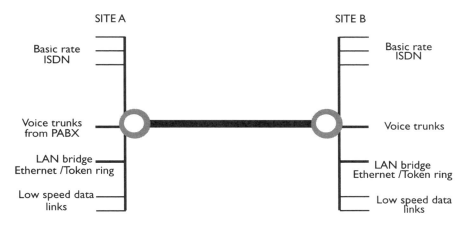

Figure 4.7 Bandwidth managers.

If the level of concurrency is low, and communication with each station is bursty, then each station may get nearly the full capacity for its bursts.

Bandwidth managers

Modern multiplexors can combine all these techniques, together with compression schemes and a 'knowledge' of the transmission patterns of different types of user devices (e.g. voice, facsimile, modem or terminal). The more complex and adaptable of these are termed **bandwidth managers**. These can provide effective linkage for all of an organization's private communications over a single high-capacity trunk line between sites (Figure 4.7).

4.5.3 *Multi-drop or tree topology*

Another approach to sharing a line, where there is a single dominant hub, is to connect stations to the shared line via branches off the line at suitable connection points or 'taps'. Such arrangements are termed **multi-drop** and the topology is called a **tree** (Figure 4.8). Typically, these arrangements are found with a central mainframe or minicomputer and a substantial number of terminals with extensive geographic dispersion – the banking and airline sectors are prominent examples.

Unlike the circuit switching and multiplexing schemes already discussed, any transmission on a multi-drop line is seen by all stations. This creates two major problems. First, a means must be found to ensure that the intended recipient of a transmission knows that it is intended for them. Every station needs to be identified with a unique physical address. Generally, each transmission will include the physical address of the intended recipient. Secondly, some scheme must be instituted to prevent too much simultaneous transmission by stations –

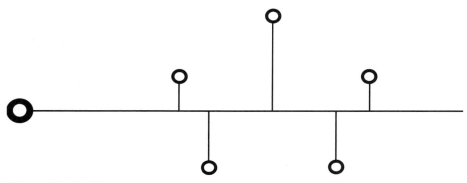

Figure 4.8 Multidrop.

as it is hard to understand two people talking at once. This calls for a scheme for controlling access to the medium, the common term for which is **Media Access Control (MAC).**

Poll-select method

One of the oldest schemes for multi-drop is called Poll-Select, already introduced in Chapter 3. This was instituted at a time when terminals had little processing capability and communicated exclusively with a central mainframe. The central system dominates activity, maintaining a master/slave relationship with the terminals. To send a message to a station, the central system must first send a SELECT message. The station then acknowledges that it has been selected, the main data message is passed, and the station acknowledges successful receipt. At frequent intervals, the central system asks each station in turn, by sending a POLL message, if it has any inbound transmission ready. These sequences are shown diagrammatically in Figure 4.9.

Contention method

A more recent scheme, now very widely used, is called **contention**. In this scheme each station transmits when it is ready, provided the channel is not in use. Contention is an 'asynchronous' method. Under such circumstances, **collisions** (simultaneous transmissions) are inevitable, but a capability for detection of collisions and their re-transmission is provided. Many modern versions of contention do not have any dominant station, but in this case transmissions contain the physical addresses of both originator and intended recipient.

4.5.4 *Bus topology*

A bus is simply a multi-drop line with no dominant station, but with the further connotation of high speed (by high speed here we mean greater than 256 kbps). The primary requirement, regardless of the type of medium used for the bus, is

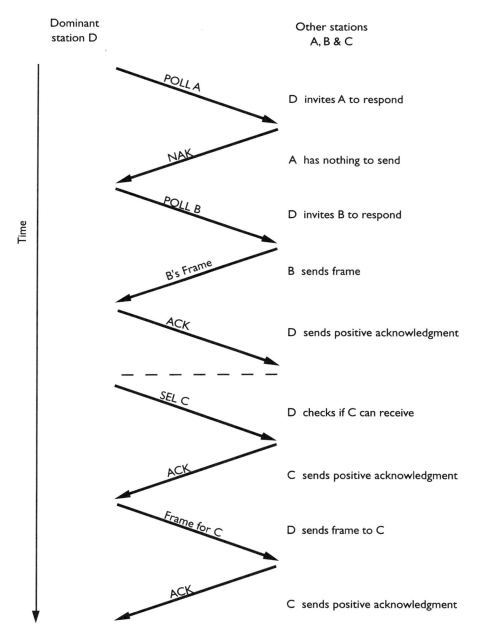

Figure 4.9 Poll-Select.

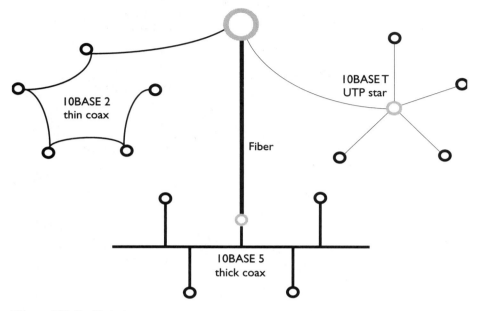

Figure 4.10 Bus Variations.

that a transmission from one station propagates to all others on the bus in a 'reasonable' time. A particular standard will specify the maximum 'end-to-end' propagation delay for a transmission, and thus effectively limit the number of repeaters, the length of a segment and the number of stations on a segment. The most common application of a bus is in local area networks.

Because the length of segment of cable being used for a bus is strictly limited, a bus is often arranged in multiple segments. The segments are connected together by **repeaters** (see 4.4.2 above) either in the form of a star or a daisy chain. Each repeater delays propagation of a transmission slightly (less than one bit time) as it passes from one segment to another (Figure 4.10).

CSMA/CD method

The most common media access control (MAC) scheme for bus topologies is a form of contention called CSMA/CD (Carrier Sense Multiple Access / Collision Detect):

- Carrier Sense – to check that the bus is not in use before beginning transmission
- Collision Detect – to detect simultaneous transmission.

This scheme is part of the Ethernet and IEEE 802.3 LAN standards.

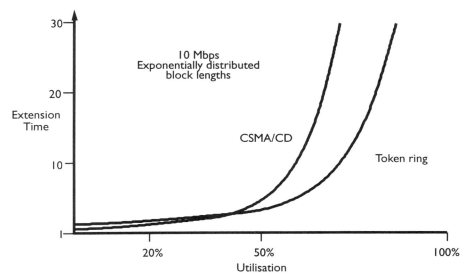

Figure 4.11 Degradation of Performance (after Bux (1981)).

While CSMA/CD performs efficiently when the bus is lightly utilized (i.e. less than 20% of capacity), the exponential increase in the number of collisions as utilization rises can cause a dramatic surge in response times and hence failure of the system. This characteristic may render CSMA/CD unsuitable for some response-critical situations, such as real-time control. The graph in Figure 4.11 plots the Extension Time (i.e. the ratio of response time to that experienced on an idle bus) against Utilization, for both CSMA/CD and the alternative of Token Passing which is described below.

Token passing method

Token passing is another MAC scheme for high-speed shared media. If used on a bus, the combination is called Token Bus. In a token passing scheme, a single small message stub is passed from station to station in a defined sequence. A station must wait until it receives the token, whereupon it may append a message intended for another station and pass the token on. The receiving station, on perceiving that the token has a message attached which is intended for it, will strip off the message and pass on, or regenerate, the token.

While a token passing scheme has, as we have just seen, some advantages over contention schemes such as CSMA/CD, it also has disadvantages because it is more complex. For example, the scheme has to provide for automatic regeneration of the token when it is accidentally lost. It must also provide for stations added to, or deleted from, the shared line.

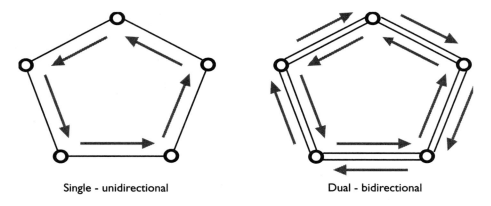

Single - unidirectional   Dual - bidirectional

Figure 4.12 Ring Systems.

4.5.5 *Ring topology*

This type of line sharing is a variation on the bus structure described earlier, where the shared line forms a complete loop. Data may circulate around the loop either in one direction only, or bi-directionally (as in Figure 4.12).

Most rings use token passing for MAC, as described above. The two most common standards are the Token Ring (IEEE 802.5) and FDDI, which are discussed in Chapter 6.

4.6 USE OF COMMERCIAL NETWORKS

Increasingly, organizations find their plans for data communications influenced by five factors:

- a large number of geographically dispersed sites, some mobile
- a number of external organizations to interconnect with
- a need to interconnect local area networks at different sites
- a diversity of traffic types and patterns within the organization
- a need to have available alternative links to increase reliability.

These factors lead user organizations to consider purchasing value-added network (VAN) services from telecommunications utility companies, instead of constructing and maintaining private networks (using lines leased from the telecommunications utility companies where necessary).

4.6.1 *Public circuit-switched networks*

The PSTN

For many individuals and small organizations, the Public Switched Telephone Network (PSTN) provides an effective service for long-distance data communications. Coverage of the PSTN network is worldwide, and reliability is good.

However, there are a number of other factors to be considered. These are:

- cost
- limited capacity
- call connect/disconnect times.

The PSTN is a circuit-switched system designed for voice communications. Costs are based on the duration of connections, the distance between the two stations, and often the time of day. The maximum capacity of a link is often no better than 4800 bps, though many times this can be achieved with compression. Call set-up involves the usual dialing, ringing, and answer sequence, which sometimes takes several seconds. In all, use of the PSTN is more suited to infrequent 'bursty' demand where the overall volume of data moved daily is small.

Because the PSTN was designed for voice communications, data communications through it must be converted by the sending station into something audible and converted back again at the receiving end. In fact, voice communications are an example of what is called **analog signaling**. In analog signaling, information is transferred by altering, in a readily distinguishable way, the characteristics (amplitude, frequency, phase) of a waveform that is being continuously generated by the transmitter. For sound, the most easily altered characteristics are the volume (amplitude) or the pitch (frequency).

Computers, on the other hand, generally use specified voltage levels to represent binary information – one voltage means '1' and another voltage means '0' – and communications between components **inside** a computer use just the significance of these voltages (plus some clock mechanism to indicate when a voltage should be 'read'). Communication where just the voltage level is altered, jumping between significant levels which signify a '0' or a '1', is called **digital signaling**. Many forms of digital signaling are self-clocking – superfluous jumps in voltage level are introduced at regular intervals to achieve this.

As an aside, it is worth noting that technology has advanced to the point where digital transmissions can be more reliably revived using repeaters than can analog transmissions – and can also be more reliably switched and routed in exchanges. Consequently the 'core' facilities of the PSTN are being converted to digital switching and transmission. With the exception of some mobile phone systems (e.g. Groupe Système Mobile (GSM)) and ISDN (see below), digital transmission has yet to reach individual premises and handsets.

So, for the past 20 years or so, and for some time yet, in order to send data between computers over the PSTN we need to convert digital signaling to analog

Figure 4.13 Using the PSTN.

signaling (in the range of 300 Hz to 3300 Hz) at one end and back again at the other. The component that does this conversion is called a **modem**. More generally, there are a variety of components which provide conversion between the common digital signaling systems used by computers and those used by specific public network systems – these components are called **NTUs (Network Termination Units) or DCEs (Data Communications Equipment)** and commonly reside on the user's premises. NTUs are signal 'translators', with a digital standard interface (such as RS232, V.24 or X.21) on the computer side and an analog standard interface (such as V.32) on the network side. A modem is just one variety of NTU or DCE. Figure 4.13 depicts the typical use of modems.

ISDN

Telecommunications utility companies are now constructing a worldwide network which should provide an integrated voice and data service, using digital signaling, to the users premises. The technology is called ISDN (Integrated Services Digital Network), and it offers a basic data interface with a capacity of 64 kbps – a considerable improvement over the usual 4800 bps – 9600 bps that is available over the PSTN. An NTU is still required for computer to computer data communications through an ISDN network, much as depicted in Figure 4.13.

While ISDNs can provide a useful backup mechanism for leased digital circuits, wholesale acceptance of ISDNs by domestic and business consumers seems unlikely. Demands by businesses for the interconnection of local area networks between sites, and for video by domestic consumers – both of which require much higher capacities than that delivered by ISDN to be effective – may see ISDN bypassed.

4.6.2 *Packet switching*

Packet switching is a technique for sharing not just a line but an entire network. Often, a packet switching service (PSS) is provided as a VAN by a commercial telecommunications company. Stations can connect to the network via switched or unswitched lines at speeds from 110 bps to 64 kbps, using clearly defined standardized interfaces (such as X.25). Because of the way these interfaces are standardized, the internal design of the network does not need to be visible to its users, and a PSS is often represented diagrammatically as a cloud. As with the PSTN, it can usually be assumed that the internal design is fast enough to cause little delay to messages traveling from one side of the cloud to another. The service can also be assumed to be very reliable – most PSS operators publish appropriate statistics. A significant contributor to a successful internal design is that all traffic through the network is packaged into data 'packets' of controlled format and limited size, enabling them to be passed from node to node in a 'store and forward' fashion – hence the name **packet switching**. The ability to intermingle packets traveling to a mixture of destinations (and belonging to a mixture of users), allows much greater utilization of trunk lines in the 'core' of the network, much as multiplexing does for a single channel, and the resulting cost savings are passed on to the users (Figure 4.14).

A PSS provides a number of facilities. The most important are:

- virtual (switched) circuits
- permanent virtual circuits
- packet assembly/disassembly.

Virtual circuits are used in a manner similar to the way one might use the PSTN. The user 'terminal' asks the PSS to connect it through to its host system, exchanges data with the host, and disconnects. This is by far the most common activity on public PSSs. Charges are generally levied for both 'connect time' and the total traffic volume.

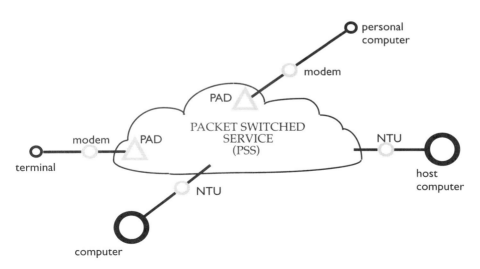

Figure 4.14 Using a PSS.

Permanent virtual circuits (PVCs) are used in a manner similar to leasing a circuit through the PSTN. Both user computers must be permanently connected to the PSS using the standard interface X.25, and they can establish a 'permanent' connection through the network.

Packet assembler/disassemblers (PAD) are provided to allow less 'intelligent' components, such as VDU (visual display unit) or POS (point of sale) terminals that transfer data character by character, to use the network. The terminal is connected, usually over a telephone line and using a modem, to a PAD facility in the network. The PAD handles the somewhat tedious business of making up packets for outgoing data, and breaking them down for incoming data. The interface to a PAD are also standardized (X.3, X.28 and X.29).

While PSSs are widely available and very reliable, they have some drawbacks:

- they only offer moderate interface capacities. Many clients end up using multiple interfaces to their mainframes in order to get enough overall capacity and PSSs may be unsuitable for local area network inter-connections
- as with most systems for sharing, when the network is heavily utilized, there can be quite long delays in the transfer of an individual packet of data from one side of the network to another
- the standards for interfacing are complex and consume significant resources in the user's equipment.

More modern commercial services, such as Frame Relay and asynchronous transfer mode (ATM)*, are variations on the packet switching paradigm, but are 'trimmed down' for higher capacities and smaller delays. They use only permanent connections (switched connections would be too slow).

4.7 DESIGN CONSIDERATIONS

Although Network Design is addressed more fully in Chapter 16, within the overall methodology for Distributed and Cooperative systems design, a few general comments are appropriate at this stage.

4.7.1 Matching supply and demand

The design of data communication facilities is primarily one of matching supply and demand. Demand is variable, and usually growing – depending on user expectations. Supply depends on the available technology and is still advancing in large steps of performance each year. Costs vary with user take-up and

---

*In this book, the acronym ATM should always be assumed to signify Asynchronous Transfer Mode – and not Automated Teller Machine – unless explicitly stated.

competition in the marketplace. It is not an area for elegant optimization – what may be best one week is quickly out of date the next.

4.7.2   *Importance of monitoring*

Very few networks experience static demand. From a network designer's point of view, it is therefore imperative that traffic levels on a network be monitored as an aid to ensuring adequate performance. Existing traffic levels and patterns of demand are used by the network designer when designing a new network or revising a network in a way that costs are minimized. They are also used to verify that patterns of demand, especially growth, are as predicted when the most recent design was completed. The capacity of the network has to be kept above the level of demand placed upon it. Thus a monitoring capability must be built into the original design, even though it increases the cost.

Network performance monitoring typically records two views:

- Efficiency measures
    - throughput (traffic)
    - utilization
    - terminal activity by transaction type

and

- Service measures
    - transaction response times
    - accuracy
    - availability

4.8   DATA COMMUNICATIONS EFFICIENCY IN THE CASE STUDIES

4.8.1   *Mr A*

Mr A's traffic is very spasmodic, and volumes are likely to be low. He is unlikely to be able to justify dedicated circuits, except possibly in his own home. He will rely on commercial networks to provide him with efficient services. Initially he is likely to use the PSTN through a modem, though if he finds himself frequently dialing out of his local calling area, he may consider subscribing to a PSS via a PAD.

4.8.2   *Bay Organic Produce Cooperative*

If the Cooperative has decided against a central computer, it is likely to be a strong candidate for a bus or ring network, since 45 lines would otherwise be needed to provide a dedicated mesh between 10 staff. Analysis of work patterns would be needed to establish the capacity needed and the appropriate type of Media Access Control.

Longer distance traffic is likely to be more intermittent, and commercial networks would be adequate.

4.8.3 Detox Pharmaceuticals

The terminals connected to the IBM AS/400 may use a dedicated network, possibly with multi-drop topology and poll-select.

The PCs and Macs on staff desks would probably best be interlinked using a bus-style LAN.

There is a dedicated link between the factory and the local refinery. If a number of different users needed to use this link concurrently, multiplexing might be justified.

4.8.4 Electric House

The Head Office mainframe will be the center of a large dedicated network, which may cover remote sites, and hence multi-drop is likely to be used.

PC users will need a shared network as traffic is likely to be intermittent.

EDI exchanges with suppliers and clients are unlikely to have sufficient traffic volumes to justify permanent links. Use of a PSS, or perhaps just the PSTN, seems most appropriate.

4.8.5 Commonwealth Open Polytechnic

Most internal needs can be met by shared networks. The exceptional needs lie in the area of video data transmission. ISDN may only offer slow-scan video, and permanent ATM links may be justified.

The network needed to support links with contractors may justify use of a PSS.

4.8.6 National Environmental Protection Board

A high-volume shared network will be needed for the headquarters, because in order to go 'paperless' high volumes of imaged documents are likely.

Wide area data interchange is relatively infrequent and low-volume, apart from any remote monitoring. Commercial networks would be adequate in most cases.

4.9 EXERCISES

1. Describe two possible consequences of failure of a data communications network to meet the demand placed on it.

2. What are the problems in estimating demand when the business process is driven by people-oriented events?

3. Why do we say that a point-to-point connection uses a dedicated line?

4. What is 'topology'?

5. Compare half-duplex and full-duplex communications.

6. What is the primary unit for describing channel capacity?

7. In what environments might the signal-to-noise ratio for data transmission be worse than normal?

8. What is the relationship between data compression and redundancy?

9. What is multiplexing?

10. Describe the five principal methods of controlling access to shared channels.

11. Show how both contention and token-passing can be used for media access control in a bus topology.

12. Would circuit-switching be a good way of supporting EFTPOS transactions?

13. What are the advantages of packet-switching? What is the most common use of networks that employ this paradigm?

14. Which parts of the PSTN use analogue transmission and which parts use digital transmission, and why?

ASSIGNMENT TASK

For the Case Study of your choice, suppose that you have a certain set of network facilities installed or subscribed to. Monitoring is starting to show that in some areas performance is dropping off as the traffic is nearing capacity. Without upgrading the capacity of the circuits, what improvements could you suggest?

FURTHER READING

This list introduces a selection of 'mainstream' Data Communications textbooks and a couple of simpler introductions.

Black, U. (1993) *Data Communications and Distributed Networks*, Prentice-Hall, Englewood Cliffs, NJ.

Croucher, P. (1990) *Communications and Networks – A Handbook for the First-Time User*, Sigma Press, UK.

Dowty (1991) *The Pocket Book of Computer Communications*, Dowty Communications, UK.

Fitzgerald, J. (1993) *Business Data Communications – Basic Concepts, Security and Design*, Wiley, New York, Chapters 3–6.

Halsall, F. (1992) *Data Communications, Computer Networks and Open Systems*, Addison-Wesley, Reading, MA, Chapters 2–3.

Keiser, G. (1989) *Local Area Networks*, McGraw-Hill, New York.

Silver, G. and Silver, M. (1991) *Data Communications for Business*, Boyd and Fraser, Boston, MA, Chapters 4–6.

Sloane, A. (1994) *Computer Communications – Principles and Business Applications*, McGraw-Hill, New York.

Stallings, W. and van Slyke, R. (1994) *Business Data Communications*, Macmillan, New York, Chapter 6.

Stamper, D. (1994) *Business Data Communications*, Benjamin/Cummings, New York, Chapter 1.

Vargo, J. and Hunt, R. (1996) *Telecommunications in Business*, Irwin, Chicago.

5 Effectiveness: reliability, accuracy and security

5.1 EFFECTIVENESS AS WELL AS EFFICIENCY

An organization can install the most efficient data communications network possible and yet still not provide effective support for the organization's business processes. Ultimately, the effectiveness of a network can be judged by its ability to enable or contribute to business activity by transferring data from one point to another in a manner which is reliable, accurate and secure.

A **reliable** network is one which consistently and accurately transfers data from sender to recipient in an appropriate timeframe. A network with long or frequent outages will almost always negatively impact on business activity. Long delays caused by saturation of some part of the network will often increase the cost of business activity, frustrate the client or, in some cases, cause the activity to fail completely. An unreliable network is often the cause of that catch-cry 'the computer is down'.

Data transfer is **accurate** if data is neither corrupted nor lost. Business decisions or other information-intensive activities may rely on data transferred across a network.

A network must also be **secure** against malicious human activity. This can include:

- eavesdropping on passing data *resulting in* loss of confidential information
- monitoring patterns of use *resulting in* disclosure of confidential facts, e.g. levels of corporate activity
- denial of service *resulting in* loss of regular business or a business opportunity
- adding, deleting, or amending messages *resulting in* benefit to the guilty party
- masquerading as someone else *resulting in* fraud or theft of computer time.

Transportation is a risky business. The level of protection that can be afforded data during transportation is inherently less that the level of protection that it enjoys in the primary or secondary storage of a computer. According to Black (1993), the most prominent factors affecting this are:

- the effects of distance
- hostile environments
- numbers of components involved
- lack of immediate control over the process.

Figure 5.1 depicts some of the common points of failure in a simple local area network (e.g. in the Small Business Case) and a simple dial-up database access (e.g. in the One Person Business Case).

Appropriate responses or counter-measures (the formal term is **controls**) to these and other threats to the data fall into three broad categories:

- prevention
- monitoring/detection
- isolation and reinstatement/repair.

In general, counter-measures involve introducing a measure of redundancy; this means adding extra data, software or hardware components.

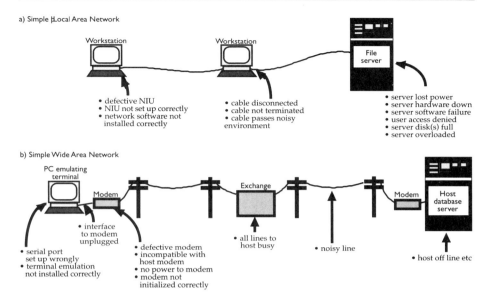

Figure 5.1 Common Points of Failure.

A cost is incurred in any redundancy. For additional components, the cost is obvious. For additional data, the cost is in lower effective data throughput. The prudent network designer will pay close attention to sources of problems (threats), the techniques (controls and counter-measures) that can be used to deal with them, and will weigh the costs of counter-measures against the potential losses.

In the next three sections, we examine in more detail reliability, accuracy and security issues.

5.2 RELIABILITY

5.2.1 Threats

Complex networks involve equipment sited at many different locations. These hardware components may be vulnerable to many external threats, both natural (Acts of God) and artificial. Electrical and other storms, flooding, loss of power and vandalism are all real threats to the continuous operation of a network, and, of course, each component may break down and need to be repaired or replaced.

The effect of a single component failing in a large network can be quite deceptive. For example, a single bridge, router, or cable may be used by almost all movements of data on a local area network and its failure will result in most activity ceasing. Another example is that the transceiver on a shared channel (such as an Ethernet or 802.3 bus) may 'jabber', transmitting continuously, thus preventing any further use of the channel by any station connected to it.

Channel components, especially cables, are very exposed to potential unintentional or malicious activity. Common threats include excavations for services, a disgruntled employee or customer with wire cutters, the power supply to a transmitter failing, or even a failure of a component of the transmitter itself (after a nearby lightning strike for example). While there are preventative measures (see section 5.2.3 below) that can be taken, common practice is to monitor loss of service at a step removed from the channel and then to have well-tested tools and procedures to repair or move to an alternative channel in the shortest possible time.

A lack of immediate, exclusive control by the originator over all components in a network complicates both preventive and remedial activity.

5.2.2 *Measures of reliability*

Availability

The most frequently used measure of reliability is called **availability**. Availability for a whole network can be defined as the proportion of:

> time the network is available to transport data (up-time)
> divided by
> total time in which the users want to use the network.

These days users typically want to use the network 100% of the time.

How does the availability of the network as a whole relate to the reliability of its individual components? The adage 'a chain is only as strong as its weakest link' might come to mind. But is it good enough to have each individual component as reliable as we would wish for the whole network? Often, the answer is no. Figure 5.2 shows two basic arrangements of components in a network.

The availability A of a network path which passes through a number of components in series is the product of the individual availabilities A_1, A_2, A_3, as expressed in the formula:

$$A = A_1 \times A_2 \times A_3 \dots.$$

If we take a system of ten components, each available 99% of the time, and each needed for the system to operate, the system's overall availability is 0.99^{10}, or just 90%. In other words, overall system availability is often considerably **worse** than the availability of any individual component taken on its own. Components in data communications have to be exceptionally reliable. This includes not just channel hardware but also such things as file server software.

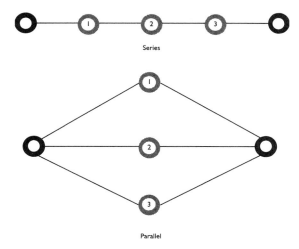

Figure 5.2 Series and Parallel.

However, dramatic improvements in availability can be made if even a modest amount of redundancy is introduced. If a number of components are connected as alternatives, in parallel, with only one needed for successful operation of the whole, then the availability of the whole is given by:

$$A = 1 - (1 - A_1) \times (1 - A_2) \times (1 - A_3) \dots .$$

For a parallel arrangement comprising just two 99%-available components, the overall availability has **risen** significantly to 99.5%. Adding redundant components, especially alternative channels over long distances, significantly increases overall reliability. Costs will increase, but these will often be more than justified by the potential for loss if the network fails.

Other measures of reliability

Many vendors refer to the twin measures of MTBF and MTTR, where MTBF is the mean time between failures and MTTR is the mean time to repair (time to diagnose the fault, get whatever spares, tools or materials are needed, and then fix the problem).

MTBF and MTTR can be related to Availability using the formula:

$$\text{Availability} = \frac{\text{MTBF}}{\text{MTBF} + \text{MTTR}}$$

Stamper (1994) also introduces a Reliability measure $R(t)$, equal to the probability of the network path not failing in a given time interval (denoted by the variable t). The formula is:

$$R = e^{-t/\text{MTBF}}$$

where MTBF is measured in the same units as the time t. The calculations for this Reliability measure when components are in series and parallel are analogous to those for Availability.

5.2.3 *Prevention*

One of the best areas for investment in pursuit of reliability (and security) is that of prevention. Significant reductions in the usual rates of post-implementation problem occurrence can be made by paying sufficient attention to the basics.

First and foremost, components should be chosen so as to be appropriately reliable. Suppliers indicate the reliability of a product by quoting a figure for its MTBF. However, the actual MTBF experienced may vary considerably from this.

Hardware components need an appropriate environment – clean, dry, not too hot and not too exposed to human hands and feet! It makes no sense to place a critical repeater in a location where it may be prone to water damage, or impurities in the air that it needs for cooling. Power supplies should be, at a minimum, appropriately conditioned and an uninterrupted power supply (UPS) should be employed wherever possible.

Software is a source of failure that is often neglected. Network software should be developed, tested, and deployed under the same stringent controls used for sensitive mainframe applications.

5.2.4 *Detection, isolation and repair*

There will be times when, despite the best preventative measures, a hardware component in a network will fail. However, our experience is that component malfunction is a far less frequent occurrence than disruption caused by inadvertent human actions. Cleaning staff, for example, may unplug NTU and repeater power cables to plug in their cleaning equipment, or disconnect cables by hooking them with the vacuum cleaner nozzle.

Rapid detection and appropriate response to a failure are crucial aspects of successful network operation, made easier by appropriate planning at the design stage. The measure of MTTR, which is as critical to Availability as MTBF, can be kept low through management action.

MTTR is derived by adding three time factors:

- time to **diagnose** the cause of the problem (i.e. which component is at fault)

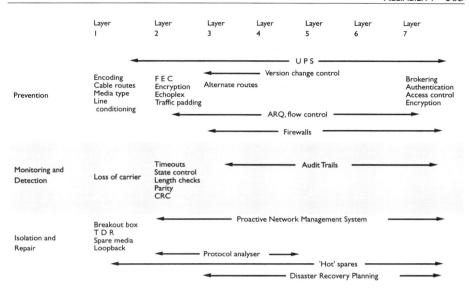

Figure 5.3 Counter-measures.

- time to get the necessary resources for repair to the failure site (**response**)
- time to effect the **fix**.

The first two of these are the primary contributors to MTTR. How long it takes to diagnose the root cause will depend very much on the provision of appropriate tools for monitoring and testing, as well as staff availability and training. Time to respond may depend on an external contractor, or the location of spare units or staff rosters.

The main point is that availability of the network does depend to a significant extent on provision of adequate services to diagnose and repair failures. Figure 5.3 shows preventive measures, diagnostic tools, and some remedial actions. 'Layers' are explained in Chapter 6.

Signal loss

The first and most obvious thing to detect is **loss of signal** on any channel. Many transmission systems are arranged so that idle periods, where there is no data to transmit, are 'filled' by the transmitter repeating an agreed signal. A receiver detecting the loss of this signal should, after a brief delay, pass an indication of the problem up the chain of command. A good example of this indication is the 'Carrier Detect' signal in interfaces between modems and computer equipment they service. For extremely secure systems, it is possible to detect the partial loss of signal that might indicate the presence of an eavesdropping device.

Loss of service

Another, often neglected, scheme is to install special software which periodically checks that critical software services are available. This software could run on a machine in the network management center, or it could report to that center using a standard network management protocol.

Auto-recovery

A prudent network designer will incorporate an appropriate degree of redundancy. Most often, this will consist of installing additional channels, creating a partial mesh where a simple star or tree might have been originally chosen. Designers often look to the telecommunications utility companies for backup services, using either the PSTN, ISDN or a PSS. Most intelligent components which are capable of switching or routing data, for example routers, bandwidth managers and mail servers, are also capable of automatically **falling-back** from a preferred channel to a less-preferred alternative. Some can balance the traffic load between alternative channels or paths.

5.3 ACCURACY

5.3.1 *Threats*

Of the three factors underlying effectiveness, data accuracy is the most vulnerable. Environments which, to the eye, look benign can be quite hostile to data transmissions which use electromagnetic signals. The radiation given off by fluorescent lights, electric motors and even some basic electrical appliances can interfere with data transmissions over twisted-pair cables. Coaxial cables can be affected by heat and humidity. Microwave transmission is affected by moisture in the air, be it fog, rain, hail or snow.

The channel is the most vulnerable part of a communications system. It often extends over hundreds or thousands of kilometers, passes through environments which are hostile to varying degrees, and often is only able to be monitored successfully at the transceivers at either end.

In addition, for many channels, there is an inverse relationship between speed and error rates. That is, we could increase the capacity of the channel if we were prepared to tolerate less accuracy in the data transported. Because 100% accuracy – minus perhaps a very small fraction of a percentage depending on application – is required, we are left with three basic strategies:

- engineer conservatively for all conditions (with a relatively low capacity as a result)

- provide for automatic, transparent, recovery from errors by adding redundant data
- adapt the speed to the conditions.

Note the similarity of these to the broad-brush responses mentioned in the introductory sections of this chapter. In practice, all these strategies are adopted at various times, often in combination. For example, Ethernets only operate satisfactorily at fairly low levels of utilization – up to 25%; and modern devices designed to operate over the PSTN, such as modems and faxes, adjust their transmission techniques/speed both before and during transmission as a consequence of detecting higher-than-desirable error rates.

Sources of channel errors

Most data errors in a data communications network are introduced through the channel. They may be caused by:

- systemic impairments, e.g. delay, distortion and attenuation
- random impairments, e.g. noise, echoes and fading.

Systemic impairments are, broadly speaking, those consequences of the physical laws of nature that we have been unable to totally surmount in physical engineering terms. The impairment of greatest significance overall is signal delay, because this generally means that all steps in the receiving process have to sit and wait at times. Our only response is to engineer conservatively around them at a step removed from the channel mechanism itself.

Random impairments are, on the one hand, a nuisance because of their unpredictability but, on the other hand, may have only a small effect on total throughput. Especially significant causes are electrical noise, often caused by seemingly innocuous devices such as fluorescent light fittings or the electric motors in lifts or pumps, and fading, for example due to a heavy rainstorm in the path of a microwave link.

5.3.2 *Prevention*

Prevention of and recovery from channel-sourced errors has been studied intensively and there is a substantial body of well-proven engineering available. We will now briefly examine some preventative measures.

Appropriate medium type for environment

In the first instance, the data communications designer or engineer should plan (within cost constraints) to use the most appropriate medium for the environment. For example, cabling on a factory floor would often be chosen to minimize interference from high-current electric motors, unusual levels of heat or moisture, or the occasional bit of rough handling. Cabling between buildings, whether in-ground or laid in a duct, would often be chosen on the basis of similar criteria. In these cases, optical fiber (being immune to virtually all electromagnetic interference) in a suitable sheath will almost certainly be appropriate. Over longer distances, cost differences between alternatives (such as coaxial cable, optical fiber, terrestrial microwave or satellite) will be much more significant, with the result that the burden of ensuring accuracy (and security) is transferred to higher 'steps' in the transport process.

Most suitable route

The route to be taken by any medium should be planned so as to avoid potential trouble spots. For example, twisted-pair cabling in a building needs to be placed away from fluorescent light fittings and, as far as possible, electrical supply wiring. On a larger scale, in-ground cabling should be routed away from likely excavation sites, in-ground high-tension power supply cables, and so on. Further up on the scale, microwave links should avoid 'growth' hazards such as uncontrolled building construction and areas of peculiar natural hazard such as storms or spontaneous fires. In a broader general sense, consideration has to be given to all paths which could pass through hazardous environments including, for example, natural hazards such as earthquake, electrical storm, and flooding, as well as artificial hazards such as unstable power supply or riot.

Filters and line conditioning

Spurious signals, noise, can often be discarded by filtering or ameliorated by pre-conditioning (adjusting the electrical properties of a channel). **Filters** are a very general mechanism, used by a 'receiver' at all levels of the data transport process. At this physical level they are used for filtering out unwanted frequencies and electrical stages, but at higher levels they are used to discard corrupted messages and reject attempts at unauthorized access.

UPS

All systems need a stable, clean, power supply. Wherever possible, an uninterruptable power supply (UPS) should be used to power all network logic components. At a minimum, even in wiring closets, a passive power line filtering device should be used.

5.3.3   *Detection*

At this most basic level, methods of error detection fall into two groups – those that involve adding redundant bits to the data stream and those that do not.

Parity checks

A traditional scheme is adding to a sequence of bits a redundant bit or bits whose value is calculated by a simple logical operation from the original group. Figure 5.4 shows how this would work for a single **parity bit** appended to an octet (eight bit group). The transmitter, in effect, attaches an extra '1' to the end of the sequence if there are an odd number of '1's in the original sequence, otherwise it attaches an extra '0'. The augmented sequence is now guaranteed to have an even number of '1's when it is sent. If it does not when it is received, then the receiver has detected an error and either discards the octet or otherwise indicates that it is defective. The redundant bit is discarded.

Note that this method of checking can only reliably detect the alteration of a single bit. If two or more bits have been altered then the parity check might not detect an error. The addition of more bits, calculated in a similar manner, can detect greater number of bits in error or even be used for error correction, as we shall see.

Cyclic redundancy checks

Modern systems typically transmit bursts of much longer sequences of bits than the eight given above, typically between 48 and a thousand or more. As a consequence they need to use many more redundant bits (16 is common) and more complicated calculations in order to detect a reasonable number of error conditions. In fact there is a substantial body of knowledge about which calculations to use in order to maximize the opportunity for detecting errors, given typical transmission impairments. Those methods in wide use are called **cyclic redundancy checks** (CRC) and are capable of adequately detecting typical errors in sequences of up to 30 000 or so bits. Choosing the most appropriate calculation from the standards available is a design activity.

State maps and timeouts

Another method of detecting errors relies on the fact that the receiver knows, as part of the basic agreement between them, that the transmitter can only be in one

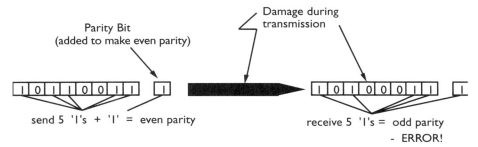

Figure 5.4 Parity Check.

of a fixed number of states, and that these states can only occur in certain sequences. Examples of such schemes can be found in token passing systems, in high-speed modems, and in the ancient art of asynchronous character transmission. A special case of this method involves checking the number of bits in a received sequence. Timeouts involve waiting a predetermined time for a response, then raising an error condition.

Flow control

Because senders and recipients are independent and work at different speeds, it is possible for a fast sender to overwhelm a slower recipient with data that they cannot process. In this case, some data may be ignored by the recipient. It is, in effect, lost or destroyed. Link protocols often incorporate **flow control** schemes, especially sequence numbering, which are aimed at prevention and detection. Lost data will be detected by aberrations in sequence numbering; backward error correction schemes are used to recover.

5.3.4 *Correction*

Because most errors result from problems with the channel, especially random corruption of data, it makes good sense to tackle the problem of correcting errors that do occur as close to the channel itself as possible. There are two basic alternatives.

Either the receiver can be given sufficient information to allow it, once it has detected an error, to make the correction without reference back to the transmitter. This is called **forward error correction** (FEC) and involves additional bits. Alternatively, the receiver can discard the erroneous chunk of data and request the transmitter to re-send it. This is called **backward error correction**. This latter alternative requires the transmitter to keep a copy of transmitted data, an overhead in itself, and it will also entail a certain amount of delay in retransmission. There are circumstances where each method is appropriate, and they can also be used in conjunction.

Forward error correction

Three instances where forward error correction is especially useful are:

- on simplex channels
- where the error rate is unusually high
- where the delay in accomplishing retransmission would be uncomfortably long.

An extension of the state mapping scheme, discussed before as a detection mechanism, also allows the receiver to make simple corrections. In effect, there is redundancy in the coding system which can be used for error detection and correction. An example of this is the trellis coding scheme used in the V.32 standard for modems (see Black 1993 p. 66).

Hamming codes make use of a complicated scheme of parity calculations and additional bits to produce codes (groups of bits) in which a maximum number of bit alterations (generally one or two) can be detected and corrected. These are special cases of a family of forward error correcting codes called BCH codes, which are themselves a special case of a yet larger family. At present the principal use for these codes is in satellite transmission systems.

Backward error correction

The more common method of error correction involves, after detection of an error by the receiver, an automatic request for retransmission (**ARQ**) to be passed back to the transmitter. The transmitter must retain a copy of data sent until such time as it is sure that it has been received correctly. Schemes for accomplishing this may involve explicit positive acknowledgment (ACK) of correctly received transmissions, negative acknowledgment of transmissions in which an error has been detected (NAK), waiting a fixed length of time (timeout), sequence numbering of transmissions, or combinations of these (Figure 5.5).

Backward error correction works best with substantial chunks of data because of the delay involved in accomplishing retransmission. It is, in effect, part of a

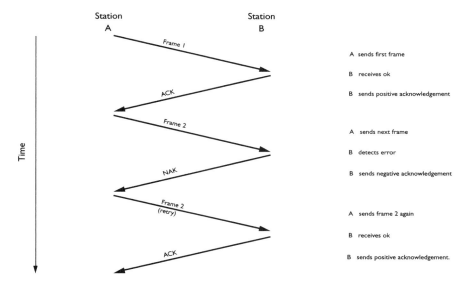

Figure 5.5 A Simple Backward Error Correction Sequence.

higher layer of activity that sits on top of the basic media access control. On multi-drop or bus channels it is often combined with schemes for addressing and flow control into an agreed protocol called a **link access protocol (LAP)**, **data link control (DLC)**, or **logical link control (LLC)**. A traditional term here which has fallen into disuse is **line protocol**.

5.4 SECURITY

Given that data can be replicated without destroying the original, and that network software components will be trusted if they are seen to perform the function for which they were designed, it is worth considering the ease with which a malicious person might modify some software component so as to tap in to the data flowing through a network.

5.4.1 Threats

Breaches of security may be intentional (e.g. a ruthless competitor, fraudster, disgruntled employee or over-zealous government intelligence) or inadvertent. Threats may be passive (electronic eavesdropping) or active (adding, deleting or amending messages).

A recent (1995) survey reported a 73% rise in reported security attacks on US organizations between 1992 and 1993. In percentage terms of attacks, 39% came from competitors, 19% from customers, 19% from public interest groups, 9% from suppliers and 7% from foreign governments. Attacks from insiders and hackers seem to have been mysteriously excluded from these figures – the suspicion is that they may be responsible for as many attacks again, most of them undetected.

A significant number of the components in a network are software processes. Software components are vulnerable to many threats, primarily because they are generally based on writeable stores, both for code and data.

A **worm** is a self-replicating program that utilizes a flaw in network software components to transport itself from one station to another over the network. A worm may be deliberately destructive to any host station software or files, or it may simply consume network resources. A **virus** is a self-replicating program that attaches itself to files or other storage objects that it can locate. Viruses are generally destructive to files on their host stations. Although a few viruses are 'network aware' and actively seek new hosts through network transmission, most are transported to new stations by human activity (as an attachment to a piece of electronic mail, or in a file copied across the network) or by locating new files on different stations on a network file system.

5.4.2 *Prevention*

Physical prevention

Transmission channels tend to pass outside any boundary that can be physically secured against malicious human activity, and so detection techniques tend to dominate. Nevertheless some physical prevention measures can be used. First, although equipment can be bought off-the-shelf to eavesdrop on any medium, some media are more resistant than others. Optical fiber emerges as the best in terms of its resistance to both eavesdropping and active interference (other than severing the cable); bus systems using coaxial cable are designed for easy addition of stations and therefore should be avoided in areas which cannot be physically secured. Secondly, physical access to areas containing cables and or transmission equipment, especially wiring closets, needs to be rigidly controlled. It is such a simple matter, having gained access, to install eavesdropping equipment or even extend a cable through to an insecure room.

Boxed network components should be afforded an appropriate level of physical protection, be they a simple NTU, repeater or file server. As they almost invariably require a power supply, physical protection should extend to that too – cutting off the power to an NTU or repeater at a critical time is just about as effective a means of causing loss to the organization as hitting the unit with a hammer!

Authentication

Authentication is used to prevent masquerades, and commonly involves password systems or digital signatures. Network services such as remote access to a local area network, access to electronic mailboxes, and access to specialist devices will often require protection through distributed authentication systems called **network access control systems**. One such system which is gaining acceptance is Kerberos, a distributed authentication and access control system developed at MIT (Cashin, 1993; Kanugo, 1994).

Encryption

Encryption is used to protect the contents of a data stream by transforming the original bit patterns, which are easily read and emulated, into seemingly random patterns. Encryption involves two components, a cryption algorithm and one or more keys which 'drive' the algorithm. The actual key (or keys) used for a particular link will be unique and it is they, when applied to a cryption algorithm, which make the resulting combination unique. The algorithms are generally in the public domain, but the key (or keys) are a private agreement between sender and recipient and must be kept secret, especially when being passed between them. The number of possible keys for a given algorithm must be so great that an eavesdropper could not simply try them all to find the one that works.

Encryption has two valuable consequences. First, it keeps data private. Secondly, it can prevent **masquerades** (where a person conducts unauthorized activity through a communications link by pretending to be a legitimate user).

DES

The most common encryption algorithm is the Data Encryption Standard (DES). It uses a 64-bit key, but only 56 of the 64 bits are used by the algorithm, the rest are used for parity checking the key itself. There are 2^{56} possible keys – more than 70 000 000 000 000 000 – so a potential eavesdropper would spend a long time trying to find the right one. However, because techniques for breaking this system are getting faster, a reasonable level of security can only be guaranteed if the key is changed regularly.

DES is what is called a symmetric algorithm. That is, the same algorithm and key are used to encode the data and to decode it.

Public key encryption

Public Key systems are asymmetric; that is, sender and receiver use different algorithms and keys. The recipient first chooses their own private key (to be used for decoding received data) then uses it to calculate a second **public** key which can be passed to the sender for encoding the data. There is no need to keep the public key secret; the system relies on the time it would take to try all possible private keys given that you know the public one. As with the DES, the prudent user will change keys at regular intervals.

Asymmetric cryptography systems have a number of advantages. First, the private key is only known to one party (which makes it easier to keep it safe). Secondly, changing keys is easier because a new public key can be sent undisguised to the sender.

One significant use of public key cryptosystems is **authentication** (proof of origin) through **digital signatures**. The best known of these is the RSA Digital Signature. Digital signatures are easy to use and not only guarantee that the sender is who they say they are, but also that the data has not been tampered with by some third party.

Location of encryption systems

Encryption systems can be employed in two ways. They can be used either:

- to protect all transmissions on a channel; or
- to protect communications of a particular type.

Protecting data on a channel generally involves the addition of hardware encryption devices between DTE (data terminal equipment) and DCE (data circuit-terminating equipment) as shown in Figure 5.6. All data passing through the channel, including flow control, is encrypted so this method can only easily be used where the channels are privately owned.

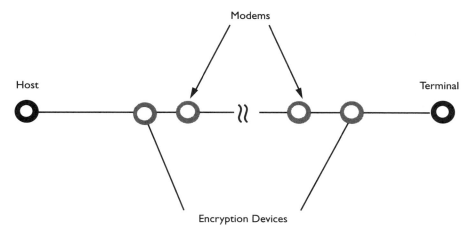

Figure 5.6 Channel-based Encryption.

Transactions of a particularly sensitive nature can also be protected by software encryption. This is more suitable for communications between two independent organizations, or where a public network is being used.

Firewalls

When a corporate network is permanently interconnected to a public network, such as the Internet, the corporate network can be very vulnerable in spite of formidable access controls on individual stations and systems within. This is due to several factors, the most prominent being:

- the large number of potentially hostile people now connected
- the length of time that a hacker could have to attempt to break in
- the difficulty in tracing access paths through other peoples networks and systems.

A **firewall** is a 'gatekeeper' station which forms the only point of interconnection. All data moving between the two networks must pass through the firewall, which imposes a rigorous access control scheme on each chunk of data by type and by source and destination address. The software of the firewall itself must be engineered and maintained to the highest security standards (Cheswick & Bellovin, 1994; Ranum, 1995).

5.4.3 *Detection and control*

Even the best preventative security measures will not deter the determined hacker or fraudster. Some see 'cracking' an organization's security as an intellectual challenge. Designing security measures for networks is like running an arms race with a band of urban guerrillas!

Good monitoring is the essence of successful security operations. Wherever possible, audit trails should be kept of all actual or attempted communications to trusted or critical components. Specifically, this should apply to network management stations and those that hold access control tables, including dial-back numbers for modems. Naturally, these audit trails should be inspected regularly.

Other than taking immediate steps to close off loopholes which have been detected, control generally consists of police or court action. In these cases, accurate records of individual transactions from identifiable physical locations may be needed as evidence if an offender is to be punished. Too often, network designers ignore the need for such recording.   .

5.5 NETWORK MANAGEMENT

In a recent US survey, it was estimated that supporting desk-top computers in organizations costs on average $3830 per seat per year. The network that links these desktops to shared computing resources – and to each other – is therefore a vital resource that needs managing. The user organization needs to ensure that its investment in data communications facilities meets the business objectives set for it.

5.5.1 *Basic tasks of network management*

The main tasks involved in managing a network are listed below.

- configuration control – maintaining inventory and topology of components, planning upgrades
- routine operation – starting-up and shutting down of the network,
  adding/deleting users and nodes, naming of devices and users
- performance monitoring – of user response, utilization of line capacity,
  errors, outages
- fault handling – detection, fail-soft, diagnosis and repair (see below)
- enforcing security – granting/revoking user privileges, analyzing logs,
  reviewing security measures
- accounting – setting up user accounts, recording levels of usage, charging
  for network use (internally or externally)
- supporting users – operating help desk, training, newsletters, wish lists,
  consultative committees.

Some of these tasks are, inevitably, largely manual procedures which do not merit detailed description here. Details can be found in other textbooks (e.g. Stallings and van Slyke, 1994; Langsford and Moffett, 1992). In this book we limit our discussion to methodologies and tools that are particular to the operation of distributed computing.

5.5.2 *Detection and diagnosis of problems*

A fault handling methodology is critical to good network management. The following four stages are typical of such methodologies.

Detection includes analyzing user complaints, monitoring component warning lights, monitoring automatic checking reports and running routine checking programs.

Fail-soft methods include isolating the problem, switching to backup facilities, partitioning the network and reconfiguring so that as much work as possible can still continue.

Diagnosis involves applying tests, analyzing logs, and continuous tracking of recurring problems.

Repair (including replacement) involves applying re-acceptance tests before restoring the full network service.

A major problem with networks is that a fault may be obscured in various ways that make timely detection and diagnosis difficult. Two factors that affect this are layering and auto-recovery.

Layering

Networks are constructed as a series of layers of software and hardware components. While each layer will have its own style of error detection and recovery, the communication of a fault indication between layers is often poorly developed. The failure to pass an indication of the original error up the hierarchy may inhibit timely detection, diagnosis and eventually manual intervention to fix the problem. As an example, the first indication of an attempted intrusion onto a channel might simply be an increase in the number of errors corrected.

Auto-recovery

Modern data communications components have embedded within them many features that detect and correct transmission errors and other faults. Employed wisely, these greatly increase the reliability of the network. But there is a downside. As we have seen, recovering from errors increases the volume of data to be transmitted, which will degrade the time it takes to transport data across the network. **Fall-back** to a secondary mode, channel, or path will also almost always result in a degradation of performance, since we naturally choose the best performer for normal operation. This degradation may not be noticed at first and it often obscures the original fault.

So it is not enough to design a network which is self-healing. It is also essential to design a network in such a way that all problems and recovery actions **at any level** are recorded and reported. These reports must, of course, be actively monitored. Typical indicators are:

- % of blocks containing errors
- number of timeouts or sequencing errors
- any loss of signal or fall-back to an alternative circuit
- numbers of retransmissions
- response times.

In addition, close attention needs to be paid to problems experienced by users. Calls to the help desk saying 'The computer is down!' need to be logged, as they often mean that there is a failure or overload somewhere in the network.

5.5.3 *Active network management*

Active Network Management is a term used to describe those methods which, as far as possible, foresee potential problems and prevent their occurrence. Such methods normally involve the use of automatic tools, which can consist of both hardware and special-purpose software.

Active network management tools include:

- monitors – for channels, user workstation activity, modems and other interfacing components, communications software and various events
- intelligent software – for analysis and reporting of monitor and log data
- quality control algorithms to warn of impending problems
- automatic reconfiguration
- testing and restoring.

To support management of complex networks, many of the above tools are bundled to provide a consistent interface to human network administrators. The result is known as a Network Management System, which operates as a 'big brother' inside the network itself. In some networks, one site in the network is set up as a Network Control Centre. This site runs the majority of the Network Management System functions, often in conjunction with smaller associated software modules on other processors and workstations. An example of suitable software is IBM's NetView.

Monitoring of problems and automatic recovery actions in any network is a difficult task and, if the network is even moderately complex, may require the employment of specialist staff. Special-purpose probes or monitoring stations may be strategically placed around the network. Remote activation of changes to the network can significantly reduce outages caused by the inevitable succession of software and hardware upgrades. Specialist skills in these areas are often in very high demand.

Many modern hardware components, except of course the communications media themselves, are built around some form of programmable processor. Even though they are engineered primarily to perform a primitive network function, such as repeating a bit stream, they are also 'intelligent' in the sense that they have the capability, as secondary function, to monitor and report on their primary activity. Some components can go further in that they can accept commands to alter that primary activity. For example, a modern multi-port repeater can be instructed remotely, from a Network Control Centre, to shut down one of its ports. Such components, which appear to be quite passive as far as their primary function in the network is concerned, appear as active stations on the network in their secondary, network management, function. Figure 5.7 shows these two views of the network.

As the reader will probably realize, there have to be standards which describe how components interface with one another for the purposes of network management. Major suppliers of network components, such as Novell and IBM, have their own standards, but easily the most common standard is **SNMP (Simple Network Management Protocol)**. This standard, originally described for TCP/IP networks (see next chapter), defines an interface between a 'manager' and an 'object' and, by implication, between a management station (i.e. network control center) and a remote station. It accommodates multiple remote stations and multiple management stations. Many suppliers provide components with SNMP capability.

It is a significant task for the network designer to select a network management standard and to design for an adequate level of management capability in the components.

5.5.4 *Passive (manual) network management*

Four aspects of network management can be identified which cannot be built into an active or automatic system. These are discussed below, together with the issue of the organization of human responsibilities for network management.

Authority

It is a critical privilege for a user to be on an organization's network. It is an important question as to who is entitled to offer or deny service to a user. There must be a system of authority that decides what the users' real needs are, whether or not the organization can afford to service them, and whether or not their usage should be limited.

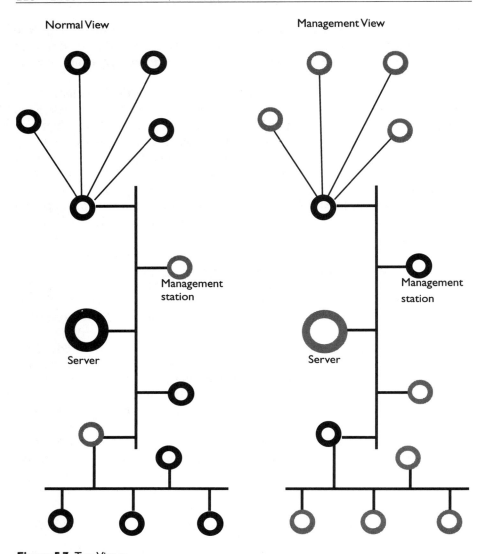

Figure 5.7 Two Views.

Service to users

A 'Help Desk' system is often used even if users' PCs are not linked to any network. As well as providing additional advice on using the network, help desks provide a vital route for monitoring user satisfaction levels, which may indicate the need for planning future network improvements. A formal system for logging, monitoring and actioning of complaints is essential practice. Many organizations use a 'Groupware' package (mentioned in later chapters) for this.

Capacity planning

Network configurations are rarely stable for long – increasing demand results in a series of upgrades in capacity, hardware and software. Rather than lurch from crisis to crisis, most organizations set up a part-time team with the task of planning a more controlled series of upgrades. This process accepts feedback from automatic and manual monitoring procedures. At the level of implementing each upgrade, the plans must allow for testing, reconfiguration and informing users about the changeover.

Disaster recovery

There will always be some threats to the network which, if realized, involve such wholesale destruction that the result is a disaster to the Information System – and hence possibly to the Business itself. Flood, fire, tornado, earthquake – not forgetting war or terrorist action – might be the cause. For mission critical networks, restoration of service goes well beyond a normal operational response to faults – a **disaster recovery plan** is called for. Disaster recovery plans for main network nodes can call for extensive planning, as a substantial number of incoming terrestrial circuits may have to be rerouted, with the assistance of the public service provider, at the last major exchange they passed through.

Organization of network management

Depending on the size and complexity of network operations within an organization, one or more staff will be assigned to network management roles. 'Network Administrator' is a common title for the leader of this function. As with a Database Administrator, the person in this role has a high level of responsibility and power. Often, both Network Administrator and Database Administrator will report to a CIO (Chief Information Officer) or 'Data Administrator'.

5.5.6 *Network management design tradeoffs*

Network administration – as well any counter-measure we may use to maintain effectiveness – costs money. The primary design question is much like insurance – what do we get for the extra premiums? All expense has to be justified in terms of the quality and value of the information system to the organization.

5.6   EFFECTIVENESS AND NETWORK MANAGEMENT IN THE CASE STUDIES

5.6.1   *Mr A*

Mr A is not too critically dependent on his network, although security could become an issue if he is to exchange data about client prospects with partners or associates.

5.6.2   *Bay Organic Produce Cooperative*

High availability is important for any sharing of data between office staff. Accuracy of lots bought and sold is also vital. Security could become important if competitors operate in the area.

BOPC would be advised to appoint someone to act as Network Administrator to cover both internal and external communications. Since the organization is small, a part-time contractor might be adequate, given a good monitoring system.

5.6.3   *Detox Pharmaceuticals*

Network reliability will be most critical in the process control area – parallel components will probably need to be considered.

The links to pharmacies and hospitals will also be important, both from the data security point of view and for high availability in order to maintain the 'easy to do business with' image.

The variety of networking needs could justify a network management system, and it is likely that a full-time network manager will be needed.

5.6.4   *Electric House*

The US company is probably already managing its network and protecting itself against threats. There will be a Network Management System and a team of staff.

With EDI, transferred money and credit card details will need protection by encryption.

The threats in Latin America may be different – availability may be more of a problem as the commercial networks may not be able to support as high an MTBF as in the USA.

5.6.5 *Commonwealth Open Polytechnic*

Network failures are unlikely to cause the organization to collapse quickly, but bad student experiences may lead to longer-term loss of business. Confidentiality is a big issue, with student details, marks, etc. Student use of Internet may need to be controlled and monitored, and COP's own systems protected from the threats of attack from remote users.

For network management, a well-qualified technical specialist may be needed, particularly to support the video applications. A network control centre at the central campus would be needed.

5.6.6 *National Environmental Protection Board*

Apart from any use of remote monitoring, network problems do not have an instantaneous effect on business. However, if the office is truly 'paperless' the administration may grind to a halt soon after a major network outage begins.

NEPB may be required by their charter to uphold the confidentiality of subject organizations, which may necessitate encryption of any data transmitted that is specific to an identified organization.

With a number of potentially different networking needs, a Network Management function is probably justified, requiring appropriate software and at least one specialist.

5.7 EXERCISES

1. Discuss the cost of network down-time to a business.

2. Describe typical threats to a data communications network in each of the following categories: malicious human activity, unintentional human action, Acts of God and systemic.

3. Describe the three types of response to threats.

4. Explain why these responses generally involve redundancy.

5. What is the effect on overall availability of a number of components being connected (a) in series? (b) in parallel?

6. How can the basic factors that affect the availability of a network be controlled by the designer?

7. What type of response to threats are parity and cyclic redundancy checks?

8. Explain the difference between forward and backward error correction schemes.

9. How can the recipient of a message be sure of the identity of the person sending the message?

10. What are the two most significant uses of encryption?

11. Describe public-key encryption.

12. Although automatic recovery measures such as error correction and fall-back appear to improve the reliability of a network, they can also create problems. Discuss.

13. What are the primary functions of a network management system?

14. Why can some components in a network be active in one view but passive in another?

15. What is the importance of a help desk system in network management?

16. What are the main tasks of a network administrator?

17. Why is the design of network effectiveness similar to taking out insurance?

ASSIGNMENT TASK

For the Case Study of your choice, draw up a table showing Risks, Detection Methods, and Counter-measures for each of the top ten threats to Availability, Accuracy and Security of the Network.

FURTHER READING

Black, U. (1993) *Data Communications and Distributed Networks*, Prentice Hall, Englewood Cliffs, NJ.

Cashin, J. (1993) *Client/Server Technology – The New Direction in Computer Networking*, Computer Technology Research Corporation, South Carolina.

Cheswick, W. and Bellovin, S. (1994) *Firewalls and Internet Security: Repelling the Wily Hacker*, Addison-Wesley, Reading, MA.

Computing (1994) Focus on network management. *Computing* (UK), 24 Feb.

Dauber, S. (1991) Finding fault. *Byte Magazine*, Mar.

Fitzgerald, J. (1993) *Business Data Communications – Basic Concepts, Security and Design*, Wiley, New York, Chapters 12 and 13.

IBM (1992) Special issue on network management. *IBM Systems Journal*.

IBM (1993) Managing a world of difference, *Seminar Notes*.

IBM (1993) NetFinity remote personal systems management. *Seminar Notes.*

Kanugo, S. (1994) Identity authentication in heterogeneous computer environments: a comparative study for an integrated framework. *Computers and Security*, 13(3), 231–53.

Langsford, A. and Moffett, J. (1993) *Distributed Systems Management*, Addison-Wesley.

Lynch, M. (1994) Safety nets (article on IS security). *Computing* (UK), 3 Nov.

Lynch, M. (1994) Code crackers publish formula for encryption key on Internet. *Computing* (UK), 22 Sep.

Stallings, W. and van Slyke, R. (1994) *Business Data Communications*, Macmillan, New York, Chapters 13 and 14.

Stamper, D. (1994) *Business Data Communications*, Benjamin/Cummings, New York, Chapters 13–15.

Unicom Seminars Ltd (1993) Securing your information network: technical and legal issues. *Seminar Notes.*

6 Implementation: layers and standards

6.1 INTRODUCTION

In Chapter 4 we saw that standards are an inescapable part of data communications. Starting with this premise, we first discuss issues and concepts that are associated with all standards; we then go on to the process of standardization and standards-creating bodies; and finally present some of the common standards that form part of the core of data communications knowledge that all IS practitioners should acquire.

6.2 LAYERS AND ENVELOPES

6.2.1 *Layers*

The complex nature of the computing technologies that underlie information systems (IS) has inevitably resulted in a fair degree of specialization of individual technologies. We readily understand and accept, for example, the division between applications programs, operating systems and systems programs, and the computing hardware and their relationships to one another; often these are presented via an 'onion skin' model.

Such specialization similarly pervades data communications technologies, although a different model is needed.

Imagine that the captains of two warships need to communicate, during a naval exercise. The entire naval exercise could be regarded as a distributed information system in operation, with the warships being processing sites. Both captains speak the same language and, if they were in the same physical location, could communicate verbally. However, the distance between the ships is a barrier to their communication. Some technological intervention is necessary to circumvent the barrier – it might be Aldis signal lamps, or a radio transmission of some kind. Each captain has a specialized task, and it is neither necessary or desirable for each to be burdened with the knowledge of how to operate this intervening technology. Secondary **agents**, called signalmen, each specialized in the use of the appropriate technology, be it signal lamps or radio or both, are employed to relieve the principal parties of the unnecessary burden (Figure 6.1).

A communication between captains will proceed as follows. The sender, Captain A, writes down or dictates a message to Signalman A, who then transmits the message, suitably encoded into Morse or similar, to Signalman B who, after reverse encoding, hands the written message (or verbally relays it) to Captain B. A similar procedure would apply for a response from B to A.

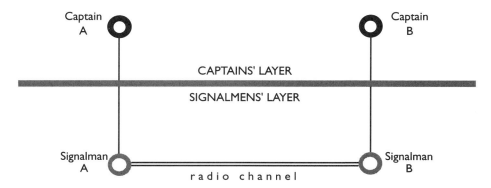

Figure 6.1 Layers and Agents.

There are five very important principles at work here:

1. If two principals do not share a communications mode that they can operate, but they both have secondary agents who do, then communication between principals can still be effected.
2. The principals do not need to know how the secondary agents accomplish their task, just that it can be done.
3. Because there is a communication between principals, albeit indirect, then they must share and utilize some common standard. They both speak and write the same language, 'Captainese' for example.
4. The secondary agents do not need to understand the meaning of the messages between principals (although they do, of course, have to know which principal the message is for). It might be in an exclusive Captain-to-Captain code, for example. To the secondary agents, the messages are simply a product (data) to be moved.
5. Although the secondary agents need not be aware of the meaning of the message between principals, they will need to embed the message inside some communication between themselves.

In effect there are two levels – or layers – of communication which are operating simultaneously; the primary layer (between Captains) and the secondary layer (between Signalmen). Both layers exist in each node of the overall system. The layers are a consequence of both specialization of communicating agents and the barriers created by distance.

Networks typically have several layers and multiple agents. The highest layer will contain agents that application programs can use to communicate. For example, these might be agents which provide for electronic mail between wordprocessors. The lowest layer will contain the physical means of transferring data from one location to another. Agents communicate with others at the same level, but until a message reaches the lowest layer in a node or station, they are always communicating indirectly through agents at lower levels.

A seven-layer descriptive system for data communication standards, the ISO OSI framework (see section 6.3 below), has been developed relatively recently. Most modern standards fit neatly into this framework, but many older ones do not.

6.2.2 *Envelopes: messages, packets, frames and cells*

A paper envelope is a container that we use to convey messages written on paper through the postal systems of the world. Data communications systems also use envelopes, although they can be called by several different names. In fact, the properties and uses of these 'envelopes' in data communications are so similar to those of paper envelopes in postal communications, that the analogy is worth further examination (Figure 6.2).

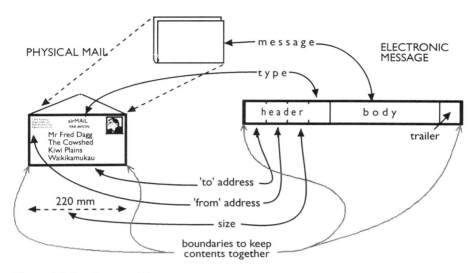

Figure 6.2 Envelopes and Frames.

A postal envelope:

- contains the paper (on which the message is written)
- keeps the paper within recognizable boundaries, keeping it together
- protects the paper from minor damage
- carries a 'to' or destination address, used by the postal service to get the envelope to its destination
- carries a 'from' or source address; also used by the postal service
- has a type (e.g. 'by air', 'printed matter only')
- has a size which reflects the volume of its contents
- often has a 'standard size'.

These same features are generally found in an 'envelope' used by data communications agents. The envelope will have a **data body** corresponding to the paper message. It has recognizable boundaries, sometimes indicated by sequences of bits reserved for this purpose. At a fixed place relative to the boundaries, there is a group of bits which is to be interpreted as a **destination address**, and a group of bits to be interpreted as a **source address**. There will probably be a group of bits that designates the envelope **type**, allowing the receiving agent to distinguish between frames carrying just control information and those carrying data as well. The control group or groups in a message will be used to implement processes such as backward error correction. There may be a group of bits that describes the **size** of the data body.

These envelopes are called by various names: **message**, **block**, **frame**, **packet** or **cell**. The basic concept, both in structure and use, is much the same, but **packet** and **cell** have a special connotation which indicates standardization of size. **Message** was the term used in the early standards when **messages** were composed of characters or bytes, and it still persists today in popular descriptions of data communications and sometimes in standards at the higher levels. The term **block** is obsolete and rarely occurs nowadays. The term **frame** generally designates an envelope of bits (as opposed to characters or bytes), and therefore tends to be common in standards at lower levels, close to the physical media. **Packet** and **cell** are terms which occur when there is standardization of envelope size, as in **packet-switching** services and **cell-relay** services. As in the postal system, standardization of envelope size reduces unit handling costs and simplifies charging for use. These and other properties make transport systems based on standard-sized packets and cells especially suitable for public carriers.

The part of an envelope before the data body is called the **header**, and the part after the data body the **trailer**. The process of composing the header and trailer and placing it around the data body (placing the paper in the envelope) is called **embedding** or **encapsulation**, and when the header and trailer are no longer required they are **stripped** (i.e. discarded).

6.2.3 *Addressing and naming*

Just as a postal envelope has to carry destination (and sender) name and address in a standard enough format so that it can be delivered, the electronic delivery system must do so as well. Two factors make the **addressing** and **naming**, which is how sources and destinations are identified, considerably more complicated in data communications networks than in traditional mail.

The first of these is layering. You can see from Figure 6.2 that the address on a postal envelope is decipherable by all those that handle it, from the person who puts the message in the envelope to the person who opens it. In layered systems, each pair of agents often have their own addressing/naming schemes. For example, when I use my workstation to send electronic mail to my colleague Fred, I use **all** the names shown in Figure 6.3.

The layers in this electronic mail system correspond broadly to people, stations, the electronic mail application programs, the Internet agents and the physical computer at each end. Each layer has its own addressing scheme, and all are used at sometime or another in passing a message between end-users.

Obviously, a name or address must be unique within the area of its use, its **domain**. In the example in Figure 6.3, neither of the names 'Chris Freyberg' nor 'IS-FREYBERG' can be guaranteed to be unique in the world; the former might not even be unique in an employing organization. However, electronic mail addresses and the Internet IP numbering scheme **are** designed to be unique in the world.

This brings us to the second complicating factor. Names and addresses are 'assigned' to agents and workstations by some local authority in each domain, just as local goverment assigns street addresses to buildings. True, for worldwide

	From:	To:
Common name:	Chris Freyberg	Fred Dagg
Workstation name:	IS-FREYBERG	GUMBOOT
Electronic mailbox:	C.Freyberg@massey.ac.nz	Dagg@cowshed.farm.org.nz
IP Number:	130.123.345.6	96.1.262.33
802.2 Address	3FDB 664E 1234	SAA2 3C78 91E3

Figure 6.3 Naming Schemes.

domains, such as the Internet (IP numbers) or electronic mail, there has to be some worldwide authority to ensure that no name/address is duplicated. The problem created by these local spheres of authority is this: when I go to send a message to Fred, I probably do not know exactly how he is referred to by those around him, and I almost certainly do not know his workstation name or his workstation's physical address (they are determined locally); but these will be needed by lower level agents to get the message to him. Somewhere along the way, translation between these naming systems has to happen. In practice, in passing a message across the world, many naming domains are traversed and translation between the various names happens at nearly every step in the process. These translations are often accomplished by reference to **name servers** – electronic phone books if you like. These servers also talk to one another using special protocols, so that they can help other agents at junction points in a network choose the correct path along which to send a message.

At the junction points in a network, there may be a variety of special stations or agents whose primary job is just to pass the message on by an appropriate route. These junction stations are also well placed to perform network management and security functions, such as monitoring demand and screening. Different terms are used to refer to these junction stations, depending on the layer they are concerned with. We have seen that at the lowest layer, between separate channels, junctions are called **repeaters**. At the next layer up, between links, they are called **bridges**; and at the next layer up again, between independent networks, they are called **routers**. In the layers above the first three, they are called either **gateways** or '**store-and-forward agents**'. Repeaters connect channels together to make a composite link, bridges connect links together to form networks, routers connect networks together and so on.

You will have noticed for the worldwide domains in the example in Figure 6.3, above, that each name/address is segmented. The electronic mailbox is something like C.Freyberg@massey.ac.nz, the IP number 130.123.345.6 where the periods and @-sign break each address up into segments. This segmentation is a convention which allows naming in a worldwide domain to be delegated, as far as it is possible to do so, to local naming authorities. For example, in the electronic mailbox name, the worldwide authority simply decrees that all New Zealand addresses will end with '.nz', and then passes authority for the finer detail inside New Zealand mailbox names over to a New Zealand authority. That authority has decreed that mailboxes in our organization shall uniquely contain 'massey.ac' just before the '.nz', and Massey University is able to make decisions about the rest. This approach is similar to that used by other worldwide naming schemes with which we are familiar, e.g. the public telephone and mail systems.

6.2.4   *Advantages and disadvantages of layered systems*

The primary advantage of layering is, of course, specialization of the agents. There is, however, a second major advantage: that agents in two adjacent layers are sufficiently independent that replacing one (with, say, a newer model) should not prove disruptive to the other. This far-reaching principle of independence can, at least in theory, be extended so that agents at a higher layer could communicate with one another irrespective of the standards being used by agents at lower layers. A consequence of these two things is improved reliability.

Another advantage is that error checking and correction may be handled in lower layers without the higher layers becoming involved in the problem. For example, nearly all the errors in a network are handled in the first two layers. Unfortunately, this is the cause of some difficulties too, because the top layers may not be made aware of the nature of the errors, or even that errors are occurring at some lower level, until they cause a total failure.

However, the main disadvantage of layered systems is that the layers impede data flow; they slow things down slightly, because of the extra software overhead, and the additional bits in the headers and trailers in the 'envelope' that have to be transmitted.

6.3   THE ISO OSI FRAMEWORK

As an aid to understanding, it is normal to position both individual standards and families of them on a background structure – the most popular template for which is the ISO OSI framework. This seven-layered framework was developed by the **International Standards Organization (ISO)**, in consultation with other standards-setting bodies, in the early 1980s. Its intent was to provide a guiding structure for the development of standards associated with open systems interconnection (OSI); that is, networking involving multiple suppliers.

Although we shall refer to this framework as just 'the ISO framework', it has many names. Most properly it is the ISO Open Systems Interconnection Reference Model, or the ISO 7498 international standard. CCITT recommendation X.200 and BSI 6568 are equivalent. It is also more familiarly called the **OSI Model** or the **OSI Architecture**.

There are seven layers in the ISO framework, from the Physical Connection (i.e. the mode) in Layer 1 through to Application Support in Layer 7 (Figure 6.4).

LAYER 7 Application	Application support services; utilities for message handling and directory services for electronic mail, file transfer and access, terminal emulation.
LAYER 6 Presentation	Provides translation between data formats; including encryption, compression, screen format conversion and code translation (e.g. EBCDIC to ASCII).
LAYER 5 Session	Establishes and maintains a session, generally involving the exchange of multiple messages over a period of time. Includes high level flow control.
LAYER 4 Transport	Provides reliable user-to-user transport of a message.
LAYER 3 Network	Provides end-to-end routing (possibly through multiple networks) of a packet of data; collects traffic data for accounting purposes.
LAYER 2 Data Link *Logical Link* *Media Access*	Provides reliable transport of a packet between two physically connected devices; including error detection and correction. Provides envelope and arranges access to a shared medium.
LAYER 1 Physical	Provides method of transporting a bit stream; converts frame into a bit stream; encoding, mechanical and electrical connection

Figure 6.4 The ISO OSI Framework.

It is very important to understand that the ISO framework really is just a framework. It is a structure on which we can locate both individual standards and also active software (and hardware) agents which instantiate those standards. Most modern standards conform well to the framework, fitting reasonably neatly within individual layers of the framework. Many standards which pre-date the framework (e.g. EIA RS232-C) do not, lying across two or more layers.

Families of standards, often called **profiles** or **architectures**, have been defined for distinct purposes. Some, such as the **TCP/IP family**, have grown with one particular artifact, in this case the Internet. Others have been developed by vendors, for example **SNA (Systems Network Architecture)** was developed by IBM. Yet others, such as **MAP (Manufacturing Automation Profile)**, have been developed for generic business processes. Some of these common profiles are described in section 6.5 below.

6.4 STANDARDIZATION AND STANDARDS-CREATING BODIES

As we have seen, standardization is an essential part of making things work together. A number of groups are involved in developing and setting data communication standards. Often, what is essentially the same standard will be adopted by a number of these bodies, each giving it their own number. Sometimes these individual, seemingly identical, standards have subtle differences – Ethernet and IEEE 802.2/802.3 are often, mistakenly, regarded as synonymous.

6.4.1 *Vendors*

Vendors, that is manufacturers of computers and communications equipment, have always had internal standards within their organizations to ensure that components such as processors and peripherals produced in different plants can be connected together successfully in the field. As clients demanded access to other vendors' specialized components, these large vendors have published their standards externally so that secondary vendors could make 'compliant' components. One of the most significant occurrences of this was the publication of the IBM PC bus standard, because it enabled secondary vendors to manufacture peripheral and other cards which could be slotted into a PC in the field – thus adding value to the IBM PC product and guaranteeing a market for the secondary vendors.

6.4.2 *Industry groupings*

Industry organizations too, have an interest in creating standards. Those large industries which are basically consumers of communications equipment will want to create a market in which a number of vendors will compete to supply their needs, thus keeping prices down and quality up. Those industries which are basically producers of equipment which incorporate communication capability – such as printers – will want common standards to enhance the market potential of their products.

6.4.3 *CCITT*

CCITT (Consultative Committee on International Telegraph and Telephone) is a grouping of organizations whose business **is** communications – many of whom have grown out of national telephone utilities or 'Telcos'. They appreciated from early on the need to interconnect their networks, especially across international boundaries. The main CCITT standards are those in the I (ISDN), Q (signaling), T (telex, fax and teletext), V (voice networks) and X (data networks) areas.

6.4.4 *IEEE*

The US Institute of Electrical and Electronic Engineers (IEEE) has also taken the initiative in standardization, and IEEE is still the acronym most commonly used for the major standards in local area networking.

6.4.5 *ISO*

The last, but by no means least, major group comprises the individual national standards organizations, which are represented internationally by ISO. One particular non-governmental standards organization, ANSI (American National Standards Institute), has in the past been very active, chiefly through its X.3 (Computers and Communications) and X.12 (Electronic Data Interchange) groups.

6.4.6 *Advantages and disadvantages of standardization*

Standards are clearly essential to all effective data communications, but not all standards are automatically cost-effective to users, or are successful in gaining widespread adoption. Adherence to standards involves overheads in both cost (hardware, software and certification) and in performance so success of a standard depends on reaching a 'critical mass' of users of that standard.

6.5 WELL-KNOWN STANDARDS PROFILES

There is no single set of standards that all suppliers of hardware and software can agree on, even though many of the individual standards, especially at low layers, are the same in several different profiles. Examples of different profiles are ISO OSI, TCP/IP, X.25/X.29, MAP, IBM/SNA and Novell.

A profile will typically be implemented on a computer system as a software procedure library or 'stack' of procedures installed alongside the operating system. Often, systems feature two or more stacks operating concurrently. For example, an IBM minicomputer or mainframe will often be using SNA for the majority of its data communications, but may be using TCP/IP – over a separate physical connection – to enable its users to have access to the Internet.

6.5.1 *ISO OSI profile*

ISO, in addition to the creation of the seven-layer OSI framework, has also created a number of standards specifically for OSI. Most of these standards were developed for and by industries as part of specific profiles, the two most well known being **MAP** (see section 6.5.6 below) and **TOP** (Technical and Office Profile). We use OSI here to illustrate the different layers as it appears to be the most comprehensive of the architectures (Figure 6.5).

In support of applications, in Layer 7, OSI contains standards for

- electronic mail handling (X.400, MHS)
- file transfer and access (FTAM)
- terminal emulation (VT)
- directory and naming services (DS and X.500).

Note that this range of application support and utility functions is typical of a number of profiles – compare for example TCP/IP below. Note also the adoption within the profile of standards created by other organizations (e.g. CCITT X.400 and X.500). We quite commonly find one standard with several labels, one for each of the major standards organizations.

At the transport and network layers, two major services are described, one connection-oriented and one connectionless. The connection-oriented service is the more complex of the two, requiring the agents at each end to maintain a two-way exchange over a period of time, using delivery confirmation and flow control to help recover from data loss, damage or duplication. A connectionless service (sometimes called a **datagram** service) simply sends the data as an 'electronic telegram' to some destination, expecting no confirmation or continuation – effectively a high-level simplex operation.

These standards interface with most of the common existing local and wide area standards for individual data links – new standards for those layers are not

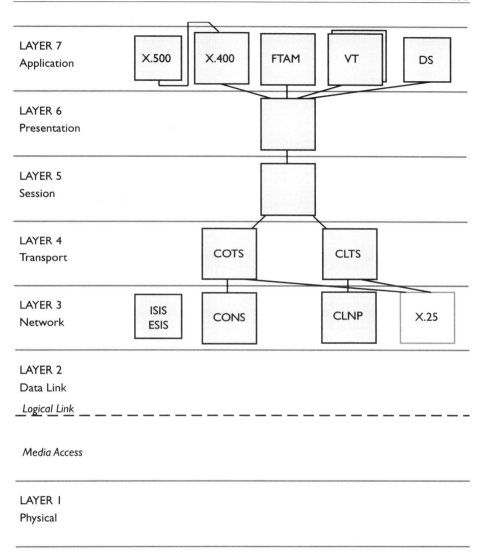

Figure 6.5 OSI Profile.

defined for OSI. This is not as peculiar as it might seem as OSI is driven by the need to interconnect disparate systems (not devices).

Although the OSI profile has been demonstrated by most of the major suppliers of computer systems, many users feel that it is too cumbersome and involves too high a performance overhead. To meet this criticism, Enhanced Performance Architecture (EPA) has been proposed to allow time-critical applications to short-cut levels 3, 4, 5 and 6.

6.5.2 *TCP/IP profile*

TCP/IP (Transmission Control Protocol/Internet Protocol) is the most common internetworking profile in use at the present time. It grew out of a series of standards for connection between UNIX systems, developed for a US defence network (DARPA) by the university/research community there. Its popularity probably results from two main factors: it pre-dates the ISO OSI initiative and it

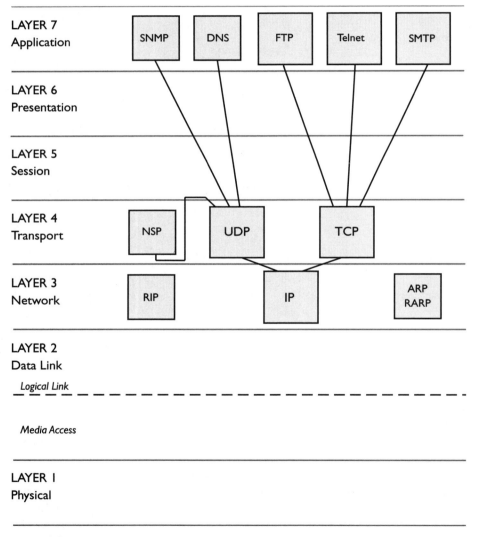

Figure 6.6 TCP/IP Profile.

is the basis for the Internet. All major suppliers of computer systems provide implementations of TCP/IP, and software is also available for most makes of workstation and personal computer (Figure 6.6).

At Layer 7, there are a substantial number of application support functions defined, of which the most commonly implemented are:

- electronic mail handling (SMTP)
- file transfer (FTP)
- terminal emulation (TELNET)
- directory services (DNS)
- network management (SNMP).

It is worth noting that SNMP (Simple Network Management Protocol) is the most widely implemented protocol for network management, well supported by suppliers of both intelligent 'passive' hardware devices (e.g. modems, repeaters, bridges and routers) and those selling software for network managers' workstations.

TCP/IP also defines both connection-oriented (TCP) and connectionless (UDP) services, both of which use a common network routing protocol (IP). As with the OSI standards, IP interfaces with most local and wide area logical link standards. Note the presence of standards for the exchange of routing (RIP) and address (ARP, RARP) information.

6.5.3 *IBM SNA*

SNA (Systems Network Architecture) is an architecture aimed at easing interworking between IBM computers. It is independent of OSI, but has a similar seven-layered architecture. In Figure 6.7, the major standards have been 'forced' onto the OSI framework so as to allow comparison.

SNA is, however, quite distinctive in recognizing three components:

- System Services Control Points (SSCP)
- Logical Units (LU)
- Physical Units (PU).

A major processor will contain all three components; an 'intelligent' station, consisting of both logical and physical units, and an unintelligent device, which is just the PU component. One common combination standard is APPC (Advanced Program to Program Communication) which comprises one logical unit standard (LU 6.2) and one physical unit standard (PU 2.1). It is used for peer-to-peer communications between user-programmable systems on PCs, minis and mainframes.

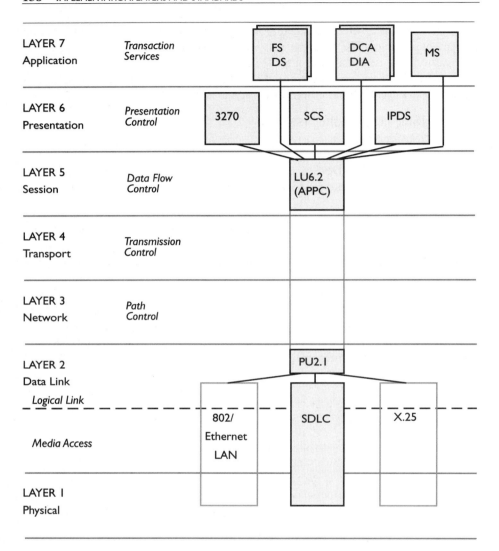

Figure 6.7 SNA Profile.

6.5.4 *X.25/X.29*

This mini-profile of CCITT standards describes the interfaces to a public or private wide-area network which uses packet switching. It was the first attempt to define a public data-oriented network system, analagous to the telephone network. Nowadays it is subsumed within the wider aegis of the ISO OSI Profile (Figure 6.8).

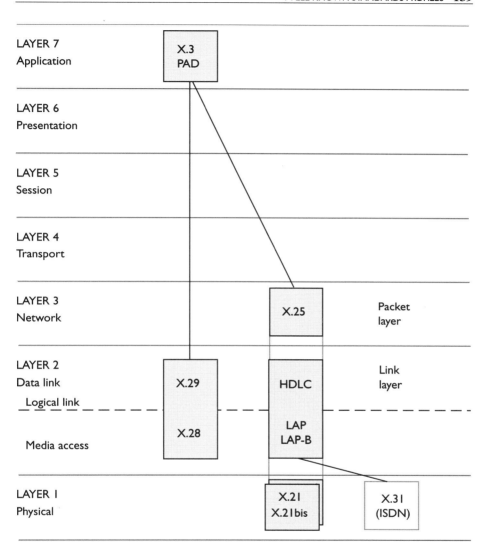

Figure 6.8 X.25 Profile.

It provides for:

- connection-oriented and connection-less services
- temporary and permanent (PVC) virtual circuits
- public and private sub-networks
- interfaces capacities from 150 bps to 64 Kbps.

X.25 describes an interface for packet-oriented communication with the network. This standard is generally used by host systems.

Terminals – or, more commonly these days, PCs with terminal emulation software – can also be connected to a PSS via a PAD. The standard for operation of a PAD (Packet Assembler/Disassembler) is defined as X.3. Also related are X.28 (which defines the dialogue between an asynchronous terminal user and the PAD) and X.29 (which defines the dialogue between the PAD and a host computer which can deal directly with packets).

Although still heavily utilized by legacy systems, X.25 is being overtaken by other developments. The first of these is ISDN (see below), which integrates voice and data services into one grand scheme (an example of convergence). The second is higher-throughput methods; because X.25 interface capacity (less than 64 Kbps) is relatively slow by LAN (local area network) standards, standard PSS is not suitable for connections which will carry LAN services. Newer, trimmer, standards such as **frame-relay** and **ATM**, both similar in many ways to X.25, are rapidly gaining popularity as they offer interface and transport capacities of 2 Mbps and more.

6.5.5 *Novell*

This is a proprietary profile (Figure 6.9). At the time of writing, Novell had over 50% of the market in LAN file systems, especially in dedicated file servers. The profile essentially provides connections in support of networking extensions to the BIOS component of PC operating systems such as MS-DOS and PC-DOS. The effect is to extend the standard DOS file system across a network to dedicated file servers.

Major network services include:

- authentication and access control
- private and shared virtual disks
- read-only virtual disks
- spooling to shared printers.

The popularity of Novell probably results from it being seen as a simple and efficient solution to the most common workgroup sharing activities. Because it integrates at such a basic level with the common PC operating systems, Novell is almost transparent to the end-user.

6.5.6 *MAP*

MAP (Manufacturing Automation Protocol), with its associated MMS (Manufacturing Message Specification) is a widely used sub-profile of OSI (Figure 6.10). It is used for messages and for linking robots with programmable devices and computers.

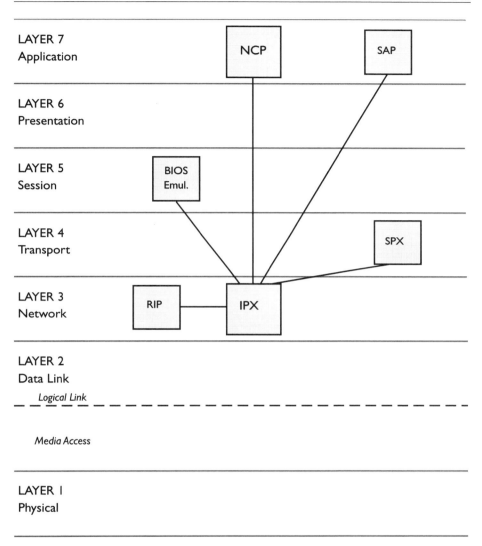

LAYER 7
Application

LAYER 6
Presentation

LAYER 5
Session

LAYER 4
Transport

LAYER 3
Network

LAYER 2
Data Link

Logical Link

Media Access

LAYER 1
Physical

Figure 6.9 Novell Profile.

6.5.7 *ISDN*

ISDN stands for Integrated Services Digital Network (Figure 6.11). It is composed of a complex set of standards (the CCITT I series) for wide-area communications in which voice and data are treated in an integrated manner. Designed primarily by the telecommunications companies, it was (and perhaps still is) seen as the next logical step in worldwide corporate networking, beyond the analogue telephone system and X.25 packet networks.

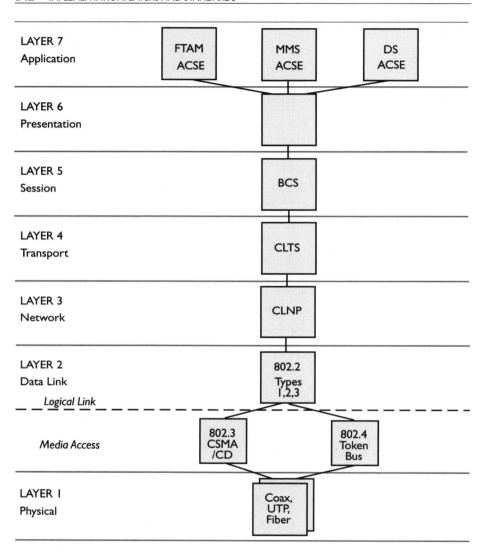

Figure 6.10 MAP 3.0 Profile.

The basic interface, incorporating 64 kbps channels for digital transmission of voice and data, is intended to extend out to every handset. This channel speed is the minimum that will permit effective transport of uncompressed voice (Figure 6.11).

ISDN has gained only limited acceptance, and is now being bypassed as increasing use of LAN-to-LAN connections and transport of video information demand much higher transport capacities.

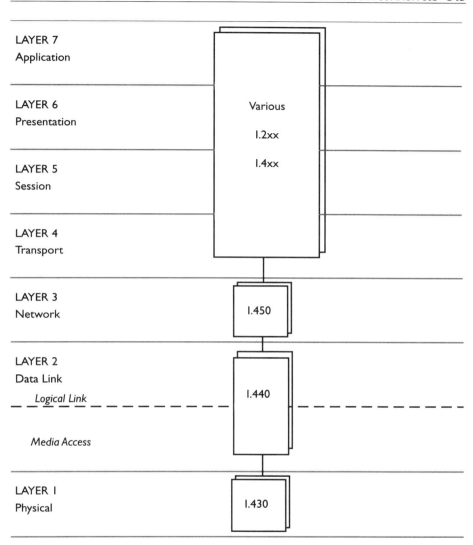

LAYER 7 Application	
LAYER 6 Presentation	Various I.2xx
LAYER 5 Session	I.4xx
LAYER 4 Transport	
LAYER 3 Network	I.450
LAYER 2 Data Link *Logical Link*	I.440
Media Access	
LAYER I Physical	I.430

Figure 6.11 ISDN.

6.6 PARTICULAR STANDARDS IN COMMON USE

6.6.1 *RS232-C, RS232-D, RS449, X.21, V.24*

These are a loosely related group of standards which describe the interface between computer equipment (DTE) and a network interface device (DCE). They basically fit into Layer 1 of the OSI framework. Of all the standards that exist, these are the ones most in evidence – such interfaces are usually provided as standard on terminals, PCs, and modems. Although these interfaces were designed primarily to connect terminals or computers to modems, they are also often used, in conjunction with a curious passive device called a **null modem**, to connect computers directly to one another or, most commonly, to connect a computer to a printer. A null modem is often manufactured as a moulded cable.

Multiple channels and multiple conductors are used. Encoding is digital, and the standard includes details of the wiring and pin/socket numbers to be used on standard connectors.

6.6.2 *V.21 through V.42bis, etc.*

The 'V numbers' are a range of standards which describe how two modems will communicate over voice-quality lines – in effect over the telephone network. Most of these standards fall in Layer 1 of the OSI framework. The standards range from the simple V.21 (300 bps in either direction, asynchronous only) to the now generally available V.34 (28 800 bps, synchronous or asynchronous). Some of the standards, such as V.42bis, describe data compression and error correction schemes. Note that there may be a significant difference between the capacity of the modem-to-modem link (say 14 400 bps) and the throughput between the attached computers (up to 72 000) because of modem-to-modem data compression. Each year the V numbers – and the speeds – go up.

A modem that you might buy 'off the shelf' today will support multiple V series standards. If it is capable of operating at 28 800 bps (V.34) then it will almost certainly be capable of operating at slower speeds such as 300 bps (V.21). In order to cope with situations where two modems, connected together, have different maximum operating speeds, most modern modems when first connected 'negotiate' between them the optimal standard to use for the time being.

6.6.3 *IEEE 802 family and Ethernet*

IEEE 802.3 and Ethernet are today used as generic labels for a variety of related standards in Layers 1 and 2 (Figure 6.12). It is important to understand that, although these are local area standards and appear to be nearly synonymous, there are significant differences and incompatibilities between the individual standards.

Ethernet and 802.2 are two distinct standards for Logical Link Control. They use slightly different frame formats, and can coexist in their use of a single channel – effectively the channel will be divided into two groups, those 'talking' Ethernet and those 'talking' 802.2. Generally a computer interface will be configured for one or the other.

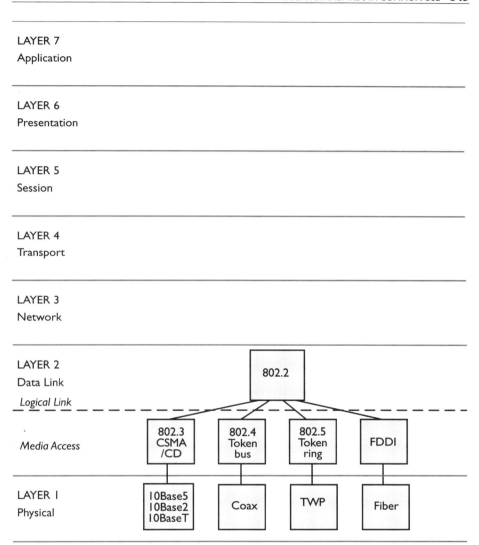

Figure 6.12 IEEE 802 LAN Standards.

There are five major media access control (MAC) schemes used by 802.2, each with a related group of standards which can provide the physical layer. The most common of these is 802.3, which incorporates a bus topology with a channel capacity of 10 Mbps and CSMA/CD (Carrier Sense Multiple Access/Collision Detect). Ethernet, in effect, incorporates 802.3. The three main media types are 10Base2 (thin coaxial cable), 10Base5 (thick coax) and 10BaseT (star-wired UTP). Often these media types are intermingled in a single installation.

Other MAC schemes are:

- 802.4   Token Bus   broadband coax or fiber   10–20 Mbps
- 802.5   Token Ring   UTP or STP   4–16 Mbps
- 802.6   MAN (dual-bus)   optical fiber   44.736 Mbps
- FDDI   Dual ring   Fiber   100 Mbps

A more recent standard which is gaining acceptance is 100BaseT ('Fast Ethernet') which runs at 100 Mbps over UTP cabling.

6.6.4 *FDDI*

After the use of optical fiber for point-to-point connections between 802.3/Ethernet repeaters, FDDI is the most widespread local area optical fiber standard. It is based on dual-ring topology and offers data rates of 100 Mbps and self-healing in the event of damage to a single fiber. FDDI is in Layers 1 and 2.

6.6.5 *X.400, SMTP, EDIFACT and X.12, X.500*

X.400 and SMTP (Simple Mail Transfer Protocol, see TCP/IP above) are Layer 7 standards for agents which store and forward electronic mail. Electronic mail standards generally distinguish between message transfer agents (MTA), which perform the traditional 'post office' function of transporting mail from place to place, and user agents (UA) which assist the user in creating, reading and replying to mail.

EDIFACT and ANSI X.12 are standards for **EDI (Electronic Data Interchange)**, i.e. business transaction messages. EDI can alternatively be described as 'electronic mail with forms'. They are generally used on top of lower layers, including X.400. X.12 provides standard transaction sets (mimicking invoices, receipts, orders, delivery dockets) for such applications as Freight Forwarding, Electrical Wholesaling, Grocery, Banking, Warehousing, and for any business involving Buying, Selling and Delivery. The primary difficulties with a business taking up EDI are, first, the two competing standards and, secondly, interfacing the exchange of electronic documents with legacy systems. The user computer system needs to acquire translation software to convert its own organization's formats into EDI message formats.

CCITT X.500 provides a standard for 'Directory Enquiries' which might be needed to support users of electronic mail. A similar but somewhat more primitive service, **Ph** is provided in the TCP/IP profile.

6.6.6 *SNMP*

SNMP (Simple Network Management Protocol) has gained popularity as the protocol for exchanging network management data. It is a Layer 7 standard belonging to the TCP/IP profile and provides for both the monitoring and control of 'manageable objects', such as a port on a multi-port repeater or router. Many suppliers of intelligent network devices now incorporate SNMP support into their products, and there are a number of suppliers of software for management workstations.

The main alternative in use is IBM NetView. ISO OSI products have so far been too cumbersome. Software bridges have been built to allow the two standards to interwork.

6.6.7 *HTTP and the World Wide Web*

The World Wide Web (WWW) is rapidly becoming the most significant application of international data communications, primarily because of its ease of use by novices and experts alike. Essentially it is a worldwide distributed database, where the objects stored in the database are small documents, and where a link can be created in one document to any other in hypertext fashion. Documents often contain colour images and sound clips, and extensions allow for moving images.

HTTP (HyperText Transfer Protocol) is the Layer 7 standard for transfer of hypertext documents, and it uses TCP (from the TCP/IP profile) as a transport service. HTML (HyperText Markup Language) is the standard which allows for a conventional text document, such as might be created by word-processing software, to have hypertext links and multimedia extensions embedded within it.

6.6.8 *Telnet*

Telnet is a Layer 7 member of the TCP/IP profile. It describes a standard for remote login from one computer, emulating a terminal to a second, host computer. It effectively determines the set of functions of a 'virtual terminal' which can operate on many different types of physical hardware. The analogous standard for OSI is VT.

6.6.9 *FTP, FTAM, XMODEM, etc.*

These are all standards associated with the transport of files, or accessing parts of a file, across a network.

FTP (File Transfer Protocol) is a Layer 7 member of the TCP/IP profile. It enables file transfer between two systems.

FTAM (File Transfer Access and Management) is a Layer 7 OSI standard. It allows transfer of both the data itself and structure details ('attributes').

XMODEM (with many improved variations such as YMODEM and ZMODEM) are commonly used with electronic bulletin boards or between home PC users. Another such standard is Kermit.

6.6.10 *ODA*

The ISO ODA (Office Document Architecture) is concerned with mixed mode documents (e.g. where sections which have been produced by different pieces of software have been pasted up on page layouts) – i.e. the classic 'Desk-Top Publishing' scenario.

The ISO ODA standard separates logical structure and layout structure. Logical structure is to do with chapter/section/paragraph structure and headers/footers, etc. Layout is to do with page sets, frames and blocks, possibly overlapping – very much like the windows on a Mac or Windows screen. Defining these structures in a standard way, together with overall document description, leads to ODIF (Office Document Interchange Format) protocol.

IBM's office information architecture is known as DIA/DCA (Document Interchange Architecture/Document Content Architecture), and is in some ways a forerunner of ODA. DIA covers the specifics of transferring documents, while DCA is mainly concerned with the formatting within the documents themselves.

6.6.11 *PICT, TIFF, JPEG, IGES, etc.*

These are all standards for passing graphics files between different programs. OSI uses IGES (Initial Graphics Exchange Standard). A more recent standard for digital video is known as MPEG (Motion Picture Experts Group). These standards are rapidly becoming more prominent as the World Wide Web expands.

6.6.12 *RDA, ODBC and SQL Connectivity*

RDA (Remote Database Access) is the ISO OSI standard for working with a remote relational database, and is based on the SQL language. ODBC (Open Data Base Connection) is a proprietary Microsoft standard. ODAPI is another standard developed by a consortium including Apple and Borland.

6.6.13 *LU6.2, RPC and DCE*

LU6.2 is part of IBM's APPC (Advanced Program-to-Program Communication) and describes protocols for program-to-program communication where neither program controls the other. It is a part of the systems network architecture (SNA).

It is one example of a category of standards known as RPC (Remote Procedure Call). Many proprietary standards exist under this name. The Open Systems Forum have proposed the DCE (Distributed Computing Environment) RPC.

OSI's counterpart is DTP (Distributed Transaction Processing).

6.6.14 *CORBA and OLE*

CORBA (Common Object Request Broker Architecture) is a standard for object-to-object messaging, the object-oriented counterpart to RPC. It has been proposed by the Object Management Group and implemented by IBM, Apple and a number of others.

Microsoft have an alternative standard called OLE (Object Linking and Embedding), which has been adopted by some other vendors including Oracle.

6.7 STANDARDS ISSUES IN THE CASE STUDIES

6.7.1 *Mr A*

Mr A is not likely to be too concerned about standards, since most of his applications are text messaging. Also, well-proven standards such as V.32 and RS232-C will be employed by his equipment in a manner which is transparent to him. However, he may need to be aware of ZModem, for example, for file transfer; and also the appropriate EDI standards for interfacing with Suppliers, Customers and the Inland Revenue.

6.7.2 *Bay Organic Produce Cooperative*

Any office LAN would involve multiple standards – often as a package deal when installing a 'vendor' LAN. If PSS were used, X.28 would be the standard for transmitting to a PAD. EDI standards might also be relevant for trading transactions.

6.7.3 *Detox Pharmaceuticals*

A variety of networks may be involved, each of which may have different standards, e.g. MAP for Process and Production Control, 802.3 for an office LAN, X.25 for PSS between sites. EDI may again be relevant for electronic trading in the future.

Transmission over the leased line to the Refinery may currently use older standards at the Data Link Layer, e.g. SDLC (an IBM SNA protocol).

6.7.4 *Electric House*

Existing networks, probably mainframe-centered, may use older synchronous protocols such as HDLC or SDLC. These protocols will differ considerably from the LAN standards involved in interlinking office users' PCs – translation will be required if the two worlds are to communicate.

X.25 or Frame Relay protocols may be relevant for long-distance networking in Latin America.

EDI standards may once again be relevant.

6.7.5   *Commonwealth Open Polytechnic*

Common LAN standards and X.25 will apply to most of the networking, with the exception of the video data. Here, ATM may be needed at the Network Layer, and video compression standards – such as MPEG (motion picture experts group) – at the Application Layer.

6.7.6   *National Environmental Protection Board*

Again, common LAN and PSS standards will probably apply for most routine networking. Special standards might be needed if remote monitoring of potential polluting sites is to be practised.

6.8   EXERCISES

1.   Describe the relationship between layers, agents and encapsulation.

2.   What are some significant properties of a data envelope?

3.   What is the primary function of a name server?

4.   Differentiate the functions of repeaters, bridges, routers and gateways.

5.   Describe the advantages and disadvantages of a layered system.

6.   Briefly describe each of the seven layers of the ISO OSI framework.

7.   Who are the main participants in the creation of standards?

8.   What is a profile?

9.   Why has EPA (enhanced performance architecture) been introduced in conjunction with the OSI profile?

10.   Draw the main components of the TCP/IP profile.

11.   What are the distinctive features of IBM's SNA profile?

2. Why are there two alternative standards, X.28 and X.29, for communication between a user computer and an X.25 PAD?

3. Explain the confusion between the terms 'Ethernet' and 'IEEE 802.3'.

4. A stand-alone modem generally has two data interfaces, one to attach to a computing device and one to attach to the telephone line. What groups of standards apply to each of these two interfaces?

5. Identify some generic functions found in the OSI Layer 7.

6. Find some examples of X.12 EDI standard electronic forms.

ASSIGNMENT TASK

For the case study of your choice, consider each User Group on the Location Model diagram. What programs might be running on computers in each User Group? What computer programs in the other User Groups might they wish to communicate with? What differences might there be between the data formats? How might the differences be resolved? Indicate which OSI layers apply.

FURTHER READING

Bennett, K. (1991) OSI tries to shake off 'boring' tag. *Communications News* (UK), May.

Black, U. (1993) *Data Communications and Distributed Networks*, Prentice-Hall, Englewood Cliffs, NJ.

Dowty (1991) *The CASE Pocket Book – OSI Introductory Booklet*, Dowty Communications Ltd.

Fitzgerald, J. (1993) *Business Data Communications – Basic Concepts, Security and Design*, Wiley, New York, Chapter 9 and pp 474–479.

Halsall, F. (1992) *Data Communications, Computer Networks and Open Systems*, Addison-Wesley, Reading, MA, Chapters 10–13.

Retix (1988) *ISO OSI and CCITT Data Communication Standards*, Wall Poster, Retix Corporation.

Scott, K. (1991) Parlez-vous TCP/IP? *Infoworld*, 7 Oct.

Sloane, A. (1994) *Computer Communications – Principles and Business Applications*, McGraw Hill, New York.

Stallings, W. and van Slyke, R. (1994) *Business Data Communications*, Macmillan, New York, Chapter 10.

Stamper, D. (1994) *Business Data Communications*, Benjamin/Cummings, New York, Chapter 10.

7 LANs and WANs

7.1 INTRODUCTION

In the previous four chapters we have introduced Data Communications from the demand point of view. We have talked in particular about the need for Efficiency, Effectiveness and Standards. Chapter 3 concluded with a section entitled 'There are many means' (section 3.6). The question now is, how do we resolve the choice of means? This can be divided into two parts.

- What is the business requirement?
- What are the alternative solutions to that requirement, and when is each appropriate?

7.2 LOCAL AREA VERSUS WIDE AREA

Before answering these questions, some discussion is needed on the traditional distinction between LANs and WANs. In most books these are addressed in two (or more) separate chapters.

The distinction arose mainly because faster network technology was developed that could be used over distances of up to 1–2 km, but not beyond. Besides this, a very large proportion of the data traffic generated by an organization stays within one site. Hence the distinction is partly one of technical history, and partly between different patterns of traffic.

However, changing patterns of supply have led to a blurring of the distinction. As satellite and fiber technology improves, and the installed base widens, the cost of wide area communications comes down. This allows businesses to contemplate higher-capacity links, especially between LANs at different sites and to mobile workers.

We already have a middle ground of MANs (Metropolitan Area Networks) using broad band coaxial cable, 802.6 and FDDI (fiber distributed data interface – see Glossary) (Figure 7.1). LANs can now also include remote and mobile stations, using such systems as Appletalk Remote Access (ARA) and Oracle Radio. Infrared by-pass channels are used to link LANs in different buildings up to 2 km apart, between which LAN cabling cannot be laid, typically because of other intervening buildings. Developments in WAN technology are also bringing

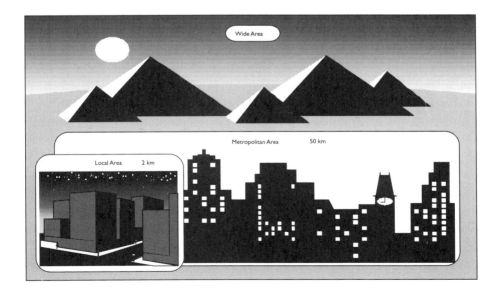

Figure 7.1 LANs, MANs and WANs.

fast wide area data highways all the way to individual workplaces; examples are ISDN and ATM (see later).

All the same, we will perpetuate the distinction just within this chapter, for ease of organization of the technical material.

7.3 LOCAL AREA NETWORKS

7.3.1 *The requirement*

The growth in use of LANs, with the prime purpose of sharing facilities amongst groups of workers who use desk-top computers, has been very rapid. Demand for the technology has outstripped the supply of people able to understand it, let alone to cope with its technical problems.

The organizational need is that of leveraging the effectiveness of team work by improving the flow of information and by sharing data resources for simple information processing tasks. In addition resource sharing saves money by sharing disks, printers and gateways to WANs.

The design problem for a user organization is one of choosing an efficient and effective structure of individual LAN elements which meet business needs.

There is usually a wide variety of applications on any LAN. Examples are:

- office automation (e.g. Email, diaries and calendars, bulletin boards)
- file sharing with files produced by PC toolkits (e.g. spreadsheets, project management, word processing and desk-top publishing)
- access to shared databases
- connection to on-line transaction processing systems
- cooperative work on shared documents (sales proposals, graphics, etc)
- workflow (coordinating the flow of administrative work)
- linking robots or sensors in a factory to a controller processor
- linking processors in computer rooms
- voice messaging and interactive voice response (IVR), with messages stored on disk
- load sharing by using idle PCs as parallel processing elements.

The typical communications traffic pattern is intermittent and bursty. A few users transmitting large files can clog up the channels for minutes on end.

Within the site, there are groups (e.g. of users or robots) within which messages in one or other of the above applications are higher in frequency and volume, but where there is less traffic between different groups. However, different applications may imply different user groupings.

7.3.2 *The alternative solutions*

Hardware

The typical technology for a LAN, as discussed earlier, is a shared bus or ring topology, using either CSMA/CD (Ethernet-type) or Token Passing protocols.

To connect the desk-top stations (PCs, Macs, etc) with the shared medium, Network Interface Units (NIUs, sometimes referred to as 'cards') are needed. 'Cards' are generally internal to the PC, but some NIUs are external, and are placed between the user devices and the cabling in the building or site; a combination of the two may also be required. Figure 7.2 shows the functions of an NIU in an Ethernet-style LAN; in such a case the NIU – the 'Ethernet Card' – would normally be internal.

The NIU:

- scans the medium for packets with matching address
- buffers data waiting to go onto (or coming off) the medium.

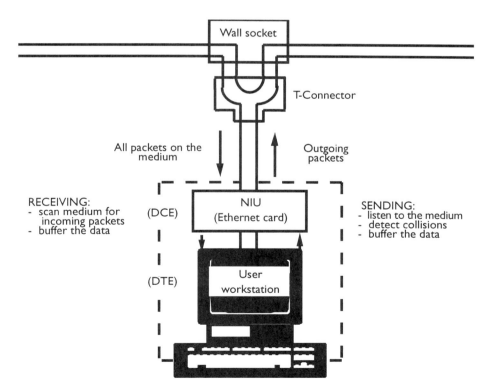

Figure 7.2 Network Interface Unit – Ethernet Style.

For the channel itself, the alternative media types are:

- unshielded twisted pair (UTP) – low cost
- shielded twisted pair (STP)
- baseband coaxial cable (thin or thick)
- broadband coaxial cable (multiple channels, better tolerance of interference)
- optical fiber (very high capacity and security)
- wireless (using radio waves or infrared, where stations are mobile or cabling is difficult).

The most common topologies are star and bus.

The wiring layout can differ from the logical topology. The least-cable solution will link locations in a linear fashion, passing from station to station by the shortest route. However, to make use of existing wiring structures, a star system of loops radiating from a single hub is quite common (Figure 7.3).

A further type of star-wired LAN is to use a PABX (private automatic branch exchange). This involves using a digital internal telephone exchange in the organization as the shared resource, instead of a bus or ring. However, capacity in such an arrangement is not high enough for heavy usage or large files. A 'Centrex' service, where the PABX is physically located in the telephone company's premises, is another variation on this.

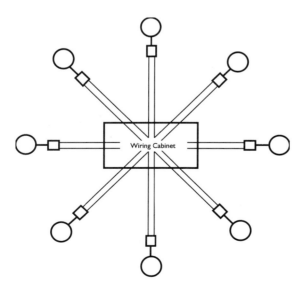

Figure 7.3 Ring Topology with Star Wiring.

The 'bargain basement' approach to linking two computers locally, for file transfer say, is to simply use an RS232-C 'null modem' cable. But it is now often better to buy a cheap LAN (sometimes referred to as a Desk- or Tiny-Area Network). A cheap version of Ethernet is now a viable option for linking home computers inside a dwelling.

The choice of LAN is governed by four factors:

- traffic peak behavior (token passing degrades more gracefully under load than CSMA/CD)
- standards already used for other LANs (cheaper to link to similar LANs)
- total distance to be covered (some media need fewer repeaters)
- special environment considerations (some approaches are more resilient).

Architecture

The underlying technology of any type of LAN places limits on the distance along the medium and on the number of connections to (sometimes referred to as 'taps'). This means that, in general, it may not be possible to connect all users and devices to one single LAN.

The simplest approach to extending a LAN is to string lengths of LAN together using repeaters. Repeaters may themselves be either simple (i.e. just extending the shared channel) or multi-port (allowing branches in a bus, resulting in a tree topology) (Figure 7.4). However, repeaters introduce propogation

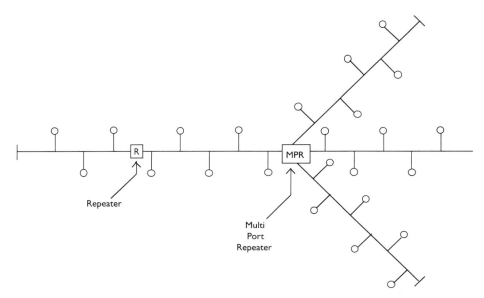

Figure 7.4 LANs Extended by Repeaters.

delays, and this will constrain both the overall length and complexity of the network.

LANs may also be 'tiered' into a hierarchical structure (Figure 7.5). This introduces the concept of a 'backbone' LAN which links a number of separate sub-LANs. Sub-LANs might be used, for example, for clusters of robots in a factory, or groups of adjacent designer workstations in a common workplace. Bridges can be placed between sub-LANs to limit the traffic crossing each bridge to messages intended for stations that are located on the other side. Backbone LANs are typically of a higher capacity than the sub-LANs, e.g. 100 Mbps rather than 10 Mbps.

A further architectural choice is that within a single LAN, the relationship between stations can be either **hierachical** (where there is a controlling station such as a server) or **peer-to-peer** (where no station has any special position).

Software

Installing a LAN involves more than just buying NIUs, cabling, repeaters and connectors. A LAN also requires software, and the technological choices here are at least as daunting as for the hardware.

Without software the user, in order to use the network, would have to write program calls to the NIU to pass and send packets. What the user needs instead is to have options in the local OS (operating system) – and preferably in the PC toolkits as well – to allow remote operations to be specified as easily as internal ones.

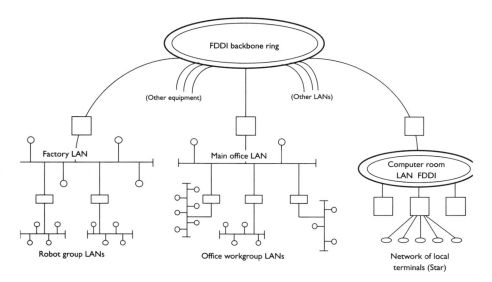

Figure 7.5 Tiered LANs.

The simplest example is the system of virtual drive addresses offered in most network software. These enable a user to access files on a remote processor as if they were located in a drive on the local machine, by using an unused drive letter such as **f:**, **h:** or **p:**. This 'Network File Server' approach should be contrasted with other more sophisticated software, where users could be enabled to access distributed databases through a single query interface.

In a peer-to-peer arrangement, each PC will have to have the same, or similar, software installed. Typical examples of software used commercially are Lantastic, Netware Lite or Windows for Workgroups. With Apple Macintoshes, if LocalTalk is used, then the software, and the NIU, are already provided.

In hierarchical LANs, the dominant or controlling station is termed a 'server'. This server will run the major part of the Network Operating System (NOS). Examples of commercial NOSs are Novell Netware, Windows NT and Banyan Vines. The NOS may still run on a PC, and its purpose is to enhance DOS by adding in the extra sharing features. Other processor types used as the server may have more advanced multi-tasking operating systems, such as IBM OS/2 or varieties of Unix. It is usually an easier task to enhance these OSs for use as LAN servers.

Even with a hierarchical architecture, a 'client' part of the NOS still has to be installed on each PC, as shown in Figure 7.6.

DOS-based PCs include a basic communications interface known as NETBIOS, which operates at Layer 5 of OSI (open systems interconnection).

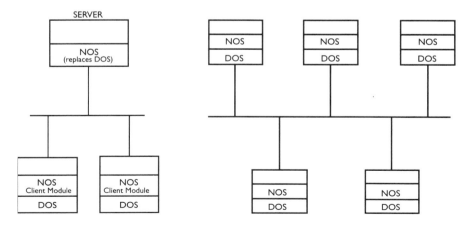

a) Hierarchical   b) P ee-to-P eer

Figure 7.6 Distribution of a Network Operating System (NOS).

This allows the PC to be network aware, but its presence is transparent to most users, who will use either the NOS client or the peer-to-peer NOS.

A number of software products have also been developed for 'bargain-basement' two computer networks as described above. Examples are Quicknet and DeskLink/LapLink.

7.4 WIDE AREA NETWORKS

7.4.1 *The requirement*

Only rarely do IS projects involve a user organization in installing physical equipment for its own dedicated WANs. Such projects are usually limited to military or other top-security microwave data transmission systems. Normally, an organization will make use of commercial or publicly available network services which contain a complex structure of lines, switches and intelligent nodes, and which cover a country and, by various arrangements, the world.

The question for the designer in the use of WANs is about how to make best use of the available facilities provided by third parties. These parties may be intermediaries, offering a service with a certain price structure on top of lines which they lease in turn from a 'common carrier', such as a telecommunications company – the dominant supplier of phone and other lines in each country or area or its competitors. Each of the two organizations involved has different interests in getting the best out of a set of lines and nodes. The supplier wants to maximize utilization of its investment and ultimately its profit; while the user organization wants to retain flexibility and spare capacity, and achieve required performance in terms of speed, accuracy, security and reliability.

We include here under WANs the concept of MANs (Metropolitan Area Networks) even though these may use technology more akin to LANs. But as these facilities are generally provided by a third party as a network service, they are more appropriately treated together with WANs.

7.4.2 *The alternative solutions*

In most cases, the user does not choose the technology – it is up to the company providing the service. The network has to be regarded as a 'cloud', in which a mixture of technologies, routes and nodes support the desired connectivity, but in a manner unknown to the user (Figure 7.7).

Most networks used for data communications are provided by either the common carriers or **VAN (value-added network)** suppliers (see below). Both digital and analog services may be offered.

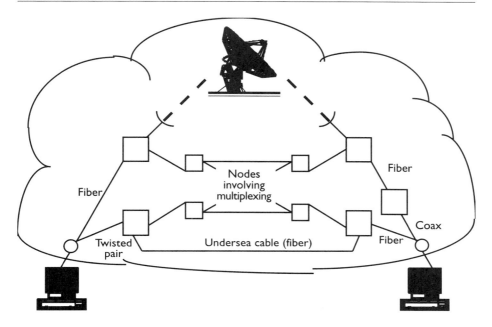

Figure 7.7 A WAN as a Cloud.

The technologies supporting today's and tomorrow's networks have, in the last decade, burst dramatically through previous capacity barriers. Fiber-Optic Cable has become the major technology for links, even across the Pacific, thus relegating terrestrial and satellite microwave links to a 'second string' with coaxial cables as the 'third string'.

WANs can be divided into two main groups – basic services and VAN services.

Basic services are where the supplier simply offers a circuit of a specified capacity between two points, the rest being left to the user organization. The two primary examples are Leased Lines and the PSTN (Public Switched Telephone Network).

VANs are commercial services, utilising lines owned by the telecommunication companies or other common carriers, which offer network services to user organizations or individuals at advertised or agreed price structures. Examples are Packet Switched Services and Frame Relay Services. Higher-level VAN services may be offered on top of these for particular applications. Examples are EDI and Computer Conferencing.

Dial-up over the PSTN

This is the first choice of most casual and home computer users, where connections are either short-distance or of brief duration. Users have to allow for potential loss and corruption of data, as well as for conforming to telephone protocols such as dialing. Modern modems can meet these requirements – the modem equipment can either be external or internal to the computer. However, data rates are limited to around 28.8 kbps, and call-time charges can be significant.

Use of analog or digital mobile phones, and of airborne communications, should be regarded as part of the PSTN for data communications purposes.

Integrated services digital network (ISDN)

ISDN represents a potential replacement of the PSTN but using digital rather than analog signaling. Traffic such as voice, audio and TV video, naturally analog, is digitally encoded and can share channels with digital data. Standard channel capacity is 64 kbps, although faster channels are available for specialist uses such as video conferencing. Both circuit and packet switching are available, and digital links to desk-top PCs can also be provided. ISDN services are marketed by common carriers.

What one needs to operate with ISDN is:

- an ISDN network termination (NT) device on the user's premises
- an arrangement with the provider to support ISDN from the user site to the ISDN exchange
- ISDN software on the user PC or Front End Processor (FEP)

Technically, ISDN carries a number of channels of three types:

- D channel – 16 kbps (one only, primarily for control information, but can also be used for slow-speed data, e.g. telemetry, videotext/teletext or terminals)
- B channels – 64 kbps (2 in the basic service, as many as 30 in primary service – for digital voice, circuit or packet switched data, Fax and slow-scan video)
- H channels – 384, 1536 or 1920 kbps (for special needs, e.g. very fast Fax or data, hi-fi audio or videoconferencing).

This all exists today, but has still to take off in a big way. The standards that were adopted when ISDN was designed may mean that it is, to some extent, already out of date.

Leased lines

For some years, organizations with more than casual data communications needs have rented dedicated circuits ('leased lines') from the common carriers, for their private use. In early years, single lines with similar capacity to telephone circuits were used. With minor 'conditioning', these lines can carry up to 56 kbps. More recently, common carriers have offered private circuits in larger units which use multiplexing to provide multiple individual circuits. The best known examples, in America, are the T-1 and T-3 facilities which support 1.555 M and 44.736 Mbps respectively. 'Fractional T-1' may be offered to user organizations with smaller needs. In Europe and elsewhere in the world, the equivalent standard is 2.048 Mbps, sometimes referred to as a 'megastream' service.

Whether or not this is an economic choice depends on the user's traffic patterns and volumes – and also the supplier's leasing prices. The user may look to carry a mixture of data, voice and teleconference over such a link by installing bandwidth managers. Increasingly though, many user organizations are buying WAN services through a VAN supplier, with Permanent Virtual Circuits (see PSS and Frame Relay below) taking over from Leased Lines.

Packet switching services

The remaining WAN solutions fall into the category of VANs rather than basic services. The most widely used is Packet Switching, which has been discussed in an earlier chapter. Transfer times when using Packet Switching can be quite variable, and depends on many choices made by the VAN suppliers, e.g. packet size, queuing rules, congestion control and routing algorithms.

User data has to be converted into and out of packets, either by software at the user's site, or by a PAD (Packet Assembler/Disassembler). The PAD device interfaces between terminals (usually asynchronous or emulating it) and a Packet Switched Network. The PAD may be provided by the network provider, in which case the user dials in or leases a line to the PAD from his/her equipment, or, if usage is high enough, the user can buy or lease a private PAD (Figure 7.8).

A user organization can also perform packet conversion on a Front-End Processor (FEP). This is traditionally a small computer acting as a communications server for a mainframe, leaving the mainframe to be more dedicated to user applications. FEP functions include message assembly/disassembly, compaction, code conversion, message switching between terminals, polling, error checking, protocol support, automatic answering to dial-in, dial-out, traffic and line availability statistics.

The cost of using a PSS (packet switching service) commonly includes both a volume-based charge and either a monthly charge (for a dedicated connection, based on speed) or a connect-time charge (for dial-up to a PAD). A Permanent Virtual Circuit (PVC) between two specific points can also be leased (see below).

Virtual private networks

One PSS supplier, New Zealand Telecom's Pacnet, advises that it is cheaper for an organization to use a PVC if it is going to use a connection for at least 4–6 hours in each day. Sets of PVCs are sometimes referred to as Virtual Private Networks, or 'software-defined networks'. The aim is to make the service look to

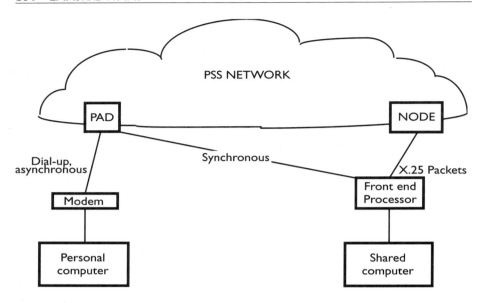

Figure 7.8 Connecting to a PSS via a PAD or FEP.

the user organization as much as possible like a private network. To provide this, the common carrier has to keep a distributed database system for control of the sharing of the physical network. The user organization supplies routing and control data to allow usage to be optimized.

Frame relay services

Frame Relay is a newer VAN service, oriented to heavy, bursty traffic, especially suitable for interconnection of remote LANs. It is technically similar to a PSS, but is based on the use of very reliable and high capacity trunk circuits. Compared with PSS it uses a minimal packet overhead and leaves error checking to the user. Capacities are up to 2 Mbps. A Frame Relay service works over a PVC between a pair of points. Charges are on the basis of the contracted and maximum data rates.

SMDS (switched multimegabit data service)

SMDS is a fast packet switching service offered by the Regional Bell Operating Companies in the USA. It offers up to 45 Mbps uses a connectionless 'datagram' approach. It can be regarded as a good transition path to ATM (see below) which, at the time of writing, is still expensive and not widely available.

ATM (asynchronous transfer mode)

For full-motion (TV quality) video, data rates of 150 Mbps are required, with 600 Mbps for a line that might need to multiplex several video files. To address this need, Broadband ISDN (BISDN) has been proposed. The mechanism proposed for delivering BISDN is known as Asynchronous Transfer Mode (ATM) or alternatively, Cell Relay.

ATM is a yet further streamlined improvement on packet switching. The packets are here reduced to small 'cells' of 53 octets. With modern digital lines and switching equipment, data rates up to hundreds of megabits, or even gigabits, per second can be achieved. Trial installations have been demonstrated, and ATM services are now available in certain selected areas (e.g. part of California) and on pilot networks (e.g. the UK's SuperJANET academic network).

The suitability of different WAN service options for different traffic patterns is summarized in Figure 7.9, which is derived from Stallings and van Slyke (1994).

Software

Having chosen the most appropriate WAN service, software is needed to link the user organization's programs with that WAN service.

On individual PCs used to dial-up remote computers, whether directly or via PADs, a basic communications package is needed to communicate through the modem. Examples of such packages are ProComm, Crosstalk XVI, Smartcom III and Vicom. Today, many integrated PC Toolkits – and even Operating Systems such as IBM OS/2 Warp and MS-Windows 95 – include such facilities.

On Front-End processors, in-house PADs, network servers, gateways or protocol converters, a number of software functions need to be supported, including:

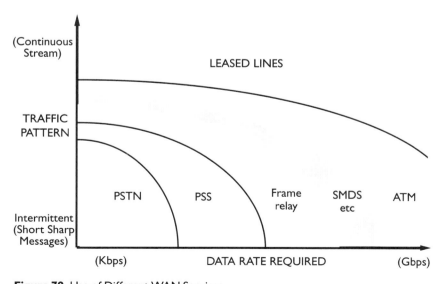

Figure 7.9 Use of Different WAN Services.

- X.25 or other protocol conversion
- handling auto-answer and incoming messages
- interfacing a 'host' computer to a network
- network management functions, including diagnostics, statistics, security, accounting.

Additional software for 'host' computers which are made available for access by remote users would include:

- a Transaction Processing Monitor (e.g. CICS – see Chapter 9) – or alternatively a Time-Sharing system
- handling of download, upload and convoyed search requests, e.g. 'Copy Management' and 'PC/Mainframe Link' software.

7.5 INTERNETWORKING

7.5.1 *The requirement*

The term 'internetworking' refers to the linking of separate networks together, so that users are only aware of a single network. 'The Internet' is one classic example, where a set of agreed standards, originally driven by the need to support cooperative defense research projects in the USA, have enabled thousands of separate networks to be linked such that the user sees only one big network or 'cloud'.

Stallings and van Slyke (1994) quote a Yankee Group prediction that the average number of LANs in the top 1000 US organizations in 1996 would range from 67 to over 200. The expectation is that all these LANs can interconnect.

LAN to LAN

Even within one site, one organization might have many autonomous LANs, very often of similar types. A large proportion of the traffic will stay within one LAN, e.g. for a Department or Workgroup. Only messages destined for addresses outside the local LAN need to be passed on to other, connected networks. The user expectation is for performance nearly as good as with a single LAN.

LAN to WAN

There are really two different requirements here. The first is to allow an organization, or a group of cooperating users which is geographically distributed for whatever reason, to behave as if it were on one site. In other words, the aim is to mimic the single-site situation by embedding WAN elements transparently within the LANs. This requirement is important for organizations split between different offices, for consortia and joint ventures, and for linking groups of homeworkers.

The second requirement is to provide users on a LAN with a gateway to specific information services which are available over WANs, such as electronic conferences and bulletin boards, on-line bibliographic databases, commercial information providers and Internet facilities.

In either case, performance approaching that of single-site systems is an aim, although users may tolerate a certain level of WAN delay.

WAN to WAN

This is less of a concern for most users, since it is normally the VAN supplier or common carrier that has the problem of ensuring that different networks interconnect. User expectation is that the Internet can do it – so what's the problem?

However, a user organization may have older WANs, designed for legacy systems. A 'star' arrangement of leased lines linked to a mainframe, to support remote terminals using a central Transaction Processing system, is a common scenario. Sometimes these old leased lines may have to interwork, at least for a time, with more modern VAN services.

7.5.2 *The alternative solutions*

LAN to LAN

Fortunately, as we have seen, there are relatively few different LAN standards in use. If the same LAN standard is used, relatively cheap interconnecting **bridges** can be used. These bridges have to be intelligent enough to recognize when a message on one LAN needs to be passed over to the other side of the bridge and repeated onto the other LAN. This emphasizes the importance of having naming systems to resolve all the potential synonyms of names and addressees.

In some cases, bridges or 'switches' with some simple protocol conversion can be used to link LANs with different physical and Media Access Control standards, but the same Logical Link Control (usually IEEE 802.2 – see Figure 7.10). A case where such bridges are used is when connecting a number of Ethernet sub-LANs to a FDDI backbone.

If the LAN standards are more different, e.g. when factory-floor LANs are involved, then a **router** has to be used. A router has to make the necessary translations of address formats and conversions of packet sizes, etc., before the message can be repeated on the other side. Routers are generally sold as special hardware/software boxes rather than as general-purpose programmable micro-computers, but they normally incorporate some intelligence.

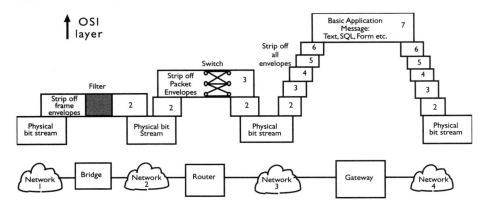

Figure 7.10 Bridge, Router and Gateway.

When linking LANs, the filtering functions of a bridge are usually merged into a router – the hybrid result is sometimes referred to as a **brouter**. However, the terminology used by different suppliers in this area is not always consistent.

LAN to WAN

Normally, internetworking between LANs and WANs will require routers or **gateways**. A router assumes that the two networks will be compatible at the Network layer (3) of OSI. A typical user installation will have routers to link, say, Ethernet or Token Ring LANs to PSS (X.25 or Internet Protocol) or Frame Relay WAN services.

Where the standards profiles are incompatible between LAN and WAN, then a gateway, which typically operates within a programmable computer, may be required. This has to strip off all the envelopes from the source network's message to reveal the basic application (OSI layer 7) data, store this, and then re-encapsulate it in the destination network's envelopes.

In the special case of supporting remote user connection to a LAN (by dial-in or radio), the gateway can either be a special-purpose box (e.g. Gator Link with Appletalk) or a server on the LAN which itself acts as the gateway.

A different situation arises where ISDN (including in the future ATM as a Broadband ISDN) is used as a combined LAN/WAN, and both local and wide area connections are made from desktop to desktop – gateways or routers would not be needed.

WAN to WAN

In the case of integrating a legacy WAN with more modern VAN services a gateway is usually necessary as the older standards (often vendor-specific) may pre-date today's commonly used profiles. The gateway may take the form of a Network Server or Front-End Processor.

7.6 SELECTING LANs AND WANs IN THE CASE STUDIES

The Case Study descriptions are fuller than normal in this chapter. This is because they form an integral part of the explanation of how one might choose between the different LAN and WAN alternatives.

7.6.1 *Mr A*

Local

Mr A has a limited need for LANs, the main need being to link his laptop to his permanent home computer in order to exchange data and share the printer. He could consider the following options:

1. pass diskettes between the computers
2. buy new computers as a pair where the laptop docks into the desktop machine
3. buy a null-modem cable, find some software, and transfer the files directly
4. install a mini-Ethernet.

Option 1 is the cheapest, but if the diskette formats are not compatible, he either has to buy a conversion package or find someone nearby with a machine that can handle both formats.

Option 2 is purpose-designed for this situation, but involves capital cost unless Mr A has to upgrade the computers anyway.

Option 3 involves only $20 for a cable with the right connectors, plus a similar sum for 'DeskLink/LapLink' software. The biggest problem might be if one of the family accidently trips up over the cable.

Option 4 may be more expensive than 3, but it can incorporate the printer and offer expandability for the future.

If Mr A's current printer is attached to his home PC, it is a bother, if he wants to print files that are on the portable, to have to transfer them to the home PC first. So it might make sense to buy a second printer cable and connect the laptop direct to the printer, possibly via a simple switch.

Remote

Mr A needs a number of casual remote connections. An auto-dial modem, with subscriptions to an Internet-connected Email/conferencing service and to the Library's OPAC (On-line Public Access Catalog), would seem worthwhile. If the fax machine is an old one, he might justify purchasing a fax modem and software for the home computer.

With a suitable internal modem the laptop could be used independently, with the ability to read the same mailbox and conferences.

If Mr A wants to make use of the World Wide Web, he has to consider subscribing to a SLIP/PPP (see Glossary for details) account with an Internet Provider and using the fastest possible modem to ensure adequate performance.

He would be unlikely to need specific EDI facilities to begin with – Email with suppliers and customers, and in future to associates, would be enough.

Mr A may still take the alternative view that hooking up computers is not justified, and that fax is enough!

7.6.2 *Bay Organic Produce Cooperative*

Local

With ten or more PC-using staff in one office that need to share access to both data and other resources, an LAN is likely to be justified.

Using floppy disks to collect each day's changes onto one PC, and then send back to every machine a copy of the new whole file is theoretically possible – this is 'SneakerNet'. But floppy copying is slow and tedious, and ten different copies of the file can also get quickly 'out of sync'.

Using RS232-C cabling might be an option for casual file transfer between two computers, but not for ten computers sharing data on a continuing, if intermittent, basis.

With a proper LAN, two main options could be considered. In the first, each machine holds a part of the data, and the telephone switchboard operator allocates calls to the desk whose PC holds the right data. If one PC then needs to look at a different part of the data, it can access those files on whichever other machine they are stored. This is a cheap solution – there is no server and traffic is minimized – but it depends on the telephone operator allocating calls to the right desk. Sharing of other resources, such as printers, may still be awkward.

The better option is to invest in an extra PC and a Network Operating System (NOS) as a Server. This would then hold a single copy of all the data, and also give convenient access to shared resources such as a printer. This solution solves most of the above problems, but at the cost of equipment, software, and ongoing maintenance. Also, it may be less acceptable to the executives who turned down the previous minicomputer proposal!

Remote

The most regular communication is to the warehouse, which may justify a low-volume leased line. Other remote links may be needed to mobile staff and to customers and possibly to some farmers in the future. Dial-up links are probably sufficient for most routes, but PSS may be justified for longer-distance or international use.

7.6.3 *Detox Pharmaceuticals*

Local

Two local networks already exist:

- the terminals (including PCs) to the AS/400 in the office
- the leased line to the refinery (we are told it is 'next door').

Any new LANs in the office may have to interface, at least temporarily, with the AS/400 system. IBM standards (the SNA profile) might be prevalent and a Token Ring might be easiest to introduce and interface. Unless agreement with the refinery could be reached to install a site FDDI backbone, a gateway would be needed to integrate with the refinery link.

In the factory, integrating the Process Control computers may require a special-purpose LAN type, e.g. Token Bus. Overall, a tiered arrangement seems called for, and this could be extended to the whole site.

Remote

The highest-volume traffic is to the local offices. However, given the size of the operation, Packet Switching with PVCs – or Frame Relay – would be preferable to leased lines.

Connections to outside organizations such as pharmacies and hospitals would be relatively occasional. It would probably be appropriate to use Packet Switching, with possibly a MAN between a local office and sites within a conurbation such as Warsaw.

7.6.4 *Electric House*

Local

Currently, local networking forms part of the overall centralized system, and those users that are connected would be on either a multiplexed or multi-drop tree network centered on the mainframe cluster or its front-end. Again, if the current hardware is IBM, SNA standards may suggest the choice of a future LAN. The same standards would probably be imposed on the Latin American offices.

A tiered LAN arrangement would be needed. The mainframe cluster would probably continue with its specialized or FDDI bus. Individual departments would also have sub-LANs.

Within stores and warehouses, independent LANs, possibly containing repeaters, would be adequate.

Remote

In North America, the existing centralized system probably involves a network of leased lines joining all the stores and warehouses. There are probably T-1 lines which multiplex the traffic into Oakland from each main direction. Protocol may be SDLC (IBM synchronous Layer 2). While some of these lines may stay, some lower volume ones – and most of the new lines for Latin America – may move towards using PSS or Frame Relay, depending on the services available in each country.

Communication with Far East suppliers is quite heavy, and it may have too high a security requirement to use the Internet. An EDI VAN should be considered.

7.6.5 *Commonwealth Open Polytechnic*

Local

The central campus needs are not extensive and a simple LAN would be sufficient. The probable choice would be a cheap version of Ethernet, as degradation under peak loads is not a disaster, and we are likely here to be a part of the 'Unix community'. Some regional centers may also justify LANs.

Remote

Being somewhat isolated geographically, the COP has to regard wide area communications as a high priority. This is because of communication with remote staff and contractors, Internet activities and Student Email. Frame Relay links to sites in the main Australian population centers are probably a good solution. It may be best to route traffic through to one of the universities in Adelaide, Melbourne and Sydney who could route traffic on to Brisbane, Perth and overseas. The regional offices could operate a local dial-in number for students and contracted teaching staff, which could be linked by MAN to the local university node.

The use of remote tutoring and other video-oriented applications forms a distinct special requirement. Negotiations would have to be made with a common carrier to provide ATM or H-channel ISDN services to designated delivery centres. Possibly, such channels could also be used to accommodate the other WAN traffic.

7.6.6   *National Environmental Protection Board*

Local

In order to achieve the goal of 'paperlessness', the NEPB has to start off with a planned LAN structure which provides an adequate level of interconnection. Some of the Departments are fairly autonomous, so a tiered arrangement at the HQ seems suitable. Simple LANs would be needed at Local Offices.

Remote

Several separate groups of needs can be identified:

- routine NEPB LAN-to-LAN traffic
- research activity – Internet, public databases, libraries, overseas legislation
- links with mobile inspectors or agents
- direct remote monitoring of emissions.

The first group can be accommodated by PSS or Frame Relay links between NEPB offices. The second would involve setting up as an Internet site through an Internet Provider with a leased line to the Provider's switch.

The third possibility would use dial-up, either by the inspectors plugging in to fixed telephone points, or by using digital mobile phones.

Since the fourth operation may involve continuous operation but only for a brief period, and several sensors at one site, a good approach might be to link all the sensors to a local server which acted as a gateway to send multiplexed messages over the PSS.

7.7   EXERCISES

1. In what sense is the distinction between LANs and WANs becoming blurred?

2. Why have LANs gained such wide acceptance?

3. What are the functions of a network 'card' or NIU?

4. How can physical wiring differ from logical topology?

5. Name four main factors to be considered when deciding which type of LAN to buy for a given requirement?

6. What restricts the use of repeaters to extend a LAN?

7. What is the main function of a bridge?

8. What is the difference between Network Operating Systems in Peer-to-Peer and Hierarchical LANs?

9. What are the differences between the supplier's and customer's objectives when considering the sharing of WAN facilities?

10. What medium should an organization choose for connecting sites on either side of the Pacific Ocean?

11. What are the limits of the PSTN as a WAN service?

12. What are T-1 and T-3?

13. How can a user's data be converted in and out of X.25 packet format?

14. When is a Permanent Virtual Circuit justified?

15. Where does Frame Relay provide an advantage over standard PSS services?

16. What is the purpose of the ISDN B, D and H channels?

17. What applications might justify choosing an ATM service?

18. When would a router be used (a) LAN-to-LAN and (b) LAN-to-WAN?

19. Under what circumstances is a gateway required, and how does it operate?

20. What software is required to allow a set of Apple Macintoshes on a LAN to connect to the Internet?

Assignment task

For the case study of your choice, where does the overall wide area traffic pattern come on the axes of Figure 7.9? Can all the traffic be treated together, or should certain types of data transmission be treated separately?

Further reading

This section is a very mixed bag with classic texts, beginners' guides and magazine articles, highlighting modern networks such as ISDN, Virtual Private Networks, Frame Relay and ATM.

Black, U. (1993) *Data Communications and Distributed Networks*, Prentice-Hall, Englewood Cliffs, NJ.

Croucher, P. (1990) *Communications and Networks – A Handbook for the First-Time User*, Sigma Press, UK, Chapter 9.

Darabi, A. and Howard-Healy, J. (1992) *Virtual Private Networks: Market Strategies*, Ovum, London.

Derfler, F. (1994) Betting on the dream (article on ISDN). *PC Magazine*, 25 Oct.

Dowty (1991) *The Pocket Book of Computer Communications*, Dowty Communications Ltd.

Fitzgerald, J. (1993) *Business Data Communications – Basic Concepts, Security and Design*, Wiley, New York, Chapter 11.

Gullo, K. (1989) McDonald's ISDN troubled. *Information Week*, 23 Jan.

Halsall, F. (1992) *Data Communications, Computer Networks and Open Systems*, Addison-Wesley, Reading, MA, Chapters 6–8.

IBM (1993) *Network Computing Today*. Consultants' Seminar, London.

IBM (1993) *Networking Systems ATM Strategy*. Consultants' Seminar, London.

Korpi, N. and Taylor, S. (1991) Frame relay goes public. *Datamation*, 1 Nov.

Lam, R. (1992) Four steps to choosing your LAN route. *Computerworld NZ*, 20 Apr.

Layne, R. and Medford, C. (1988) McDonald's serves up global ISDN strategy. *Information Week*, 15 Feb.

Lynch, M. (1995) SuperJANET puts ATM service in five colleges. *Computing (UK)*, 16 Feb.

Marney-Petix, V. (1994) *Business Strategies for the 1990s and ATM (B-ISDN)*, Wellington, NZ Center for Educational Research.

McClanahan, D. (1992) Preparing your LAN for client/server. *DBMS Magazine*, Nov.

McCusker, T. (1991) The latest in high-speed protocols. *Datamation*, 15 Jan.

NZ Telecom (1992) *Guide to Data Communication Services*, New Zealand Telecom.

Scales, I. (1994) ATM is dead – long live ATM. *iText Magazine*, 1(1).

Silver, G. and Silver, M. (1991) *Data Communications for Business*, Boyd and Fraser, Boston, MA, Chapters 9–11.

Sloane, A. (1994) *Computer Communications – Principles and Business Applications*, McGraw-Hill, New York.

Stallings, W. and van Slyke, R. (1994) *Business Data Communications*, Macmillan, New York, Chapters 7–8.

Stamper, D. (1994) *Business Data Communications*, Benjamin/Cummings, New York, Chapters 4–8.

Stephenson, P. (1991) Mixing and matching LANs. *Byte Magazine*, Mar.

Stevenson, I. and Almeida, A. (1994) *Strategies for LAN Interconnect*, Ovum UK.

Part Three
Styles and Themes in Distributed and Cooperative Systems

The previous five chapters have concentrated on the Data Communications (DC) facilities needed to support business requirements. While DC encompasses some software elements as well as physical network equipment, we have not so far addressed the question of 'systems'.

Design of Information Systems (IS) is the primary subject of this book, so it is now time to consider the nature of IS which will use the DC infrastructure.

The immediate observation is that there is no single pattern to Distributed Systems. From time to time a particular fashion holds sway and becomes more or less equated with Distributed Processing in many people's minds. The most recent example has been 'Client/Server', though there are signs that this may be on the wane. Earlier fashions have included mainframe/minicomputer hierarchies and 'processor pools'.

The next five chapters examine the different styles of Distributed and Cooperative systems. Chapter 8 offers a taxonomy of the possible styles, analyzed in a number of different dimensions. Following this analysis, we identify four major themes which are adopted by a large proportion of today's Distributed Systems.

Chapter 9 discusses Transaction Processing, Chapter 10 addresses Client/Server, Chapter 11 surveys Distributed Databases and Chapter 12 deals with Message Passing.

A standard structure is used for Chapters 9–12:

N.1 Introduction and definitions
N.2 Business needs
N.3 Alternative flavours
N.4 Technical issues
N.5 Software
N.6 Assessment
N.7 Potential use of this theme in the case studies
N.8 Exercises

8 Rationale, styles and examples of distributed and cooperative systems

8.1 RATIONALE

Distributed and Cooperative computing has arisen from a combination of application needs, technical advances and struggles in the Information Technology market place. The effectiveness of many remote, centralized systems has been judged by users as inadequate. Data Communications facilities and services have developed to the point where it is now fast, reliable and cheap to transport data, as and when required, from secure storage to users' working locations. Desk-top and lap-top computers have acquired almost unbelievable power at very low prices, while large central computers, with their high costs of purchase, development and maintenance, are seen as risky investments.

These developments have forced huge changes on the style of Information Systems (IS) being developed, but it seems that the art of developing systems has yet to catch up. There is no clear 'plateau' in IS patterns comparable with the Batch Processing and Centralized On-Line Transaction Processing (TP) of earlier generations. Instead there is a whole range of *styles* and *themes* that are gradually sorting themselves out.

The aim of this chapter is to review the current scene in Distributed and Cooperative computer systems, and to clarify the differences between the various styles of processing included. A number of illustrative examples are considered, both from common business applications and from the Case Studies.

8.1.1   *Advantages and disadvantages of distribution*

The advantages of distribution fall under the following headings:

- application trends
- autonomy
- reliability
- performance
- modular growth
- lower communications cost
- low capital cost
- resource sharing.

Application trends means that distributed systems more naturally model the increasingly distributed nature of business applications needs, themselves caused by the swing in management styles.

Autonomy also aligns with the above trend and results in better motivation for users, who can then talk in terms of 'our system' rather than 'the system'.

Reliability means that crashes are more 'graceful', i.e. not all the system goes down when one element (e.g. the mainframe) does. There can be the option to re-route to a different processor, or to make do with a partial system using only the local server or workstation.

Performance means giving faster response where it matters, i.e. the user's workstation. Processing may still be slow, but an intelligent workstation can monitor this and give the user assurance rather than appearing to 'hang'. Also, a mix of specialist processors can give a better balanced throughput than a single general-purpose one.

Modular growth means that it is easier to add new sites, functions and processors, since the overhead of an environment that allows multiple cooperating computers has already been paid for.

Lower communications cost is achieved because one does not have to transmit all the data to a central processor, e.g. when processing is only relevant to one site, or simple site-to-site message passing.

Low capital cost arises from the fact that cheaper, smaller processors can get through the same number of MIPS a lot more cheaply than mainframes – this is the classic 'downsizing' argument. Software for the smaller computers is usually cheaper too.

The snags of Distribution have also been well aired, mainly under the following points:

- technical complexity and risk
- techie-ocracy
- duplication of resources
- loss of consistency.

More technical complexity and risk arises because one is using new products and crossing many more interfaces between systems that were not primarily designed to collaborate with 'foreigners'.

Techie-ocracy means getting into the clutches of communications experts and other 'techies', with counterproductive effects – many anecdotes could be supplied.

Duplication of resources arises because we are providing certain things at many sites instead of at one central one.

Loss of consistency, in which two parts of a system may give different results, is a risk that can arise if a distributed system is developed, on the cheap, without adequate overall consistency checking.

Some experts maintain that there is a 'down side to downsizing', the main argument being that the capital cost savings are often wiped out by the additional costs of the people needed to administer and support distributed systems.

8.1.2 *Advantages and disadvantages of cooperation*

The arguments for structured cooperation between autonomous systems, rather than total autonomy, are rather less well known.

The main advantages are:

- enabling cooperation among different users in a number of locations
- reducing duplication and inconsistency between otherwise isolated systems;

while the disadvantages are:

- overhead in having to conform to protocols
- technical complexity and risk – 'techie-ocracy' again.

Few people would seriously advocate total PC anarchy, but managers may feel that not all efforts to integrate independent systems are justified, since it brings a renewed technical risk that independent PCs avoided.

8.1.3 *Distribution and cooperation – same result?*

If a 'Distributed System' is a single system that someone decided was better split over several processors, and a 'Cooperative System' is one where several formerly independent processors were brought together to achieve some common goal, is there any difference in the result? Given a set of interconnected processors, can we decide whether it is 'distributed' or 'cooperative'? Does it matter?

The short answer to these questions is 'no'. However, many systems, like people's clothes, betray the fashions prevalent at the time they originally flowered. Finding an ideal distribution style for a system is not just a matter of selecting one of these old fashions, it is a series of choices in several dimensions. We will therefore spend a little time looking at these dimensions as well as a wide range of distribution fashions.

8.2 DIFFERENT DIMENSIONS OF CLASSIFICATION

At the highest level, the biggest contrast is not so much between Distribution and Cooperation as between:

- **Hierarchical** and **Peer-to-Peer**
- **Hot** and **Cool**
- **Tight** and **Loose**
- **Non-Redundant** versus **Replicated**

Each of these contrasts is addressed below.

8.2.1 *Hierarchical versus peer-to-peer*

In a **hierarchical** system, one station exercises some level of direct control over what happens on another. One processor feeds data to, and makes requests of, its

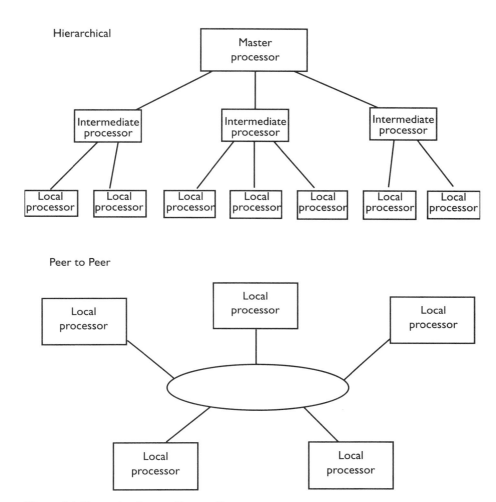

Figure 8.1 Hierarchical versus Peer-to-Peer.

controlling processor. These request or control relationships can form a hierarchy, as shown in the first part of Figure 8.1.

The classic example of this is CAM (Computer Automated Manufacturing), where a Global Resources processor may control a number of Departmental processors which in turn control Process Control computers which operate robots and sensors. Another term for this style is **Vertically Integrated**.

Hierarchical distribution usually reflects a central management control structure over the area of business.

In a **peer-to-peer** system, relationships between stations are balanced. Processor B is just as likely to make a request of processor A as vice versa. Peer-to-peer distribution is often associated with the existence of different spheres of management control, interest or ownership, or of 'chinese walls' between organizational groups.

An illustration of this distinction is the difference between the different philosophies for LAN operation. In server-based LANs, all non-local tasks pass through the nominated Server which runs a multi-tasking Operating System (OS). In peer-to-peer LANs, all processors are potential servers and run the same OS.

8.2.2 *Hot versus cool*

Hot means that any changes to one part of the system are instantly – or at least, very quickly – propagated throughout the whole system. A non-distributed, centralized on-line system is always *hot*, since there is only one copy of data, which is always up-to-date (Figure 8.2).

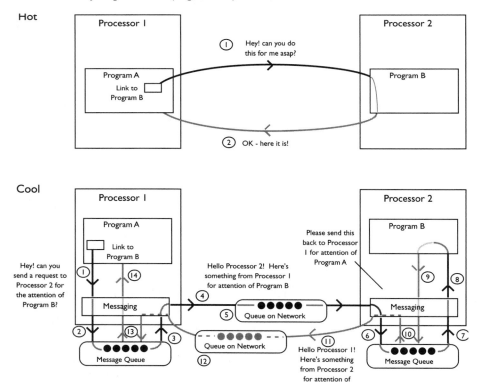

Figure 8.2 Hot versus Cool.

In a **cool** system changes may take some time to be available at all sites. The details will filter through when computing resources are available and priorities permit. There will be queues of changes originated by a source site waiting to be actioned at a destination site.

In the lower half of Figure 8.2, the numbers 1–14 indicate a sequence that might be followed in a *cool* approach.

The term **warm** is sometimes used to imply some intermediate approach.

8.2.3 *Tight versus loose*

In a **tight** system, the user's view is of a single service with no awareness of there being many processors, communications links and so on. 'Single image', 'seamless' and 'single logical view' are equivalent terms used to describe this. In the extreme, the set of processors may behave as if there is only one computer. Examples of this are multiprocessors and parallel architectures such as Pyramid, Sequent and others.

In a **loose** system, the user is aware that he or she is dealing with a number of separate systems. Examples include the use of Electronic Mail or File Transfer, where the user is aware of the different locations of users and host computer files. Another example occurs when accessing a number of specific remote Relational databases.

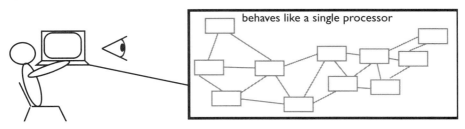

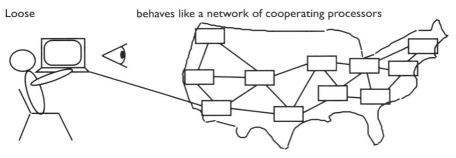

Figure 8.3 Tight versus Loose.

Further along the scale of looseness, individual participating processors may retain the option to disconnect themselves from the arrangement. This is, for example, the case with LAN users who may have turned off their *file sharing* facilities – or even shut down their whole computer.

Tight versus *loose* is usually a distinction between different cooperative or *federal* approaches. It is less relevant where a system is deliberately distributed (Figure 8.3).

8.2.4 *Non-redundant versus replicated*

To the database specialist, non-redundancy is usually seen as an advantage – there is only one copy of the data, hence query results are always consistent wherever the query originates. In practice, the need for high availability and fast response often outweighs this consistency argument. A system with only a single copy of data or procedure is also more vulnerable to breakdown or loss than one with multiple copies.

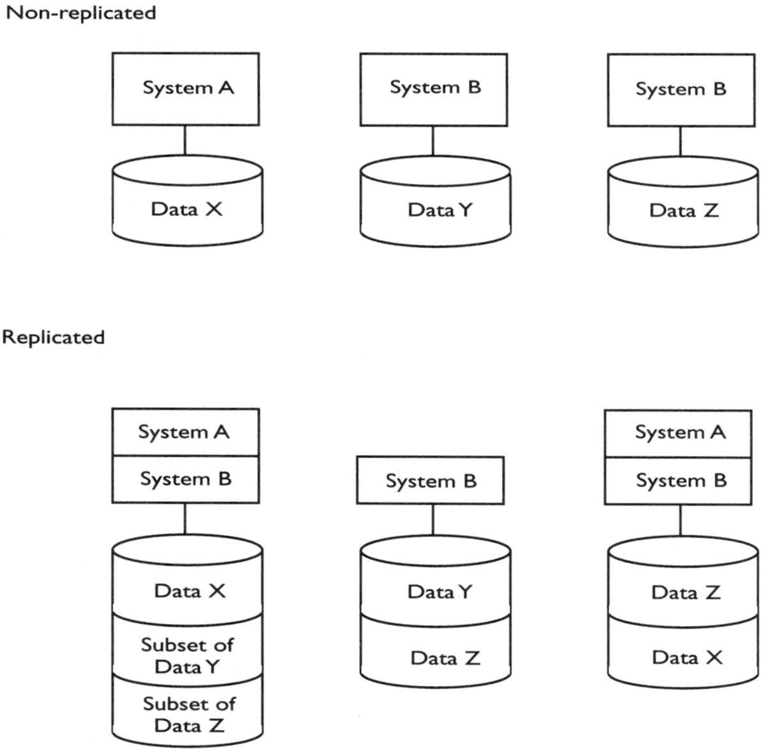

Non-replicated

Replicated

Figure 8.4 Non-replicated versus replicated.

Replicated means that the same programs and data, in total or partial duplicate, appear on a number of sites. This means that every geographical site holds most of the resources it needs locally. The chief reason for doing this is speed of access to data. Sometimes there are other factors such as security against data loss if a processor is disabled (Figure 8.4).

An example application would be a Military Command and Control system where any given command post might be 'taken out' and the communications (probably radio) interrupted. Sites gathering data would have to attempt to send update messages to all the other sites as soon as possible (Figure 8.5).

Many variations on *replicated* databases are possible – examples are given in Hansen and von Halle (1995). We regard replication as a dimension in Distributed Processing rather than a style in itself. It is a design feature which could be combined with any of the styles discussed below.

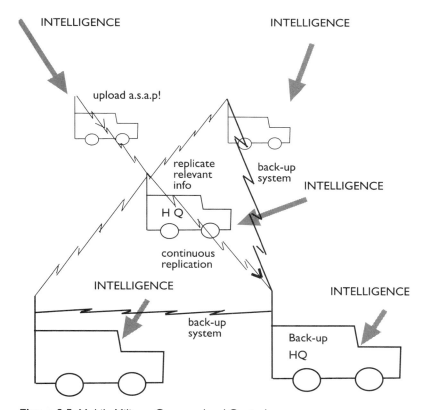

Figure 8.5 Mobile Military Command and Control.

8.3 A TAXONOMY OF DISTRIBUTION STYLES

The previous section discussed dimensions of classification. This next section takes a different viewpoint, looking at fashions or styles in Distributed Computing that have gained general recognition in the market. Figure 8.6 shows a pattern of evolution in styles of Distributed and Cooperative processing. There are two main derivations:

- from integration of previously independent computer systems
- from devolution of a logically central system.

In the diagram, the seven styles can be re-assembled to form four 'current themes' which represent 'hot topics' in Distribution which are discussed in the following chapters.

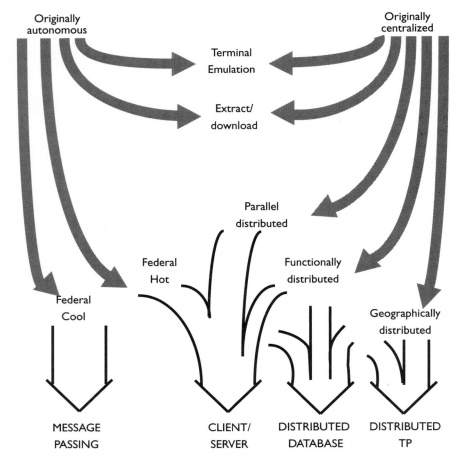

Figure 8.6 Pattern of Evolution of Distributed Systems.

Within each style, each of the following may be distributed:

- the user or robotic devices
- the data
- the application functions.

8.3.1 *Autonomous*

This is one extreme of the spectrum: each site, unit or function does its own processing independently of any other site. One could argue that this is Distributed but not Cooperative. This pattern is rarely the result of planning – it is more likely to have resulted from independent user action in implementing the system they want – without waiting for the IT professionals to get round to providing it within an integrated system.

8.3.2 *Terminal emulation*

Terminal emulation is an early style of Distributed Processing, which keeps a user's local PC independent for most of the time, but allows it to be logged on as a terminal to a central system (Figure 8.7). In this mode, the PC is not using any

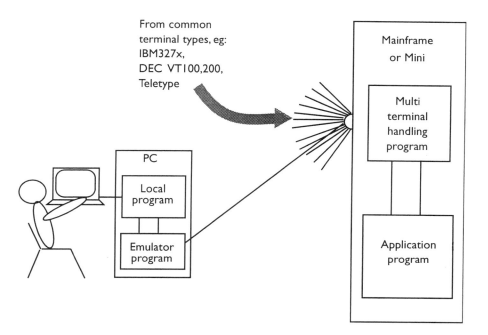

Figure 8.7 Terminal Emulation.

of its own software – it is totally under the control of the host. The PC as a terminal may be able to capture or transmit data from/to the host, and, after switching to local mode, process that data using its own programs.

Such an approach provides a minimal connectivity for cooperation. As an integrated approach it is becoming obsolete, though fuller capabilities can be built into the emulation (see Extract/download below).

8.3.3 *Extract / download*

This style, common in organizations which have both centralized mainframes and local PCs, can be seen as a transition to a more planned Federal or Client/ Server system (Figure 8.8).

The approach assumes a contrast between 'worker' systems – running on a shared mainframe or minicomputer – and local query, reporting and 'what-ifs' –

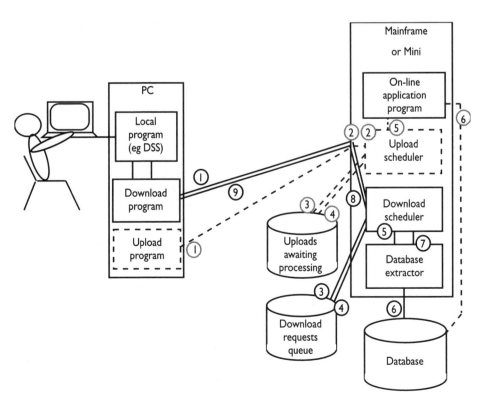

Figure 8.8 Extract/Download.

running on PCs or an Information Center. Extracts or copies (either by communications link or on diskettes) are taken from the worker databases on a regular basis, typically daily or weekly, and the local queries are all on an 'as at ...' basis. A common example would be the overnight downloading of Accounts or Sales data onto spreadsheets for analysis. Local processors may also have their own 'database' as well as application programs.

Two sequences of numbers can be followed on Figure 8.8. A download process is represented by the heavy lines, while the shaded lines denote possible uploading. Uploading is not necessarily included in this style of processing, but if it is required to submit corrections or other updates to the worker system, then these should be uploaded as a file and submitted to the normal input and validation process of the worker system.

Since a wide range of possible user queries has to be catered for, a greater volume of data has to be transmitted in this approach than with 'hotter' approaches discussed later. But these transmissions are less frequent, and are usually scheduled for quiet or cheap times of day. A variant of this approach is to allow on-demand extracts, but to use a queueing system so that several requests for downloads can be convoyed into a single pass of the worker database. A further variant is to put a shared computer in between the worker system and a set of PCs, so that direct interference between PCs and worker system is minimized.

The PC-to-Mainframe style is less fashionable than in the 1980s, but there is still useful software available, for example Trinzic Corp's Info Pump. This allows periodic extracts to be scheduled from a variety of different sources and to be downloaded into a local shared database server.

Some of the problems in this approach are:

- coordination of extracts and of uploads
- consistency of data between the different PCs
- access control to ensure that only authorized use is made of the data.

8.3.4 *Federal cool*

The previous two styles have assumed a *hierarchical* relationship between PCs and Mainframe or Minicomputer hosts. If the cooperating computers are in more of a *peer-to-peer* relationship, the method involving the least loss of autonomy is for them to limit interchange to the sending of messages which are queued until the receiving computer is ready to accept and process them. Requests to another computer are simply filed into a suitable 'in-tray' file on the recipient. An application can then pick up waiting tasks at a time which suits the recipient computer.

In practice, this approach leads directly into *Message Passing*, which is one of the four key themes identified in this book, and which is discussed in more detail in a separate chapter (Chapter 12).

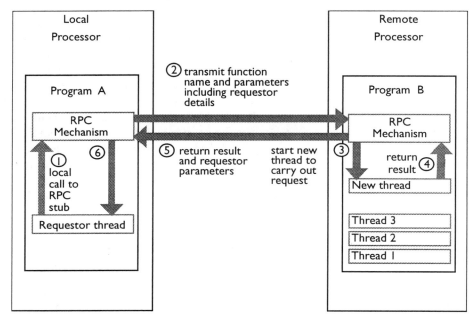

Figure 8.9 Remote Procedure Call (RPC).

8.3.5 *Federal hot*

This term is used to describe a form of processing where sites or functions agree to interchange data by more immediate means such as remote on-line query or updating. It is 'hot' because it is on-line, in contrast to the delayed transmission of Extract/Download or Federal *Cool* message passing.

Usually, a *Remote Procedure Call* (RPC) by a program on the requesting computer invokes a program on the receiving computer to do a certain job for the requestor – and then return the results. This is illustrated in Figure 8.9.

A typical example is the linking of a simple database application on one computer to make remote SQL calls to a Relational database held on a separate computer. Application-level standards such as ISO RDA (Remote Data Access) and Microsoft's ODBC (see Glossary for details) apply here.

Federal *Hot* can also be regarded as analogous to *Client/Server* (see Chapter 10), except that here the style is more *peer-to-peer* – since the processors involved usually pre-date the federation.

8.3.6 *Centralized*

In this approach, all processing takes place at a central server, which is the antithesis of 'distributed'. Today, however, few terminals and devices are 100%

dumb, and most have at least some performance-improving functions such as screen formatting, which may reduce the amount of data transmitted. Of course this category closely relates to Terminal Emulation, i.e. where intelligent workstations act dumbly, for example an Apple Mac emulating a Teletype.

In the next three styles we are talking about planned, rather than born-again, Distributed Processing. A conscious decision is taken to split the whole application and database on one of three bases.

8.3.7 *Geographically distributed*

In this style, the same application and data structure is installed for a number of different geographical or departmental organization units, but the data held at each site is limited to objects of local concern. These could be just what is captured at the site, or what the site is responsible for maintaining.

It is possible to have some parts of the database that are replicated, but any objects appearing in more than one site must be allocated to one or the other for data administration responsibility.

An example is a Bank whose branches keep their own accounts on a local system. Because customers are on the move, some transactions against these accounts arise at different locations, though hopefully a high proportion of transactions will be local (Figure 8.10).

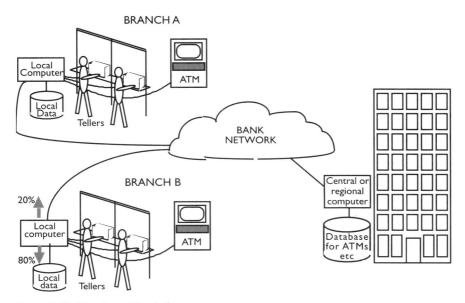

Figure 8.10 Distributed Bank Computing.

8.3.8   *Functionally distributed*

In this style, different functions in the application are installed on different computers, and data is usually stored with the function that creates and updates it, and is shipped to other functions on demand.

Functional *distribution* is often not widely dispersed geographically, although it is quite common for different functions within an organization to be concentrated in different workplaces within a local area (e.g. Inventory Control in the Warehouse, Production Control on the Shop Floor).

Functional distribution can split the overall system in either hierarchical or peer-to-peer fashion. An example of a hierarchical functional split, in a CAM (Computer-Automated Manufacturing) environment, is between Operational Process Control (lowest), Production Control and the Management Information System (highest). An example of a peer-to-peer functional split is between time recording for contracted staff and progress reporting on projects in a Staff Contracting application (Figure 8.11).

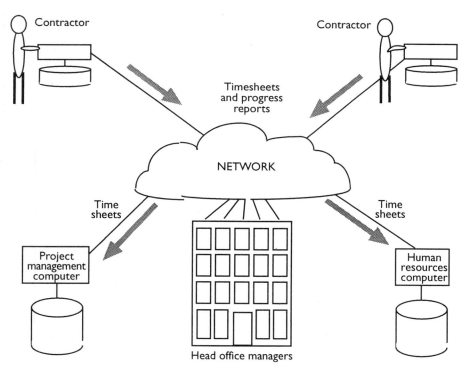

Figure 8.11 Example of a Peer to Peer Functional Split.

8.3.9 *Parallel distribution*

In this style a server process or database is distributed between a number of computers so as to allow parallel threads of execution – thus improving performance. This can be regarded as the computing equivalent to having a team of clerks to which a given batch of office work is allocated.

One example is the speeding up of relational joins in a database, by working on different parts of one table simultaneously – many sophisticated join algorithms exist. Another is the farming out of tasks onto processors which are sitting on a network doing nothing (IBM Heidelberg or Kiwinet style) (Figure 8.12).

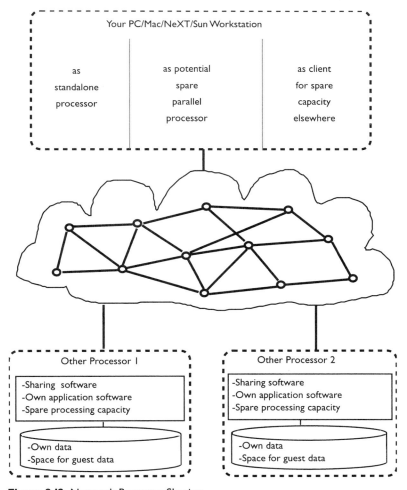

Figure 8.12 Network Resource Sharing.

This approach is sometimes referred to as **multiprocessor** or **processor pool** distribution. It is similar to *parallel processing* but perhaps without the same level of 'tightness' and without the implication that the user only sees a single processor.

8.4 FOUR KEY THEMES

As shown in Figure 8.6, this analysis of styles leads us to identify four main themes in Distributed Processing which are widely used or talked about today. These four themes do not themselves represent a classification, rather they are *fashionable tendencies* which have been enabled by the availability of software, standards and not a little hype.

8.4.1 *Distributed TP (transaction processing) – Chapter 9*

This theme covers the *hot* aspects of Federal processing, or of Geographical or Functional distribution. The aim is to give the user an On-Line Transaction Processing (OLTP) service comparable to what would be offered by a single system on one central processor – in other words, a fairly *tight* style.

This involves a relatively sophisticated level of technology, including software. Standards, such as DCE/DME and CORBA, have appeared relatively recently. However, there is a suspicion that such *hot* processing is not always cost-justifiable, and is sometimes more about keeping IT experts in jobs.

8.4.2 *Client/server – Chapter 10*

Strongly fashionable, this approach is effectively a modern development of the Terminal Emulation and Extract/Download styles. It has similarities with Functional Distribution and Federal *Hot* styles, but the relationship between the processors in Client/Server is one of a hierarchy of requested services, rather than of peer-to-peer inter-operation.

Much software, a few standards and a lot of hype are in evidence. Technology levels are not as high as in Distributed TP, though RPCs are employed below the surface. The net effect is often just a replacement of mainframes by cheaper hardware and software, but not always cheaper overall system operating costs.

8.4.3 *Distributed database – Chapter 11*

This theme arises from Geographic or Parallel Distribution, where the Data itself is split across processors. Cooperative databases are sometimes included, but they are often termed **federal databases** or **multi-databases**.

Software and standards have appeared, but as a fashion the idea shows signs of being somewhat dated. In one possible view, a Distributed Database is a special case of Client/Server where the communication between Client and Server is between one DBMS on the Client and another DBMS on the Server. This may make sense for a system which is largely 'database-centered', but is not appropriate to many applications which are more 'process-oriented'.

8.4.4 *Message passing – Chapter 12*

This final theme arises from the Federal *Cool* style and the realization that *hot* Distributed TP and Client/Server are often too expensive a means of meeting the real need. The ubiquity of Electronic Mail, especially on the Internet, as a means of passing requests and responses between computers has also led to a surge in this approach.

There is not a lot of basic software yet, but there are some standards, such as those for EDI. As a fashion it is 'coming in' on the back of the Internet and generally improved networking.

8.5 EXAMPLE APPLICATIONS

These examples, from a variety of organizations, are intended to illustrate the styles discussed earlier.

8.5.1 *Travel reservations*

Airline booking has in the past been one of the most quoted examples of *centralized* OLTP (On-Line Transaction Processing) (Figure 8.13). As well as fitting in nicely with mainframe capabilities once random access disks were available, it matches the business pattern in which any customer anywhere could want a seat on any flight. However, it relies on a concentration of booking clerks at one location who answer 0800 calls.

Before OLTP, however, practices were different. In 1985 Indian Airlines, one of the last large airlines to install computer bookings, still kept their passenger lists manually at the departure airport of each flight. Bookings and changes would be phoned or telexed through to that site. This was *geographically* distributed. Whether today it could be worth returning to this pattern for a computer system would depend on what proportion of transactions for a flight arose near the departure location – our guess would be not too many.

Other types of travel booking may need to follow different business patterns. Train, bus and package tour seats would probably always be *centralized*.

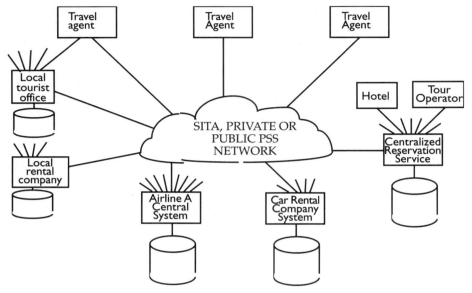

Figure 8.13 Travel Reservations Example.

Computerized Rental Car booking services are partly centralized and partly *geographically* distributed, depending on the localization of business by rental site.

Nowadays, access to travel booking systems is not limited to dumb terminals. Some possibilities (both for agents and frequent customers) are:

- PCs simply emulating mainframe terminals – *terminal emulation*
- independent PCs sending and receiving booking requests – *federal cool*
- PCs running presentation software and other tools – *client/server*.

Also, at a centralized site, the database computer may in fact be a multiprocessor exhibiting *parallel* distribution.

8.5.2   *Materials and parts stockholding*

Traditionally, this has been an area of *centralized* systems. Typical stockholdings are of auto spares or building materials. The growth of chains and franchises providing nationwide coverage has meant a trend to cooperating multiple warehouses. A customer will contact his or her nearest warehouse, and if local stock is not available, transfers from neighboring warehouses may be initiated, or the request itself may be re-routed (Figure 8.14).

This situation is typically addressed by either *geographical* distribution or a *federal hot* approach, depending on whether or not one management group has

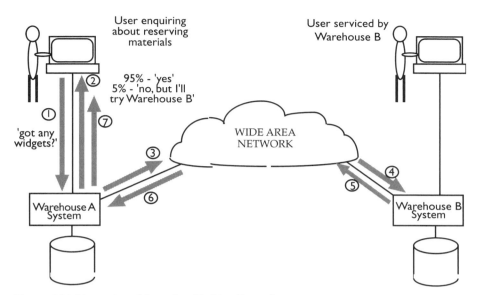

Figure 8.14 Materials and Parts Stockholding Example.

full control over the systems at the different warehouses. Many customer departments or organizations may also want to access the distributed system from their own computer systems – *federal cool* may be appropriate for many transaction types.

8.5.3 *Computer integrated manufacturing (CIM)*

Many manufacturing companies install robots to carry out manufacturing, materials handling and assembly operations, in conjunction with a number of automatic sensors measuring positions, lengths, stresses, temperatures, currents, etc. Each *cell* of related operations is controlled by a small computer (Figure 8.15).

Each department in a factory controls the work of its cells for purposes such as job routing, load balancing and maintenance scheduling. This may be done on a tightly coupled computer platform, which may often use *parallel* distribution in order to provide high availability.

At the global factory level, a database is kept with the order book, delivery schedules and production plan, covering approaches such as 'making for stock' or 'just in time'.

Distributed processing, both *functional* and *geographic*, is natural because the various machine groups use different – sometimes special-purpose – processors. Also, information processing operations are highly localized – there is little reference to another computer's data apart from periodic summaries and plans.

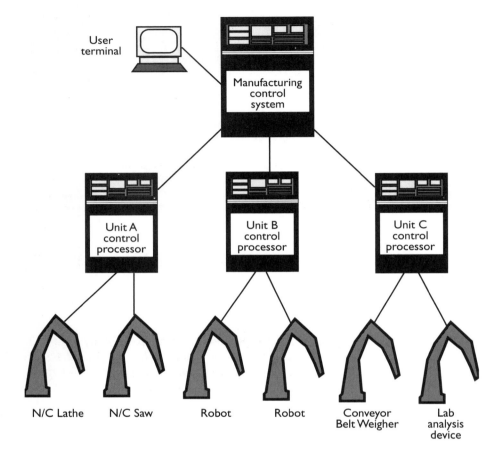

Figure 8.15 Computer Integrated Manufacturing Example.

The distribution is a hierarchical one, *hot* rather than cool. All levels in the hierarchy have their own specific application programs.

8.5.4 Bank transaction processing

A typical Bank has a number of branches which have management responsibility for their own accounts. Generally, a high proportion of the transactions against these accounts are made locally. However, there is a significant percentage of transactions made against remote accounts. Refer back to Figure 8.10 for an illustration.

Many banks have introduced *geographically* distributed processing. Remote transactions must then be routed through to the processor holding the right account data. Bank staff should not have to spend time and effort sorting out the routing – the whole service should appear as a single system.

The advent of Automated Teller Machines has brought the need, for performance reasons, to locate the data on daily account balances in one or more *centralized* computers. The user should ideally be unaware of such optimization.

8.5.5 *Insurance policy selling and renewal*

Insurance Companies do their business through a mixture of Head Offices, Branch Offices and independent Brokers, depending on the type of business. The locality of transactions at Branches and Brokers is higher than with banks, so there are stronger arguments for distribution. Just as with banks, the Head Office needs to control risks and exposure, so there is still some interaction, but less than with banks. The most likely pattern would be hierarchical, with *geographical* distribution, and loosely coupled. Even at head office, individuals or groups may concentrate on a range of account numbers and the data for these could be *extract/downloaded* to that group's database or file server (Figure 8.16).

Brokers, being independent, may be held at arm's length by using a *federal cool* approach. Another alternative would be to enable Brokers' PCs to *emulate* Head Office terminals. They could also run their own brokering software, in conjunction with the company's databases, in *federal hot* mode, as a client/server application.

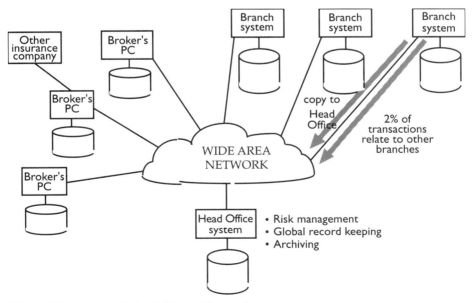

Figure 8.16 Insurance Policy Selling and Renewal.

8.5.6 *Retailing*

EFTPOS machines at checkouts are usually controlled by a cluster of processors which are tightly coupled and replicated to give high availability. Other store functions are inventory, shelf restocking, special offers, cards, money-off vouchers and staff planning (Figure 8.17).

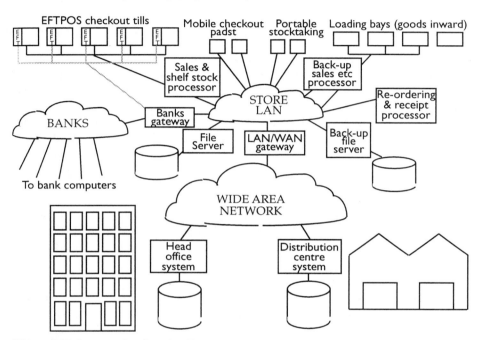

Figure 8.17 Supermarket Retailing Example.

Warehouses will probably have Inventory and Transport Scheduling systems. The Head Office would have Personnel, Finance, Decision Support, Executive Information Systems (EIS), etc.

Within stores, one could have *federal hot* or *functionally* distributed sub-systems at each store. The link to banks needs to be very hot because of the need to check availability of funds. EDI (see 8.5.7 below) could be introduced to link suppliers. Links from stores to warehouses could use either *federal cool* processing or *terminal emulation* for on-line TP.

8.5.7 *Electronic trading*

Groups of businesses may agree to do business with each other – or with the electronically connected public – by direct computer-to-computer means (with or without human moderation). Some trading can be highly timing-sensitive (e.g. currency or security dealing), other trading moderately so (orders, acknowledgements) and yet others less so (e.g. receipts, invoices, money transfer). The ruling style here is *federal cool*, as business relationships are generally peer-to-peer (except maybe Home Shopping) and immediate treatment of the transaction is usually not required. A possible exception to this, however, is a financial or commodity trading market, which would require a different type of system.

In EDI (Electronic Data Interchange), business transactions in each participant's systems are converted to standard trading documents – the range is now quite wide, covering such things as purchase orders, invoices, delivery notes, bills of loading, etc. Examples include wholesaling, regular purchasing, inter-bank processing and home shopping. Even EFTPOS can be regarded as a form of EDI (Figure 8.18).

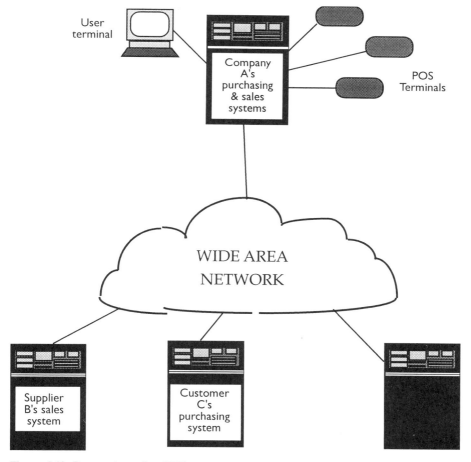

Figure 8.18 Electronic trading (EDI).

Security is, of course, very important if money is changing hands, so that both encryption and use of PIN numbers are normal.

Early EDI initiatives have used VAN services such as IBM Information Network, AT&T Easylink, CDC Redinet, GEIS INS Tradenet, British Telecom (ex McDonnell Douglas), British Banks IDX and Singapore Tradenet. Some example costings are shown as Figure 8.19. More recently, EDI using email has been used, but improved security arrangements for this are still being developed.

8.5.8 *Mobile sales force management*

A recent fashion among companies with sales forces has been to give salespeople notebook computers with modems as their 'portable office'. The aim is to allow

Initialization fee	$250.00
Mailbox fee	$ 75.00 per month per site
Communication charges	
Connect time	$ 0.45 per minute connected
Processing charges	
Data sent	$ 0.005 per data segment
Data Received	$ 0.005 per data segment
Format translation	$ 0.005 per data segment
Minimum monthly charge	$100.00
Discounts on amount of monthly spending:	
$0 - $999	no discount
$1,000 - $3,999	10% discount
$4,000 - $6,999	20% discount
$7,000 +	30% discount

Figure 8.19 Example of an EDI Charging Structure. (ORDERNET Services Inc. – as quoted by Stallings and van Slyke (1994)).

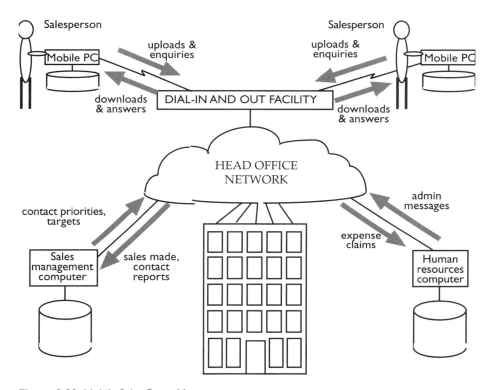

Figure 8.20 Mobile Sales Force Management.

them to give good quality information service to potential customers 'on the road', but also to link up to the sales office when appropriate. Overnight, there is an upload of orders taken and other intelligence, and an *extract/download* of the next day's targets, special deals, changed guidelines, etc. (Figure 8.20).

The notebook computer carries software to enable complex quotations to be evaluated on the spot, but the sales representative may need to login to the office system in order to confirm quotations or reference shared files.

This is *geographically* distributed, but the distributed processing is not required to be immediate. Most operations are purely *message passing*, but some could involve on-line queries or a link to a remote system.

8.5.9 *Air traffic control (cooperating regional centres)*

Each regional air traffic control center typically has a tightly coupled cluster of computers which keep flight plans for flights passing through its area (Figure 8.21). Flight plan data is likely to be replicated. Neighboring regions need to trade

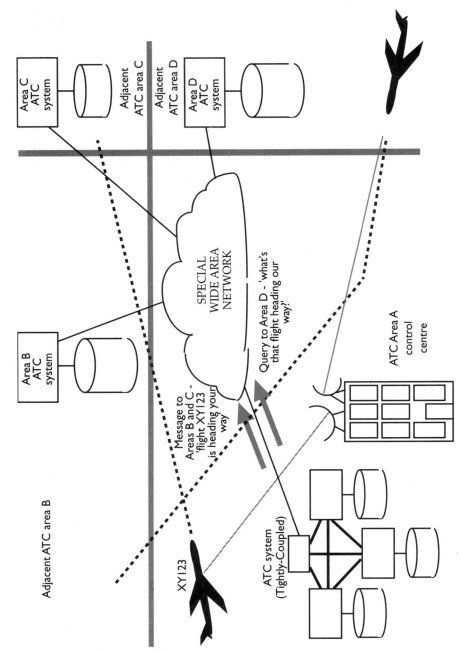

Figure 8.21 Air Traffic Control Example.

individual flight plans, and regions may replicate neighbors' data as insurance against failure of one center. Controllers in one region may also have a need for remote access to another region's database.

8.5.10   *Inland Revenue service*

Processing of Inland Revenue returns and accounts is ideally suited to *geographical* distribution, since each taxable individual or company usually deals with one IR office at one site, allowing of course for transfers (Figure 8.22). A characteristic is that assessment data is not accessed frequently – usually only once in an annual life cycle – which would suggest a *federal cool* style. Occasionally the Inland Revenue (or dare one suggest another Government Department) needs to find an individual by searching across all sites. This could involve *federal hot* access to a distributed database.

Some Inland Revenue Services are now also allowing EDI or file transfer facilities to electronically connected individuals, both to deliver blank forms and to collect returns. This would be using the *federal cool* style.

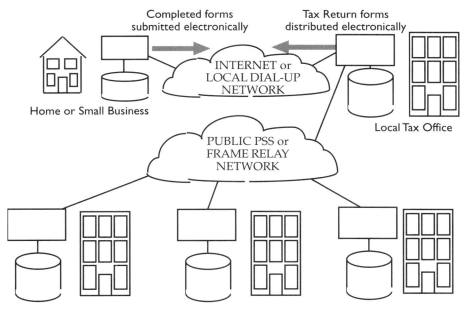

Figure 8.22 Inland Revenue Service Example.

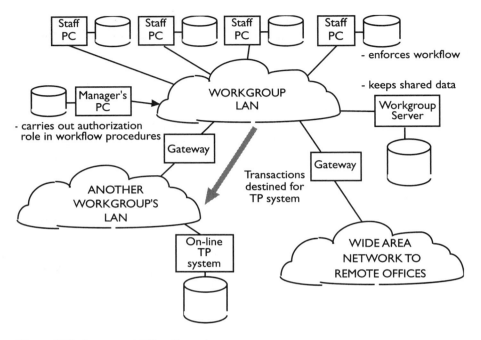

Figure 8.23 Automated Office Example.

8.5.11 *Automated office*

Typical office work is a mixture of formal procedures and *ad hoc* work (Figure 8.23). Formal procedures include such things as enforcing an authorization sequence for a purchase order or expense claim, fixing a meeting (physical or electronic), preparing routine status reports, or recording data into databases. *Ad hoc* uses include word-processing, spreadsheet modeling, drawing diagrams and electronic mail. PC packages can be used in both cases, but some cross-application scripting is needed to control formal procedures (i.e. *workflow* systems). Multiple applications may also share resources such as databases.

Distribution in these cases is a mixture of *extract/download* and *federal*, both *hot* and *cool*. It is also *geographical* in that there are typically many separate desk-top PCs.

8.5.12 *Research and cooperation over a network*

This covers both use of simple email and conferencing between researchers, and also the use of public information services such as CompuServe and the Internet,

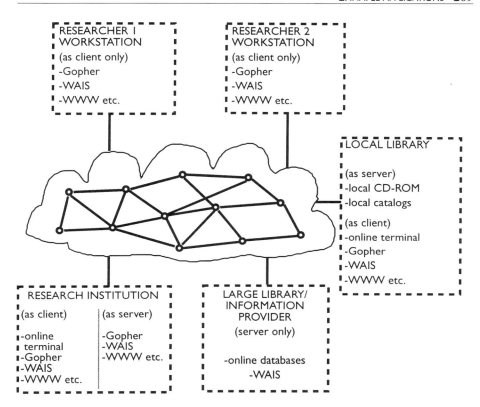

Figure 8.24 Research and Cooperation over a Network.

where such facilities as FTP, Gopher, WAIS (see Glossary) and WWW (World Wide Web) are commonly used (Figure 8.24).

Worldwide electronic mail is now widely available to researchers over the Internet (which was originally a research network), although there are other public services such as Dialcom. However, Fax still provides the most convenient means for many users wishing to do general inter-organization message passing.

The Internet tools, e.g. FTP, Gopher, WAIS and WWW can best be regarded as *federal*, since independent software runs at both requestor and host, and is at least fairly *hot*!

8.6 TYPES OF DISTRIBUTED OR COOPERATIVE SYSTEM RELEVANT TO THE CASE STUDIES

8.6.1 *Mr A*

As a freelance, Mr A's way of working is fundamentally a cooperative one, and much of his use of computer systems consists of exchanging messages with external contacts. If, in the future, Mr A gets involved with Partners or Associates, those people cooperating on a project will need to have access to shared data, e.g. client contact records or product specifications.

In terms of internal systems, there may be subsets of data which Mr A will wish to replicate onto the portable PC, so that he can work when he is away from home. He may also want to access other data which has not been replicated. If the business grows, it is possible that more than one person may need to simultaneously access data and use a printer for administrative tasks.

In terms of the four dimensions, Mr A's potential future systems are mainly *peer-to-peer*, *cool*, *loose* and *replicated*.

The most appropriate distribution style would seem to be *federal* **cool**. However, there could be scope for *extract/download* of some external databases, e.g. Suppliers' catalogues and prices.

The dominant theme is *message passing* with possibly some *client/server* access to shared files.

8.6.2 *Bay Organic Produce Cooperative*

Even though the management are against a centralized computer system, the main information systems are logically centralized, because most of the access needs arise from users who do not specialize in particular subsets of the data. If this assumption were reversed, then the pattern could be different.

In terms of the four dimensions, BOPC's planned systems are mainly *hierarchical* (because of the logical centralization), *hot* (because staff are dealing with suppliers and customers on-line), and *tight* (because we do not want to be concerned with which processor is doing the work). The choice between *replicated* and *non-replicated* could be deferred as a matter for performance tuning.

The most appropriate styles would seem to be *extract/download* (to exchange data with portable PCs operated by traveling staff) and *centralized*.

The main themes are *TP* (several clerks may need to access the same data simultaneously) and *client/server*, with some *message passing*.

8.6.3 *Detox Pharmaceuticals*

At the Factory, computing is already distributed at the Process Control level, but a more centralized view is needed for Production Control at the overall factory level. Warehouses and Local Offices are relatively independent, but their systems also need to cooperate and align with a central view.

In terms of the four dimensions, Detox's future systems are a mixture of *hierarchical* and *peer-to-peer*, and of *hot* and *cool*. Coupling will generally be *loose*, and mostly *non-replicated*.

The pattern of systems use calls for both *geographic* and *functional* distribution. There will be some element of *federal cool* with more casual data sharing.

All four of the themes could be relevant in the different areas of Detox's IS.

8.6.4 *Electric House*

The US Operation is relatively hierarchical, and management culture may wish this to continue in future systems. Warehouses and Stores have some autonomous systems needs, but are also hierarchically subordinate to the Head Office. Salespeople may have portable PCs and would need to link to a Head Office mainframe or other server. EDI with suppliers and large-volume clients (see 8.5.3 above) is a likely option. In-cab computers could be considered to improve Transport Fleet management.

The pattern in Latin America after the merger may be rather different. A greater level of autonomy may exist in specific countries.

In terms of the four dimensions, a *hierarchical* pattern predominates, with more *hot* than cool processing. *Tight* coupling may be used for central systems, but otherwise linkage will be *loose*. The balance would be towards *non-replication*.

The most appropriate styles would again seem to be *geographic* and *functional* distribution. *Terminal emulation* might be used to allow desktop PCs to access legacy TP systems. The TP systems may be able to make use of *parallel* distribution. Some *extract/download* might be used for salespeople's PCs. *Federal cool* may also be relevant for inter-site information.

TP would be very big in Electric House, with *client/server* and *distributed database* as possible options, especially if new systems are built for Latin American operations. Home shopping is likely to operate on a *message passing* basis.

8.6.5 *Commonwealth Open Polytechnic*

The main campus is mainly concerned with routine administration, which suggests central databases of students and contractors. Each regional center could be semi-autonomous as regards enrolments and student administration, but there might be global limits on student numbers for remote supervision and examining purposes.

In terms of the four dimensions, there is a big contrast between the *hierarchical* administration systems and most other IS which are *peer-to-peer*. Most processing will be *cool*, as there is less immediate pressure from clients or physical processes. Videoconferencing would be a rather special exception to this. Coupling would generally be *loose*, and *replication* variable.

The most appropriate styles would seem to be *centralized* for most administration, and *federal*, mainly *cool* for teaching and other academic work, but occasionally *hot*. *Terminal emulation* may apply to the use of remote Library Public Access Catalogs for bibliographic query.

Except for limited *TP* in administration, the main themes would be *message passing* (e.g. distribution of teaching material over the Internet) and *client/server* (staff access to administrative systems).

8.6.6 *National Environmental Protection Board*

Inspectors could use a system on portable PCs to record measurements for later transfer to regional or central shared databases. Regional offices and HQ Departments will have a need to interchange data both for regular and *ad hoc* purposes. Researchers will use PCs and make casual access to external databases. Processing of questionnaire returns is likely to be geographically delegated to regional centers. Regular interchange of data with subject organizations could use EDI.

In terms of the four dimensions, the business is relatively *hierarchical*. Most processing is *cool*, and coupling *loose*. Some systems may justify a degree of *replication*.

The most appropriate styles would seem to be *extract/download* (e.g. for inspectors' data), *federal cool* (e.g. for queries to external reference data) and *geographical distribution* (e.g. processing of questionnaire returns).

The main theme will be *message passing*, with some *client/server* and only a little *TP*. *Distributed database* is an option for regional collections of inspection and questionnaire data.

8.7 EXERCISES

1. 'The concept of Cooperative Processing is a marketing lifeline for computers and systems that have passed their "use by" date' – discuss.

2. Is adequate management control of data possible in a Peer-to-Peer approach?

3. What is the difference between 'Functionally Distributed' and 'Client/Server'?

4. Would the wide adoption of a single Data Communications technology all the way to the Desk-top PC affect the balance of styles of Distribution and Cooperation?

5. What style of distribution would you expect in a 'workflow' system, i.e. a system which routes electronic documents to the humans who must process them?

6. Local processors in Process Control systems are usually relatively passive. How does this affect the classification of the system to which they belong as 'distributed' or 'centralized'?

7. In the examples in sections 8.5.11 and 8.6.2 above, what difference does it make if office workers specialize, rather than act as generalists who can perform any of the tasks?

8. In Detox Pharmaceuticals, what style of Distribution/Cooperation would be suitable in a system for feeding sales forecasts into the production plan for the factory?

9. What style of computing would be appropriate to support the management of an Advertising campaign for the Electric House/Casa Electrica merger in Latin America?

0. Discuss the operation of a system for electronic submission, marking and return of student assignments at the COP.

1. What centralized management control of enrolments is needed at the COP and how can it be managed through an information system?

2. What sort of system could ensure that changes in Government Legislation are reflected quickly in the NEPB's central database?

ASSIGNMENT TASK

For your chosen Case Study, review the classifications suggested in section 8.6. Can you envisage an application that contradicts them?

Further reading

Apple (1994) *VITAL*. Statement of Direction, Apple Corporation.

Barker, R. (1994) *Managing Open Systems now that the Glass-house has Gone*. British National Conference on Databases (BNCOD 12), Springer Verlag, Berlin.

Barr, J. (1994) Developing large-scale cross-platform applications. *Cross-Platform Strategies*, **1**(1).

Coulouris, G. and Dollimore, J. (1988) *Distributed Systems – Concepts and Design*, Addison-Wesley, Reading, MA.

Hall, J. (1994) Distributed systems – a European perspective. *Data Management 94* (BCS DMSG), Cambridge, UK.

Hayward, D. (1994) Desktop faces the downside of its own success. *Computing (UK)*, 10 Nov.

König, W. (1994) Distributed information systems in business and management. *Information Systems* **19**(8).

O'Brien, J. (1993) *Management Information Systems: a Managerial End User Perspective*, Irwin, Homewood, IL.

Sawitzki, G. (1992) The NetWork project: distributed computing on the Macintosh. *Apple Technical Journal*.

Stallings, W. and van Slyke, R. (1994) *Business Data Communications*, Macmillan, New York, Chapter 3.

9 Transaction processing

9.1 INTRODUCTION AND DEFINITIONS

The need to record and process transactions, which are the essential units of any business or organizational activity, has been with mankind for a very long time. As Gray and Reuter (1993) open their book, 'Six thousand years ago, the Sumerians invented writing – for Transaction Processing'.

A **transaction** is defined as a collection of changes to the state of a business which together are to be regarded as an atomic unit. Simple examples are selling or buying something, paying or receiving money, etc. Examples of more complex transactions include taking a sales order, receiving an invoice from a supplier, or applying a 10% salary raise to a selected set of staff.

Historically, transactions have been processed using paper, quill pens and manual filing systems (nail marks on clay tablets for the Sumerians). Mail, telephone and telegraph successively improved the practice of processing remote transactions. Computer systems were introduced to ease the problems of processing very large, and expanding, numbers of transactions. Early computers struggled for many years to support the Transaction Processing (TP) need in Batch Processing mode, and were generally restricted to daily updating cycles. With the arrival of random-access storage devices, time-sharing and multi-tasking operating systems, on-line TP systems took over and became the single biggest area of computer application. With the first data communications links (Telex and early modems) came the concept of 'Tele-processing', or, processing-at-a-distance, which in some quarters is what 'TP' originally stood for.

The concept known as TP has been one of the most cost-effective applications of computers. In order to realize the economies of scale, many organizations developed, in recent decades, large, central computer systems in which a very large database is available for access by hundreds or thousands of staff or agents. Transactions have been relatively simple, and while accuracy and 'no loss of data' have been paramount, speed of response has also been important. Early examples of such systems include the reservation systems operated by major airlines.

TP often carries the connotation of thousands of 'dumb' terminals subordinated to a single central mainframe computer running a single application software system. This picture is changing fast. An ever-increasing proportion of user terminals are now PCs, which may emulate terminals, but can also run their own software and communicate to the TP system in client/server mode. Also, the single mainframe may be a cluster or parallel architecture. The mainframe workload may even be geographically distributed on a number of computers that are remote from each other.

This chapter aims to provide an appreciation of the principles of Transaction Processing (TP), which are fundamental for most shared systems whether centralized or distributed. It also discusses the issues which affect TP in a Distributed or Cooperative environment.

9.2 BUSINESS NEEDS

9.2.1 *The one-person business concept*

It is an essential business requirement to 'know how things stand' at any point in time. To do this, the manager has to bring together all the records of state and changes of state in his area of control, and process them into a single 'document' which contains the summary, exceptions and trends as well as the detailed figures. Data sources are essentially distributed (changes originate at many locations) but the decision making process, and hence much of the output, is relatively centralized. Figure 9.1 illustrates what has been called the 'one person business' concept, in which the manager's need is to be able to control a large-volume business as if it were a small concern in which he or she was the sole employee (Figure 9.1).

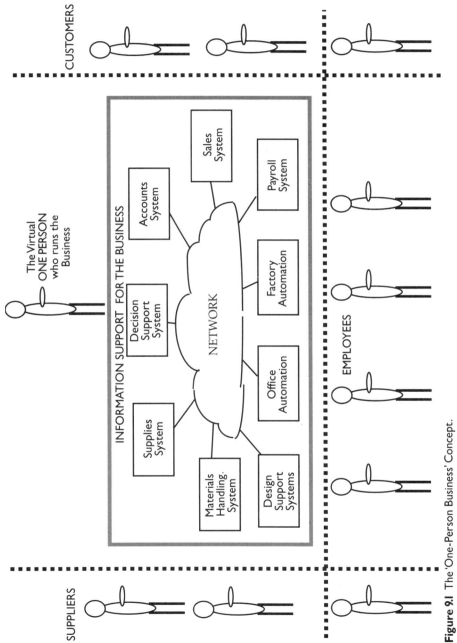

Figure 9.1 The 'One-Person Business' Concept.

An important advantage of this concept is that it enables the manager to enforce policies which the 'one person' or the Board have decided, for example with respect to pricing or credit, by standard procedures. A single, centralized record of transactions is also easier to audit.

Modern business requirements look to extend this concept to situations with hundreds or thousands of separate sources of data. Furthermore, speed of processing, as well as accuracy of recording, has been added to the business needs. Distance is no longer a justification for customers having to wait for their transaction to be handled.

More recently, the expectation has grown up that computers can enable transactions across the boundaries of one company or organization.

9.2.2 *Critical success factors for TP*

The major factors in determining whether or not a TP system – centralized or distributed – will be a success are:

- Speed of Response
- Availability
- Manageability
- Security
- Accuracy.

Speed of Response is important for two reasons. One is the need to be as quick as, or quicker than, the competition in dealing with client enquiries and interactions. The other is to ensure that staff have the incentive to record things using the system and not to resort to pen and paper! The user is not only interested in getting sub-second response some of the time – he also needs consistency.

Availability is important for the same two reasons. The business cannot afford delay in money transactions since a few seconds in a volatile money market could mean millions of dollars lost. Most of us have at some time stood at an airline desk to be told that the computer is 'down'. We as clients don't accept this as an excuse for the airline not being able to process our request; we expect them to have some backup system like aeroplanes themselves have. A related measure is 'fault tolerance', i.e. the ability not to go 'down' in the first place – possibly by providing a reduced service until repair is achieved.

Manageability means being able to run the system easily in normal operation, coping with problems, and making changes when the system grows or alters. Changes may include such things as adding users, increasing the range of transaction types, and including additional servers.

Security matters to the business both because it wants its view of the business to reflect input from authorized agents only, and also because it does not want to be defrauded. The business is also likely to have to demonstrate the system's security to auditors.

Accuracy is essential because the organization needs accurate data to make good decisions. As with security, regulatory bodies (e.g. auditors, tax inspectors) will require a high level of accuracy to be demonstrated.

9.2.3 *The 'ACID' test of a TP system*

The accuracy of TP systems is often discussed in terms of the so-called 'ACID Properties' (Figure 9.2).

- **Atomicity** means that either the whole transaction succeeds or else none of it does (i.e. a half-complete transaction is not allowed).
- **Consistency** means leaving the state of the system, database, etc. in a valid state (e.g. not violating any rules, constraints, relationships, etc).
- **Isolation** means that it appears to any one transaction that it happens independently of other transactions. This is equivalent to requiring that the transactions appear to proceed in a strict sequence – this is called 'serializability'.
- **Durability** means that once a transaction succeeds, the changes are never lost.

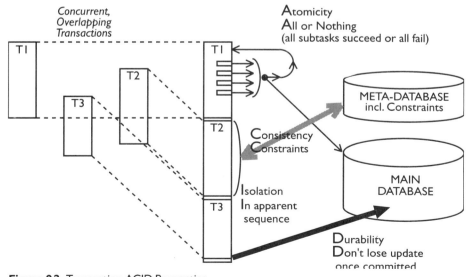

Figure 9.2 Transaction ACID Properties.

What ACID is really about is defining adequate 'failure semantics', i.e. making sure that all types of failure are properly catered for. To paraphrase Gray and Reuter (1993), 'no ACID means that work gets lost'.

9.3 ALTERNATIVE FLAVORS

As discussed earlier, the classic style of TP is the centralized mainframe with a single database and suitable software for both TP and DBMS. User workstations are assumed to be unintelligent – if not totally dumb, than of the IBM3270 or Digital VT100 type.

While the task at the remote locations was originally limited to simple data capture, the activities at these locations are often now themselves part of a local computer system. Workstations are more often than not powerful PCs. Some parts of what are logically 'transactions' from the business viewpoint may be carried out across more than one processor. The centralized part of the processing is reduced and becomes a specialized server (in modern parlance).

In geographically distributed systems, transaction processing will primarily take place on a processor at a local site, but there are usually likely to be some 'cross-site' transactions. The prime example of this is Customer Accounting in Banks (for more detail, see the previous chapter).

Another development with TP, especially with high levels of concurrency, is to retain geographical centralization but to introduce a processor pool structure as discussed in the previous chapter.

Application software which might previously have operated entirely on a mainframe is often now devolved by separating 'transaction server' functions (which perform process sharing and enforcement of ACID) from 'database server' functions, onto two specialized computers.

Things are more complex in cooperative systems, where the computer architecture has evolved from one of independent processors to a federal system with sharing of resources. The introduction of certain computers into the federation as shared servers brings a need for TP facilities, since each request by one computer to another for provision of a service can be regarded as a transaction. The problems of concurrency, contention and queuing, which mainframe TP systems cope with as second nature, should therefore apply just as much in the world of shared servers. However, it is questionable whether many of today's client/server systems have addressed these fully.

Other flavors are concerned with the positioning of hardware and software units within the technical infrastructure for the TP system. These will mainly

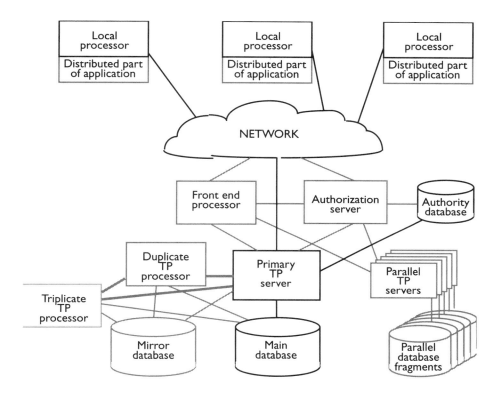

Figure 9.3 Technical Infrastructure Options for TP.

affect speed and availability or 'fault tolerance', but will also impact the scalability of the system. Typical options include (Figure 9.3):

- use of specialized processors, e.g.
  - front-end processors to handle incoming/outgoing messages
  - authentication servers
- use of parallel servers for performance or for fault tolerance
- moving more or less of the application software to run locally on user workstations (see also Figure 10.4).

Closer to the physical level, TP systems often vary in approach to optimizing use of the communications resources available. There are a number of ways of balancing variable traffic loads onto the available link capacity. This affects speed of response where it is subject to most delays

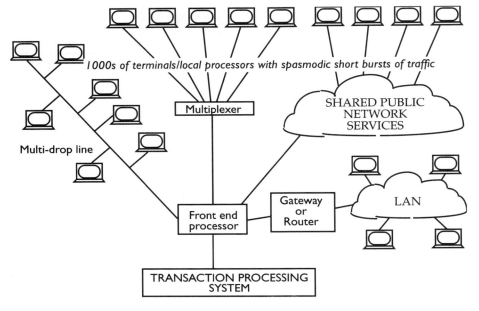

Figure 9.4 Optimizing Line Usage with TP.

and variations, namely the network. Options include using such methods as (Figure 9.4):

- multiplexing usage of a leased link
- multi-drop with polling over leased link
- use of shared WAN services such as a Packet Switching Service
- LAN media access control methods.

9.4 TECHNICAL ISSUES

9.4.1 *Performance*

The main performance issue in high-concurrency TP systems is their degradation in response time at peak periods. A lot of effort is put into the development of efficient software for TP. This is to ensure that resources such as processors, disk channels and storage, which may form bottlenecks and hence cause queues, can be utilized as efficiently as possible.

At normal loadings, this concentration on efficient use of computing resources helps to defer the point at which degradation of performance starts to occur. These situations can be analyzed through queueing models which are discussed later.

In distributed TP there may be more opportunity than with single-processor TP to even out peaks by load-sharing among the multiple processors. However, prediction of response times with multiple processors is an even more complex task than in the single-processor case.

9.4.2 *Enforcement of ACID*

The following methods are normally used to achieve each of the four ACID properties.

Atomicity: clear marking of beginning and end of transactions, with a Commit/Abort decision depending on the success or failure of the whole transaction. This may be complicated by sub-transactions (see section 9.4.3 below). With distributed processing, commit operations involve passing of a series of messages between the multiple sites that may be involved in a transaction.

Consistency: declaration of constraints on what constitutes a consistent state, and evaluation of constraints prior to Commit/Abort. With distributed processing, evaluation of constraints may involve multi-site queries.

Isolation: a 'pessimistic' locking system in which only one transaction can operate on a resource at a time; or an 'optimistic' system in which all transactions go ahead but are checked for interference before Commit/Abort; or an enforced sequence using time-stamping. With distributed processing, locks may have to be held and released across sites, again involving a messaging overhead.

Durability: a system of logging changes, usually through 'before' and 'after' images of the database, which can be applied following a failure so that no committed changes are lost. With distributed processing, there has to be confidence that all the sites involved in a transaction write to their logs.

In the distributed situation, all these methods have to be adapted for multiple processors and therefore carry extra overheads. A recurring problem is that of 'who controls the global position?' The two main alternatives are either a nominated 'controller' site, or the site originating the transaction.

One particular method of note is that of 'Two-Phase Commit' (2PC) which is used to control distributed Atomicity. In the first phase, all the sites involved in a distributed transaction are asked whether they vote to Commit or Abort. If all the votes received by the controller are for Commit, then all sites are told to Commit, otherwise they are all told to Abort.

Enhancements to this protocol, and distributed approaches to Isolation, are discussed in Chapter 11 on Distributed Databases.

9.4.3 Transaction structure

Transaction structure is the main area of design within a TP System. In practice, we cannot always insist on implementing 'logical' transactions as they appear in the business requirement. For example, real-world accounting systems often have to introduce Suspense Accounts to cater for 'things we don't know where to put'. From the Consistency point of view, not all constraints on the status of the system or database are best implemented as 'hard' constraints. We may want to allow them to be temporarily broken while we fix a problem with the data. Other variations on transaction structure include (Figures 9.5 and 9.6):

- nested transactions (one transaction kicks off sub-transactions)
- chained transactions (one transaction kicks off the next)
- long transactions ('sagas')
- batch processing with intermediate checkpoints
- cooperative transactions (e.g. multi-participant design support)

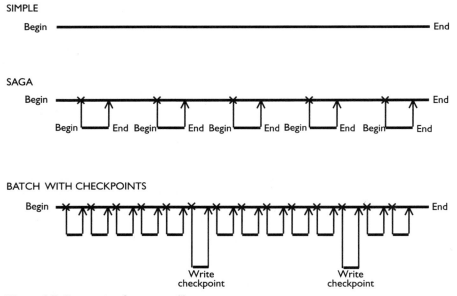

Figure 9.5 Transaction Structures (I).

This analysis is relevant to distributed systems because a distributed transaction is naturally broken down into the sub-transactions that will run on each individual computer. Cooperative transactions involve a different aspect, namely of two transactions on cooperating computers that are initiated independently, but share a combined sub-transaction.

Transaction structure can also be varied to provide users with 'receipt of request' feedback and progress reports on long transactions – this has a strong effect on how the user perceives performance.

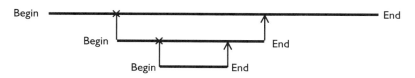

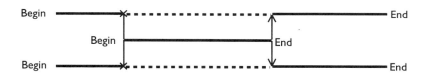

Figure 9.6 Transaction Structures (2).

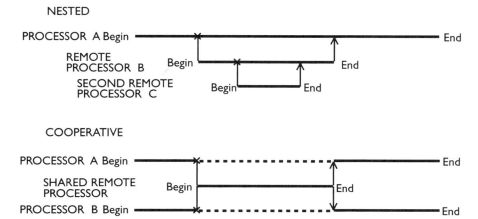

Figure 9.7 Distributed Transaction Structures.

Distributed transactions (Figure 9.7) are naturally nested or chained, in that there is a natural sub-transaction each time a task has to be started on a different processor. For cooperative systems a more de-coupled structure is appropriate, but the problem is that Atomicity as defined for centralized transactions is not powerful enough to cope with cooperative transactions, and more sophisticated protocols (e.g. 3-phase commit) have to be used.

9.5 SOFTWARE

9.5.1 *TP monitor principles*

Just as a Database Management System (DBMS) controls sharing of data, a TP Monitor is a piece of software that controls sharing of computer resources on the processing side. In a typical TP system many terminals want to perform the same process at the same time. To manage this, the software has to balance the load on various resources, such as shared program storage, and to control queues for resources that may be busy. These issues can be critical in applications with hundreds or thousands of terminals or workstations, especially where different terminals may need to use separate threads of the same application program.

With early Operating Systems (OSs) usually being geared to centralized batch processing, many TP Monitors supplement – or in fact partly replace – the OS. Perhaps the best known is IBM's CICS (Customer Information Control System – pronounced 'kicks' – or in Italy, 'cheeks'). With many TP systems using databases to store the shared data, some DBMS have included an associated TP (or 'DC') package (e.g. IMS-DC, IDMS-DC) while others use whatever TP Monitor is provided on the host (e.g. CICS).

Later OSs are more multi-user oriented, and TP Monitors such as DEC's ACMS and Tandem's Pathway work in conjunction with OS facilities, in a fashion which is more appropriate for Distributed TP. Unix is also multi-user oriented, though possibly with fewer facilities for resource sharing and re-entrancy. These have been improved recently with extensions such as Unix Systems Lab's Tuxedo. In some cases the OS itself now includes TP facilities, e.g. Tandem Guardian, and recent versions of DEC VMS.

Another approach is that of TP Generators, an example being Tandem's Pathmaker.

There are also TP systems geared to Open Heterogeneous systems, e.g. Transarc's Encina (extension to Unix) which works with OSF (Open Software Forum)'s DCE (Distributed Computing Environment) standard.

Recently, IBM have been remarketing their originally mainframe-oriented CICS system as a Server environment – which demonstrates the convergence between TP and Distributed Processing!

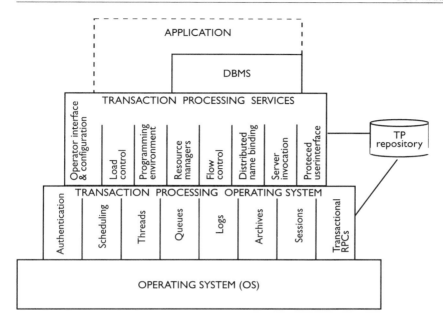

Figure 9.8 TP Monitor Architecture (based on Gray and Reuter, 1993 — by permission).

Figure 9.8 shows a TP Monitor Architecture as suggested in Gray and Reuter (1993).

Figure 9.9 shows an operation structure for a typical TP Monitor from the same source.

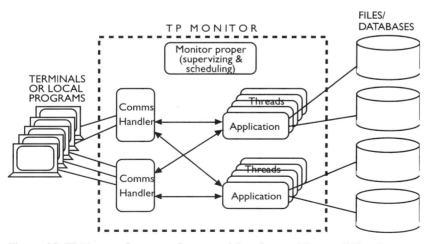

Figure 9.9 TP Monitor Operation Structure (after Gray and Reuter, 1993 — by permission).

9.5.2 *Facilities expected in a TP monitor*

To give a flavor of TP Monitor facilities, and to show where choices of facilities might be exercised, the following lists are offered. They are based on the Cullinet IDMS-DC System developed in the early 1980s (Cullinet, 1983), with further material from Gray and Reuter (1993).

a) Configuring the system

Set tuning options, e.g. size of program and storage pools, level of multitasking

Add/remove/reallocate users and terminals (can be 'physical' or 'logical')

Identify programs, tasks, scratch areas, queues

b) Operations control

Begin/end tasks

Deal with abnormal terminations

Change priorities

Inter-program communication – two alternatives are usually offered:

LINK (i.e. call as a subroutine and expect to return)

TRANSFER (pass control unconditionally)

Posting and waiting for events or timed activities

ENQUEUE/DEQUEUE transactions into/from a queue for a specific resource

Snapshot dumps

Send messages to terminals

Sign terminals on and off

Slow transaction replay for diagnostic purposes

Write transaction logs

c) Presentation services

Design user interfaces (screens, etc.)

Specify mapping of screen data to database

Display screens to user

Control input of data from user interface

React to user response (keyboard, function keys, menu choice, mouse)

The way most of these facilities work is for the programs to call specific TP functions, typically by using embedded commands which are pre-processed (like embedded DML or SQL calls in a database). For example, Encina has a language 'Transactional-C'. The SQL-oriented 4GLs which are marketed with many Relational DBMSs also provide these facilities, e.g. Sybase TransactSQL. Some Application Generators and Lower CASE tools also allow calls to common TP Monitors such as CICS.

The critical factor is whether or not the result will be efficient and accurate when 1000+ users want to enter transactions simultaneously. Therefore a large part of the software has to address the exceptions rather than the routine processing. Exceptions have to cover abnormal results, aborted transactions, partial or total breakdowns, queues, timeouts and so on.

9.5.3 *Facilities expected in other software for distributed TP*

In classic centralized TP, the TP Monitor often includes facilities for mapping data to screen displays (see section 9.5.2 c above). However, with the advent of intelligent terminals, PCs and client/server approaches, this task has gradually moved away from the TP Monitor site. Instead, the challenge now is to provide interfaces with heterogeneous remote presentation services. Particular facilities to look for are:

- Gateways – these are means of linking to other, possibly heterogeneous clients or servers in a network. Encina, for example, has gateways for DCE RPC, IBM SNA LU6.2 and X/Open. These gateways may appear in programs as 'middleware stubs'.
- Authentification – since a distributed TP Monitor has to act as a broker for transaction requests coming in from all sorts of clients, an authentification system is needed with suitable encryption and digital signatures. Encina uses the DCE Kerberos proposal.
- Support for load sharing and consistency checking among multiple TP servers, when making use of parallelism (processor pool) or mirroring (duplicating the system for fault tolerance).
- Distributed 2PC – this is discussed in Chapter 11 (Distributed Databases).

9.6 ASSESSMENT

TP is not a theme that goes away when a user organization turns its back on mainframes and centralized processing. The need for ACID still applies where there is multi-user updating of shared data even if data and processes are distributed. In any proposed design for a distributed system, the question must be asked – 'where is the ACID provided?'

Another question is whether immediate TP is really needed, rather than a 'cooler' system of message passing with queueing of updates. Obviously if the workstation user has a client standing in front of them, or waiting on the end of a telephone line, then things need to be 'hot'. Otherwise what we need to determine is what Chorafas (Chorafas, 1994) calls the 'Real Enough Time'.

9.7   POTENTIAL USE OF TRANSACTION PROCESSING IN THE CASE STUDIES

9.7.1   *Mr A*

Mr A's TP needs are limited to sharing his databases with at most one other person, namely Mrs A or a 'temp' he occasionally calls in at peak periods. Concurrency is always likely to be low. The multi-user facilities that come with multi-user versions of some PC Database software are quite adequate.

9.7.2   *Bay Organic Produce Cooperative*

The Cooperative has approached things from a Federal angle, with the need to share data between autonomous PCs. If a database server is introduced, the DBMS sharing facilities may be adequate for the fairly low level of concurrency, but the provision of ACID will need checking. If certain of the staff specialize (e.g. in a group of Farmers, Markets or Buyers), then BOPC could allow each of these PC users access to another PC's database when required, on a peer-to-peer basis.

9.7.3   *Detox Pharmaceuticals*

Assuming regional offices keep separate databases of Orders, there may be low to medium concurrency with multiple clerks or salespersons updating the database. A server-based DBMS, with adequate ACID support, would probably suffice. The Head Office does not necessarily need to have up-to-the-second information about Orders placed. Similar comments apply to Product Inventories at Warehouses.

The main TP need is in the Production Control systems in the factory. At the Process Control level, concurrency control can be assumed to be already provided in the existing control-room systems. At the level of Process Group Scheduling and Monitoring, the timescales may be longer, so that any TP used is 'warm' rather than 'hot'.

Administrative Systems are conceptually batch-oriented, although *ad hoc* queries and immediate validation of single updates are often needed. This fits a similar pattern of low-urgency TP.

9.7.4   *Electric House*

Transactions at Store Checkouts involve TP in that they affect Store Inventory levels, but the concurrency level is limited – the number of Checkouts in one store is in tens rather than hundreds. Also, since the intervals for reordering from the

Warehouse are unlikely to be more frequently than hourly, the timescale is not too critical. Obviously fast response, including EFTPOS, has to be provided to the customer.

Wholesale and Home-Shopping Orders need to be answered quickly, and immediate updating is desirable so that the same stock is not reserved twice. If all inventories are handled centrally, transaction rates may be fairly high, but in terms of transactions per minute rather than per second. An alternative architecture would be to route all stock status enquiries to the Warehouse nearest the customer, dealing with as many requests as possible locally. This would still leave a certain level of concurrency in the re-routing of requests that could not be fulfilled by the local warehouse.

9.7.5 *Commonwealth Open Polytechnic*

Student databases, assuming they are kept centrally, need to be kept up-to-date (perhaps to the hour or day rather than the second) in order to support access by both administrators and students phoning in. The number of system users accessing the system at one time is potentially high, but contention where two concurrent transactions want to access the same student's details would be rare.

Other uses of TP might be in the area of remote login to assignments, but these are more in terms of file transfer than updating a shared data collection.

9.7.6 *National Environmental Protection Board*

There is very little requirement for online TP, although some *ad hoc* queries need supporting.

If the NEPB were to get into the business of installing meters at critical sites, and reading them remotely during special monitoring exercises, an interesting choice would have to be made between immediate TP and batching of meter readings.

9.8 EXERCISES

1. 'Most of the problems with TP only arise because we are trying to over-centralize our computing' – discuss.

2. What are the arguments for and against the 'one-person business' concept?

3. Is there ever any justification for a shared database that does not have ACID?

4. What would be likely to happen in an airline seat booking system if the TP system did not have an effective Isolation mechanism? As an example, consider

two travel agents who, at roughly the same time, try to book the last seat on a certain flight.

5. What is meant by 'two-phase commit'? Which of A, C, I or D does it relate to?

6. Why are sub-transactions relevant to distributed TP?

7. What are the main complications to the supporting of ACID when TP is split among several computers?

8. Give three examples of software packages commonly used for TP support. In what sort of special environment might each of these packages be used?

9. Why is a such a large part of a TP Monitor concerned with the processing of exceptions?

10. At my bank, the teller behind the desk gives me an account balance as at the previous midnight. However, the automated teller machine gives me an up-to-date balance, even including my last transaction. What does this tell me about my bank's TP systems?

11. Give three application examples from the case studies where updates must be 'up-to-the-second'.

12. In which application example from the case studies is the Availabilty requirement the strictest?

13. Compare the risks for Detox between centralized and regionally distributed TP systems security.

14. Two authorized Electric House Order system users representing wholesale clients are on-line, trying to reserve stock for delivery. The first user gets a list of availabilities, but while she is thinking about it, the second user comes in and reserves so much that the first user is now short. What are the pros and cons of locking out other users once the first user has started the transaction?

15. Discuss options with the potential to improve TP performance for the Electric House Home-Shopping application.

16. What problems might arise in linking Electric House's TP Systems with those of Casa Electrica (which might use different software and standards)? What solutions should be considered?

17. What might be the advantages in introducing parallel processors to support the COP Student Registration TP system?

18. What sort of TP system does the COP need to control and account for students' remote use of computer facilities?

19. For the NEPB's database of Companies needing to comply with legislation, would a non-TP system (e.g. all transactions queued first and subsequently submitted in strict sequence) be any less useful in business terms than a full on-line TP system?

20. Discuss further the requirements of the proposed TP system needed to control remote meter reading in NEPB as described in section 9.7.6 above.

ASSIGNMENT TASK

For your chosen case study, identify the application area where there is most need for TP with ACID. What are the likely levels of:

- immediacy of response (seconds)
- workload (transactions per second)
- concurrency (number of users active at one time)
- contention (number of users trying to access the same piece of data at one time)?

If you need to make extra assumptions about numbers of transactions and data volumes and other details, please state these clearly.

FURTHER READING

Betz, M. (1994) Inter Operable Objects – Laying the foundation for Distributed Object Computing. *Dr Dobb's Journal*, Oct.

Brodie, M. (1994) *Distributed Object Management – A Core Technology for Future Computing*. Tutorial, Extending Database Technology (EDBT), Cambridge, UK.

Coulouris, G. and Dollimore, J. (1988) *Distributed Systems – Concepts and Design*, Addison-Wesley, Reading, MA.

Cullinet (1983) *IDMS-DC User Manual*.

Gellersen, H.-W. (1993) Graphical design support for DCE applications. *Proc. International DCE Workshop, Karlsruhe, Germany*, Springer Verlag, Berlin.

Gray, J. and Reuter, A. (1993) *Transaction Processing*, Morgan Kaufmann, Cambridge, MA.

Haney, C. (1994) Database strategies overlook DCE doubts. *Computing (UK)*, 3 Nov.

IBM (1988) Special issue on SAA. *IBM Systems Journal* **27**(3).

Mohan, C. (1993) *High Performance Transaction Processing*. Tutorial, Very Large Databases (VLDB), Dublin, Ireland.

Schill, A. (1993) *DCE – The OSF Distributed Computing Environment*, Springer Verlag, Berlin.

Xephon (1994) *Beyond Client/Server: Cooperative Processing for TP Systems*. Xephon Ltd, UK.

10 Client/server processing

10.1 INTRODUCTION AND DEFINITIONS

The essential elements of a Client/Server approach are as follows (Figure 10.1):

- several (but sometimes just one) computers, often incorporating a user interface, which need to call on other computers in order to meet fully the users' requirements; this is the **client** role
- one or more computers which process a limited variety of requests from other stations for a specialized, shared service; this is the **server** role
- a network linking the computers, usually a LAN
- additional software which facilitates the formulation and movement of requests and responses.

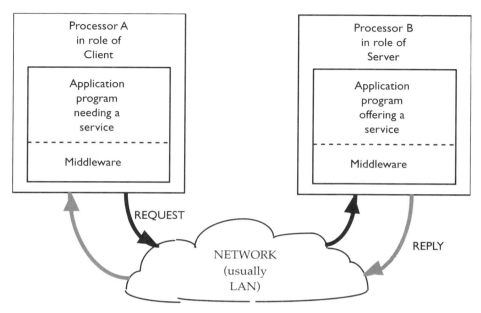

Figure 10.1 Typical Elements of a Client/Server Approach.

The approach also allows the same computer to be a Client for some services and a Server for others as shown in Figure 10.2 below. The path marked **1** shows the simplest case, with a user workstation as client and a single specialist server. Path **2** shows the use of another user's workstation in the server role. Path **3** shows a computer already in the server role taking also the client role for further specialist services; an example could be for TP on a mainframe acting as a 'super-server'. Path **4** shows a further second-tier client/server relationship involving a WAN rather than a LAN.

In the taxonomy of Chapter 8, Client/Server can best be regarded as *federal hot* processing where there is a hierarchy of client-to-server role pairs. Alternatively, it can be thought of as *functional* distribution where parts of the application that are better located near to users (the clients) make requests of other parts (the servers) which are shared by many users.

The primary purpose of this chapter is to review the concept of Client/Server, putting it into the context of Distributed and Cooperative IS. Different styles of Client/Server are examined, and the technical implications considered. We also take a look at the very lively market in Client/Server software. Finally we consider the difficulties in getting good business value out of the approach.

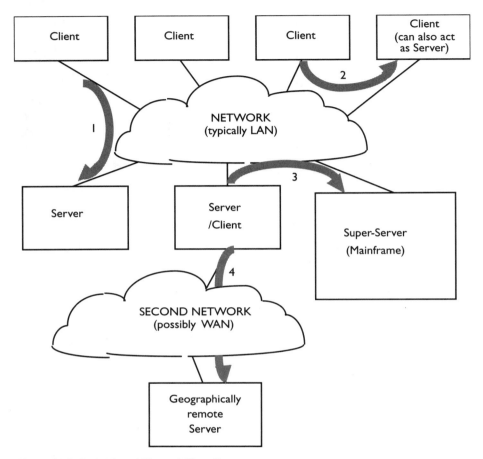

Figure 10.2 Examples of Chained Client/Server.

10.2 BUSINESS NEEDS

Chorafas (Chorafas, 1994) suggests three main business drivers for Client/Server, the first of which looms largest for user organizations.

- mainframe replacement by 'downsizing'
- better modeling of the organization, through functional distribution
- opening the way for reusability of 'plug-in' hardware/software modules

To these we add:

- enabling use of modern graphical user interfaces (GUIs) in conjunction with existing software.

The first driver, mainframe replacement, means cutting IT costs by distributing the application on to multiple, smaller processors, purchased from a better 'window' on the price/performance curve. This also has the huge side-effect of slimming down the vast ranks of IT 'techies' that have traditionally attended mainframe computers.

Cynics say that 'Client/Server' is no more than a fashion-word, hyped up by IT Consultants and Service Suppliers, in an attempt to drum up business from user organizations that have become reluctant to spend money on traditional computer developments. The carrot dangled before the user is the chance to escape the large mainframe bills and instead to pay the much lower initial costs associated with PCs. Whatever the Client/Server is sold as technically, 'downsizing', and hopefully 'downcosting', is the common thread.

To justify claims of a reduction in cost, it is a good idea to show comparisons with an 'equivalent mainframe solution'. There has to be some realistic sizing of the transaction rate each small server can handle, and proper statistics on what happens at peaks. For the personnel costs, which are often the largest part of the total, we need to allow for staff maintenance time spent by local users of PCs as well as IT Department specialists. A possible checklist/form for the comparison is shown in Figure 10.3.

Cost Item	Client/ Server	Equivalent Mainframe

1) One-offs:
        Server processors
        User workstations
        Network upgrading
        Software licence
        -    client application
        -    client middleware
        -    server middleware
        -    server application
        -    server DBMS
        System Dev't charges
 	
2) Continuing:
        Suppliers' maint. fees
        IT Dept support
        User staff maintenance		

Figure 10.3 Skeleton Form for Calculating Client/Server Trade-Off.

The System Development estimates must also include costs of integration of the various technologies used in each case.

10.3 ALTERNATIVE FLAVORS

10.3.1 Client/Server – 'all things to all men?'

The trouble with using the term Client/Server is that it is applied to such a wide range of processing architectures and that as a consequence its value as a marketing label is quickly declining. Various authors have distinguished a number of sub-styles of Client/Server, and have attempted to attach more specific names to them. The difference between these sub-styles is generally based on different placement of the various components which make up the software system.

The best known classification is the so-called Gartner Diagram (Figure 10.4), which shows a whole spectrum of sub-styles. This version is based on additions

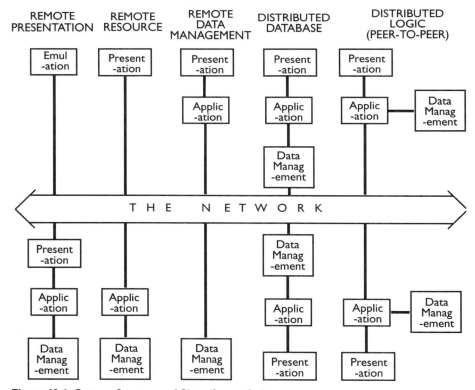

Figure 10.4 Gartner Spectrum of Client/Server Styles.

suggested by SEER Technologies (Seer, 1993). The Gartner Diagram has been added to in subtle ways by a number of authors (Figure 10.4).

In 'Remote Presentation', the client simply runs emulation software, and all other software operates on the server. In Chapter 8 terms, this is terminal emulation. In 'Remote Resource', the GUI is devolved to the Client, but all the application logic is still on the server. In 'Remote Data Management' the application logic now runs on each client, and only calls the server for database services. The server in this configuration is often referred to as a 'database server'. In a 'Distributed Database' each computer runs its own DBMS and request/response takes place between DBMSs. The client's DBMS acts as an 'agent' for accessing data regardless of location. This is the subject of the next chapter. Finally, in 'Distributed Logic' the application software itself is split, and request/response takes place between application programs.

The philosophy of Client/Server, which implies a hierarchy of roles between processors, contrasts with 'peer-to-peer' approaches (e.g. Appletalk, LANtastic and Novell Netware Lite), where every processor is presumed to be both a potential client and also a potential server.

10.3.2 *Types of role allocated to servers*

To gain the claimed advantages of Client/Server, the designer has to decide what is a suitable split of functionality, eg what tasks are 'shareable' and can be devolved to a Server. The commonest form of Client/Server computing these days (Figure 10.5) is to have a number of PCs as Clients with a single Server supporting a shared database service.

However, Client/Server is not limited to a 'database' approach. Some other common Server functions are described below – though not all will necessarily have dedicated computers.

a) File service

A trivial variant of a Database Service is 'File Server' or 'Virtual Disk'. In this approach, data can be stored on a different computer, but accessed as if they were resident on the client. This function is normally embedded in a Network Operating System (e.g. Novell or NFS) where file space on other computers in a network is visible to the client as 'virtual' disk drives. These systems also allow private, as well as shared, virtual disks. File Service can be regarded as a form of Database Service where only simple File Management functions (e.g. Open, Close, Read Block, Write Block) are allocated to the Server.

b) Print service (including spooling and queueing)

A Print Service provides spooling to shared printers – usually Lasers. A Print Service will often reside in a Server computer together with other services, often as part of the Network Operating System (e.g. Novell Netware).

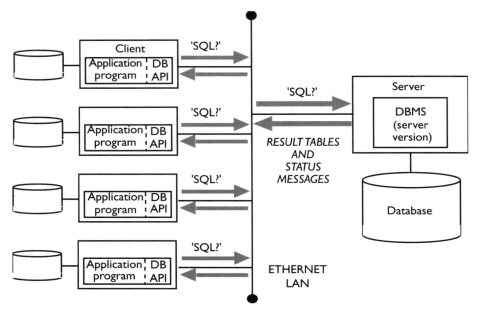

Figure 10.5 A Typical Database Server Architecture.

c) Mail service

This provides electronic mail boxes for a group of users, and often a gateway to a public transportation system for electronic mail. Functions include mailbox storage, alerting user workstations of incoming messages, and translation of names and addresses.

d) Network gateway service

A Server can also be used to link a group of Clients on a LAN to wider Network destinations through a WAN. Although Bridges and Routers can also be regarded as cheaper, dedicated-hardware Network Servers, they do not allow programmed control of the internetworking, such as might be required in a 'Firewall' security system where a Gateway Server could be set up as a so-called 'Bastion Host' (Ranum 1995; Trusted, 1993).

e) Network management service

A common Resource Management requirement is to deal with Network Management, System Administration and Usage Accounting. Network Management software has traditionally been provided by LAN vendors, and is sometimes combined with the Network Operating System. In some heterogeneous networks, a dedicated server is used.

f) Authentication service

User Access Control and Authentication have often been included in one of the previous three services. Recently, with the rise in usage of networks as a means of passing business transactions between different organizations, the need for better authentication of messages has led to the use of dedicated servers.

g) Report library service

Where a large number of batch reports or other extracts (e.g. for microfiche, downloads) have to be run overnight against one or several databases, a library of reports/queries is often used. Users can request a run of a given report from the library (optionally with parameters) or update and add report specifications. Report requests can also be triggered by calendar or other events. Such a service is often attached to a Database Server, although report libraries can sometimes operate across multiple databases.

h) Internet public access service

Some of the software that is widely available over the Internet is split into Client and Server elements. Each site offering public access to data will operate one or more Servers for each type of service, e.g. FTP servers, Gopher servers and WWW (Hypertext) servers.

i) Application-specific services

This covers a whole range of possible functions. One common situation is Business Rule (or Constraint) enforcement, where it may be inappropriate to attach rules to the Database. Another is handling the interface between different types of system, e.g. between real-time data collection and decision support.

Figure 10.6 shows a possible situation in a Foreign Exchange and Money Market Dealing System for a Bank. A number of processes are distributed to user workstations, but a number of shared control functions (e.g. checking traders' positions against exposure limits, sampling and aggregation of real-time data feeds from Financial Information Services) are allocated to separate servers.

10.3.3 *Choosing between alternatives*

The main areas for design choice in a Client/Server system are:

(a) Which major functions should be shared on Servers?
(b) Which software components go on the Server and which on the Client?
(c) How many different levels of Server should exist?
(d) What level of parallelism in the Servers is desirable?

Choice (a) depends on how the whole system can be modularized, and where there are common levels of resource sharing. This is discussed in more detail in Chapters 14 and 15.

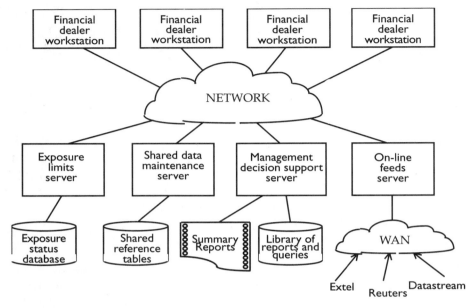

Figure 10.6 A Non-Database Client/Server Example.

Choice (b) concerns the fine tuning of software placement. With Client/Server Databases generally, the more logic the designer can put into the database procedures, the better the system will run and the greater the integrity enforce nent on the shared database. However, this means more work on the Server and possibly more contention and queueing. Ideally, some system of modeling is needed for evaluation of these options. Evaluation of alternatives is discussed further in Chapter 18.

Choice (c) depends on having a good model of the message passing structure between the software modules identified above (possible with some Object-Oriented design methods).

Choice (d) depends on building a reliable model' of multiprocessor performance, and is not discussed further.

10.4 TECHNICAL IMPLICATIONS

The technical requirements of a Client/Server approach can be summarized in terms of the four elements introduced in section 10.1 above, namely:

- Clients
- Servers
- LAN
- and usually, Middleware (bridging software)

Functions which have to run on the client usually include presentation logic and a share of the application logic. To this has to be added the additional bridging software or Middleware that enables the client software environment to communicate with the server environment, which may be of a different type. Clients which are also user workstations are typically PCs running some form of MS-Windows. Other common alternatives are Apple Macs and Unix workstations and – in the future – 'Internet Appliances'. Some upgrading to the stand-alone configurations may be needed to support the additional workload.

The servers must run a multi-tasking Operating System of sorts – plain MS-DOS is not enough, but it can be used with appropriate add-ons. Other common options for the Server are Novell NetWare, Windows NT, IBM OS/2, or some variety of Unix. Some of these, e.g. SCO, can still run on PC compatible hardware processors and handle, as well as the server function software, multiple concurrent requests and the bridging software.

A shared application server must give adequate TP performance and behavior (e.g. ACID, as discussed in the previous chapter). A database server must provide all DBMS functions below the SQL statement level. It should also have means of supporting Integrity Constraints, Triggers and embedded Database Procedures.

Because Client/Server processing may involve the transport of large volumes of data (whole files from a file server, whole tables from an SQL server), the capacity of the LAN must be substantial (preferably at least 10 Mbps). Ethernet and Token Ring systems are common. If usage is intensive, faster technologies such as FDDI or fast Ethernet may be necessary.

Middleware is discussed below in section 10.5.3.

10.5 SOFTWARE

In any conversation about software for Client/Server, the first word that gets mentioned is usually 'Middleware'. This concept forms most of the following discussion, but we first mention the facilities that are used specifically on Clients and on Servers.

10.5.1 *Client software for Client/Server*

Client facilities used in Client/Server applications are most commonly programs or tools that may have been used previously on user PCs or workstations in a stand-alone environment. Of course they may continue to be used in this mode, as well as being linked in with the Client/Server environment. Examples of such products are:

- Graphical User Interfaces (GUIs), e.g. Windows, Mac, OS/2 PM, XWindows

- Common workstation tools – Word Processing, Spreadsheets, Graphics, Project Management, Desk-Top Publishing
- Personal 'databases', e.g. Paradox, MS-Access, dBase, DataEase, Omnis, with their associated 4GL, query and report tools
- Specialist reporting and query tools, e.g. R&R
- 'Fourth Generation' language with links to many DBMSs
- Programming language, e.g. C, Delphi, Visual Basic or COBOL.

Middleware functions are often added on to the above tools, as discussed in section 10.5.3 below.

10.5.2 *Server software for Client/Server*

A large proportion of Server software in Client/Server systems is purely for database management. Other server functions were discussed in section 10.3 above, but the use of Servers for Databases (taking the wider sense that includes flat files) seems to outweigh all the others.

A Server DBMS must accept requests in some data language (usually a form of SQL), and pass data in a standard format (usually Relational tables). Otherwise the functions are much the same as for any multi-user DBMS in a centralized environment. Indeed, many Database Server products derive from mainframe equivalents.

There is a very lively market for Database products in the Client/Server arena. Examples of products on the market are:

- DB2 family   (IBM – merging a number of variants)
- SQL Server   (Microsoft – ex partnership with Sybase)
- SQLBase   (Gupta Technologies)
- Netware SQL   (Novell)
- XDB   (Xerox)
- InterBase   (Borland – geared to dBase and Paradox)
- Informix
- Ingres   these last five products are Server versions
- Oracle   of established Relational DBMS which run
- Progress   most typically on Unix or DEC VAX VMS.
- Sybase

Most of these will run under more than one OS – the most common options are:

- OS/2
- Windows NT
- Unix (57 varieties?)
- DEC VAX/VMS.

Other possible server platforms are Novell NetWare, Apple Macintosh, IBM OS/400 and even DOS (though as Van Name and Catchings (1989) comment 'limitations of one process at a time and 640 kbytes of memory make DOS a poor server platform').

A number of other 'personal' database products, sometimes sold as 'PC DBMS' (a slight contradiction in terms as a Database is about shared data), are now evolving in one or both of the following two directions:

(a) as client-based application generators, with SQL interfaces to talk to more substantial Server DBMSs

(b) as smaller-scale Database Servers on a LAN.

Examples of products evolving in this way are DataEase, Omnis, Microsoft Access and Paradox.

A final group of database server software runs on specialized 'back-end' processors, such as Teradata's DBC1012, both of which are a tightly coupled processor cluster.

Virtually all Database Server software types these days are SQL Servers, i.e. they work with some standard form of SQL (e.g. ISO RDA, Microsoft ODBC, IBM DRDA or IDAPI) and relational tables. Non-relational DBMS can still be used, but almost always with a relational front-end. This is how Adabas offer their database as a Server – using a product named Entire.

The market for server software, other than database, does not have the same coherence. Possible exceptions to this are the emerging markets for independent Network Management software and Authentication servers. For the sampling and aggregation of real-time data feeds, e.g. from Financial Information Services, Lotus Corporation has offered a software product named 'Realtime' to complement its '123' Spreadsheet.

Anything application-specific will normally have to be coded or generated in conjunction with a TP Monitor (as discussed in the previous chapter).

10.5.3 *Middleware*

The need for Middleware arises, as discussed earlier, when the software running on Client and Server cannot communicate. The incompatible software usually originates from different suppliers who have adopted different data passing conventions. There is therefore a need for software to bridge the gap.

Middleware can be regarded as including any software that provides an API (Application Program Interface) – either RPC (Remote Procedure Call) or Message Passing mechanism – which allows a Client Application to make requests from a Server Application. Figure 10.7 below shows one view of a Middleware structure.

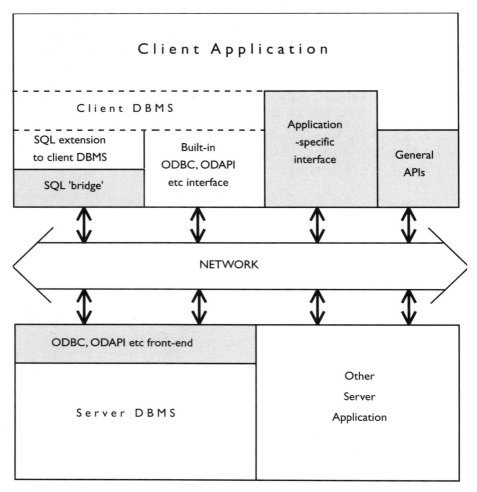

Figure 10.7 Simple Middleware Structure.

A narrower definition includes only those products which are independent of any Client or Server software already in operation, implying a cooperative evolution path to Client/Server. In practice, much Middleware is embedded in, or is in an add-on to, Client or Server software or Operating Systems. In the view of some authors, distinct Middleware products could vanish from the market-place in a few years' time. The vendors of Client and Server products will bundle in a large number of 'hooks' to allow them to link to other vendors' software.

Most authors distinguish between RPCs ('synchronous' or 'hot' Client/Server) and Message Passing ('asynchronous' or 'cool', allowing queueing for Server resources). This corresponds to the distinction drawn in Chapter 8.

The starting point for the RPC approach is the class of program-to-program invocation protocols such as IBM's LU6.2 (SAA) and its TCP/IP and OSI equivalents. The difficulty with these is that, since they are quite detailed, they require good programming skills and may not give high productivity for the majority of common Client/Server calls. LU6.2 is said to have 32 verbs, some with 100 parameters, and there are 1400 error conditions to be monitored. There are simpler products addressing a similar need, such as Message Express. Since a lot of the required RPC functionality is now provided in both TP and Database Servers, the Client APIs can safely become a bit simpler. Examples are Server versions of CICS, and another CICS-derived product, Encina (see the previous chapter).

When linking Client SQL requests to Database Servers, the Middleware market is well developed. Many Database Server vendors offer Network software that allows a reasonably wide range of SQL dialects from a Client to be recognized and actioned. Examples are the 'NET' products of Ingres and Oracle, and the basic Client/Server facilities of Sybase/SQLServer. As an alternative to these vendor-driven standards, there are also independent standards. The RDA (Remote Data Access) OSI standard has been incorporated in recent versions of the SQL standard and in many client SQLs. While not exactly vendor-independent, Microsoft's ODBC (Open Data Base Connectivity) and Apple/Borland's ODAPI have gained some status as DBMS-independent standards.

Another widely-used Middleware product is Information Builders EDA/SQL, which offers a version of the Focus 4GL on both Client and Server, and takes advantage of the long history of Focus in being able to access data in as many as 50 different DBMS and file systems, both relational and non-relational. This provides a path to the large volumes of data residing in organizations' legacy systems using software such as IMS DL/I, IDMS, VSAM and COBOL BOFs (Boring Old Files).

In the reality of today's marketplace, a number of 'any-to-any' Middleware toolkits following the RPC approach have been offered. Examples are Microsoft Q + E Lib, Oracle Glue, Rumba and Gnosis SequeLink. These allow connection between a wide range of popular Client packages and languages and a number of key Servers. Figure 10.8 shows, as an example, what was offered by Q+E Lib in one specific advertisement. However, such lists of possible linkages are always growing.

The OSF (Open Systems Foundation), which includes several major suppliers such as IBM, HP, etc., has proposed a standard called DCE (Distributed Computing Environment). This is geared to a standard RPC mechanism for TP-type applications, primarily in a Unix environment. It proposes the structure of Client and Server RPC 'stubs' which are the pieces of code on either side of the gap which allow each of the communicating programs to behave as if the whole application was at one site (Figure 10.9). A

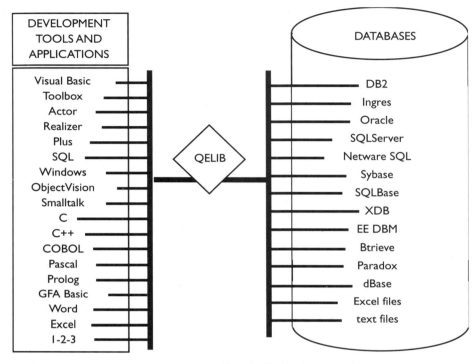

Source: Pioneer Software Advertisement

Figure 10.8 Example of Commercial Middleware Connectivity.

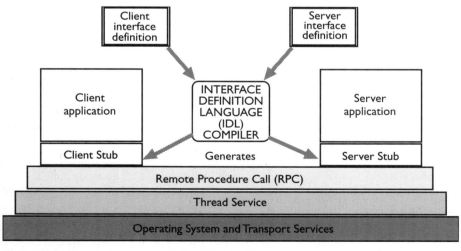

Figure 10.9 Open Software Foundation DCE Architecture.

version of DCE for MS-Windows has already been produced. Windows NT already includes an RPC mechanism.

Object-Oriented systems are by nature oriented to a Client/Server view. The Object Management Group (another consortium of suppliers) has published CORBA (Common Object Request Broker Architecture) which provides a mechanism for transparent inter-object communication where objects may reside on different processors. The architecture (Figure 10.10) is not too dissimilar from that of DCE. A number of key vendors, known as the OpenDoc consortium, i.e. Digital, Hewlett Packard and Apple, as well as IBM with DSOM, have announced CORBA-compliant products. Microsoft have proposed their own standard, OLE (Object Linking and Embedding), which has also been endorsed by Oracle. A programming interface – and some early products – have already appeared. Although users may have to dodge the stray bullets in such a commercial fight, plans for CORBA to interface with OLE have now appeared.

The Message Passing approach to Middleware is still uncommon, but this is now changing. Client/Server technology is still at the moment being pushed by programmers who have grown up with RPCs. However, it is doubtful whether 'hot' links are always justified. Organizations with less critical timescales are

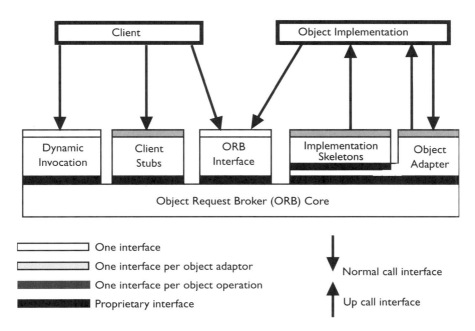

Source: Object Management Group, Inc

Figure 10.10 CORBA – Middleware for Distributed Objects.

looking at simpler messaging systems, even including the Internet's SMTP (simple mail transfer protocol), as a means of passing information and requests. A Message Passing approach is also said to be easier to program. It is addressed in more detail in Chapter 12.

Middleware appearing on clients

The best-known examples are the SQL add-ons which are available with local DBMSs such as Paradox, Access, Omnis. These add-ons enable the excellent presentation and quick application development facilities of these packages to be used against a genuinely shared database on a Server. As a result, these packages are undergoing some degree of market repositioning – away from being purely a DBMS, and towards being Application Development, Report Generation or Query tools. Some (e.g. DataEase) are also offering Server versions.

Similarly there are extensions to common workstation tools, most frequently spreadsheets, to allow them to access Server databases. For example, Lotus 123 has a Novell NetWare SQL add-on. These offer an alternative to access using Middleware from independent suppliers. Other examples of client middleware include dBXL/Quicksilver and Lotus Data Lens.

Middleware appearing on servers

This is usually manifested as extensions to the server software. Typical examples are the 'add-ons' which allow a DBMS to accept ODBC or ODAPI calls to a database server.

10.6 ASSESSMENT

10.6.1 Cost per seat

There is a lively argument these days, especially in former mainframe IT Departments, as to whether or not the Client/Server approach really brings any cost/benefit improvement. One IBM-oriented education provider recently ran a series of seminars entitled *The Down Side of Downsizing*, and quoted audit reports that showed increases, rather than decreases, in the total cost of providing the information system.

In an article in *IS Audit & Control Journal*, David Crowell (1994) quoted a First Boston study which calculated the 'cost per seat' at $15 000 – where it had been $4000 with traditional mainframes. He also suggests that many Client/ Server installations may be hiding the real cost, since they have shifted many control functions from a centralized IT Group to the End-User Groups, which increases the burden on the latter.

10.6.2 *Performance*

Client/Server systems have an inherent advantage over centralized ones in that more of the processing can take place locally, without using communications lines. However, adverse effects on performance can also arise from:

- mushrooming use of the network, hence contention for line capacity
- contention for shared server functions with under-sized server processors
- excessive data transfer by clients downloading large tables
- overheads of the RPC or Message Passing mechanism
- overheads of the GUI
- 'impedance mismatch' between the different software architectures of the client and server functions.

The Network in a Client/Server installation often has to be upgraded at a further cost. Even with proper network design it is difficult to estimate the traffic generated by a Client/Server arrangement, especially in the 'take-off' stage of usage growth.

Contention in the Server may be a problem if the Server software is not optimized to the right mix of transactions. Centralized TP monitors like CICS have had many years of practice in ensuring good performance even with large volumes. The Server software you buy cheaply for a PC or small Unix server may not be as advanced.

It is virtually impossible to predict in advance the effect of the last two factors. The most appropriate course of action would be to benchmark two or three alternative software sets using a small part of the same application. This could be a good task to contract out (see Chapter 19).

10.6.3 *Development difficulties*

The move to Client/Server has produced a new blip in the graph of failed system developments. There have been a number of abandonments and what are euphemistically called 'project redefinitions'. The main problem is that there is no longer a single homogeneous technology for the target system. The fact that it is also difficult to predict performance (see section 10.6.2 above) means that confidence that a design will perform optimally – or even acceptably – is limited. In the end, all that many organizations are doing in the name of 'Client/Server' is just front-ending a legacy TP system with PC-based GUIs.

A number of Client/Server methodologies have been proposed, e.g. IBM/Seer Technologies HPS, Blueprints (Inmon), Client/Server Engineering, ODAM diagrams, etc., but as Inmon (1993) points out, one approach is rarely appropriate for all types of Client and Server; he illustrates this by contrasting 'transaction processing' and 'decision support' parts of a system. As yet, there are few well trodden paths – many of the Client/Server methodologies are 'proposed' or 'piloted', rather than 'tried and trusted' – and that goes for those in this book too. In fact, claims to have produced THE Client/Server methodology are almost certainly premature at this stage.

A further comment is that, with development work for a Client/Server system being split between different groups of people, there are difficulties in providing a secure and consistent development process for what may be a vital corporate system.

10.6.4 *Maintenance responsibility 'holes'*

Problems with Client/Server can also occur at the Maintenance stage of the Life Cycle. This is again because of the greater diversity of underlying technology. Users often find that a software engineer called in to look at the Client part of the system will say 'you can't expect much better if all you've got on the Server is XXX!' and of course the Server software engineer will say the same about the Client.

The other maintenance issue is that end users often have to waste their working hours 'fixing the system', when they should be performing the specialist tasks for which they were hired. This problem emerged with the uptake of PCs and has become worse – the cost of this to organizations is potentially enormous as already mentioned in section 10.6.1 above. The other problem is that the fixes made by the users are often less durable than those made by the IT professionals.

Larger organizations have 'help desks', and the compelling argument of the 'anti-downsizers' is that such teams have a lot more work under Client/Server than they ever had under centralized mainframes or stand-alone PCs.

10.6.5 *Change management*

A common objection to adopting Client/Server architectures is that the organization can easily lose control and consistency because not all users are using the same version of the Client software. This can be critical, given the fast rate of appearance of new versions of such software – the symptom is sometimes referred to as 'versionitis'.

Some organizations have bitten this bullet and gone in for ESD (Electronic Software Distribution) (Figure 10.11). If all workstations are permanently plugged in to the network, or can be left connected at a set time, the new versions can be centrally downloaded. However, where there are remote nodes on a LAN, or where workstations are portable, or where the management structure is decentralized, some users may still escape the process and retain inconsistent versions.

Another solution to the problem is to force all Clients to download their executable software, at the start of each session, from a single copy located on a file server.

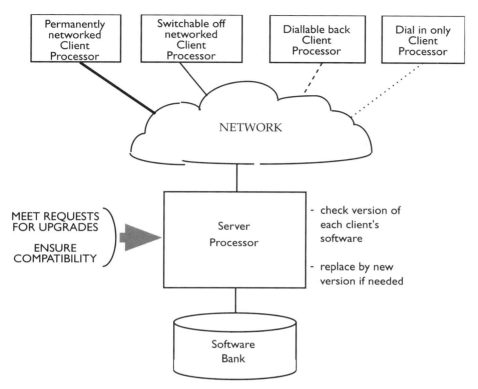

Figure 10.11 Electronic Software Distribution for Client/Server.

10.7 POTENTIAL USE OF CLIENT/SERVER IN THE CASE STUDIES

10.7.1 *Mr A*

Until he has quite a few partners, Mr A is unlikely to have the level of sharing that might justify dedicated servers. In the meantime he can consider offering certain services (e.g. data access and laser printing) on the home PC, given suitable peer-to-peer facilities.

10.7.2 *Bay Organic Produce Cooperative*

Given that the majority of staff users do not specialize in particular functions or data, a Client/Server approach to accessing the shared data would seem to be an ideal answer. Network-capable OS options would be Novell, OS/2, small Unix, etc. If the PCs already have client application software (e.g. spreadsheets or PC databases) or tailored programs, then some Middleware will be needed.

10.7.3 *Detox Pharmaceuticals*

The PC culture is not yet well developed, so immediate use of Client/Server, other than simple file service in the office, is limited. A database server could be introduced to allow managers to have PC access to sales data collected from the Regions.

10.7.4 *Electric House*

Stores have a mixture of intelligent and dumb terminals, so there may be a need to include a 'checkout controller' as a front-end server linked to the back-end database server. Centrally, the issue is less clear as immediate updating is not so important. A more cool federal approach may be preferable.

10.7.5 *Commonwealth Open Polytechnic*

Administrative users and teaching staff with PCs may wish to access the student records database. There are some doubts as to whether or not Client/Server is really justified. It may be more appropriate for user PCs to emulate terminals under the control of the central TP system.

10.7.6 *National Environmental Protection Board*

Local offices may justify Client/Server databases to share data about Subject Organizations between Inspectors. At HQ, however, timescales are rarely that critical and message passing may be adequate.

10.8 EXERCISES

1. 'Client/Server has won the battle against mainframes, but not against peer-to-peer PC message passing' – discuss.

2. Is the argument for 'downsizing' proven or not?

3. Compare and contrast 'remote presentation' and 'distributed logic' in terms of the Gartner diagram.

4. What is the main disadvantage of merging a report-library service in with the database server?

5. For a research center that offers both FTP and World Wide Web services to both internal and external users, what are the implications for Client/Server?

6. Why might user workstations have to be upgraded to link into a Client/Server system?

7. Contrast Client/Server as defined above with the use of a Front-End Processor (see Part Two).

8. In a Client/Server approach, where should the procedures for validating input data reside?

9. In a Client/Server approach, where does the responsibility for ACID (see Chapter 9) lie?

10. What difficulties can you foresee in SQL (e.g. ODBC) being the *de facto* standard for Client to Server communication?

11. 'Client/Server APIs and RPCs are letting the hackers back into Application Development – and CORBA/OpenDoc/OLE will be worse.' Is this assertion fair?

12. What are the main disadvantages of Client/Server and how would you set about minimizing them?

13. What policy might Bay Organic Produce Cooperative adopt to keep development costs on a Client/Server database application down to a minimum?

14. Technical experience in Detox is limited to traditional IBM mainframe skills. Should this affect their choice of architecture, or of the type of server hardware and software chosen?

15. Discuss the problem of issuing software upgrades to Electric House and Casa Electrica stores and warehouses.

16. COP Course Controllers want to extract student lists and marks for the current teaching period from the central system, and to post new marks back. They use spreadsheets for their own processing. How strong a justification for Client/Server is this?

ASSIGNMENT TASK

For your chosen case study, identify the application area most suited to a Client/Server approach. Decide which functions could justify being specialized, shared services. Suggest a way in which these could be grouped on to server computers.

Making your own assumptions about the software currently being used, what enhancements and additions will be necessary?

FURTHER READING

Atre, S. and Storer P. (1995) Weaving your client/server security blanket. *DBMS Magazine*, Feb.

Barry, W. (1994) Moving to client/server application development: caveat emptor for management. *NZCS Journal*, Sept.

Byte (1990) Multiuser databases. *Byte Magazine*, May.

Chappell, C. (1994) The missing link (article on middleware). *Computing (UK)*, 1 Dec.

Chorafas, D. (1994) *Beyond LANs – Client/Server Computing*, McGraw-Hill, New York.

Crowell, D. (1994) An introduction to the client/server environment. *IS Audit and Control Journal* **III**.

Datamation (1991) Microsoft's client/server challenger. *Datamation*, Jul.

Dudman, J. (1992) Valued client. *Computing (UK)*, 7 May.

Edelstein, H. (1994) Unravelling client/server architectures. *DBMS Magazine*, May.

Finkelstein, R. (1995) The new middleware. *DBMS Magazine*, Feb.

Goodwin, C. (1993) Divine distribution (article on electronic software distribution). *Computing (UK)*, 23 Sep.

Haney, C. (1994) Client-server hype faces users' doubts. *Computing (UK)*, 22 Sep.

Hugo, I. (1991) An architecture still open to interpretation. *Computing (UK)*, 31 Oct.

Hugo, I. (1993) Division of labour. *Computing (UK)*, 7 Oct.

IBM (1993) *Application Development for Client/Server*. Consultants' Seminar, London.

Inmon, W. (1993) *Developing Client/Server Applications*, Wiley, New York.

Jones, R. (1995) Challenging the real cost of client-server. *Computing (UK)*, 16 Feb.

Korzeniowski, P. (1993) Make way for data (article on middleware). *Byte Magazine*, Jun.

Lynch, M. (1994) Client-server problems fail to discourage users. *Computing (UK)*, 3 Nov.

Manchester, P. (1994) Where's the plumbing? (article on middleware). *iText Magazine*, **1**(1).

Parry, D. (1993) Middle management. *Computing (UK)*, 30 Sep.

Pearson, D. (1994) *State of the Art Client-Server Systems*. Data Management 94 (BCS DMSG), Cambridge, England.

Quinlan, T. (1995) The second generation of client/server. *Database Programming & Design*, May.

Ullman, E. (1993) Client/server frees data. *Byte Magazine*, Jun.

vanName, M. and Catchings, W. (1989) Serving up data. *Byte Magazine*, Sept.

Ward, M. (1994) IBM turns spotlight on client-server strategy. *Computing (UK)*, 17 Nov

Youett, C. (1995) Muddleware or middleware? *Computer Contractor (UK)*, 11 Jan.

11 Distributed and federal databases

11.1 INTRODUCTION AND DEFINITIONS

The theme of Distributed and Federal Databases was introduced in Chapter 8. One definition includes all situations where we want the potential to integrate dispersed data into single user 'views'. Another definition includes any database which, although geographically or functionally distributed, is nevertheless managed as a single collection or as a 'federation'. As with Distributed and Cooperative processing, the difference between the two alternative names 'distributed' and 'federal' may be a reflection of the previous history of the data.

Distributed Database was also included as a variation of Client/Server in the Gartner diagram, where the DBMS functions are split between Client and Server, and where DBMS talks to DBMS across the Network and the Middleware.

In this chapter we aim to bring an understanding of the methods and tools available for managing dispersed collections of data which need to be integrated for some purposes. By looking at the details of how some of the key problems are tackled, the reader can come to appreciate how decisions about distributing a system can be affected.

11.2 BUSINESS NEEDS

In the introduction to this book, we pointed out that the resources which constitute the data of interest to an organization are naturally scattered, and that the Network itself is often 'THE Database' in its original meaning, i.e., the mechanism for providing all the information that the organization needs. Distributed Processing, Transaction Processing and Client/Server Processing, as seen in the previous three chapters, can all improve the cost/benefit ratio in an organization. But the issues of control and integration of the shared information, at a level adequate for business needs, now need to be discussed. The concept of a Distributed Database – together with its less formal variations such as Federal Database and 'Multi-database' are approaches to dealing with these issues.

Many of the naturally decentralized organizations discussed in Chapter 8 and elsewhere have dispersed collections of data which they need to integrate. Often, this need to relate the data has arisen after many databases were first designed.

The business objectives of distributing or federating data include:

- speed of response for local users
- reduced operating cost (through downsizing),
- disaster prevention (through replication)
- reduced development cost (through ability to federate existing databases).

Any IS and software should reflect the organizational needs appropriately. If the Distributed Database is too closely controlled, the organization may constrain itself excessively and pay a high price. Too little control, and the value of the information deduced from the combined data may be very low.

11.3 ALTERNATIVE FLAVORS

11.3.1 *IBM's categorization*

IBM recognized at an early stage that a Distributed Database is an evolutionary rather than an absolute concept. In an article (IBM, 1989) entitled *Milestones on*

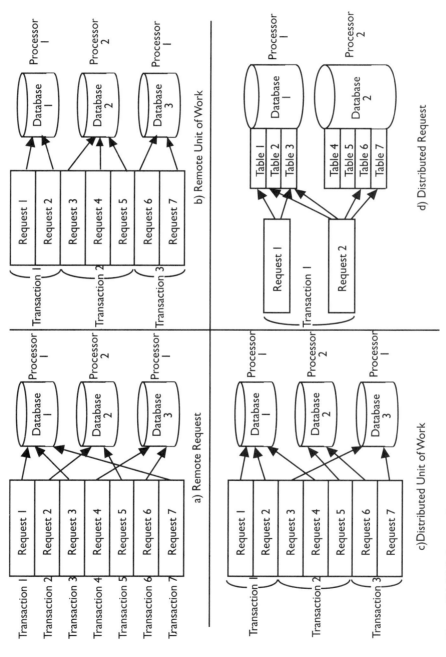

Figure 11.1 IBM's Steps to Distributed Databases (by permission, DBMS magazine).

the Road to Distributed Database and in other publications, they show a progression of sophistication (Figure 11.1).

- Remote Request – this means sending one command (e.g. an SQL statement) at a time to a named remote site. This may cause concurrency problems if the 'unit of work' that is needed to get to a COMMIT contains several such requests.
- Remote Unit of Work – this is a more advanced approach, allowing multi-request units of work, provided the requests are all to a single remote processor.
- Distributed Unit of Work – allows requests to multiple sites as long as they can be committed or recovered as a single unit. A single SQL command must still be restricted to one site.
- Distributed Request – allows one SQL statement to access data across multiple sites, which takes us nearer to the theoretical ideal of a Distributed Database.

Variations in approach can also occur in positioning of metadata. A central schema is an option, but this loses a lot of the advantages of distribution, since the bottleneck is simply shifted from the central DBMS processor to the processor managing the schema. Other options, mentioned in the same IBM article, are full replication of the schema, local schemas supplemented by a guide to what is held by other sites, or a combination of these based on frequency of remote reference.

11.3.2   *Bell and Grimson's categorization*

Another good discussion of the alternative types of Distributed Database appears in the book by Bell and Grimson (1992, pp. 44–54). A somewhat similar taxonomy is proposed by Sheth and Larson (1990). A composite version of these taxonomies is shown here in Figure 11.2. Particular distinctions that these authors draw are:

Distributed DBMS versus distributed systems with multiple DBMS

In the first category (left-hand side of Figure 11.2) users are under the impression that they are dealing with a single DBMS. In the second category they are aware of a 'trading' of data between a number of separate DBMSs.

Homogeneous versus heterogeneous

This refers to whether all sites' DBMS are the same or not. If they are, it is obviously easier to build up a 'single image' Distributed DBMS (abbreviated to DDBMS).

Integration 'via systems' versus 'via gateways'

Some DBMSs allow heterogeneous distribution by providing a set of 'gateway'

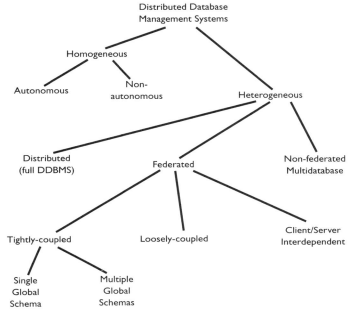

Figure 11.2 A Taxonomy of Distributed Databases (after Bell and Grimson (1992)), Sheth and Larson (1991)).

software modules which translate the 'foreign' databases and allow the overall database to be treated as a homogeneous one. Others have built in the ability to cope with heterogeneity into a DDBMS package which is used at all sites.

Federated versus non-federated or multi-database

The majority of Distributed Database systems only partially meet the goal of a 'single image' DDBMS. These are what most authors term 'Federated', though both Sheth and Larson (1991) and Bell and Grimson (1992) have the concept of non-federated 'Multi-databases', where each database is autonomous.

Tightly-coupled versus loosely-coupled versus interdependent

Some Federated systems work with a **Global Schema** which describes the structure of the whole data collection – these are referred to as tightly-coupled. In loosely-coupled systems, a Global Schema is regarded as compromising the benefits of distribution – so these systems work with a mechanism often referred to as an **Export Schema**. This describes the structure of a collection of data that one site makes available for access to other sites.

The category 'Interdependent' is introduced by Sheth and Larson to cover the loosely-coupled case where a remote database acts in a 'server' role to a local database. The signficant difference is that the sites are not now strictly autonomous, as client/server dependencies may exist.

11.3.3 *Date's 12 rules*

The principle of a 'classical' or theoretically complete DDBMS is that, although its data and processes may be distributed, it behaves to the user as if it were a non-distributed database. Date has 12 rules, which are more properly 'goals' (Date, 1990). We restrict our discussion to the bare essentials of each.

1. Local autonomy – no dependence on another site in order to be able to operate.
2. No reliance on a central site – sites are all peers (see comments below).
3. Continuous operation – no operations, e.g. adding a new site, upgrading to new DBMS release, should require the system to stop running.
4. Location independence or transparency – users should see the database as if it were stored entirely at their own site.
5. Fragmentation independence – users should not be aware that tables may have been split across sites, either column-wise or row-wise.
6. Replication independence – users should be unaware that multiple copies may exist at different sites – the system will organize updating of any duplicates.
7. Distributed query processing – the system will optimize the execution of a query that involves sending data from site to site.
8. Distributed transaction management – the system must be able to handle transactions that cross sites, and in particular must synchronize them (e.g. using two-phase commit – see later).
9. Hardware independence – the system should run across many suppliers' hardware – several DBMS can do this.
10. Operating system independence – the same system should run across multiple operating systems – also possible in some cases.
11. Network independence – the system should hide all details of what sort of network, or networks, links the sites.
12. DBMS independence – the system should offer a single user interface, even if it sits on several DBMS, e.g. SQL on top of Ingres, Oracle and DB2.

Under rule 2 above, there may be a global schema, distribution tables and cross-site applications, but sites should have their own copies of these. However, there are many DDBMSs in practice which do have centralized elements. This may be acceptable as long as failure of the central machine does not cause all the other sites to wait; for example, these sites may be able to continue capturing 'provisional' data.

11.4 TECHNICAL ISSUES

11.4.1 *Overview of issues*

Taking our definition of Distributed and Federal Databases to include all situations where we want the potential to integrate dispersed data structures into single-user views, then the key concerns are as follows:

- If we refer to attributes with the same name at different sites, will they have the same meaning?
- How do we find equivalent attributes at other sites, which might be under a different name?
- Will queries across two or more sites give us the whole picture, or does some of the meaning of data get lost in the reduction to a common model?
- Are the different sites in step, i.e. do they jointly form a consistent database? This implies three sub-questions:
  - can we be sure that no updates have been lost?
  - are all copies (replications) of the same attributes equal in value?
  - when we make a query, will the data at different sites be up-to-date 'as at' the same time?
- What sort of reduced database query service will we get if we lose a site, or a part of the network?

The first three issues are addressed under the general heading of 'Schema Translation' in section 11.4.2 below. The 'consistent database' issue is discussed in section 11.4.3, and 'partial availability' in section 11.4.4.

In addition to these issues, there is the question of achieving the expected user performance. If the business operation requires 'hot' processing, then we need to ensure that the overheads of DDBMS do not impact performance unduly. In other situations, user expectations may be 'cooler', often because they are aware that the data is distributed, and will accept the computer responding with a message such as 'I acknowledge your request, and will let you know when it's done'. A comparison can be drawn with use of the World Wide Web. The user knows that the system is going all over the world to follow the link or find the URL (Universal Resource Locator) implicitly or explicitly specified. Messages such as 'Contacting host...' and '50% of page read' are acceptable. Many other applications of Distributed Databases could take the same approach.

11.4.2 *Schema translation*

Sheth and Larson (1991) and Brodie (1993) use the acronym HAD (Heterogeneous, Autonomous, Distributed) to describe the typical situation for most future database developments. If this is true, then the ability to translate between

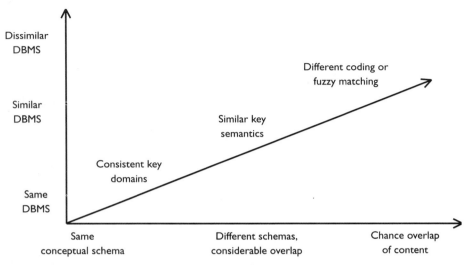

Figure II.3 Three Dimensions of Data Description Differences.

data in different schemas, with possibly differing semantics and different DBMSs, is vital if single-user views of distributed data are to be offered.

Differences between Schemas

Schema differences can be categorized in a number of ways. Here we concentrate on three classification schemes, one by similarity of DBMSs one by similarity of Conceptual Schema, and the other by similarity of keys (Figure 11.3). The first axis describes the degree of similarity between component DBMSs.

- same DBMS – the simplest, homogeneous, case
- similar DBMS, e.g. Relational–Relational, Codasyl–Codasyl. Most of the semantics will be treated similarly, but there may be exceptions
- dissimilar DBMS, i.e. Relational versus Codasyl versus IMS versus VSAM versus Adabas versus Bibliographic versus Object Oriented. In these cases some of the semantics may be held variously in Relationships, Constraints, Active Rules, Methods or Embedded Text.

The second axis depicts the range of differences in the scope and structure of the data itself.

- same conceptual schema – the differences should all be resolvable
- different schema designs, but with highly overlapping content and semantics, suggesting a similar original purpose
- some chance overlap of content, suggesting federation of databases developed for different purposes.

The third axis signifies similarity or differences among the keys which might be used during relational Joins between the sub-databases.

- there are common keys in the sub-databases which use consistent coding systems. This occurs where databases are autonomous but are within a single span of management control
- keys represent a similar domain, but have different coding and detail; matching is likely to be fuzzy (e.g. 'Home Counties' versus 'London and the South East'). This occurs where federation is unplanned, e.g. in research or crime investigation.

Incidentally, not only may DBMSs be different, but there may be further differences in the associated metadata structure, which may be based on a separate software product (e.g. a commercial Data Dictionary System such as MSP's DataManager). This is critical because the first stage in any translation is usually the matching of data names. There have been some proposals for standards for interworking between Data Dictionaries, e.g. IRDS (Information Resource Directory Standards) and PCTE (Portable Common Tools Environment). To date these have not been widely adopted. An alternative approach is for the translator program to read Data Dictionary files as if they were in simple Relational table form.

With or without a Global schema

Translation between different database descriptions is easier in the presence of a Global Schema that acts as the source of all user views. The requesting user's query is first translated into Global Schema terms, and then into queries against the local database structure at each site.

Figure 11.4 shows the pattern of schemas (data descriptions) that might be used in each of three approaches – a homogeneous DDBMS, a tightly-coupled federated system and a loosely-coupled system (or multi-database).

Depending on the approach taken, a number of different names are used to describe the various Schemas used – these are based on Bell and Grimson (1992).

- A **Local Schema** describes data available within one site.
- A **Fragmentation Schema** describes criteria on which the database is broken up into sub-databases.
- An **Allocation Schema** maps fragments to individual computers.
- An **Export Schema** describes the structure of a set of data that one site makes available to other sites.
- An **Auxiliary Schema** provides conversion rules for mapping between local and global data descriptions when a site is part of a heterogeneous federation.

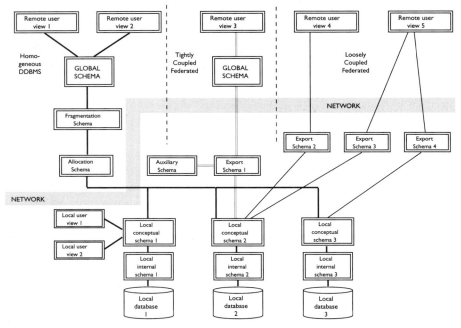

Figure II.4 Schemas Used in Translation in Different DDB Approaches.

Some approaches may have no formal Global Schema at the DBMS levels, but might include a DBMS-independent Global **Conceptual** Schema in a Data Dictionary, which acts as a system-wide reference point. Such Conceptual Schemas may best be represented in a special form such as a Semantic Model or Nijssen's Universal Information Model (Nijssen, 1989).

The simplest situation is the homogeneous DDBMS as shown on the left (thick lines). Note the split between local 'conceptual' and 'internal' schemas, representing the logical and physical data structures respectively. At each site, local users can derive their separate views from the local conceptual schemas.

In the tight federation in the center (double lines), a copy of the Global Schema might be held at all sites. The Export Schema shows the structure of the data each site makes available, with the Auxiliary Schema to assist in the translation to the Global Schema.

The biggest problem with all approaches based on a Global Schema is the amount of 'up front' development work needed. This usually involves having to obtain formal agreements between managers who may act like rival factions in organizational battlegrounds. For this reason many organizations are ruling out this approach. The right-hand option (thin lines) shows how a loose federation might operate, without the use of a Global Conceptual Schema. Remote users derive their views directly from one or more Export Schemas.

Incomplete mappings

When translating between two different DBMSs, we may be able to use a default mapping for that particular pair of DBMSs. However, it is too optimistic to expect that such mappings will be complete and will preserve all the semantics of both data descriptions. Mappings can be categorized as:

- complete two-way, i.e. a translation is available in both directions in which no semantics are lost. This is only likely where the two DBMSs are essentially clones of each other (e.g. the same version of Oracle on different platforms), or are very close to the same standard
- complete one-way, but partial with some loss of semantics in the other direction
- partial two-way, i.e. some loss in both directions
- effectively non-mappable – the structures are too different (e.g. between a text database for bibliographic Information Retrieval and a fixed column formatted DBMS).

Figure 11.5 shows these four possibilities in the context of a direct translation between two local DBMSs.

Relational-to-relational mappings are usually fairly complete, and mappings between Relational and any of Codasyl, IMS, VSAM or flat files are also workable. Many of these problems were resolved some years ago by commercial software vendors. Good examples are Information Builders Inc's EDA/SQL

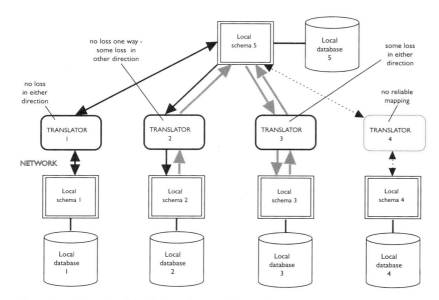

Figure 11.5 Four Possible Grades of Inter-Schema Mapping.

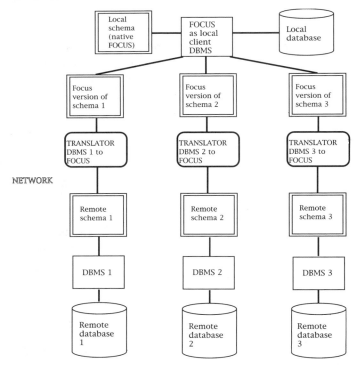

Figure 11.6 EDA/SQL Transformation Approach.

(Ricciuti, 1991), which is based on the Focus 4GL (Figure 11.6); and the Ingres DBMS gateways.

Even if such mappings can be made, we still have to sort out whether the same data name means the same thing in each DBMS, and whether different data names in the different databases may in fact still refer to the same data. This is discussed in the next section.

Name, description and context matching

In cases where Federation is loose and there is no Global Schema, a different approach is needed. If inter-operation is likely to be frequent, each site could build up rules about how to interpret the structure of the other databases.

The first stage in such a translation is to compare lists of table/file names, attribute/field names and so on and, if available, definitions and descriptions of their use. We want to be able to deduce which data items are equivalent – exactly or approximately. Artificial Intelligence techniques may help us to parse compound data names or descriptions and find the best matches. Figure 11.7 attempts to illustrate this situation.

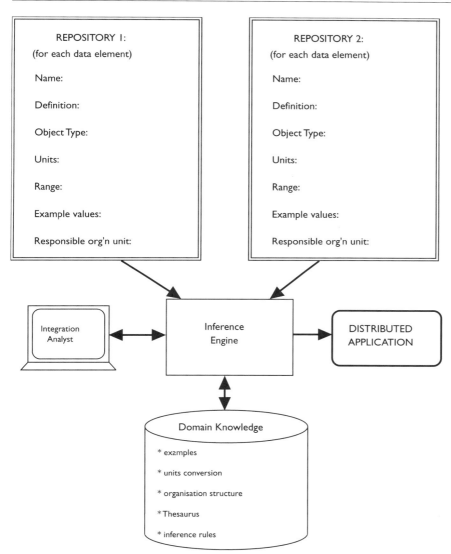

Figure 11.7 AI-driven Semantic Schema and Data Matching.

Even if meanings are similar, value systems may still not be compatible. One typical example is the ranges of values in scientific data, e.g. ages, temperatures, lengths, etc. Another problem is with different units of measurement. In some cases the values may be terms in common parlance but which can have different interpretations, e.g. 'Greater London', 'Bay Area', 'Wellington' (NZ). Sometimes the connection has to be made on a name that could be typed in different ways, e.g. 'ICI', 'I.C.I.' or 'Imperial Chemical Industries' or simply misspelt, e.g. 'Schneidermann', 'Shneiderman', etc. Within one organization or a consortium, management may be able to enforce a global Naming convention, but this does not help if the system is a cooperative one, covering several organizations.

11.4.3 *Consistency of a distributed database*

Any DDBMS has to maintain Database integrity across sites (see rule 8 of Date). If a single transaction can update data at more than one site, there are extra difficulties in ensuring that the system passes the 'ACID' test (see Chapter 9). Examples of the problems are:

- deadlock may occur across sites and may not be detectable by any site
- updates may be lost between sites and not accounted for
- processing of distributed transactions may be incomplete
- replicated copies may get out of step.

Kroenke and Dolan (1988, p 545) quote a paper which states 'More than 20 concurrency control algorithms have been proposed for DDBMSs, and several have been, or are being, implemented. These algorithms are usually complex, hard to understand, and difficult to prove correct – indeed, many are incorrect'.

Serializability (ACID – isolation)

In all forms of Transaction Processing (see Chapter 9), multiple concurrent transactions can incur problems such as Lost Updates and Inconsistent Reads). A general view of these problems is that the results are inconsistent with what would have happened if the transactions had been executed one after the other, i.e. serially. The search for solutions then revolves around trying to find sequences of execution which are equivalent to a serial set, i.e. are 'serializable'.

The problem of ensuring Serializability with concurrent access (e.g. avoiding lost transactions, etc.) is dealt with in TP systems by one of three methods: Locking, timestamping and Optimistic Concurrency Control.

Two-Phase Locking (2PL – not to be confused with 2PC below) is a traditional TP approach in which all locks are acquired in a first 'growth' phase, where transactions are only allowed to acquire locks, and a second 'shrinking' phase, where transactions are allowed to release locks but not acquire them. Unless there is a central site scheduling all locking, each site must operate 2PL for all requests originating from that site.

Distributed 2PL and Deadlock Resolution algorithms have been discussed by a number of authors, e.g. Kroenke and Dolan (1988) and Ricardo (1990). Ricardo proposes four alternative procedures and discusses their relative merits. The procedures are:

- Global locking (one site, the requesting site, controls all the locking of rows/tables at any site involved in the query): this is reliable but very expensive in message transmission
- Primary copy (in cases of replication, one site is designated as 'dominant' and locking is based on what is going on at that site)
- Majority consensus (using timestamps instead of locks, an update goes ahead if the majority of sites accepts it)
- Multi-protocol (a complex hybrid using timestamps, used in CCA's SDD-1 DDBMS prototype).

Details of these procedures are not discussed further. The designer needs to be aware that this is a 'leading-edge' area when proposing high-concurrency distributed database systems.

Recoverability (ACID – atomicity)

In databases in general, the principal recovery approach is based on the use of atomic transactions (alias 'success units'). Recovery is based on keeping logs of changes to the database which survive most catastrophes. In Distributed Databases, schemas (whether central or distributed) must also be subject to careful locking procedures.

Most approaches to ensuring Atomicity are based around the idea of 'two-Phase Commit' or '2PC'; see for example Kroenke and Dolan (1988).

1. The coordinating transaction asks all agents at sites to 'Prepare to Commit' (i.e. be able to Commit or Abort) by force-writing all logs (i.e. not doing anything else until the Operating System has confirmed that the logs have been written successfully on non-volatile storage). They then reply 'OK' or 'Not OK.'
2. The coordinating transaction force-writes its own log, recording whether the decision is Commit (all OK) or Abort. Each site agent is then told to Commit or Abort immediately.

For Distributed Databases, the 2PC protocol works well in most cases, but under certain conditions, if some sites go down in the middle of the process, it is subject to 'blocking'. It can also impose an overhead on transaction performance. Many variations on the basic 2PC have been proposed, including 'Presumed Abort' (used in the RDA (Remote Database Access) protocol – see Ceri (1990)), 'Cooperative Termination Protocol' and 'Decentralized 2PC' (see Bell and Grimson (1992)). All have their advantages in minimizing overheads and blocking, but none is perfect.

To avoid blocking, two possible improvements (Constantinidis, 1995), have been proposed, namely:

- 'three-Phase Commit', where an extra 'pre-commit' phase is introduced (see Bell and Grimson (1992)). This avoids blocking, but carries an extra message overhead

- 'Replication Server', where the blocking problem is by-passed by having several copies of the data; however, this approach is not strictly 'atomic'. It is an option in some versions of Sybase, Ingres and Adabas.

11.4.4 *Partial availability of a distributed database*

Further difficulties can arise when there is a network failure and, as a result, the system is divided into two isolated partitions. In these cases there is a conflict between complete correctness and maximum availability. To prevent these difficulties, even the 3PC procedure needs to be enhanced – one example is the 'Quorum-based 3PC' proposed by Ceri (1990). An alternative approach is to rely on detection and recovery rather than prevention. An example of this is to use the 'optimistic' protocol, where both partitions of the distributed database are allowed to continue running separately, but they must keep graphs of all changes made, which are analyzed and resolved when the network comes up again.

If the network does become partitioned, there is a need to ensure that availability is kept as high as possible, and that any processing that can take place is allowed to proceed. This means building in some ability for sites to monitor connectivity of the network and for partitions to reconfigure themselves.

11.5 SOFTWARE

Compared with Client/Server Middleware, where immediate market stance is all-important, DDBMS and Federal Database software are still waiting for a real market take-off. Many of the products which can be discussed are in computer research laboratories and universities rather than the marketplace.

An analysis of the state of the art in DDBMS is provided in Chapter 3 of the book by Bell and Grimson (1992). A few example systems and proposals are evaluated, in terms of their taxonomy discussed earlier. A summary is shown in Figure 11.8.

11.5.1 *Full DDBMS*

Full DDBMS are fairly thin on the ground, the main ones being the distributed versions of single site RDBMS, i.e. Ingres/Star, SQL*Star (Oracle), and also Tandem Non-Stop SQL. Chris Date collaborated with RTI (the original

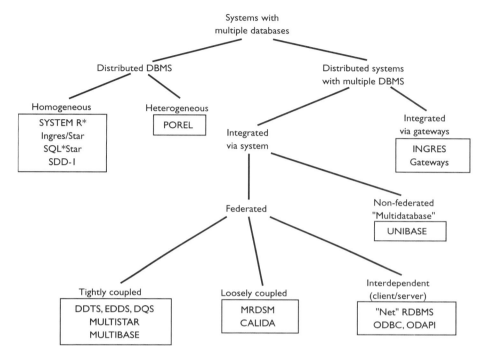

Figure 11.8 Examples of the State of the Art in Distributed DBMS (after Bell and Grimson (1992), Sheth and Larson (1991)).

company selling Ingres), and hence Ingres/Star went further down the Date path than most others. Tandem had the services of Jim Gray, one of the leaders in Distributed TP.

Early products were often short of some basic features, such as global query optimization or 2-PC. Among the more developed prototypes were CCA's SDD-1, which was used on US Navy ships, and IBM's System R*. Distributed versions of IDMS were marketed for a time, and Oracle and Ingres still offer SQL*Star and Ingres/Star respectively.

11.5.2 *Network-linked DBMS and client/server*

If a user organization is prepared to forgo the need for 'location transparency', i.e. it is prepared to program in the addresses of the other sites to whom remote requests for data are to be sent, then it can use a less-sophisticated software tool. This is not dissimilar to using a Client/Server approach.

In the case of Ingres and Oracle, for example, the 'Net' (rather than 'Star') products have been used in this way, although the marketing of these products is now usually in terms of 'Client/Server'. The snag is that sites originating transactions must now take responsibility for Serializability and Atomicity, which they will have to do either in their own application software or through nominated Transaction Servers.

A large number of products, not only DBMS but also ESS (Executive Support Systems), have gateway software which allows their own DBMS to access a remote database under a different DBMS.

11.5.3 *Tightly-coupled Federal*

The classic example in this category is the Multibase system built by CCA for US Military applications. It was designed as a single software environment but yet is geared to Federal rather than true DDBMS style. It uses an Auxiliary Schema for mapping Local Schemas to the Global Schema needed for queries. However, as a market product, its potential may be limited since it is based on the Functional Model, which has many academic adherents but virtually no commercial ones.

Some other prototype systems are:

- DDTS (Honeywell) – manufacturing applications
- Mermaid (SDC – Systems Development Corporation) – illusion of a single DBMS
- IISS (Arizona State U) – common Entity-Relationship data model on top of different IBM, DEC and Honeywell Databases
- ADDS (Amoco) – Extended Relational
- DQS (CRAI, Italy) – IBM only, but relatively high autonomy.

11.5.4 *Loosely-coupled and others*

- MRDSM (Honeywell) – no global schema, but the Database Administrator defines a 'Dependency Schema' for one schema on another
- Calida (GTE Labs) – uses 'intermediate' language

11.6 ASSESSMENT

Distributed Database is a classic example of the 'cocktail' concept – put any two successful ideas together in a single phrase and propose it as the next advance in the technology!

In the case of Distributed Databases, theoretical development has run well ahead of successfully implemented technology. In spite of Date's rules, there is no single, uniform paradigm of Distributed Databases. The widely held view on

Date's rules is that they formalize an ideal which is never likely to be widely realized. As Jim Gray, architect of many TP and Database systems with Tandem and Digital, has said, 'such transparency is too liberal'. In other words, trying to meet all the rules costs too much, and does not bring enough benefit. The technical issues, as we have seen in section 11.4, are complex. Many user organizations have taken the view that adopting Distributed Database technology, with its high cost and risks, is not justified.

Distributed DBMS products, which should have reached maturity by now, still have a decided 'prototype' feel. Evidence suggests that the number of users of the flagship DDBMS products is low, and that fashions are moving towards the more federal and 'multidatabase' architectures, or to redefine problems as Client/Server. In the area of non-tabular data, there has been a move towards Groupware as a substitute form of Distributed DBMS.

11.7 POTENTIAL USE OF DISTRIBUTED DATABASES IN THE CASE STUDIES

11.7.1 *Mr A*

There is no real case for distributed databases for Mr A. There might be cooperative databases between Associates in the future, which could be Federal with a Global Conceptual Schema. Other loosely cooperating databases would be Mr A's Information Sources, but there would only be casual message passing.

11.7.2 *Bay Organic Produce Cooperative*

Only if the cooperative grew to several times its current size might there be a case for some functional distribution of the database between Farmers, Markets and Buyers. Geographically, Farmers could be served by local sub-offices and the Warehouse could also have its own database. There would be some argument for such distribution being reasonably well-integrated if the organization wished to retain a single management structure.

11.7.3 *Detox Pharmaceuticals*

Databases of sales and warehouse data are highly geographically distributed. The schemas should be the same for each Sales Office and for each Warehouse. Whether a formal distributed or federal database is justified depends on how many inter-site transactions will take place. Location transparency at the level of Date's rule 4 does not seem to be required, unless there will be transactions wanting to update 'all sales to Organization X' or 'all stocks of drug A'.

11.7.4 *Electric House*

Most of the data will be distributed geographically at Stores and Warehouses. As in Detox, we can suppose that schemas between different Stores and Warehouses within Electric House proper will be consistent. However, we could guess that Casa Electrica will be using one or more DBMS that are not the same as Electric House's, and that the Schemas will not all show a standard structure. Bar codes for products sold in stores are also possibly different from those in the US. This suggests that some schema translation might be needed, at least until migration to a standard DBMS was completed. Again, there does not seem to be a demand for full location transparency, and a federal 'cool' processing style would probably be adequate.

11.7.5 *Commonwealth Open Polytechnic*

The database containing student details and marks could be geographically distributed to Regional Centers. These databases would be homogeneous both in DBMS and Schemas. As decision timescales are rarely immediate, the level of integration between databases does not need to be 'hot'.

11.7.6 *National Environmental Protection Board*

The database containing Subject Organization details and Inspection records requires access from both Head Office and Local Offices. Geographical distribution of the database is an option, but the need to access other databases would probably be low in volume and not 'hot'. The Research and Intelligence database used by technical staff at the Head Office is likely to consist of a very loose, unfederated collection with largely unplanned inter-operation. Because there could be several dissimilar DBMS and data structures, schema translation using an AI-based tool might be considered. A third distributed database possibility involves cooperative access to documents across a large number of user workstations – a possible example of Groupware being used as a distributed DBMS.

11.8 EXERCISES

1. How do the four IBM milestones show the path to distributed databases?

2. Should 'unfederated multi-databases' be included in a dicussion of distributed databases?

3. Relate each of Date's 12 rules to a business need.

4. For what style of business do you think Date's 12 rules are intended?

5. What is the purpose of an Export Schema?

6. What is the significance of the acronym 'HAD'?

7. What is the advantage of having a Global Schema when translating between two databases in a federal system?

8. What methods can you suggest when two databases you wish to access together may have comparable data but under different names? Or that the data under the same name may have different meanings?

9. Are the advantages of a location-transparent distributed database negated if we have to hold a Global Schema?

0. From the point of view of the consistency of a Distributed Database, is deferred updating any safer than immediate locking with two-phase commit?

1. Under what circumstances might optimistic concurrency control be preferable to a pessimistic approach (i.e. using locking or Two-Phase Commit)?

2. What are the main alternatives for avoiding blocking in distributed database Atomicity support?

3. What is the difference between 'Star' and 'Net' products offered by Relational DBMS vendors?

4. 'Groupware represents the database that organization staff involved in informal and creative activities really want – just look at the relative sales volumes of DDBMS products and Lotus Notes' – discuss.

5. If the Bay Organic Produce Cooperative went for a Distributed Database, evaluate the business need for location transparency. How would transparent and non-transparent systems look different to the user?

6. Suppose Casa Electrica have several countries with data stored under IBM's IMS database, whereas Electric House has largely moved to Oracle. How would you describe the schema translations in terms of one-way/two-way and complete/partial?

7. At the NEPB, the information they wish to integrate in their Research and Intelligence database (a Relational DBMS) is available over a network but is held in the STATUS Bibliographic Information Retrieval format. What can you suggest as possible approaches to integrate the two sets of data?

18. The NEPB has to produce an Annual Report summarizing all its activities in a number of tables with comments. The Director wants this to be as automated as possible. What advice do you have?

Assignment task

For your chosen case study, select the application area which, in your opinion, is most suitable for a distributed database. Characterize the requirement in terms of the following factors:

- homogeneous versus heterogeneous
- federated versus single DBMS view
- consistency of data descriptions (schemas)
- consistency of keys and coding systems
- immediacy of user response, i.e. 'hot' versus 'cool'
- frequency of inter-site transactions.

What sort of software do you think is most suitable for this application?

Further reading

Atre, S. (1992) *Distributed Databases, Cooperative Processing and Networks*, McGraw-Hill, New York.

Bell, D. and Grimson, J. (1992) *Distributed Database Systems*, Addison-Wesley, Reading, MA.

Brodie, M. (1993) *Interoperable Information Systems*. Tutorial, Very Large Databases (VLDB), Dublin, Ireland.

Brodie, M. (1994) *Distributed Object Management – A Core Technology for Future Computing*. Tutorial, Extending Database Technology (EDBT), Cambridge, UK.

Ceri, S. (1990) *Distributed Databases*. Tutorial, Extending Database Technology (EDBT), Venice, Italy.

Constantinidis, V. (1995) *A Critical Analysis of Distributed Database Recovery Protocols*. Proc. 6th Australasian Database Conference, Adelaide, South Australia.

Date, C. (1990) *An Introduction to Database Systems,* Addison-Wesley. Reading, MA, Chapter 23.

Davis, R. (1989) Sharing the wealth. *Byte Magazine*, Sep.

Hsiao, D. (1990) *Federal Databases and Systems*. Tutorial, Very Large Databases (VLDB), Brisbane, Australia.

IBM (1988) *Concepts of Distributed Data*. SC26-4417-0, IBM.

IBM (1988) *Introduction to Distributed Relational Data*. GG24-3200-00, IBM.

IBM (1989) *Milestones on the Way to Fully Distributed Data. DBMS Magazine Supplement*.

Kroenke, D. and Dolan, K. (1988) *Database Processing,* Science Research Associates, Chicago, Chapter 15.

Nijssen, G. and Halpin, T. (1989) *Conceptual Schema and Relational Database Design*, Prentice-Hall, Englewood Cliffs, NJ.

Oxborrow, E. (1989) *Databases and Database Systems,* Chartwell-Bratt, UK, Chapter 6.

Özsu, T. (1991) *Distributed Data Management: Unsolved Problems and New Issues.* Tutorial, Very Large Databases (VLDB), Barcelona, Spain.

Ricardo, C. (1990) *Database Systems – Principles, Design and Implementation*, Macmillan. New York, Chapter 15.

Ricciuti, M. (1991) Universal Database Access! *Datamation,* 1 Nov.

Sheth, A. and Larson, J. (1991) Federated database systems for distributed, heterogeneous and autonomous databases, *ACM Computing Surveys,* 22(3).

Tagg, R. (1994) *Distribution of Data and Processing.* Proceedings of Data Management 94 (BCS DMSG), Cambridge, UK

Valduriez, P. (1990) *Distributed and Parallel Database Systems.* Tutorial, Very Large Databases (VLDB), Brisbane, Australia.

Waters, G. and Read, B. eds, (1992) *Distributed Databases.* Seminar Notes, IEE (UK) Colloquium, IEE, London.

Wing, K. (1993) Distributed object database management systems. *Object-Oriented Programming,* Mar–Apr.

12 Message passing

12.1 INTRODUCTION AND DEFINITIONS

Message Passing is a term used to describe systems where the passing of messages between cooperating elements of the system is of primary importance. In simple terms, this means more like electronic mail and less like an integrated transaction processing system. Our definition of Message Passing here is slightly restricted, and refers to a type of distributed processing where the requests and responses between different processors are limited to 'cool' (alias 'queued', 'asynchronous', 'non-immediate' or 'store-and-forward') messages. The sending of a message to another processor invokes only limited server functions (Figure 12.1) such as:

- file the message passively for further reference
- store the message into an appropriate position in the folder/directory structure

- queue the message as an asynchronous standard transaction to a given program
- submit the message as an asynchronous database query.

These are distinct from active functions such as directly invoking an on-line program.

Message Passing is not so much to be contrasted with Client/Server, since it is one alternative for communication between Client and Server, but the more significant contrast is with Remote Procedure Calls (RPCs). It also relates more strongly to cooperative, peer-to-peer styles than to hierarchically distributed patterns.

Message Passing is one of the fastest growing aspects of Distributed and Cooperative IS for two reasons. One is the realization that not all processing has to be 'hot' – 'real-enough time' is all the user needs. The second is the advent of Object Oriented technology, which can be stretched to a Message Passing view of systems.

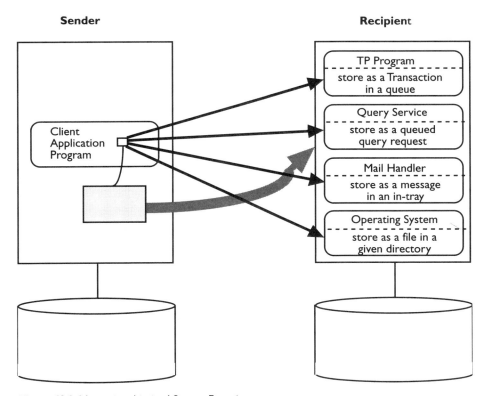

Figure 12.1 Messaging: Limited Server Functions.

In this chapter we introduce the range of different applications that can be built on top of a messaging service. We also discuss some of the software which supports this form of cooperative processing.

12.2   BUSINESS NEEDS

In the three previous themes of TP, Client/Server and Distributed Database, the usual assumption has been that things have to happen 'immediately', i.e. that the Distributed System is fully on-line (or real time). This puts a high cost on computing resources which the business need does not always justify.

Today, many business ventures are cooperative, with different participants having different ownership and management. One partner does not necessarily expect another to respond immediately to every request. The receiver will have different priorities from the requestor for the order in which information tasks should be handled.

Independent business ventures may not be ready to commit themselves to a level of integration which guarantees responses in a specific timescale or format. That is, they may not be willing to re-engineer their existing systems to meet constraints imposed by full integration. However, there is a need to make some commitment to respond appropriately to another's business needs. Examples might be research institutions sharing results or references, or companies trading through electronic commerce (e.g. along the supply chain).

A messaging approach, in which requests and messages are passed to a queue (e.g. a mailbox, in-tray, pending file, etc.) is more appropriate in these circumstances. Yet the whole still forms a Cooperative Information System.

As well as saving cost compared with 'hot' Client/Server processing, Message Passing can also be seen as an opportunity to close the gaps in office document flow which prevent full benefit from being achieved from the 'paper-less' office (or rather the 'less-paper' office). If documents have to be printed, annotated, authorized and physically signed, even over a small part of the life cycle, one does not achieve the big gains in timescale. However, recent applications such as Groupware and Workflow systems, with Authentication and Digital Signature processing, now offer a chance to have optimum computer-supported coverage.

12.3   ALTERNATIVE FLAVORS

12.3.1   *Basic electronic mail (email)*

This well known application is the simplest form of messaging. The metaphor used is essentially that of a postal service, where messages are delivered to a 'mailbox', from which an addressee can pick up and read the messages.

Features of the basic application, most with parallels in ordinary mail, include:

- mailboxes stored at a remote server computer (electronic post office boxes or *poste restante*)
- forwarding and immediate reply
- multiple recipients and 'copy to'
- enclosures or 'attachments', i.e. files of any type appended to messages.

Email is currently on a big surge in popularity, due to the:

- low cost of commercial services (from around US$10 per month)
- high level of home ownership of PCs (and coverage of office desktops)
- cheap modems and mailer software
- critical mass of users reachable over the Internet
- stunning growth of information and services available through VANs and the Internet
- well-developed standards.

12.3.2 *Electronic conferencing*

In this book, we take 'Conferencing' to include a variety of applications such as Bulletin Boards, News and Mailing Lists (or 'Reflectors') as well as true Electronic Conferencing and 'Chat'. All these applications could be regarded as a form of email with a shared mailbox.

Bulletin Boards are simply structured shared mailboxes to which subscribers can 'post' notices and read what everyone has 'posted'. Many of these were originally accessed by dial-up.

News is similar, but usually works over a Network Service such as CompuServe or the Internet. It also has a formal subject structure – for example the Usenet News, available on the Internet, has a hierarchical naming system for news groups, e.g. **alt.scifi.startrek**, which suggests a group for 'trekkies' in the 'scifi' sub-heading within the 'alt' (alternative) major heading.

Mailing Lists are mailboxes at a server which automatically forward copies of each incoming message to all subscribers on a Mailing List file (Figure 12.2). The program also accepts single-line messages (which should be sent to a separate administration mailbox) asking to join or leave the Mailing List. Such a message obviously has to include the subscriber's details, e.g. **join bpr-list r.m.tagg@-massey.ac.nz**. Mailing list software also provides primitive directory services (for identifying subscribers) and FTP repositories.

True Conferences also act like mailboxes, but they contain additional internal structure. In the CoSy system developed at the University of Guelph, Canada, which is also used by a number of Commercial Conference services, each conference is divided into 'Topics'. Within each topic there are 'Threads'. When a subscriber posts a message, it can either be a comment to a previous posting (in

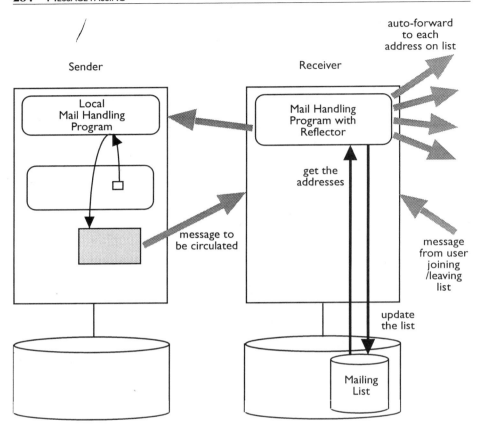

Figure 12.2 Operation of a Mail Reflector.

which case it is added to that Thread), or it is an independent idea, such that if anyone else comments on it, then a new Thread has been started (Figure 12.3).

Some conferences provide the impression of being a participant for only as long as the subscriber can afford to stay logged on. The Eurokom system based in Dublin, Ireland sends a message to each currently logged-on subscriber each time any other individual has joined (or left) the conference. The same facility can also work with just two people – such a facility is sometimes called 'Chat'.

In all of the above applications, restrictions may be placed on both reading and writing, if only to ensure that subscribers are registered or 'pay up'! 'Read-only' conferences are a misnomer – it really means that just one person or group (usually the administrator of a service) has permission to post messages. 'Private' conferences are limited to closed user groups – in CoSy these are run by 'Moderators' who decide which people can actually join the conference.

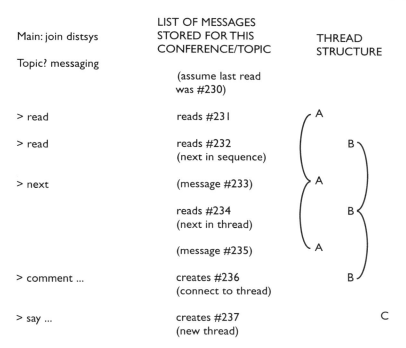

Main: join distsys	LIST OF MESSAGES STORED FOR THIS CONFERENCE/TOPIC	THREAD STRUCTURE

Figure 12.3 Electronic Conference Session with Multiple Threads (example based on CoSy).

12.3.3 *Inter-application message passing*

Strictly speaking, in all applications which use message passing, messages are always sent between two application programs. However, in the case of Email and Conferencing, the receiving application is limited to treating the message as an entry to be stored in a file such as an 'in-tray' or 'conference thread'. If a file is being downloaded or attached to a message, this too is simply put away in the directory structure. The file then just sits there until some other action initiated by the recipient picks it up.

In some applications, however, the messages which are passed could be intended as 'transactions' for some TP or batch system on the recipient processor. This is distinct from Client/Server and other 'hot' approaches in that the sender wishes to keep at 'arm's length' from the action, perhaps not even requiring an acknowledgment or an answer.

The best-known example of this is EDI (Electronic Data Interchange). We use this term here in its narrow sense of meaning 'Business-to-Business Transactions' or 'Email with Forms'. Examples are:

- passing money (paying bills, transferring investments, etc.)
- passing requests for money (invoices)

- ordering goods or services (buying, commissioning, booking resources)
- informing potential customers of stock availability
- passing inspection reports (goods received, maintenance)
- bills of lading and other transhipment documents
- customs clearance
- submitting Inland Revenue returns.

The formats used in EDI tend to emulate existing standard documents. Standards are therefore needed to enable diverse TP systems at sender and receiver to interpret the same semantics in a given EDI message.

Until recently, it was envisaged that EDI should run over Value-Added Networks (VANs) using Packet Switching and possibly higher-level messaging protocols such as X.400. There is certainly experience of running EDI over X.400, but with the current high prices of EDI VAN services and lack of security in public networks, user uptake of EDI may not reach a critical mass.

Seen as basically message passing, there is no reason why EDI needs much more than simple Email in terms of a delivery mechanism. However, a Form (paper or electronic) in transit has more significance as it represents a commitment and may be worth money. The legal status of EDI documents is not yet stable. 'Doing business over the Internet' is a big slogan at the time of writing, but the informal nature of the Internet (e.g. the lack of security, no guarantee of delivery, and no-one to sue!) may act as a brake to other than mail-order operations.

Another example application of inter-application message passing is in the Financial and Commodity sectors, where 'Front-Office' on-line dealing systems have to be coordinated with 'Back-Office' Transaction Processing – a process which, however, does not need to be on-line. An internal EDI approach, posting front-office transactions asynchronously to an 'in-tray' on the back-office processor, is sometimes used (Figure 12.4).

This application example is a specific case of what could be termed 'cool replication'. If a Distributed Database needs to have full or partial replication at different sites, but immediate refresh of changes is not vital, then messages which cause changes can be passed asynchronously by the originating site to the other sites. If a Client site were to need an up-to-the-second status, it could issue a distributed query instead of its normal local one.

12.3.4   *Global information retrieval*

This group of applications includes those where an individual can carry out searching, browsing and, in some cases, interaction in a wide variety of information sources and services which are connected to Commercial Networks and the Internet. It represents application-to-application message passing where the recipient action is limited to database query.

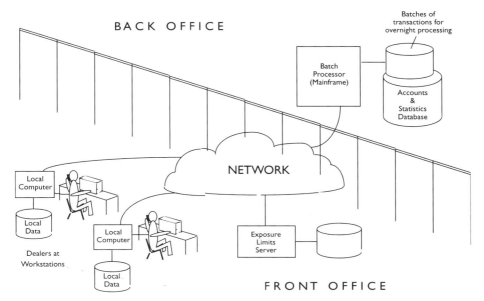

Figure 12.4 Example of Message Passing through 'Internal EDI'.

We are not including here tools which involve remote sessions such as Telnet, since these are not really message passing systems. However, services like Gopher and WWW offer fixed pages (much like postings in a conference) which you as client fetch to your processor, and then decide what to fetch next. This approach is relatively 'arm's length', and has similarities in style to conferencing or 'chat'.

12.4 TECHNICAL ISSUES

12.4.1 *Message passing infrastructure*

Message Passing approaches are generally less demanding on technical resources than 'hot' approaches such as Distributed TP, Client/Server and Distributed Databases. However, software support for Message Passing comparable with Middleware in the Client/Server approach, has been slow to develop, although there are recent signs of a surge.

Ideally, transparent support should be provided for message-enabled applications, so that the user does not have to switch into a separate messaging program in order to initiate message sending. In Mac or Windows terms this can be achieved by including an extra option of 'Send' in the 'File' pull-down menu, or an icon in a toolbar. One example is the Microsoft Office suite. The function of the above option is to cause the current File or highlighted Selection to be transmitted asynchronously to the recipient (who in turn would be chosen from a sub-menu). The user would not have to type the address or even know what means of transmission would be used, e.g.

- various email systems via various mailers
- dial-up or use fixed LAN connection
- fax
- commercial EDI service.

In effect, the mail application will know the best way to contact a particular correspondent, including the use of a fall-back route if the primary means is unavailable.

12.4.2 *Authentication servers*

The prospect of transacting business over the Internet means that some extra provisions have to be made for acknowledgment, encryption, authentication, non-alteration and non-repudiation (Figure 12.5).

What is needed is an Authentication process, in which there is a protocol by which both sender and recipient can have confidence that the message is really

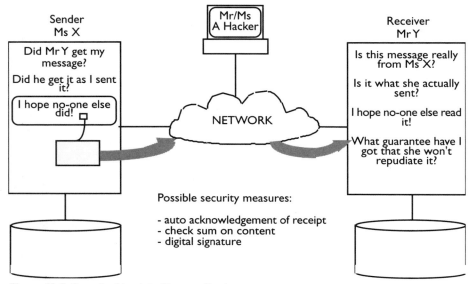

Figure 12.5 Security Needs in Message Passing.

being sent by the right person or agent to the right person or agent. Apple (1994a) has proposed such a protocol for two-way authentication in future applications software, based on Kerberos (Cashin, 1993). This protocol uses a system of encrypted 'credentials' obtained from the Authentication Server together with generated random numbers.

Other possible roles for an Authentication Server include the issue of Public Keys for encryption; and the issue of Certificates for use with Digital Signatures. For further details see Stallings and van Slyke (1994) or Stamper (1994).

12.4.3 *Higher-speed access to Internet*

For users who are not on a LAN, and who usually dial-up to a VAN which operates Internet mailboxes, data rates may be too slow to download WWW pages and FTP files in a reasonable time. In these cases a leased line is needed for linking to an Internet Service Provider. User workstations will generally need extra software to enable them to work directly with TCP/IP.

12.4.4 *Standards for graphics and multimedia*

As the proportion of messages that are not representable in the standard ASCII code increases, standards are quickly becoming vital. However, at the time of writing there are several alternatives. Current examples of standards for graphics are PCC, TIFF, EPSF, JPEG and GIF; and for video, MPEG, and QuickTime.

12.5 SOFTWARE

12.5.1 *Client mailers*

These are the programs that we as individuals run on our desk-top, lap-top or home computer. Some come with the modem we buy or the Commercial Information Service we sign up for. Others are widely sold commercial products like ProComm or Vicom. Yet others are 'shareware', e.g. Matrix in the UK. For an illustration of the structure of such software, see Figure 12.6.

The main components of such software are:

- an editor for browsing and composing messages, with interface (e.g. cut-and-paste) to other local applications

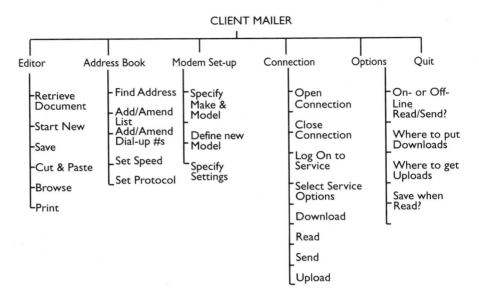

Figure 12.6 Structure of a Typical Client Mailer.

- an address book with Email addresses and dial-up telephone numbers
- set-up details for a modem or other communications device
- connection and disconnection
- message management, i.e. replying, forwarding, copying, redirection, autoreply, file handling of attachments
- mailbox management of in- and out-trays, filing, purging
- options and usability aids, e.g. start-up sequences, macros, off-line reading, nicknames, signatures
- a function to quit the mailer program.

Some programs only allow on-line access, while others incorporate an Off-Line Reader which accepts a single-user command to logon, downloads any unread mail from a mail server, uploads any outgoing messages waiting to be dispatched, and logs off. Many also include a 'scripting' language in which the user can develop his/her own macros to control the behavior of the mailer.

As well as supporting LAN connection or dial-up to a Mail Server, a Client program will often also support both sending and receiving facsimile. The program can divide the current file (text or image) up into pages, and add a cover page, headers, footers, etc. Incoming Faxes can be handled in any of four ways:

- displayed or printed in image form
- stored in a file in a standard image format, e.g. PICT, TIFF
- converted to text using extra OCR (Optical Character Recognition) software
- converted to a formatted structure using applicant-dependent software.

12.5.2 *Mail servers*

These operate either on a LAN or with dial-up. The server has to maintain disk space to store unread incoming and untransmitted outgoing messages. It may also keep all messages until these are expressly deleted by the end-user or are purged through passage of time. Since the server will usually be operating a shared service, then it will also have to manage accounts, access rights, passwords, etc.

Mailing List Managers (see section 12.3.2 above) are programs which automatically generate new outgoing messages to members of a distribution list, when triggered by messages arriving for a given address. Example uses could be for acknowledgments, apologies for absence, changes of address, forwarded copies to a 'stand-in', forwarded copies to members of a group. These programs are also often operated in conjunction with a Mail Server. One widely used product is Majordomo.

12.5.3 *Conference administration*

There are a number of programs used to support various Electronic Conferencing services – an example already mentioned is CoSy. These include a lot of the same features as mail servers, and may indeed be used in a dual-purpose fashion. Extra facilities are needed to cover Moderators, Topics, Threads, etc.

Mail Reflectors, or Client Mailer scripts, are sometimes also used to simulate some Conferencing requirements.

12.5.4 *Directory and name servers*

Name Servers, which operate directories of addresses for message sending (e.g. all Email subscribers on a Mail Server with their aliases) may share a processor with the Mail Server. However, for messaging generally, there may be other types of directory, e.g.

- personal directories of nicknames and formal addresses
- addresses for sending messages to cooperating applications
- the global (distributed) database of all potential message recipients.

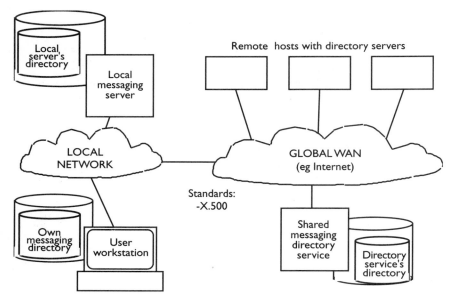

Figure 12.7 A Global Web of Directories.

While the first two types of directory may be managed on the client or a local server, the third type will generally be spread over a range of servers, either within the user's organization or in the public domain (Figure 12.7). One way of accessing these global directory servers is to use the WWW and navigate outwards from the user's local Directory page. Some software vendors offer specialist Directory search programs.

12.5.5 *Application message enablers*

This class of software aims to support mail-enabled applications, and would be installed on both senders and recipients. Since the interface operates at OSI Layer 7, the communicating programs need not be concerned about what message passing mechanism is actually being used – it need not even be Email. An example of such software is the Apple Open Collaborative Environment (AOCE), which can support several different Mail or other Delivery systems (Figures 12.8 and 12.9). Similar products are Microsoft Messaging API (MAPI), Lotus Vendor Independent Messaging (VIM) and the X.400 AI Association's XAPI.

Another, partial, example of message-enabling is the Global Village Fax Modem program, which, when the Option key is depressed within any application such as Word Processing, Spreadsheet or Paint/Draw, shows 'Fax' instead of 'Print' in the File Menu.

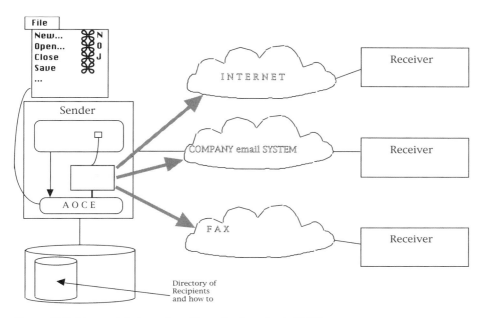

Figure 12.8 Network-Independent Messaging (e.g. Apple OCE).

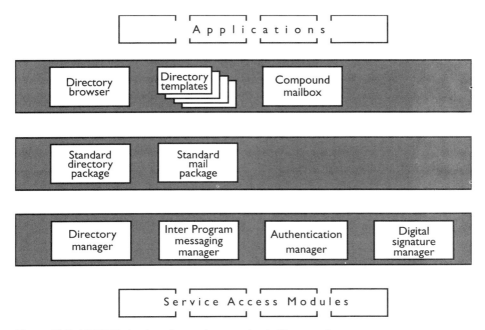

Figure 12.9 AOCE Technology Layers (source: Apple Computer).

Some of the newer software in this category also aims to provide an Authentication Server as discussed in section 12.4.2 above.

12.5.6 *Translators and 'messaging middleware'*

The applications area with the most common need for translation software is in converting from messages in a user's TP system into messages in standard EDI formats such as X.12, and vice versa. Packaged translators are usually available for the best-selling ranges of commercial application packages, which includes subsystems for such things as accounts payable and receivable, taxation and movement of goods documentation. EDI translators are also available with some of the popular DBMS. However, for many legacy systems it may be a case of DIY (Do It Yourself).

To link other heterogeneous application systems for messaging purpose, 'middleware' allowing different software to be 'message enabled' is not yet widely available, and today's products may be limited to one vendor's OS environment. As an example, to allow applications enabled for Apple OCE (Open Collaborative Environment) to work with non-Apple messaging standards like Novell's MHS or Lotus VIM, CE Software's QuickMail (enabled for AOCE) can be used as a glue.

Recently, a number of vendors have begun to collaborate through MOMA (Message Oriented Middleware Association).

12.5.7 *Browsers for IR applications*

These are client programs that give the user a convenient interface for navigating ('surfing') through networks when doing global information retrieval. This is currently an area of great development and there is an enormous surge in the amount of literature being written, e.g. Krol (1992). There are a number of News readers that allow a user to define his or her scope of interest and to alert the user when new articles are posted. For the WWW, there are Netscape, Mosaic, Cello, Spyglass and the WWW Worm, together with specialist search tools such as Lycos or Web Crawler. Browsers are also available for other Internet tools such as Gopher and WAIS, and even FTP will involve a client program. There are also a range of specialist X.500 Directory browsers, one example of which is Veronica.

12.6 ASSESSMENT

Message Passing is a growing topic, more appropriate to Cooperative than Distributed systems. It offers a cost-effective solution when there is less need for 'hot' processing. It may also offer a more cost-effective form of linkage between user workstations and legacy systems than Client/Server. The WWW has shown the practicality of the approach on a global scale, and we may expect substantial corporate adoption of 'Intranets' and 'Internet Appliances'. However, the technology and methodology are both still immature, and its take-off will depend on the establishment in the marketplace of suitable support software.

12.7 POTENTIAL USE OF MESSAGE PASSING IN THE CASE STUDIES

12.7.1 *Mr A*

Mr A's business is highly dependent on messaging in various forms, especially Email (to the Home Office, Customers, Sources of information). He will also be involved in conferencing, web searching and news groups. EDI, with Suppliers or Tax inspectors, is also of interest, but the volumes are very small, and the cost and overheads of any software would have to be low. Good client software is important.

12.7.2 *Bay Organic Produce Cooperative*

If some of the staff specialize in Farmers, Markets and Warehousing, then there will be a good case for Application-to-Application message passing between staff PCs in a peer-to-peer arrangement. Updating will have to be fast enough to avoid double selling though. Groupware might be a suitable approach.

12.7.3 *Detox Pharmaceuticals*

Messaging between Warehouses (for stock transfers), and between Regional Offices and the Center (for summaries and big orders), is likely to be appropriate for Detox. EDI VANs may be slow to penetrate in Poland, so EDI with customers at Hospital Boards or Group Practices would probably need to use standard PSS or Internet. This would bring up security considerations, authentication, etc.

12.7.4 *Electric House*

Much of the inter-site traffic could be more appropriate to message passing than using 'hot' approaches. Much of the traffic is of predefined types, and therefore could use program-to-program messaging rather than pure Email or file transfer. EDI is likely to be limited to Wholesale Customers – the Far East suppliers may be limited to Fax, but special network arrangements with the top suppliers could be considered. Home shopping would all be based on message passing.

12.7.5 *Commonwealth Open Polytechnic*

Except for remote tutoring and videoconferencing, most data transfer is not 'hot'. Email is fine for most casual messaging between students, Regional Center staff, Campus staff and Contractors. Transmission of whole files, some large and incorporating multimedia, is likely to be common. Regional transactions may trigger messages to the Campus systems.

12.7.6 *National Environmental Protection Board*

Apart from remote monitoring, most of NEPC's data communication could be treated as message passing. Examples are Inspection reports, reminders to Subject Organizations, and communications with external Research Laboratories. Questionnaires could be submitted by Subject Organizations using EDI. Researchers would be frequent users of Internet facilities.

12.8 EXERCISES

1. Does message passing completely remove the need for RPCs (Remote Procedure Calls)?

2. Why does an organization expect immediate response for internal information when it does not expect it from an external organization?

3. Account for the recent surge in popularity of Email. Is the bubble likely to burst?

4. What problems may there be in sending files as attachments to Email messages?

5. What are the differences between an Email service with Mailing List Managers and a true Electronic Conference?

6. What are the likely legal and political issues of passing messages electronically between separate organizations?

7. What are the remaining obstacles to achieving a paperless office?

8. Can Internet services like WWW and Gopher be satisfactorily classified as Message Passing?

9. Who does the user sue in the courts if Internet fails to deliver a key message?

10. What is the importance of an Authentication Server in Message Passing?

11. Describe the purpose and modes of operation of an Off-Line Reader for Email.

12. What are the tasks of a 'moderator' in an Electronic Conference?

13. How can a workstation user find out the correct Email address of someone they know by surname in a foreign university?

14. How does the Apple Open Collaborative Environment differ from a typical electronic mail system?

15. What does it mean to say that an Application is 'message enabled'?

16. How can a company using a commercial Accounts Receivable package send invoices and receive payment notifications electronically from its clients?

17. Should Mr A get a PPP (point-to-point protocol) or SLIP (serial line Internet protocol) account, or should he continue to access the Internet through dial-up to the CIX Conferencing Service?

18. What security measures would you suggest to Detox if they plan to transmit sensitive data over dial-up links in Poland?

19. Discuss the different types and frequencies of message passing between Electric House and its Far East Suppliers.

20. Suggest what facilities the NEPB needs in a Mail Server.

ASSIGNMENT TASK

For your chosen case study, list the application areas where there is most need for:

- electronic mail
- global information retrieval
- EDI
- 'cool' inter-application message passing

indicating what hardware and software facilities might be needed in each case.

Would these solutions be more cost-effective than the 'hot' equivalent (OLTP with Distributed Databases or Client/Server)?

FURTHER READING

Apple (1994) *Apple Open Collaborative Environment*. Apple Corporation.
Apple (1994) *OpenDoc*. Apple Corporation.
Baum, D. (1993) Apple Open Collaboration Environment. *Infoworld*, 31 May.

CompuServe (1994) *Introductory Membership*. CompuServe, Columbus, Ohio, USA.

Computing (1994) Novell reaffirms faith in OpenDoc. *Computing (UK)*, 13 Oct.

Computing (1995) Focus on electronic data interchange. *Computing (UK)*, 26 Jan.

Cronin, M. (1993) *Doing Business on the Internet*, Van Nostrand–Reinhold, Princeton, NJ.

Dettmer, R. (1995) Anyhow, anywhere – the rise of open distributed processing. *IEE Review*, Jan.

Dykman, C. *et al.* (1991) Turf wars: managing the implementation of an international electronic mail system. *Journal of Systems Management*, Jul.

Harding, C. and Frangon, G. (1989) Worldwide interchange (article about EDI over X.400). *Connexion (UK)*, 5 Jul.

King, J. (1994) Conferences seek to raise EDI awareness. *Computing (UK)*, 31 Mar.

King, J. (1994) IBM joins the race to launch EDI service. *Computing (UK)*, unknown.

Knight, J. (1990) *EDI – an Overview*. 2nd Australian Computer Abuse Research Bureau Conference.

Krol, E. (1992) *The Whole Internet*, O'Reilly & Associates, Sebastopol, CA.

Linthicum, D. (1995) Reconsidering message middleware. *DBMS Magazine*, Mar.

Lynch, M. (1994) Electronic shopping to be offered on Internet. *Computing (UK)*, 22 Sep.

Lynch, M. (1994) Government review represents serious threat to EDI funding. *Computing (UK)*, 25 Aug.

MacMillan, G. (1993) Royal Mail sets the seal on its EDI services range. *Computing (UK)*, 7 Oct.

Ranum, R. (1995) *Thinking About Firewalls*. Glenwood, Maryland, USA, Trusted Information Systems Inc.

Schatz, W. (1988) EDI: putting the muscle in commerce and industry. *Datamation*, 15 Mar.

Tasker, D. (1994) It's how you say it (article on object message passing versus subroutine calling). *Database Programming & Design*, Nov.

Telecom (1990) *Business Information Services on Telecom Gold*. British Telecom, London, UK.

Viehland, D. (1994) *The Growth of Information Services: A Vision of the Future of the Internet in New Zealand*. Public Internet Seminar, Auckland, NZ.

Viehland, D. (1995) E-mail bonding (article on mail reflectors). *CIO Magazine*, Jun.

Part Four
A Design
Methodology for
Distributed and
Cooperative Systems

The final, and largest, part of the book provides the 'payoff' in terms of fulfilling the promise of this book's title, in which the primary word is 'Designing'.

The authors have suffered, over many years, in being forced to treat Distributed Systems Design as either an inconvenient appendage to traditional methods (most of which even today pre-suppose a centralized system) or as a 'physical' issue which should be left until all the possibilities for Analysis, Conceptual Design and Logical Design have been exhausted.

The remaining chapters, therefore, represent an attempt to integrate distribution and communications network design into the same framework as data and process design. Given today's environment where Distributed and Cooperative Systems are the norm rather than the exception, we believe that the result forms the basis for a methodology for **any** IS Design.

We say 'basis' because the book does not specify every detail of a prescriptive series of steps. In our definition, methodology is not that sort of thing. Our preferred approach is what we term 'open toolbox', in which we emphasize the need for certain stages to be addressed, but leave the precise choice of method, tool and even sequence up to individual designers.

Chapter 13 is introductory and introduces the principles underlying our proposed methodology. The five chapters that follow address each of five main stages of design:

- Information Strategy Planning
- Technical Architecture Planning
- Network Design
- Shared Data Design
- Design within an Individual System or Sub-system

Each of these chapters has a common layout, namely:

N.1 Rationale for this Design Stage
N.2 Inputs to this Design Stage
    N.2.1 Starting Points (i.e. what you need to have before starting this stage)
    N.2.2 Nature of the Alternatives (which could be considered)
    N.2.3 Evaluation Criteria (for choosing between alternatives)
N.3 Design Tasks at this Stage
N.4 Description of Individual Techniques
N.5 Application to the Case Studies
N.6 Exercises

The final chapter is rather different, and deals with the practice, commonly adopted with distributed systems and advanced communications, of using external tendering as part of the Design process.

13 Overall methodology

13.1 RATIONALE FOR YET ANOTHER VIEW OF METHODOLOGY

Methodologies for computer-oriented IS development have always been an active topic in literature. Many leading gurus have made their names this way – Yourdon, Gane and Sarson, James Martin are people that come to mind. However, no methodology, however well-championed, has ever kept a monopoly on the truth for very long. Both the Technology and Business Application ends of IS have been so fast moving that the 'design equation' is always changing. This may also account for the fact that Academics have never really broken into IS Design in a big way – there are no elegant, timeless theoretical solutions for all occasions.

In practice, most IS designers, until recently, have been able to attach themselves to one or other of a number of 'schools', of which the three best-known are:

- the structured school
- the database-driven school
- the real-time process school.

So far, none of these schools has offered many ideas for Distributed or Cooperative Systems. Observation suggests that when networks and multiple processors begin to be considered, design technique downgrades into what can be termed 'design by configuration'. This means that, rather than generating alternatives and choosing the best, the designer pulls a set of technology out of the hat (or his favorite supplier's handbook) and hopes that no-one else knows enough about that technology to challenge it.

In other words, distribution and networks have found themselves excluded from the mainstream design process at a time when they are almost certain to be an element of any newly designed system.

Another reason for a rethink about methodology is that fewer organizations go for big-bang developments these days. That is because they cannot afford to completely replace many systems. There are no 'green fields', except in start-up companies, and even they should probably be going for low-risk package-oriented approaches rather than hand-crafted developments.

A landmark in development methodology came in the late 1980s, when IBM launched an initiative known as AD/Cycle, AD standing for Application Development. The idea was to produce a family of tools – from different suppliers in a partnership – that would interwork and thus support the whole development process. Although the AD/Cycle partnership collapsed, it generated a 'baby' that should not be washed down the plughole with the proverbial bath water. This 'baby' is the truth that, for decentralized organizations, only a component-based approach to methodology has any realistic chance of success.

Each time a new methodology is proposed, it makes difficulties for the development teams that are already working in organizations. Individuals' ability to learn new techniques is limited. No IS Development Group can ever expect to totally jettison its existing methodology for a new one. Both timescales and quality may be risked every time there is a change. Also, methodology is often tightly bound up with the use of tools (e.g. CASE), and a change in methodology often entails a change of expensive CASE software and an enormous meta-database and repository conversion.

Hopefully the proposals in this book can be regarded as being incremental and inter-operable with existing practices. We are not in the business of proposing a fundamental revolution in IS development, only a reorganization of the toolkit and a resequencing of some of the operations.

13.2 PRIORITIES FOR AN IMPROVED METHOD OF DISTRIBUTED SYSTEMS DESIGN

Between the different schools of design methodology, there is a difference in balance between the various design factors (Figure 13.1). With traditional process flow-chart methods, the biggest factor was the speed of in-memory processing and the space occupied by both code and data buffers. With

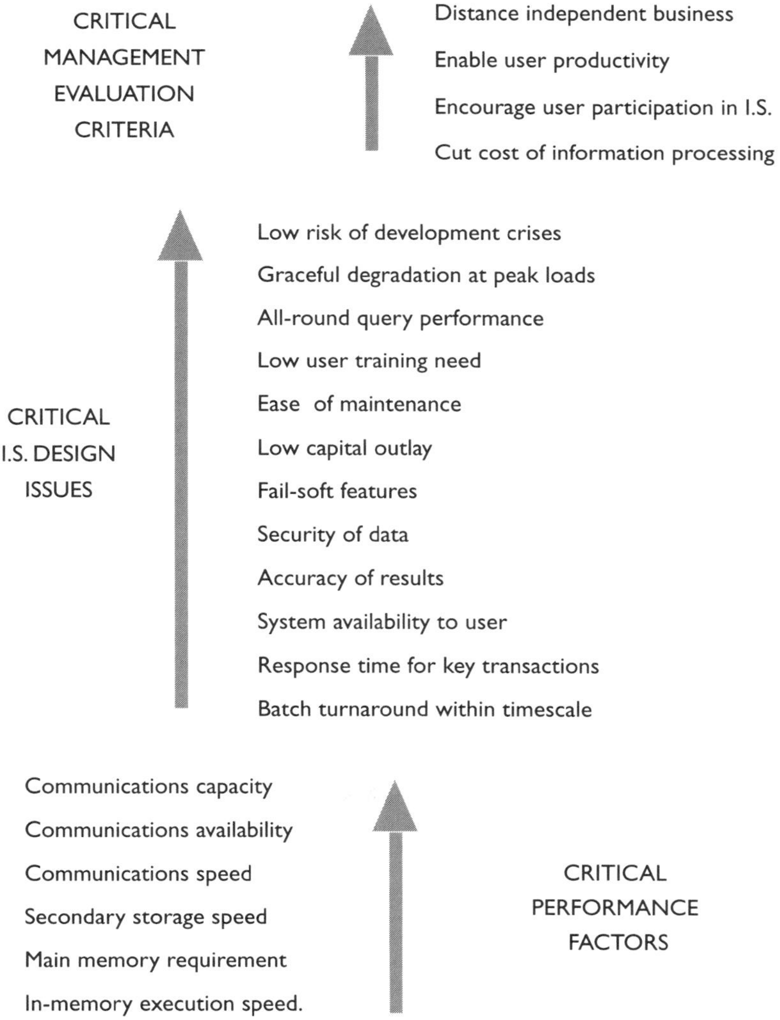

CRITICAL
MANAGEMENT
EVALUATION
CRITERIA

Distance independent business

Enable user productivity

Encourage user participation in I.S.

Cut cost of information processing

Low risk of development crises

Graceful degradation at peak loads

All-round query performance

Low user training need

Ease of maintenance

Low capital outlay

Fail-soft features

Security of data

Accuracy of results

System availability to user

Response time for key transactions

Batch turnaround within timescale

CRITICAL
I.S. DESIGN
ISSUES

Communications capacity

Communications availability

Communications speed

Secondary storage speed

Main memory requirement

In-memory execution speed.

CRITICAL
PERFORMANCE
FACTORS

Figure I3.I Change in Importance between Design Factors

structured methods the hot decision area moved towards quality and maintainability. With database-driven methods, the use of a good conceptual model, mapped to an efficient storage and retrieval system, was of greatest concern. With real-time, the need to operate within the time constraints, and to have foolproof backup paths, was the key.

We have identified five major imbalances which need to be redressed in an improved design method. The majority of traditional IS design methods are:

- geared to centralized processing and take little account of the location dimension
- oriented to commercial data processing and not to other application styles and objectives
- based on specifications of the information system and less on the underlying business process
- oriented to pure performance and not to other measurable goals
- assuming that 'logical' decisions must always come before 'physical' ones, regardless of the wide variation in lead times and costs for different decision areas.

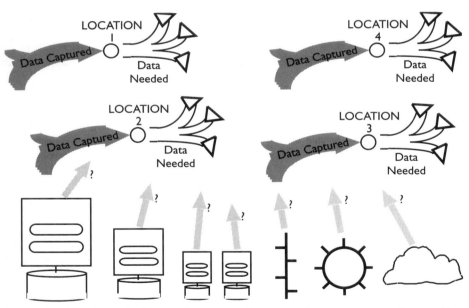

Figure 13.2 The Design Problem in the Location Dimension. (squares represent data needs)

13.2.1 *The location dimension*

With the arrival of Distributed and Cooperative computing, an extra design dimension, namely Location, is clearly present.

Given a set of data captured in one set of locations, and a number of users (or robots) requiring information in another set of locations, there is clearly an optimization task – where do we put units of data and processing in order to meet all the functional requirements, satisfy all the design constraints, and optimize the cost-benefit ratio? This is illustrated in Figure 13.2.

User organizations are – as they have been for some time – geographically dispersed. This is true both within one geographical site and over a wider area of the globe. Also, what has to be considered in the IS goes beyond the boundaries of the organization being studied. In some organizations, IS involving external business networking may be as important as internal ones. The difficulty is that the organization has little or no managerial control over these external data sources (Figure 13.3).

13.2.2 *Different application styles and objectives*

Different existing design methodologies tend to reveal a bias towards a particular style of application. The structured and database-driven schools are mainly geared to on-line TP systems which handle what used to be called 'commercial data processing' and are now often classed as 'legacy systems'. Designers trying

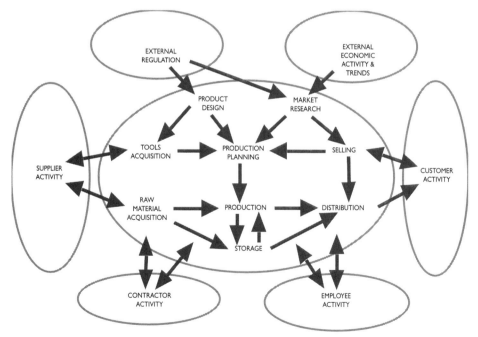

Figure 13.3 Internal and External Business Processes (example from a typical manufacturing company.)

to build a real-time Process Control system, or even a Command and Control system, often tend to use different approaches. The Cadre Teamwork CASE tool offers a different module for Real-Time applications. The new Object Oriented Design (OOD) methods also seem to specialize in these other areas – the examples used in Booch (1991) for example, discuss a Home Heating system and a Remote Weather Monitoring system.

Today's balance of applications is still changing, and we now have Design Support applications like CAD/CAM, those built around Groupware, interactive Multimedia systems – all of which did not exist a few years ago.

Applications can be characterized by their primary objectives. A few interesting examples are shown below:

- improve management control of a large, complex real-world system
- speed delivery of accurate information to decision-makers
- offer a shared information service (commercially or otherwise)
- offer a gateway to external information resources
- support the optimization of management decisions, including group decision making
- support research (which usually involves access to fuzzily indexed material held in various locations)
- support soft objectives such as 'group consensus building'.

Because these design objectives vary so widely, the evaluation criteria, because they have to be aligned with these objectives, will be very different. Also, the technical bottlenecks and resource restrictions, where the designer has to work hardest to find a good solution, will not be the same.

13.2.3 *The business process influence*

Like it or not, Business Process Re-engineering (BPR) has come into play as the new lever to enforce organizational rationalization – although not without some criticism. It seems that today's organizations, especially public ones, find a need for a 'talisman' with which to justify making the type of wholesale changes that usually result in a lot of job losses and redeployment. In earlier days 'the Consultant says' was good enough. Then we had 'the Consultant says, based on James Martin's Information Engineering'. Now we have 'the Consultant says, after a BPR exercise'!

BPR includes the modeling of work flows through processes. High importance is placed on defining the processes and coming up with improved flows so that the value chain from inputs to end-users is optimized. This represents a contrast to the database-driven school. If the designer is in an environment where BPR is being used, then the methodology must be better aligned to processes and work flows.

Another cause for change is that many methodologies take a very 'army-style' model of how business operates, with objectives being passed down the layers of management in a top-down hierarchical manner. However, management consultants have for some years recognized that this is becoming less and less appropriate. Flatter hierarchies, with more autonomous work groups and profit centers, are now the norm. A federal, rather than hierarchical, approach is a better model for today.

To accommodate this change, more emphasis has to be put on the boundaries of management control, since there may no longer be a single sponsor who can authorize implementation of the whole of a designed system. The designer will have to consider such issues as:

- enterprise boundaries
- scopes of formal and informal cooperation between different organizations, including information resource exchange and sharing conventions
- use of public information sources and facilities, whether commercial or free of charge
- organizational and social structure of workgroups and individuals.

13.2.4 *Measurable delivery goals*

Unfortunately, many Analysis and Design methods are all too often characterized by clever diagrammatic or optimization techniques, but with little regard to what the real requirements of the project are. The implicit assumption is that one simply has to satisfy the client-stated functional requirements, but any experienced designer instinctively knows that things are not that simple. We can fairly easily formalize functional requirements, and possibly produce cost and performance models, but this leaves many other goals unsatisfied – which can easily sink the system.

Tom Gilb, in his book *Principles of Software Engineering Management* (Gilb, 1988) makes the establishment and monitoring of all these goals the main thrust of his method. It does not matter that he is talking about Software Engineering – his remarks apply to any sort of Engineering. In fact, one can regard Gilb's approach as 'Information Engineering' in the true meaning of the phrase.

The following are examples of Tom Gilb's suggested dimensions for these goals (or 'attributes' as he somewhat confusingly calls them):

- development timescale
- ease of use (for some user group)
- security (against some named threat)
- development delay risk
- marketability
- system availability to users
- maintenance cost
- extensibility
- technical risk
- development cost
- packageability
- connectivity to other systems

- independence from hardware
- independence from software
- consistency
- worst case response time
- error rate in output data
- new technology failure risk
- return on development investment
- capital expenditure
- infrastructure manageability.

- bug free-ness (zero defects)
- normal response time
- peak load response time
- daily workload capacity
- supplier failure risk
- level of system breakdowns
- user productivity gains
- user training hump

Gilb states that if any of these could possibly be critical, then there should always be some measure for it. Otherwise there is no basis for quality control, inspection and acceptance.

Not all of the above goals may be critical in all projects. What is needed is a set of priorities or weights for each goal. Some may have too small a weight to be included, and too many goals means too complex a design process. However, we have to be careful about leaving goals out. Most designers know of systems that were successfully designed to meet all the main objectives but then failed when measured against other goals that had not been addressed.

13.2.5 *Lead times and costs of different decision areas*

Many authors have pointed out that in design, one should make decisions early about the things that:

- take a long time to implement and
- take a lot of cost, effort and time to change later

while other design decisions should be deferred so that they are taken 'just in time'.

The following 'league table' highlights where some of the decision areas rate on both lead time and cost.

	Lead time	Cost scale points (e.g. 6 means $\sim\$10^6$)
Change whole methodology or architecture	1–2 years	6
Introduce new data collection procedures	1–2 years	6
Build major system from scratch	1–2 years	6
Upgrade a mainframe-based installation	6–12 months	6
Change the distributed processing architecture	2–3 years	5
Change Data Dictionary	6–12 months	5
Change Operating System	9–12 months	5

Collect/load back data for database	3–12 months	4
Change DBMS	3–6 months	4
Change to new WAN technology	6–9 months	4
Change a network protocol	3–6 months	4
Re-engineer a major system	6–12 months	4
Integrate new software package	3–6 months	4
Install new LAN	2–3 months	4
Install new server	1–2 months	4
Design a database for efficient sharing	2–4 months	3
Change one method in a design toolkit	2–4 months	3
Prototype new TP subsystem	1–2 months	3
Install new workstations	2 weeks	3
Amend database structure	1–2 weeks	3
Produce new report	1 day	2
Produce new query	1 hour	1

Experienced readers will no doubt have different ratings from their own experience, or may have additional 'teams' that they would add to this league.

The problem is that with the advent of Distributed and Cooperative Systems we are not always taking proper account of these lead times. With the 'database-driven' school, we have tended to think of logical database design as up-front, procedure design after that, and anything physical, including data placement, networks, archiving, etc. as fairly insignificant last minute optimization.

The solution is to bring forward some of the long lead-time, high cost decisions into earlier design stages. It means that we have to have some preliminary physical design.

13.3 THE OPEN TOOLBOX CONCEPT

The overall approach we propose (Figure 13.4) is what we call the 'Open Toolbox'.

It is a 'Toolbox' because we take the view that any individual design tool or method should be selected for its fitness for purpose. It is 'Open' because we do not ever wish to close the door on the addition of new tools.

Not everything in the toolbox is strictly a tool, some things are materials used to assemble bits of whatever we are constructing – the equivalent of nuts, bolts and glue. Other things are more like 'kits' than single tools. This analogy holds up well for the Design toolbox.

What needs to be in the toolbox for developing Distributed and Cooperative IS? Here is an initial 'packing list':

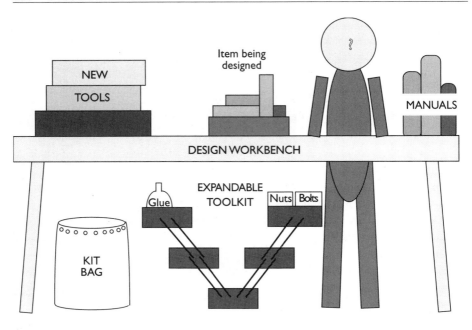

Figure 13.4 The Open Toolbox Concept.

- Modeling kits (data structure, data flow, procedure, object, state transition, message passing)
- Model cross-checkers (including matrix processors)
- Process simulation tools (manual or computer)
- Screen and report layout painters
- Statistical analysis tools
- Report generator
- Query languages in various styles (command, menu, form, hypertext or graphical)
- TP application generators
- Database schema generation tools
- Reverse and re-engineering tools
- Various program generators
- Code development, editing and debugging tools
- Performance monitors (within both processor and network)
- Scripting language (glue)
- Middleware (glue).

Things that could be 'added' to the 'open toolbox' include:

- extra models for specialized types of requirements, e.g. Information Rich Pictures when using Soft Systems Methodology (SSM)
- bought-in Application Packages
- in-house utilities supporting development (e.g. DBMS bridgeware).

Any toolbox also needs to be kept in order and uncluttered, so sometimes we need to tidy it up, or even throw some unused or obsolete tools out, or at least put them into a museum.

There is the question of whether or not we should decide on a single paradigm – either 'Object Oriented' or 'Procedure on Data' for using the toolkit. We believe that this is not practicable, as no organization will succeed in making an instantaneous and total switch of paradigm. Therefore, there must inevitably be a period when the two paradigms exist side-by-side.

An interim approach consists of allowing, within the traditional 'Procedure on Data' approach, some Entity Types to have Procedures attached to them. These procedures could be limited to the simple Create/Read/Update/Delete ('CRUD') (Figure 13.5).

In the alternative Object Oriented approach, Jacobson's three-way division into Entity, Control and User Interface Objects (Jacobson *et al.*, 1994) allows independent Procedures to be packaged into Control object classes (Figure 13.6).

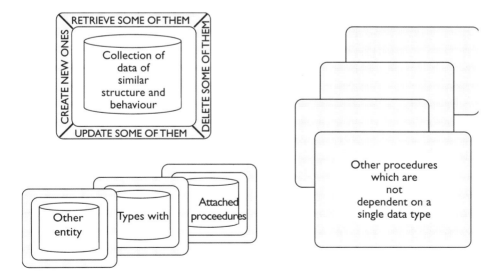

Figure 13.5 Packaging Procedure with Data.

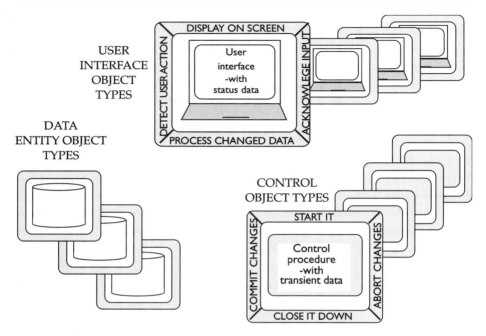

Figure 13.6 Object-Oriented: Jacobson-style.

13.4 DEVELOPMENT OF THE ENGINEERING PARADIGM

We regard methodology as a general philosophy of how to use a development toolkit. As the basis of a suitable methodology for Distributed and Cooperative systems, we use the Engineering paradigm because we feel it best describes our preferred approach of fashioning something to a specification by using a selection of available tools.

Although we do not prescribe development by numbers, we think that the Design Team Leader – who is effectively the 'Chief Engineer' for the project – may wish to specify the sequence of tasks for that particular project. We do suggest some task sequences, but the overall process should be regarded as evolutionary wherever possible, i.e. proceeding iteratively from one partly adequate product to another, improving or adding to the detail at each stage. In particular, we do not wish to leave any impression of a methodology where all of one stage (e.g. Analysis) has to be completed before another stage (e.g. Design or Programming) can start. We do not have good experiences with user-signed-off specifications, and prefer to rely on frequent user feedback from prototypes.

However, we do have some sympathy for Spiral methodologies such as Boehm's (Boehm, 1988) (Figure 13.7).

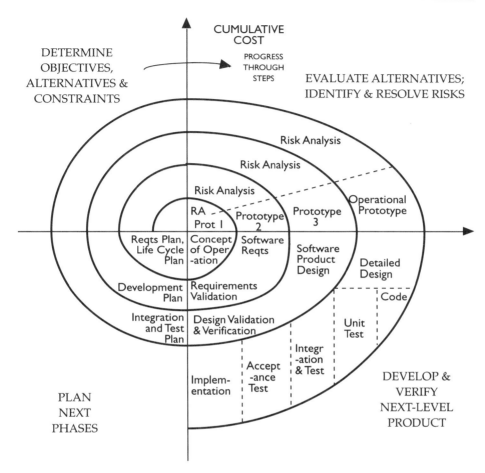

CUMULATIVE COST

PROGRESS THROUGH STEPS

DETERMINE OBJECTIVES, ALTERNATIVES & CONSTRAINTS

EVALUATE ALTERNATIVES; IDENTIFY & RESOLVE RISKS

Risk Analysis

Risk Analysis

Risk Analysis

RA Prot 1

Prototype 2

Prototype 3

Operational Prototype

Reqts Plan, Life Cycle Plan

Concept of Oper-ation

Software Reqts

Software Product Design

Detailed Design

Development Plan

Requirements Validation

Code

Integration and Test Plan

Design Validation & Verification

Unit Test

Integr-ation & Test

Implem-entation

Accept-ance Test

PLAN NEXT PHASES

DEVELOP & VERIFY NEXT-LEVEL PRODUCT

Figure 13.7 Boehm's Spiral Model of Software Development (by permission, Barry W. Boehm 'A Spiral Model of Software Development and Enhancement' IEEE Computer, May 1988, © 1988 IEEE).

In our engineering approach, we draw a contrast between 'Great Leaps Forward' and 'Incremental Steps'. Figure 13.8 shows these as a process of climbing up a series of plateaux. The point is that not every design task in IS is a grand one. We need to apply the same toolbox concept to the small steps as to the major projects. We also need to recognize that every project is incremental – even a Great Leap Forward has to start from an existing Information System, whether that system consists of handwriting in manual ledgers or a ten-year old TP system that has run out of steam.

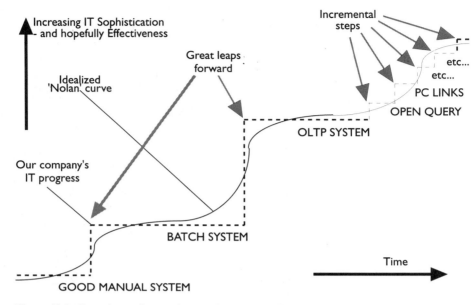

Figure 13.8 Great Leaps Forward versus Incremental Steps.

Incremental Steps are not all of one type. Some are like miniature application developments, for example add-ons to a system's functionality. Others can be limited to the infrastructure and not associated with any particular functional requirements. For example:

- network expansion and modernization
- the organization and training of users
- procedures for the non-computer aspects of systems
- maintenance of equipment.

A final distinction is between Architecture and Detailed Design. The meanings we apply in the IS context are analogous to their meanings in House Construction. The main purpose of Architecture is to enable the user organization to plan its progress through a Great Leap Forward so that the longer-term objectives are met. The Detailed Design generally follows the Architecture, but an infeasibility or an opportunity to save big money at a lower level of detail has to be permitted to feed back into the Architecture.

13.5 STAGES INCLUDED – AND NOT INCLUDED – IN THIS BOOK

Figure 13.9 shows a number of traditional methodology stages pictured in a 'house construction' metaphor. This is a widening of James Martin's original Information Engineering 'cube' (Martin, 1990a) to cater for styles of development other than those oriented to 'green field' shared TP applications.

IS Strategy Planning is seen as the task of creating and maintaining an IS strategy that correctly reflects the overall Mission, Objectives, Strategies and Critical Success Factors (MOSC) of the organization. It also needs to take account of Business Process Re-engineering (BPR), Technical Opportunities and so on. The primary output of IS Strategy Planning is a series of priority projects for early development. These can be implemented in a number of different styles, depending on the work involved.

Technical Architecture Planning is an outcome of Information Strategy Planning which looks at the technical consequences of the Information and Systems Architecture which are identified during the Strategy Planning task.

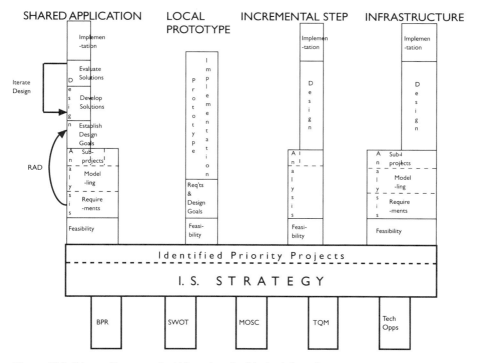

Figure 13.9 'House Construction' Metaphor for Methodology Stages.

Information Strategy Planning is discussed in Chapter 14, while Technical Architecture Planning, because of its increased importance in a distributed environment, is treated separately in Chapter 15.

Feasibility is taken to mean ensuring that at least the most critical goals of any IS project can be met, before committing too much effort to Analysis, Design or Implementation. It can also establish which other dimensions may come into play as a side-effect of meeting the chief ones. We do not treat Feasibility separately in this methodology, instead, we regard it as part of the evaluation phase at early design stages.

Analysis is treated in a very limited way in this methodology. In this book we restrict it to the collecting of requirements and the modeling of these requirements into a suitable form which is independent of potential design solutions. We regard this process as an evolutionary one and we envisage that more detailed requirements will be collected iteratively as the design gets into more detail. For this reason we have not included an Analysis chapter in this book.

Design is defined as the creation of a workable blueprint for an individual system or sub-sytem that meets a certain set of formalized requirements that have been established through an Analysis process at some stage and level of detail. Design is considered in three main stages:

- Network Design (Chapter 16)
- Shared Data Design (Chapter 17)
- Design within an Individual System or Sub-system (Chapter 18).

This sequence should not be regarded as immutable – there may be good arguments for using a different sequence in some cases.

Each design stage is regarded as having four main phases:

- establishing the starting point (e.g. results of previous design work, statements of requirements from Analysis work, measures of required performance)
- generating alternative solutions
- evaluating the alternatives
- refinement of the solutions.

Implementation includes any purpose-built coding of software programs, acquisition and installation of hardware, software and communications facilities, conversion of data files, documentation and training, and also various levels of testing, acceptance and commissioning. It is not addressed in this book.

13.6 POSSIBLE APPROACHES TO METHODOLOGY IN THE CASE STUDIES

13.6.1 *Mr A*

Since low overhead is likely to be a critical success factor (CSF) for Mr A, he cannot afford a front-heavy methodology. He therefore has to prototype, using as reliable a set of tools as he can find. He has to make all development timescales short ones – he cannot weather a long changeover period (not, at least, until he has several Associates).

13.6.2 *Bay Organic Produce Cooperative*

Again, low overheads are paramount – we know that they have already turned down a mainframe or minicomputer. The methodology is likely to have to be evolutionary, i.e. always building on what is already there. For example, if they decide to share data, we should look to add software to the existing client systems, rather than to design a new system from scratch. Low risk in any development is also important, as such a small organization might not weather the shock of a failed system.

13.6.3 *Detox Pharmaceuticals*

In Detox's case we have a legacy of traditional systems analysis and design, but a need to move towards client/server and distributed databases. However, it is likely that Business Process Re-engineering will be needed to establish an efficient value chain. This implies a good amount of up-front Analysis and Design in the methodology. Systems for the Regional Offices and Warehouses are also going to be duplicated several times, so it is important to have a low error rate.

13.6.4 *Electric House*

Use of a formal methodology can probably be assumed to be quite well established in Electric House proper, but the situation may be more variable in Casa Electrica. The new systems that will need to be designed will be mainly for the companies in the Casa Electrica group, and we may have to cater for a different profile of end-user skills from that in the USA. This may necessitate a high level of prototyping of user interfaces.

13.6.5 *Commonwealth Open Polytechnic*

There is likely to be a big dichotomy between the 'bread and butter' systems that enable the COP to operate, and DIY systems developed by and for individual staff members. The methodology needs to be quite formal on the first type of system, to ensure a sound base for all users of the data.

13.6.6 *National Environmental Protection Board*

The opportunities for formally developed systems in NEPB are possibly quite limited. Groupware may be a big element, and translation between different data sources may be a more pervasive need than formal systems. A 'special' approach to methodology may be called for.

13.7 EXERCISES

1. Why have academics rarely been the source of successful IS design methodologies?

2. What is meant by 'design by configuration'?

3. If AD/Cycle was such a good idea, why did it fail?

4. Give some reasons why IS development teams in organizations might be suffering from 'methodology fatigue'.

5. What is meant by the 'location dimension'?

6. Mention two methodologies that provide better support for Process Control and Command and Control systems.

7. What effect should BPR have on IS development methodology?

8. In what units might one measure the Gilb Goals listed in 13.2.4?

9. Introducing new data collection procedures is very high in the league table for timescale and cost of change. Why?

10. Why does Analysis have a less major role in the proposed methodology, compared with other approaches?

11. What is the main shortcoming of the 'database-driven' Analysis and Design methodologies, which are often used in conjunction with large database implementations, for distributed organizations?

12. Consider the analogy between a distributed information system and a large road transport (trucking) company. Each collects a commodity from a number of sources and delivers it to the users. How might we design the company's operations? Can any useful parallels be drawn?

13. In what sense does the proposed methodology follow an Engineering paradigm?

14. Suggest features of a methodology that would minimize changeover disturbance as a primary requirement, as required by Mr A and BOPC.

15. If Detox is to implement new Process Control systems, what arguments govern the type of methodology to be used?

16. What special methodology features or tasks might be needed when compatible systems have to be introduced in a number of geographic locations, as with Detox or Casa Electrica?

17. In the COP or NEPB, a lot of application development will be left to end-users. What methodology can still be enforced or encouraged?

18. The NEPB estimates that it requires 20 person-years of effort to load up the back data it needs to get its initial database ready to use. What effect would this have on your recommendation for a methodology?

ASSIGNMENT TASK

For your chosen case study, assume that at least some existing methodology is in place. What are the main business arguments for considering changing this methodology in order to cater now for Distributed and Cooperative IS?

What is the relative importance of each of the main development stages (e.g. IS Strategy, Feasibility, Analysis, Design, Implementation)?

Which of Gilb's Goals are likely to be the most important?

FURTHER READING

Avison, D. and Fitzgerald, G. (1988) *Information Systems Development*, Alfred Waller, UK.

Boehm, B. (1988) A spiral model of software development and enhancement, *IEEE Computer*, May.

Booch, G. (1991) *Object Oriented Design with Applications*, Benjamin/Cummings, Redwood City, CA.

Davis, C. (1991) Systems analysis for data communications networks at an electric utility. *Journal of Systems Management*, Jul.

Gilb, T. (1988) *Principles of Software Engineering Management*, Addison-Wesley, Reading, MA.

Hugo, I. (1994) Breaking the speed limit (article on Rapid Application Development). *Computing (UK)*, 6 Oct.

IBM (1985) *Planning for Distributed Information Systems*. GE20-0655-1, IBM.

Inmon, W. (1993) *Developing Client/Server Applications*, Wiley, New York.

JMA (1991) *RAD Handbook*, James Martin Associates, Ashford, Middlesex, UK.

Oberweis, A. *et al.* (1994) Income/Star: methodology and tools for the development of distributed information systems. *Information Systems*, Elsevier, Amsterdam.

Seer (1993) *Systems Development with Seer·HPS*. Seer Technologies, Cary, NC.

14 Aligning the information strategy to the business

14.1 RATIONALE FOR THIS DESIGN STAGE

Information Strategy Planning (ISP) started life in the mid-1970s. It arose partly because user management felt that piecemeal one-project-at-a-time Analysis and Design was resulting in too many lost opportunities. The IT function did not make a sufficient effort to align itself to the whole organization's business strategy and needs.

As already observed in the previous chapter, IS should follow the needs of the Business or Organization; but at the same time, because IT can in turn bring

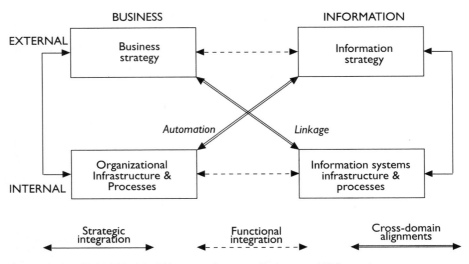

Figure 14.1 MIT '90s' Model of Alignment between Business and IS Strategies.

Business benefits, it should have some feedback into Business Plans. This process is well illustrated by the diagram in Figure 14.1 which was developed as part of the '1990s' project at MIT (Morton, 1991).

One problem with this 'business-based' ideal is that many businesses are not in a stable enough state to say 'these are our Mission, Objectives and Strategies' or even 'this is the way we do business'. Many have muddled along for some time, and are only now, with the recent recessionary times, starting to ask fundamental questions. Some leading companies have recently embraced Business Process Re-engineering (BPR), and are in the process of making fundamental organizational changes. But many not-for-profit organizations have modes of operation which involve service, rather than profit, responsibility; and their process models may be quite different from those of commercial companies.

Sometimes the timing of planning major IS developments fits in nicely with the timing of organizational re-thinking such as BPR exercises. This makes sense because IS are often a Critical Success Factor for the new process model. But the timing is not always so fortunate. Often, it falls to IT Staff and Consultants, who are around when the need for a Strategic IS Plan arises, to carry out some Business Strategy Review or 'substitute BPR' – a task for which they may not be qualified and which sometimes leads to awkward impasses between the organization's top management and the staff involved!

In typical cases, Information Strategy Planning (ISP) is normally carried out as a 'one-off' exercise, at a point in time when senior managers, both IT and non-IT, feel that the organization is at a 'cross-roads' as regards IS deployment.

Typical exercises take 3–6 months, and set plans for a 3–5 year timescale. They involve considerable collection of data on user requirements. The analysis is done largely through building a series of process and data structure models, which are complemented by a large number of matrices showing the interactions between data, processes and organizational units.

It is not the intention in this chapter to propose in any detail yet another procedure for Information Strategy Planning. A generic task structure will certainly be discussed, and suggested improvements will be highlighted, so that users can take better account of BPR and the Location Dimension, within the chosen ISP method.

14.2 INPUTS TO THIS STAGE OF DESIGN

The current approach of the IT community to ensuring that IS Plans are business-based is to appoint a multi-disciplinary team, combining both IT and Management skills with knowledge of the Organization, to carry out an ISP project as described above. A series of techniques from Management and IT are combined to deliver a series of outputs:

- an information architecture
- identification of strategic systems
- organizational implications
- a schedule of priority IS development and infrastructure projects
- an organizational learning experience.

The Information Strategy Plan itself is the schedule of projects which need to be carried out in order to move an Organization's Information Systems from where they are now to where they should be, in order to best meet the Organization's Business needs. These projects fall into the following groups:

- Analysis Projects, where, for each area of the Business that has some natural coherence in Information terms, more detailed analysis of requirements is carried out. Analysis projects may in turn each give rise to one or more:
  - Systems Design Projects
  - Implementation Projects.
- Technical Infrastructure Projects, where enhancement of Hardware, Software and Data Communications platforms is carried out.
- Organizational Infrastructure Projects, where changes are made to Organization Unit Structures, Peoples' Roles, and Data Collection and other Procedures.

The Design and Implementation Projects may take very different forms, depending on the approaches or tools to be used, e.g. Structured Analysis and

Design, Joint or Rapid Analysis and Design with Prototyping (JAD and RAD); and the use made of CASE tools, Generators, 4GLs, Packages, etc.

14.2.1 *Starting points*

ISP exercises do not have any standard starting point. There is usually a combination of factors which build up gradually to a point where top management is agreed that 'we must do something fundamental about our IS for the future'. Many different events can trigger this, for example reorganizations, mergers, increased competition, fundamental changes in markets or unfavorable auditors' reports.

14.2.2 *Nature of the alternatives*

Alternative Strategy Plans can usually be assessed in two dimensions, which can be characterized as 'Ambition' and 'Urgency', as shown in Figure 14.2.

The most **ambitious** plans are those which go for high benefits but with high risks. Supporters of these plans are looking for IS to lever the organization into a quantum leap in competitiveness or effectiveness. At the technical level they may involve leading-edge hardware, software and communications. They also involve wholesale restructuring of people's work, whether in IT, elsewhere in the company, or in business partners. At the other extreme of this dimension are plans which involve doing just what has to be computerized (or what is being done currently) and doing it as cost-effectively as possible.

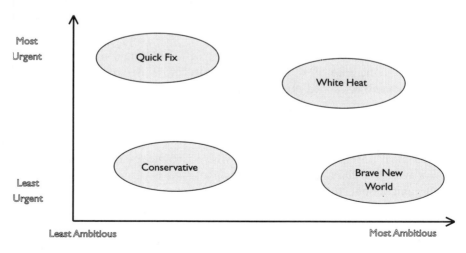

Figure 14.2 'Ambitious' and 'Urgent' Information Strategy Plans.

On the **urgency** scale, the high scorers are plans which include a lot of new or upgraded systems in a short space of time, using contractors and off-the-shelf solutions if need be. The low scorers are those which try to even out the rate of IS change to what the organization and its IT resources can cope with.

In two dimensions, it is sometimes appropriate to attach names to the options, as in Figure 14.2. No-one to our knowledge has yet proposed a 'back to clerks with quill pens' alternative!

There may also be variations in the relative priorities given to 'formal' systems (e.g. TP and Process Control) compared with informal ones such as Groupware, Research Support and *Ad hoc* Information Retrieval.

14.2.3 *Evaluation criteria*

The most important criterion for selecting a good Information Strategy Plan is that the top management feels not just happy with it, but will commit to its implementation. It must demonstrably address the management's concerns, and must propose specific schedules, which give at least a rough estimate of cost and benefit.

Cost and benefit are key aspects which must be addressed, but a third item, risk of failure, is also important. Many directors and top managers have already been through at least one IS development crisis which was caused, at least in part, by the IT practitioners 'biting off more than they could chew'. Risk of failure also relates to feasibility, which implies that at least some Technical Architecture planning and Organizational Implications analysis should be included in the ISP exercise.

14.3 DESIGN TASKS AT THIS STAGE

14.3.1 *Tasks in a typical ISP methodology*

Most of the methods for ISP share a common set of core tasks. The following list shows one example, based from the TI Information Engineering methodology:

1. Scope and Planning of the Study
2. Analysis of Business Strategy
3. Collection of Information Needs and Priorities
4. Assessment of Existing and Planned Information Systems
5. Formalization of the Structure of Information Needs
6. Identification of Areas for more Detailed Analysis
7. Identification of Natural Systems and Data Stores
8. Proposal of a Technical Architecture

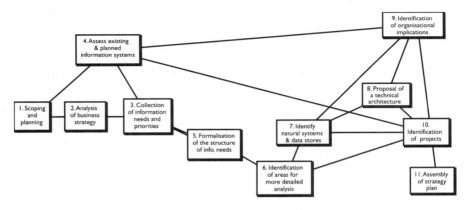

Figure 14.3 Dependencies in a Typical IS Planning Methodology (as Critical Path Network).

9. Identification of Organizational Implications
10. Identification of Projects
11. Assembly of a Strategy Plan.

While these tasks as listed indicate a general passage of time, they do not form a strict 'waterfall' sequence – a typical task dependency chart is shown in Figure 14.3.

Some of the techniques that are commonly used include:

	Task Numbers
CSF (Critical Success Factor) Analysis	2
Value Chain Analysis	2
SWOT (Strengths/Weaknesses/Opportunities/Threats) Analysis	2 and 4
Entity Relationship and Process Modeling	5
Clustering of Two-Dimensional Matrices	6
RAEW (Responsibility/Authority/Expertise/Work) Matrices	9
Risk Analysis	10
Critical Path Analysis	1 and 11.

14.3.2 *The ISP market place*

ISP Methods tend not to be sold directly to user practitioners, but are jealously held by major consultancy companies who provide expert staff to carry out these very sensitive projects. This mode of operation is perhaps more akin to Management Consultancy than to IT Consultancy.

Some of the main practitioners worldwide include:

- Arthur Andersen & Co
- Price Waterhouse
- Ernst and Young
- Texas Instruments Software
- James Martin & Co
- EDS
- Oracle Corporation.

The methods used by these companies do not remain static, and are currently changing by taking particular account of the advent of Business Process Re-engineering and Object Oriented approaches.

14.3.3 *Shortcomings in current methods*

In practice, all the methods appear to concentrate heavily on the building of a high-level conceptual data model. This tends to steer the Organization towards database-oriented thinking. This is often no bad thing as a counterbalance to purely procedural thinking, but it still represents a bias. As a result, the Plans produced are strong on the sort of IS that go with databases, e.g. Data Storage and Retrieval, Commercial Data Processing, and Transaction Processing. The methods are less suited to Real-Time and Control systems, Office and Text systems, Groupware and Cooperative systems, and Decision Support. Consequently, these may be given short shrift in the Information Strategy Plan.

All methods seem to pre-suppose the existence (or relatively quick and deterministic discovery) of statements of Business Strategy. As discussed in the introduction to this chapter, this is not always possible.

Most methods also ignore the location dimension, thus resulting in plans which are prejudiced towards centralized processing. Admittedly, many Distribution decisions are to do with solutions rather than requirements, but Distribution can also be a requirement, e.g. multiple Factories or Retail Outlets, or Suppliers and Customers at different sites.

The practice in ISP studies is to interview (or otherwise involve) all managers. This brings a danger in that many managers still occupy 'staff' rather than 'line' roles. This is not necessarily wrong – the wheels of any efficient machine need oiling. But there is sometimes too great a reliance on such wheel-oilers. The result is a picture of the business which lacks the 'mission-critical' perspective.

Lastly, many ISP studies suffer from over-tight scoping. This arises from a natural reluctance by managers who sponsor ISP exercises to let the study loose on the awkward boundaries with other managerial empires. However, in current business, many IS have to extend beyond the organizational boundaries as they exist at present in order to achieve their pay-offs.

14.3.4 *Recent trends in combining ISP and BPR*

Realizing the overlap in practice between BPR and ISP, some of the leading consultancies have been evolving their ISP methods to incorporate some BPR approaches. Typically, an ISP team finds that the Organization's Business Strategy is not settled, and that part of the reason the study has been set up is because there is a problem over Business Processes. Sometimes, there is also a market struggle between Management Consultants trying to recapture this area from database consultants!

In a recent book (Jacobson *et al.*, 1994), Ivar Jacobson and his colleagues at Objectory have proposed a combined approach based on User-oriented Scenarios (called 'Use Cases') and Object Models. This approach distinguishes an external model of the Business (expressed in terms of Use Cases) from an internal model (based on Objects of three types: Entity Objects, Control Objects and Interface Objects). Despite this promising improvement, these authors still favor use of an 'ideal' object model, in which Location is ignored, over a 'real' object model which includes Location.

14.3.5 *Proposed ISP methodology improvements*

In the context of this book, the single, most important change needed is to improve the treatment of Location as a factor in identifying elements of the Strategic IS Plan. Figure 14.4 illustrates the Location Dimension in relation to ISP.

A second area of change is the involvement of the ISP team in BPR or BPI (Business Process Improvement) studies.

The third important change is to capture a better balance of all types of Information System that might be needed, and to avoid over-concentration on commercial TP systems.

The overall task structure is not altered, but the orientation of certain tasks is somewhat changed.

- now Task 2 (formerly, Analysis of Business Strategy) is re-named 'Analysis of Business Strategy and Processes'. The additional tasks are described in section 14.4.1 below.
- Task 3 (formerly, Collection of Information Needs and Priorities) is re-named 'Information Needs and Location Analysis'. This represents the greater emphasis to be placed on where the users of the information are located and where the source of the original data lies. This is discussed in section 14.4.2 below.
- Task 5 (Formalization of Structure of Information Needs) retains its name, but the scope of 'Structure' is extended to include a Location model. This is discussed in section 14.4.3 below.

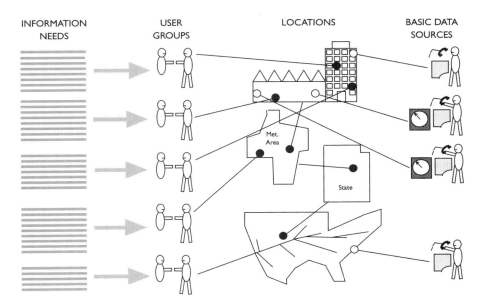

Figure 14.4 The Location Dimension in Information Needs.

- Task 6 (formerly, Identification of Areas for more Detailed Analysis) is re-named 'Identification of Clusters for Future Development and Distribution'. The clusters are formed at multiple levels in order to distinguish IS areas for each of the following purposes:

  - Network – areas that might justify being on different networks
  - Analysis – areas that are logically separate enough to form separate sub-projects for further Analysis
  - Shared Data – areas that could be regarded as potentially separate databases
  - Sub-system – areas that could be regarded as different sub-systems by virtue of their data coverage, application style, alignment with pre-packaged solutions.

  This multi-level clustering is discussed further in section 14.4.4 below.

- Task 7 (formerly, Identification of Natural Systems and Data Stores) is re-named 'Identification of Natural Systems'. A wider view of 'Natural Systems' is taken here which includes data maintenance systems. This is discussed further in section 14.4.5 below.

The new task list is as follows:

1. Scope and Planning of the Study
2. Analysis of Business Strategy and Processes
3. Information Needs and Location Analysis
4. Assessment of Existing and Planned Information Systems
5. Formalization of Structure of Information Needs
6. Identification of Clusters for Future Development and Distribution
7. Identification of Natural Systems
8. Proposal of a Technical Architecture
9. Identification of Organizational Implications
10. Identification of Projects
11. Assembly of a Strategy Plan.

The content of the new/amended tasks 2, 3 and 7, and recommended changes within other tasks to allow for the Location dimension, are detailed in section 14.4 below.

14.4 DESCRIPTION OF INDIVIDUAL TECHNIQUES

14.4.1 *Involvement in BPR/BPI*

We are not suggesting here that BPR/BPI techniques should replace the use of methods such as Mission/Objectives/Strategies, CSFs, SWOT, etc. – the techniques proposed are additional and complementary to these. The precise sequence in which the different sub-tasks should be performed is not predictable, and depends on the situation in the business at the time.

The initial Scope and Planning task will consider the timing of the ISP study in relation to any BPR or BPI work. It is a possibility that the Board will decide to incorporate a BPR study as a preliminary to ISP; or it may limit the project to a study of areas where particular opportunities are offered by IT.

Figure 14.5 shows a possible dependency structure of sub-tasks in the revised Task 2 (Analysis of Business Strategy and Processes), assuming that this task has been aligned with BPR/BPI work. Each of the seven sub-tasks is described below.

Identifying key processes

This means identifying what is 'mission-critical', i.e. the processes without which the organization could not do business. To many businesses, the threat of losing Customers drives many of the priorities. Key processes are likely to be in the areas nearest to the primary value chain, and will very often have stringent timing requirements.

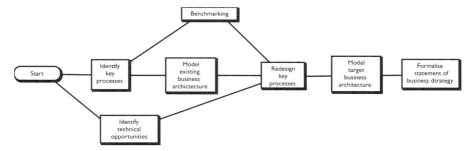

Figure 14.5 Sub-task Structure of 'Analyze Business Strategy and Processes'.

Identifying technical opportunities

ISP methods tend to be relatively strict in their adherence to the principle of 'business needs before technical solutions'. However, there is often a lot of pressure on management to consider the business opportunities of adopting a particular new technology, such as fast data communications, intelligent data capture devices, multimedia, etc. In many businesses, information itself is often one of the main commodities being traded, and is itself part of the value chain. Much of the potential cost-benefit of today's IS arises from the enabling power of Data Communications.

We still take the view that Business requirements should be paramount, but that technical opportunism in connection with a mission-critical requirement should not be inhibited. We advocate early use of Delphi techniques, in which imminent technology leaps are discussed and then examined for potential opportunity for the organization.

Benchmarking against other similar organizations

This depends on defining suitable measures of performance and getting data from associated companies, public sources or information brokers. It can involve considerable elapsed time, as scanning of data about competitors is becoming increasingly difficult.

Modeling existing business architecture

Modeling requires a suitable set of concepts and diagrams, but the concepts used for the process side in many ISP methods are generally weak or little-used. Process Dependency and Work Flow diagramming techniques are the most suitable conventions available. Recently, a very large number of proposals for Process Modeling have appeared (e.g. Spurr *et al.*, 1994), but no clear standard seems yet to have emerged.

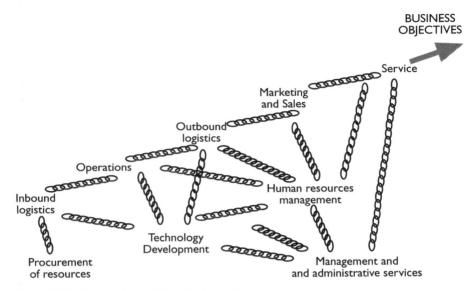

Figure 14.6 Typical Primary Value Chain in a Business.

Redesigning the key processes

Process Redesign usually succeeds by rationalizing Process Flows on or near the Primary Value Chain of a Business, which is typically the main route running from Supply to Customers. In Figure 14.6, the uppermost sequence of links, starting from Procurement of Resources, would be regarded as primary. A common result of such redesign has been that Groups of business partners, which were formerly external to the Organization's IS, must now be included in Process Models, and hence involved more closely in the planning of the Organization's IS.

Modeling target business architecture

This involves building a model of the re-engineered processes using the same concepts as for the existing architecture. The two models should be compared and the proposed improvements checked.

Formalization of business strategy

An organization may have a formal statement of its Mission, Objectives, Strategies and Critical Success Factors (MOSC for short) before involvement in BPR/BPI. In fact the BPR/BPI exercise may be constrained by such a statement.

Following BPR/BPI, however, amendments and greater details of the Business Strategy are likely to be established. Besides the basic 'MOSC', the organization may develop Goals and Action Plans, Cycles of Planning and Control, and Process Dependencies.

The relevance of the Location Dimension at the Business Strategy level is not necessarily of prime importance, but an expanding business may well set itself the objective of being 'Geography-proof'. This is used in the sense that remoteness is not an obstacle to the organization doing business. Competitive edge is also often gained by the effectiveness of the organization's communication with its customers, its suppliers, its own workforce and its means of collecting data, all of which is location-dependent.

Whitten, Bentley and Barlow's 'Enterprise Network Model' (Whitten *et al.*, 1994), which was introduced in Chapter 2, offers a high-level management view of relevant business locations. The case study example diagrams in Chapter 2 demonstrate this.

14.4.2 *Information needs and location analysis*

An 'Information Need' is defined as any expressed requirement of a user for information, as long as it can be justified by the fact that it supports one of the following measurements:

- progress against a mission statement, objective, strategy, goal or action plan
- the status or level of a critical success factor, inhibitor or assumption
- evaluation of a documented critical decision
- execution of a business process on a value chain
- performance of a required and documented planning and control function.

A collection of Information Needs may include several different types. Some of the most common types are:

- key statistics (single figure indicators, trends over time, comparisons between categories)
- alarms and exception messages and reports
- formal tabular reports
- interactive forms (on a video screen)
- data files (or views or extracts)
- alerter signals.

Some needs may be expressed as general descriptions of some area of data, e.g. 'profitability'.

Many needs may share the same underlying data – sometimes one need may be simply a summarized form of another more detailed need that is required by a different set of users.

The 'name' of an Information Need can be described in two parts:

1. the name of the attribute or group of attributes (e.g. 'staff absence')
2. the 'breakdown', which indicates the detail and periodicity needed (e.g. 'by department by month').

For each Information Need, a number of attributes may be relevant:

- Title (description and breakdown)
- User(s) who have declared that they require it (initials or roles)
- User Location
- Type (categories such as measurement, transaction, exception, summary)
- Volume – average, peak, growth rate – per time interval (see below)
- Time Interval (e.g. hourly, daily, yearly or *ad hoc*)
- Response Time (e.g. sub-second, overnight)
- Up-to-dateness (e.g. up to the second or 'as at' some cut-off time)
- Interaction Mode (e.g. paper, keyboard/screen, touch screen, process control display, robotic interface, alarm, etc).
- Process (the real-world goings-on that the users want information about)
- Process Location (i.e. the source of the information)
- Objective, CSF, etc. which this Need helps the user to monitor
- Importance Factor/Priority (based on the above)
- Current Coverage (e.g. existing system)
- System Replacement Priority (based on the above)
- Overall Priority.

The set of Information Needs that have been collected for an individual User (or all the Users working on a Process) can be documented in a CASE tool or on a paper form. The example in Figure 14.7 shows how some of the Information Needs in the ABC software company (described in Chapter 2) could be entered.

Information Need	Function Requiring it	Location	Level S/P/C/O	MOSC item Supported	Current System	Impor-tance	Dissat-isfaction	Priority Factor
Profitability by Product Group (M)	Manage Product Gp	HQ Board HQ Fin	P	Obj- ROC > 15%	none	4	3	12
Market Share by Product Group (Q)	Manage Product Gp	HQ Mktg	S	Obj- Mkt share>30%	none	4	3	12
Beta test site assessments (W)	Implement Product	Lab Mgmt	C	CSF- success reports from beta test sites	WP and email	5	1	5
New commitments (D)	Gain Commitment	Reg S Off HS Sls	O	Goal- each sales region's target	Sales processing	3	2	6
Product Development Progress report (W)	Implement Product	Lab, HQ Mktg	C	Goal - each prod devt team's target	Project Manager Workbench	3	1	3

Figure 14.7 Extract from the Information Needs List for ABC Software Co.

The total set of the whole Organization's Information needs can usefully be arranged on an Information Needs Map, the format of which is shown in Figure 14.8. The columns represent the top level functions of the organization, while the rows represent the four management categories:

- Strategic (top)
- Planning and Analysis, alias Tactical
- Control and Monitoring, alias Operational Control
- Operational.

This grid is used here so that the mapping between Information Needs here and Natural Systems later in the ISP process can be compared (see section 14.4.5 below). The letters shown indicate that different users may have different needs within one grid cell.

Some additional comments are required on the two Location entries used with Information Needs. The first Location is that of the users who need the Information. It is not so much a purely geographical location as a 'type of workplace' or 'user group'. Examples are 'Head Office' 'Finance Department' 'Salaries Section' 'Sales Office' 'Customer Premises' 'Home' 'Mobile' 'Factory Floor Location' 'On Site (e.g. Construction Location)'.

The other Location applies to the 'sources' of the information. This can either apply to the location of the 'process' of collecting information (e.g. by a human taking readings or transactions), or the location of automatic measuring equipment.

14.4.3 *Including the location dimension in the information structure*

Most ISP methods include the preparation of an 'overview' Information model incorporating major Entity Types, though some stop short at a simpler form which is only broken down to 'Subject Data Areas'. In either case the model assumes a logically centralized single collection of data, since physical location is not considered an issue at this stage.

However, matrices are commonly drawn up showing how the Entity Types (or Subject Data Areas) support Information Needs, which **are** Location-dependent. Obviously, every Information Need should be supported by at least one Entity Type. Also, every Entity Type should support at least one Need (or it is not 'of interest to the organization'). Some Needs may require a 'join' of two or more Entity Types.

Using the connections between Needs and Locations, the use of Entity Types at different Locations can be expressed in an Entity Type/Location matrix – an example from the ABC software company is shown in Figure 14.9.

	Division Management	Product Management	Selling	Designing	Pricing	Purchasing	Communicate
S - Strategic	******(CEO) ******(MD)	******(PD)		********	*****	*******	
P - Plan & Anal	****** ******** ***** *******	***** ******** ********	******(SD) ******(RSM)	******** ******** ****** *****	******** ******** ******** ******** *****	******** ******** ********	*****
C - Control & monitor	****** ******* ****	****** ******* ***** *****	****** ******** ******* ******** ******** *****	******** ***** ******	****** ***** ******	******** ***** ***** ********	****** ******** ********* *******
O - Operational	******* ******	******** ****** **** ********	****** ********	***** ******** ****** **********		****** **** ********	******** ****** ***** ****

Figure I4.8 Example Layout Pattern for an Information Needs Map.

Location -> Entity Type	H Auckland	Research Lab P.N.	User Site	RSO Perth	RSO Adelaide	RSO Melb'n	RSO Sydney	RSO Brisbane	RSO Auckland	RSO W'ngton	RSO Ch'ch
Advert Medium	X										
Commitment	X			X	X	X	X	X	X	X	X
Competitor	X	X									
Competitor Product	X	X									
Customer	X		X	X	X	X	X	X	X	X	X
Customer Survey	X		X	X	X	X	X	X	X	X	X
Design Project	X	X	X								
Financial Transac'n	X										
Geographic Zone	X										
Market	X										
Market Need	X										
Market Research	X										
Portfolio Strategy	X										
Product	X	X									
Product Application	X	X	X								
Product Group	X	X									
Product Price	X			X	X	X	X	X	X	X	X
Purchase Order	X	X									
Sales Target	X			X	X	X	X	X	X	X	X
Supplier	X	X									
Supplier Product	X	X									

Figure 14.9 Entity Type/Location Matrix for ABC Software Co.

← Business → ← ──────── Scope of company A management control ────→ ← External →
   partners   info sources

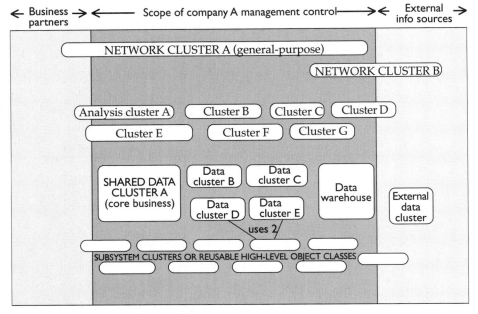

Figure 14.10 Four Levels/Types of Cluster.

14.4.4 *Clustering IS requirements*

The 'engine room' of most ISP methods is a 'clustering' of the information requirements collected so that the IS Plan can identify smaller units of further development work which are relatively self-contained and which can be packaged as separate Projects.

A problem with many of the existing methods is that they only provide one level of clustering, namely into 'Business Areas' for detailed Analysis. But as we discussed in the previous chapter, this is often too strict a view of the development life-cycle.

The method proposed here allows for potentially four levels of clusters (Figure 14.10).

1. Network – these are sub-divisions of the business for which it makes sense to have separate Networks, designed independently (they can always interlink through Gateways or Routers). Examples are where there are totally different kinds of business, or autonomous units managed at arm's length. In most organizations that are not conglomerates, there will only be one Network cluster.

2. Analysis – these are parts of the business on which it makes sense to do Analysis together. This occurs where groups of departments or activities

have their own processes and data, betweeen which there is relatively light interaction.

3. Shared Data – these are parts of the overall stored data requirement which it makes sense to design together. This is determined not only by the logical separation as in Analysis clusters, but also by the type of data and the responsibility for their management. Shared Data clusters are usually sub-sets of the scope of Analysis clusters.

4. Sub-systems – these are parts of the overall IS processing function which it makes sense to design together as a System or Sub-system (always smaller than Analysis clusters, sometimes within a Shared Data Cluster, sometimes using several).

Clustering in many ISP methods also tends to be based only on the Matrix of Entity Type versus Function or Process. The problems with this are:

- It takes no account of Location, therefore is of limited use where distribution is likely to be an issue – which nowadays means in most cases!
- It suffers from the fact that many of the Functions in such Matrices tend to be artificial information-handling ones of the 'Maintain XXXXX Data' variety, which skew the clustering against genuine coincidences of information use.

The second problem can be helped by taking an Object Oriented approach to ISP, so we will consider two complementary clustering approaches, i.e. the established Entity Type/Function Matrix and Object/Location multi-dimensional distance function.

Clustering by Entity Type / Function Matrix

The Entity Type/Function Matrix (Entity/Function or 'CRUD' matrix for short) has each Entity Type as a row, while the functions which form the columns are those at the bottom level of the Function Hierarchy for the organization (i.e. the lowest level of task in business terms before starting to talk in data processing terms). An example for the ABC software company is shown as Figure 14.11.

The letters C, R, U or D in the cells of this matrix denote whether the Function Creates, Reads, Updates or Deletes instances of the Entity Type. If more than one letter is applicable, the most significant one is entered – the significance order being C, D, U, R. Every Entity Type should be created (C) by one Function (sometimes more, but never zero!), and used (R, U, D) by at least one other. This process provides a further validation in both Entity Type and Function models.

Clustering is a process of reordering the rows and columns of the CRUD matrix to form clusters such that most C, D and U cells (and as many Rs as possible) are grouped into rectangular blocks, preferably arranged on the downward diagonal (Figure 14.12).

Entity Type \ Function	Amend Contract	Analyze Research	Assess Credit	Communicate	Conceive Product	Develop Product	Develop Spec ific'n	Develop Tech Sale	Estab Sales Target	Gain Commit ment	Identify Needs	Implement Product	Manage Pub. Rel	Manage Prod Group	Manage Vert Mkt	Negotiate Sale	Plan Research	Purchasing	Set Prices	Track Design
Ad. Medium				U																
Commitment	C					C	C			C						C		C		
Competitor											C							C		
Compet. Prod											C									
Customer	U								C					C						
Cust. Survey									C	U		C			C					
Design Project								C							C					U
Financial Tr.			R													C		C		
Geog. Zone																C		C		
Market															C					
Market Need		U									C									
Mkt Research		U																		
Portfolio Strat										U				C					C	
Product					C							U							R	
Prod. Applic'n					C							U								
Product Group					C							C		U						
Product Price																			C	
Purch. Order	C					U	C			U						U		C		
Sales Target									C											
Supplier																		C		
Supplier Prod																		C		

Figure 14.11 ABC Software Co's Entity Type/Function (CRUD) Matrix before Clustering.

Function / Entity Type	Gain Commitment	Amend Contract	Develop Product	Purchasing	Negotiate Sale	Develop Spec'ific'n	Conceive Product	Implement Product	Manage Vert Mkt	Estab Sales Target	Assess Credit	Manage Prod Group	Set Prices	Manage Pub. Rel	Communicate	Identify Needs	Analyze Research	Plan Research	Develop Tech Sale	Track Design
Commitment	C	C	C	C	C	C														
Purch. Order	U	C	U	C	U	C														
Supplier Prod				C																
Supplier				C																
Financial Tr.				C	C						R									
Product							C	U					R							
Prod.Applic'n							C	U												
Product Group							C	C				U								
Cust. Survey	U							C												
Geog_Zone								C	C											
Market									C											
Customer		U							C	C	U									
Sales Target	U									C										
Portfolio Strat												C	C							
Product Price													C							
Ad. Medium												C			U					
Competitor																C				
Compet. Prod																C				
Market Need																C	U			
Mkt Research																	U			
Design Project																			C	U

Figure 14.12 ABC Software Co.'s Entity Type/Function (CRUD) Matrix after Clustering.

Automated tools are often used for the clustering process, but manual interpretation and adjustment is always recommended. A frequent problem is that of 'hinge' Entity Types, which have Cs or Us against many Functions and have to be dropped out of the clustering to form a 'hinge' at the bottom of the matrix. Examples often have names such as 'Plan' and 'Diary Entry'.

Clustering by Object / Location Matrix

In this alternative matrix, high-level Object Classes form the rows, and User Groups (or Device Workplaces) form the columns. Following Jacobson, the Object Classes include Entity, Control and Interface Objects. The Entity Objects include all the simple CRUD as methods. Control Objects include multi-object transactions and event triggering. User Interface Objects which are of major importance are also usefully included, since they are strongly tied to the User Group Locations.

The Location columns include all the generic workplaces for users and sources of the information. Cell entries are simply Xs (with optional little xs for minor involvement).

Clustering in this case is not symmetrical as above, and is a one-dimensional grouping of the Objects. The basis for clustering is the Association Factor between objects, based on the level of message passing between pairs of Objects. An example for a company operating in the Financial Futures market is shown in Figure 14.13.

Inter-cluster Dependencies

For Object-based clusters, the flow of messages between Objects in different Clusters can be accumulated into 'Inter-cluster Dependencies'. Obviously it is part of the clustering task to minimize these.

	Object Classes	User Groups Feed Suppliers	Dealers	Managers	Support Team
IFH	Input Feed Handling	X	x	x	x
DLS	Dealing Support		X	x	
CAM	Customer Account Maintenance		x	x	X
XPM	Exposure Position Maintenance		x	X	
XLA	Exposure Limit Adjustment		x	X	x
MGQ	Management Enquiry			X	

Suggested clustering:

A) Input Feed Handling
B) Dealing Support
C) Everything else

Figure 14.13 Example of an Object/User Association Factor Matrix.

On the clustered Entity Type/Function CRUD matrix, Inter-cluster Dependencies are suggested by the arrangement of the Rs which lie outside the clusters. These represent the fact that data is created/maintained by functions in one Cluster but is read by functions in a different Cluster. To draw these dependencies on the clustered CRUD matrix, L-shaped lines are drawn from one cluster to another via each group of off-diagonal Rs. The direction of the dependency is horizontal first, then vertical.

Figure 14.14 shows a simplified example of this for the ABC software company. The original CRUD entries have been removed and cluster boundaries drawn in. A name has been given to each cluster except two, where more detailed analysis is needed.

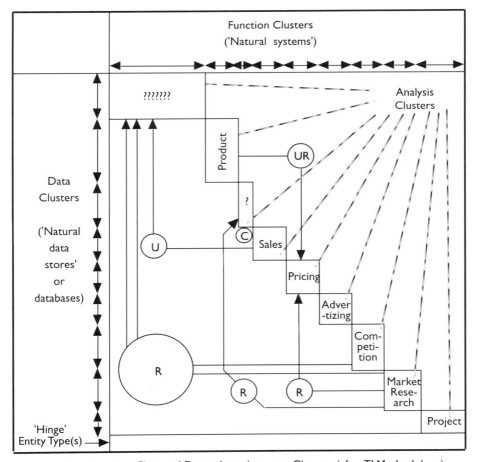

Figure 14.14 Information Flow and Dependency between Clusters (after TI Methodology).

14.4.5 *Identifying natural systems*

The results of the various clustering exercises are used not only to define reduced scopes for follow-on projects in the IS Plan, but to identify 'Natural Systems'. These Natural Systems can be identified as follows:

- Whole clusters which contain a homogeneous processing pattern
- Subsets of clusters where the processing pattern is split, e.g.
  - 'hot' versus 'cool'
  - formatted data versus text/multimedia
  - TP versus Information Retrieval
- Major 'off-diagonal' clusters of R entries
- Hinge entity types.

The 'off-diagonal' clusters are often recognized as Decision Support systems, while the 'hinges' can be interpreted as general or cooperative systems such as Project Planning, Diary/Calendar, Workflow and Groupware systems.

A set of Natural Systems may be represented diagrammatically on the grid of the Information Needs Map discussed in section 14.4.2 above. Figure 14.15 is a possible Natural Systems Architecture for the ABC software company. Note how the informal 'Contract support' system forms a long sausage that crosses several Function columns at the middle level of management.

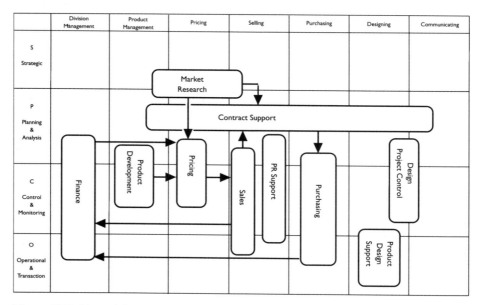

Figure 14.15 Natural Systems Architecture Diagram for ABC Software Co. (after TI Methodology).

This diagram is commonly used when presenting ISP results to management, to demonstrate schematically how a proposed set of systems can cover the set of Information Needs.

14.4.6   *Technical architecture planning*

This task of assessing the technical requirements of future systems which may support the defined Business Areas is not well covered in many methodologies. Some do include an approach to Technical Architecture Planning, but their methods of deciding on the desired level of distribution are often sketchy, and the development of candidate architectures owes more to personal conviction than to reasoned evaluation. However, any Information Strategy Plan ought to be checked for technical feasibility. This area is the primary topic of the next chapter.

14.4.7   *Organizational implications*

It is also well understood that a new medium-term plan for IS development is likely to have significant impacts on the job structure of many user staff who will be involved in the new IS. In fact, there may be organizational infeasibilities just as there may be technical infeasibilities. BPR will have already identified a number of human and organizational implications. In an ISP exercise, we concentrate on those humans and groups whose work is directly involved with IS. This means not just the IS Department itself, but all the users whose main job is in handling information and interacting directly with computers (perhaps excepting stand-alone personal computing).

A tool commonly used for this purpose is RAEW Analysis. This involves building a Matrix of Information Management Functions (rows) versus User Groups (see example in Figure 14.16). The Information Management Functions (or jobs) are relatively standard from Organization to Organization. Each cell consists of a 2×2 grid showing four possible codes:

R   Responsibility – the person(s) responsible for this job being done successfully
A   Authority – the person(s) with authority to sanction work on this job
E   Expertise – the person(s) qualified to do the job
W   Work – the person(s) who actually do the job.

Classic problems are suggested by A without R, or W without E, or vice versa. Also, if one User only has R and A for a Function, then there must be another User or Group to which it delegates E and W. The planning process involves changing the Matrix which represents the current position to an improved Matrix (Figure 14.17), by changing the scope of the Information Management work done by some User Groups, or creating new Groups. Obviously these changes have to be made subsequently in the real world!

IS Functions \ I.S. Orgn Units	Board of Dirs	V.P. of I.S.	IS Dept Head Off.	IS Production	IS Marketing	Internal Consult.	Maintenance	Network Group	Operations Section
Long Term Planning	R A	R E W	E W	E W	E E W				
Tactical Planning			R A E W	R E E W	R E W				
Systems Development				R A E W			E W		
Development Coordination				R A E W					
Systems Packaging					R A E				E W
Marketing Sales			R		R A E W				
Network Management								R A E W	
Doctor/Office Management			A	R	W		W	E	
User Training					R E W	R A E W			
User Support					E W	R A E W			
Operations/Network			R A E W					R A E W	R A E W
Distribution Support			R A E W	E W					
Facilities Management	A	R	R E W						

Figure 14.16 Example of an Initial RAEW Matrix for an IS Organization.

IS Functions \ I.S. Orgn Units	Board of Dirs	V.P. of I.S.	IS Dept Head Off.	IS Production	IS Marketing	Internal Consult.	Maintenance	Network Group	Operations Section
Long Term Planning	A	R A / E W	E W						
Tactical Planning		A	R / E W						
Systems Development			A	R / E W			E W		
Development Coordination			R A	E W					
Systems Packaging			A		E				R / E W
Marketing			A						
Sales					R / E W	E W			
Network Management								R A / E W	
Doct/Office Management			A	R / W	W		W	E	
User Training				E W	E W	R A / E W			
User Support				E W	E W	R A / E W		E W	
Operations/Network								R A / E W	R A / E W
Distribution Support			R A	E W					
Facilities Management	A		E W						

Figure 14.17 Example of a Target RAEW Matrix for an IS Organization.

The Location Dimension affects RAEW analysis, in that the User Groups used in the analysis are the very means by which Location is represented in a location-dependent ISP study.

14.5 STRATEGIC PLANNING IN THE CASE STUDIES

14.5.1 *Mr A*

Most of the formal part of Mr A's ISP could be written down fairly quickly. However, his business is currently very low-volume, and it is too early to draw diagrams which suggest strong patterns. Much of his activity will be of the type 'do whatever we have to do'. That said, some of his predictable Information Needs can be listed, together with sources. As far as clustering is concerned, a few administrative areas can be identified, and the rest is 'informal document and plan processing'.

14.5.2 *Bay Organic Produce Cooperative*

The cooperative's way of working, by contrast, is relatively settled, although there are still a few peripheral but important areas (e.g. Overseas Buyers) where there may be few patterns and low volumes. The CSFs are likely to highlight good contact with both Farmers and Buyers, so it would be unwise if the Coop were to draw the boundaries for its ISP to exclude these. The critical management decision, mentioned in previous chapters, is whether staff will specialize or not. This decision has a profound effect on many subsequent decisions.

14.5.3 *Detox Pharmaceuticals*

Cost-competitiveness is very high on the list of CSFs, and movements in Market Share will be key measurements. The priority for systems is therefore likely to be in the Sales area, but the decision timescale is daily rather than second-by-second, which only really applies to Process Control.

14.5.4 *Electric House*

In the IS Planning timescale, success of the merger is probably the paramount CSF, and this offers really challenging design problems. As with Detox, Market Share will also be a key factor. On a shorter timescale, managing Store Inventory will demand good on-line checkout data collection to detect early when sales patterns are atypical and may result in empty shelves. A large amount of the user access to data will be limited to local sites only.

14.5.5 *Commonwealth Open Polytechnic*

IS priorities could vary depending on the charter of the COP, and how it regards the competing objectives of course quality, growth in student numbers, cost-effectiveness to sponsors, etc. One strategy may be to keep administration simple and decentralized, as experienced staff may be hard to attract to Broken Hill. This may place a high priority on integrated capture of all details on enrolments, course performance, etc. User access patterns are split between local responsibility for enrolments and tutoring, and central responsibilities for course planning and assessment.

14.5.6 *National Environmental Protection Board*

The goal of a paperless office sets a stiff target for IS design, especially as a high proportion of the Board's work is not particularly structured to a fixed pattern. This suggests that 'hinge' Entity Types will be critical, with importance on groupware and diary operation on long projects and exercises. As with the COP, local and central access will overlap.

14.6 EXERCISES

What events might lead an organization to initiate an ISP exercise?

What are the outputs of an ISP exercise?

What is the difference between 'ambition' and 'urgency' when describing alternative IS Strategies?

Discuss the importance of risk when evaluating IS Strategies.

The ISP market seems to be sewn up between large Accounting firms and Software Houses. Is this desirable?

Is BPR anything more than a slogan used to justify drastic cost-cutting?

What are the main shortcomings in earlier ISP methods?

Can one capture any useful location-dependent requirements during Analysis of Business Strategy and Processes?

What options are available when the Board of Directors does not have a formal Business Strategy?

10. The chief sponsor of an ISP study is keen to look for opportunities of gaining competitive advantage from new IT techniques, but is harder to pin down on business benefits. What would you suggest?

11. Why does an 'Information Need' have potentially **two** locations associated with it?

12. Draw up a Value Chain for Detox, and suggest where Business Processes might be improved.

13. Describe the cycles of Planning and Control for Electric House's operations.

14. What are the four types of cluster in IS requirements?

15. What is the significance of 'off-diagonal' clusters of R entries?

16. How could a 'hinge' entity type be interpreted?

ASSIGNMENT TASK

Note: this series of sub-tasks might be suitable for a longer student assignment.

A1. Using your chosen case study, write down a formal list of Mission, Objectives, Strategies and Critical Success Factors/Inhibitors (MOSC).

A2. Indicate the main means of measuring how the organization is doing against these factors.

A3. Make up a list of 20–30 business functions which cover the business processes. Start by drawing up a function hierarchy if desired.

A4. Draw up an Information Needs List for part of the organization, bringing in at least one Need relevant to the MOSC list.

A5. Create a rough list of 20–30 Entity Types which would support the needs.

A6. Draw up a matrix of Entity Type against Location.

A7. Draw up a spreadsheet showing Entity Type against Function, marking in the CRUD entries.

A8. Cluster the matrix by shuffling the rows and columns of the spreadsheet.

A9. Identify a set of Natural Systems.

FURTHER READING

Bartholomew, D. and Caldwell, B. (1995) Top priority loses its lustre (article on BPR). *Infotech supplement to The Dominion (NZ)*.

IBM (1985) *Planning for Distributed Information Systems*, Report no. GE20-0655-1.

Jacobson, I. *et al.* (1994) *The Object Advantage – Business Process Reengineering with Object Methodology*, Addison-Wesley, Reading, MA.

JMA (1987) *ISP Handbook*, James Martin Associates.

Martin, J. (1982) *Strategic Data Planning Methodologies*, Prentice Hall, Englewood Cliffs, NJ.

Martin, J. (1990) *Information Engineering I*, Prentice Hall, Englewood Cliffs, NJ.

Morton, M. S. (ed) (1991) *The Corporation of the 1990s*, Oxford University Press, Oxford.

Spurr, K. *et al.* (eds) (1994) *Software Assistance for Business Re-Engineering*, Wiley, UK.

Tozer, E. (1988) *Planning for Effective Business Information Systems*, Pergamon Press, Oxford.

15 Preparing a technical architecture plan

15.1 RATIONALE FOR THIS DESIGN STAGE

The introduction of a Technical Architecture stage is relatively novel in IS Design methodologies. Traditionally the thinking has been 'settle all the logical things first, and leave physical decisions until as late as possible'. The assumption behind this view seems to be that the lead times between design decision and implementation are always shorter for installing equipment or tuning performance than for designing databases or software.

In practice, many equipment or tuning design decisions, especially with Network development, may have timescales as long as, or longer, than Database or Software development projects. Not all physical design decisions can be telescoped down into a short, late and frenzied bout of design.

A Technical Architecture is an overview of the longer-term goals for hardware, software and communications infrastructure for an organization, which reflects the organization's IS strategy. It is a generic description of the type of facilities that are planned to be used. There are no names of products or suppliers, and even capacities should be left flexible. The Technical Architecture forms a framework which guides, and helps to evaluate, some of the later, more specific design decisions.

15.2 INPUTS TO THIS DESIGN STAGE

15.2.1 Starting points

In some methodologies, Technical Architecture Planning is counted as part of ISP (Information Strategy Planning) as described in the previous chapter. In other methodologies ISP stops with the identification of Clusters for further analysis. Inevitably, organizations following these latter methods often then initiate a Technical Architecture Planning exercise.

In either of the above situations the starting point is much the same. However, in some cases a Technical Architecture Plan, or a review, can be developed outside the orbit of an ISP exercise. This sometimes occurs where an organization has already carried out some form of 'logical only' review of its information. In such a case the designers will have to establish some of the following starting-point details before proceeding.

Performance requirements

At some previous stage we need to have established the performance and behavior requirements for each Natural System. At this stage we are more interested in system averages than in individual transaction and query types. Figures needed include user response, peak volumes, availability, accuracy, security, development timescale, risk – all the sorts of things emphasized by Gilb and listed in Chapter 13 above. Once again a formal means of documentation is useful (see the example in Figure 15.1).

Location model

This was introduced in the previous chapter. We use a combined model of Geographic Locations, Location Types and User Groups, in a somewhat similar way to that suggested by Whitten, Bentley and Barlow (Whitten et al., 1994), but with additional views. The Location information can also be documented as a

NATURAL SYSTEM: Purchasing Support	UNIT OF MEASURE	TARGET VALUE	WORST ACCEPTABLE
USER RESPONSE	Seconds at non-peak hour	2	5
	Seconds at peak hour	5	15
THROUGHPUT	Transactions per hour	2000	1500
	Prob. of overnight completion	99	97
AVAILABILITY	MTBF hours	1000	500
	MTTR minutes	10	30
ACCURACY	Percent of uncorrupted output	99.9	99.5
UP-TO-DATENESS	Hours	24	48
SECURITY	Mean time between breaches	10000	8000
	DoD Classification	IIb	IIa
USER FRIENDLINESS	Days of Training Course	1	2
	Percent of staff OK in 1 week	80%	60%
PORTABILITY	$$ to move to another platform	5000	1000
ENHANCEABILITY	$$ to add benchmark feature	10000	12000
DEVELOPMENT COST	$$ to get 1st system operational	50000	60000
DEVELOPMENT TIMESCALE	Elapsed months	6	7
DEVELOPMENT RISK	Prob. of completion in < +10%	98	95
	Percent of system up in time	80	65
	Prob of cost within budget +10%	90	80
MAINTENANCE COST	$$ per annum	50000	70000
VALUE FOR MONEY	Return on investment %p.a.		

Figure 15.1 Natural System Performance Checklist.

User Group/Location matrix such as in the example from the ABC software company in Figure 15.2.

We also need to record the volumes of the data arriving or being used through each User Group. Whitten, Bentley and Barlow (Whitten *et al.*, 1994) include a diagram marking volumes on links between geographic locations. These volume figures should be available from the Information Needs List.

Clusters and natural systems

We finished the previous chapter with a set of Clusters at different levels. For Technical Architecture, the preferred level of clustering is that of 'Natural Systems' (which may include some of the Natural Databases as 'Data Server Systems') separately from the functions which use them.

User access patterns

The user activity requirement for each Natural System by each User Group can be expressed in a Matrix. The example in Figure 15.3 is based on the Financial Futures trading company introduced in the previous chapter.

A more complex coding system than simple Xs is used here, because the mode of use of the systems can vary from location to location, e.g. local on-line transaction capture, regular reports, *ad hoc* querying across sites, etc. The code is in two parts, the first representing the **type** of access (in fact it is just a slight variation of the CRUD system used in the previous chapter); and the second representing the **locality** of access, i.e. whether the users access only their own local data (L), data from foreign sites occasionally (F), or are equally likely to access data from any site (T). This coding system is also used in later design stages.

Technical opportunities

The philosophy of the 'MIT 90s' model discussed in the previous chapter is that the influence between Business Needs and IT should not be one way. Many methodologies consider, more or less formally, the opportunities for organizational gain that IT can offer. If the IS Designer does not suggest it, the business people certainly will.

There is no obvious formalism for documenting Technical Opportunities. The three-level approach shown in Figure 15.4 is based on O'Brien (1993).

Service Achievement is concerned with the apparent improved service that the organization can operate as a result of the Enabling Technology. Business Opportunity is the real pay-off, the 'bottom line' or the answer to the question 'so what?'.

For a particular organization, the arguments can be summarized as a three column table, in which for each Enabling Technology in column 1, the resulting Service Achievements and Business Opportunities are entered in columns 2 and 3. Most of this information will have been collected in the early stages of an ISP exercise.

User Group	Head Office	Research Lab		Sales Office	Mobile		External Premises	
Location Type		Office	Labs		Car	Home	Supplier	Client
Finance Managers	X							
Receivables Clerks	X							
Payables Clerks	X							
Sales Managers				X				
Salesmen				X	X	X		X
Lab. Managers		X						
Product Researchers		X						
Product Developers			X					
Supplier Contacts							X	

Figure 15.2 User Group/Location Matrix.

Natural System	User Group	Feed Suppliers	Dealers	Dealing Managers	Financial Managers	Support Staff
On-line Feeds		CU L	AB L	BS LT	BS T	S T
Dealing Support			CUA LT	ABS LT	BS T	
Exposure Control			A L	CUABS L	BS LT	S T
Limit Maintenance				UAB L	CU T	
Management Reporting and Query				ABS L	BS T	
Transaction Accounting				BS L	BS T	CUABS T

Key:
    C=Create U=Update/Delete (as in CRUD)
    A=Ad hoc (retrieve 1 at a time)
    B=Browse (retrieve a set of occurrences in some sequence)
    S = Summarise (retrieve summaries over a set of occurrences)

    L=Local (each user to own site)
    F=Foreign (other sites as well as user's own)
    T=Total (access any site's data)

Figure 15.3 Example User Group Access Pattern Matrix.

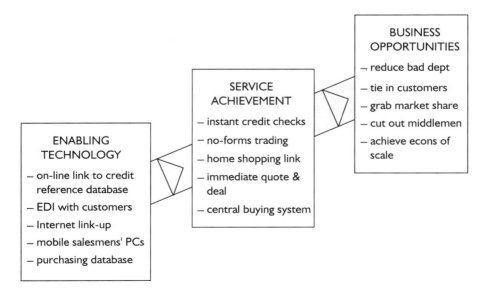

Figure 15.4 Technical Opportunism (based on O'Brien (1993)).

15.2.2 *Nature of the alternatives*

Many earlier texts characterize the Technical Architecture decision as being a straight choice between Distributed and Centralized. In today's world of intelligent workstations and cheap multi-processor-based servers, this is usually too simplistic. One possible alternative is to think in terms of a two-dimensional space of possible solutions (Figure 15.5).

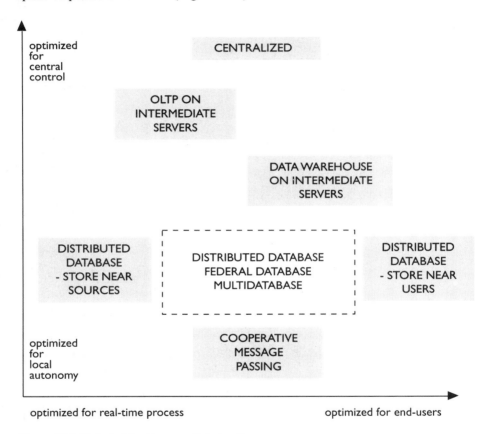

Figure 15.5 Technical Architecture Solution Space.

In one dimension, optimization can favor central control or local autonomy; in the other dimension it can be oriented to a real-time process or to end-user data retrieval.

At the left hand end of the *x*-axis, data is kept as near as possible to where it originates, assuming little or no knowledge of how users want to use the data, and most processing of the data takes place near to the users (Figure 15.6).

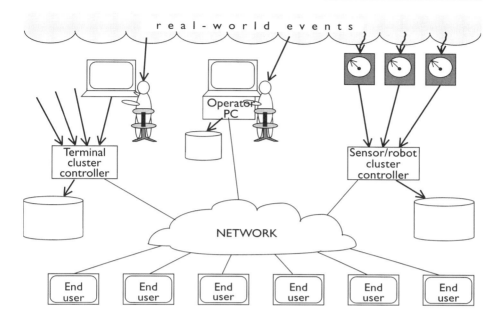

Figure 15.6 Keeping Data Near its Source.

At the right-hand extreme, all the data is automatically processed and shipped to be easily accessible to each user, which assumes advance knowledge of what information the users want (Figure 15.7).

Intermediate solutions may well be cheaper and better (in various ways) than these extremes. A totally centralized solution introduces one single intermediate node (Figure 15.8) but as we all know, this has the drawback of creating a potential bottleneck and a single point of failure which could cause total loss of system availability.

Other intermediate solutions do more or less work at a number of intermediate nodes (e.g. Figure 15.9).

A totally different categorization is provided by the Gartner Client/Server spectrum already introduced in Chapter 8, here reproduced as Figure 15.10. As observed earlier, not all the colors here are truly Client/Server.

A combined set of 'standard' alternatives is shown in the following list. An additional slant has been added in that the 'solution flavors' refer to the immediate, partial or deferred processing of data.

- storage near data sources, processing at clients
- data processed immediately and passed to client workstations
- data processed immediately, passed to one central site, then processed by clients

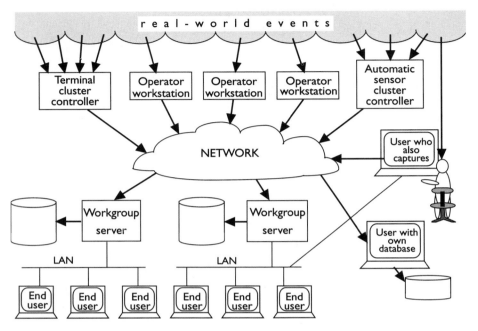

Figure 15.7 Storing Data Near its Users.

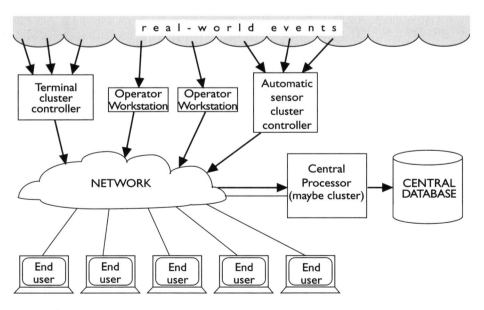

Figure 15.8 Centralized Architecture: Introducing a Single Intermediate Server.

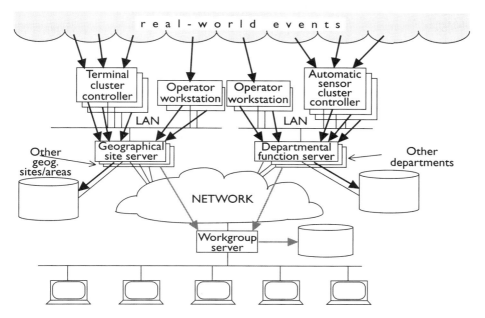

Figure 15.9 Several Intermediate Servers.

- data processed immediately, passed to one central site, then processed at central site from client transaction messages
- data partly processed and cleaned up, passed to a 'data warehouse' located on a workgroup server.

Other flavors can be considered, including replication (or non-replication) of data with immediate (or deferred) propagation of changes to the copies.

Not all these options may be worth considering. Seven or more boxes (as in Figure 15.5) are too many to evaluate. Normal practice is to identify three to five 'serious candidates' and to work through the hardware, software and communications requirements that arise from them.

15.2.3 *Evaluation criteria*

At a high level, we need to evaluate quickly whether a particular alternative architecture is a 'goer' or not. This is more likely to depend on a few key measurements, such as:

- performance on the most frequent transactions which support business activities on the 'primary value chain', e.g. making a quotation for a telephone sales order

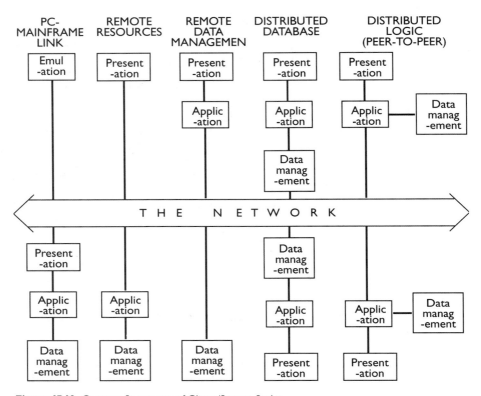

Figure 15.10 Gartner Spectrum of Client/Server Styles.

- business opportunities enabled
- contribution to success or failure of business operations
- level of technical expertise required
- flexibility if the business or technology changes
- the overall security level as seen by the auditors
- the overall cost of the IT infrastructure
- the technical risk involved in the architecture as a whole.

15.3 DESIGN TASKS AT THIS STAGE

15.3.1 *Reviewing involvement of natural systems at different locations*

One can summarize these requirements in a matrix of Natural System by Location, as in the example in Figure 15.11 for the ABC Software Company.

System \ Location	H Auckland	Research Lab P.N.	User Site	RSO Perth	RSO Adelaide	RSO Melb'n	RSO Sydney	RSO Brisbane	RSO Auckland	RSO W'ngton	RSO Ch'ch
Contract Support	X										
Purchasing	X	x		x	x	x	x	x	x	x	x
Finance	X			x	x	x	x	x	x	x	x
Product Devt	X	x	x								
Sales	x			X	X	X	X	X	X	X	X
Pricing	X			x	x	x	x	x	x	x	x
PR Support				X	X	X	X	X	X	X	X
Market Research	X			x	x	x	x	x	x	x	x
Product Design Supp		X	x								
Design Proj Control	x	X	x								

Key: X=major involvement
x=minor involvement

Source: Clustered CRUD matrix
Function / Organisation Unit matrix
Organisation Unit / Location matrix

Figure 15.11 Natural System/Location Matrix for ABC Software Co.

15.3.2 *Consideration of special technical needs of natural systems*

This task involves listing, in purely generic terms, some of the technical components which are 'indicated' in order to meet the requirements of the Natural Systems. This involves preparing a checklist, which is often in table form, of any special requirements that arise from the nature of the Systems identified. Example rows include special terminals, data sharing software, development toolkits, packages, etc. It is not essential to complete every cell in the table, since that may be pre-judging a choice which should be made later in the design process. An example is shown in Figure 15.12, also for ABC Software Co.

Technical opportunism can be considered at this point. Use of leading-edge technology for systems brings not only benefit (in terms of competitive advantage, etc.) but also cost and risk. One wants to encourage technical opportunism with proper cost-benefit consideration, but not technology for technology's (or IT staff's) sake.

15.3.3 *Shortlisting of options*

Ideally, we should consider all the options for each Natural System and then every combination of these for the total management scope. However, it is more common to look for groups of Systems which have similar usage patterns, and to take a 'global' view of the Technical Architecture alternatives, within which different flavored Systems can still co-exist.

Normally, we try to look for a 'short list' of no more than three to five alternative technical architectures. A grouping suggested in the Texas Instruments Information Engineering methodology is:

- minimum technical risk and cost
- white heat of the technological revolution
- middle-of-the-road, a compromise between the above.

An alternative partitioning, more in line with the traditional Distributed versus Centralized argument, is:

- very centralized
- very distributed
- balanced, part-distributed.

A third approach is to take the alternative overall solutions as those which optimize for each of a number of major user groups.

The three to five short-listed architectures will often be a combination of the above three partitionings.

Existing expectations and practices may also impose constraints on a totally free choice, for example:

- most users have PCs on their desks and will not go back to dumb terminals

Technical System Area	Contract Support	Purch-asing	Finance	Product Devt	Sales	Pricing	PR Support	Market Research	Prod Des Support	Des Proj Control
Hardware type									Co-proc'r	
User workstations				Graphics	Mobile	Hand held	Graphics (Design)		Graphics (CASE)	Graphics (CPM)
Comms facilities local									Wireless LAN	
Comms facilities remote					Cellular					
OS type									Unix	
TP Monitor type	Medium concurrency	Medium concurrency								
File Management/ DBMS type									Versioning	
Application software						Quotations Stats	Design DTP		CASE CAD/CAM	Project Control
Development method	Tailored	Package	Package	Tailored	Package	Package	Packages	Packages	Toolkit	Package
Development tools	CASE			4GL		Stats tool				
End User development	Reports	Queries	Queries	75%	Queries	Stats work	90%	80%	Macros	

Figure 15.12 Special Technical Needs of Natural Systems (ABC Software Co).

- users either have Internet, WWW, etc., or know about them, and can't see why their organization should give them any less sophisticated service!
- EDI or Electronic Commerce may be forced on the organization by dominant business partners.

As we eliminate the infeasibilities, we may find that the more extreme architectures are dropped, and then we can explore more subtle intermediate architectures in this area of the decision space.

15.3.4 *Preparation of technical architecture diagrams*

The next task is to complete the details of the hardware, software and communications facility types that would be needed to make each architecture work. It is helpful to do this on a Technical Architecture diagram. The pattern shown in the skeleton in Figure 15.13 (and the subsequent completed examples) is based on the James Martin Associates version of Information Engineering (James Martin Associates, 1987). Other conventions for such diagrams are also possible.

These Technical Architecture diagrams are based on a grid whose rows are a spectrum of group usage of information within the organization. The traditional rows used are 'Shared General', 'Shared Workgroup' and ' Individual', with sometimes 'External' as well. The columns represent styles or categories of

	Process Control	Transaction Processing	Professional Support	Messaging
Shared General				
Shared Workgroup				
Individual Workplace				
(External)				

Figure 15.13 Technical Architecture Diagram: Skeleton Structure.

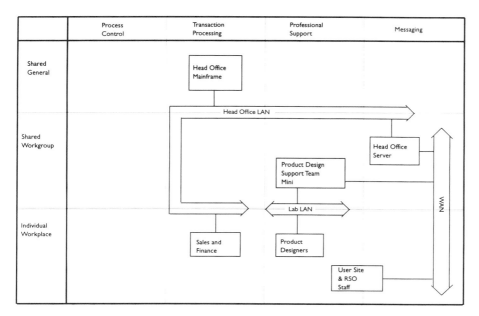

Figure 15.14 Technical Architecture Diagram: Completed Example I (ABC Software Co.).

Information System application, and the titles traditionally used are 'Process Control', 'Transaction Processing', 'Professional Support' and 'Messaging' (though other categorizations may be preferred).

In Figures 15.14 and 15.15, boxes represent computing or other information processing facilities, with larger boxes, usually showing the hardware platform, containing smaller boxes representing significant software or ancillary facilities. Connecting these platforms are 'tubes' which represent communications facilities. The main tubes usually sit horizontally along the boundaries between the rows, but there are usually other tubes both horizontal and vertical (e.g. for MAP messaging between manufacturing process control and TP or management support areas). Figure 15.14 above is based on the ABC Software Co. Figure 15.15 was originally based on an oil refinery.

The usual approach is to draw rough sketches for each of the three to five shortlisted Technical Architectures. In conjunction with the evaluation forms described in section 15.4 below, the alternatives can then be discussed with management, who will usually guide the planner towards the direction they favor.

The Technical Architecture Diagram should not be confused with a Network Diagram – it is a higher-level, and more generic form of documentation, and shows no names of products or suppliers.

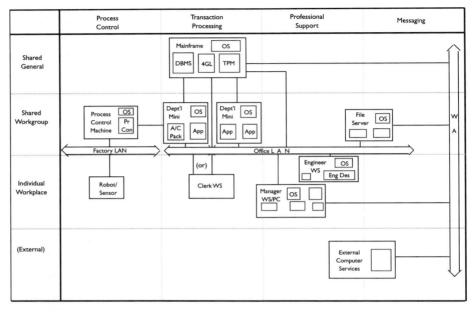

Figure 15.15 Technical Architecture Diagram: Completed Example 2.

15.3.4 *Evaluating alternatives*

Each alternative architecture needs to be evaluated under a number of categories, which cover the criteria listed in section 15.2.3 above. To make it possible to do this evaluation, one may have to assume that one 'might' be using certain typical products, makes and models of hardware and software. But the principle at this stage is still 'no names', because we want to retain the option to go to tender for supply of the Technology, or to evaluate different suppliers' solutions against an independent statement of requirements.

Three evaluation methods, namely Factor Tables, Weighted Evaluation Spreadsheets and Overall Security Reviews are described in the Techniques section in section 15.4 below.

15.4 DESCRIPTION OF INDIVIDUAL TECHNIQUES

Choosing an architecture is rarely a straightforward, deterministic procedure. Not only are there a number of possibly conflicting objectives but the chosen solution has to carry the support of the people that have to make it work. This is why we do not apologize for presenting a number of quite disparate evaluation approaches, all of which have been applied in practice.

The methods that we shall consider are:

- technical conviction
- factor tables (heuristics)
- level of data-sharing analysis
- James Martin's distribution analysis technique
- weighted evaluation spreadsheets
- query performance evaluation
- overall security review
- algorithmic optimization.

15.4.1 *Technical conviction*

This name gives an impression of an obscure criminal judgment, which cynics might say was totally appropriate! However, as stated earlier, the chosen solution has to carry the support of the people that have to make it work, so perhaps we should treat it with some seriousness.

In a recent ISP study which included Technical Architecture, one of the authors found the client IT Manager pressurizing him into a 'centralized IBM mainframe' architecture. The author counter-proposed two other architectures, one (with the help of two Digital salesmen) based on a number of minicomputers, and another based on a network of cooperating OS/2 servers supporting the users' PCs. Even against good cost and performance arguments, the IT Manager won the day through his conviction that he could make the mainframe solution work, but wasn't sure about the others.

More common, and less creditable than the above, is the conviction that some new technology (usually Client/Server or Object Oriented) is THE way to go, regardless of processing patterns. The same author was once asked for advice by a company wanting help on a client/server database with two users, increasing to four, where there was not even a high priority on immediate updating.

15.4.2 *Factor tables (heuristics)*

Moving to a slightly more formal level, some methodologies (particularly James Martin's) use 'factor tables' to suggest what should or should not be distributed (see example in Figure 15.16).

Each row is a heuristic rule which says that, if this condition applies, then that aspect of the system (processing, storage, development, etc.) should be centralized or distributed. James Martin's diagrams use the following letter codes in the cells of the matrix shown:

NATURAL SYSTEM OR DATABASE / DISTRIBUTION FACTOR	Product Management	Customer Order Operations	Customer Records Maintenance	Supplier Records Maintenance
Largely same data at all locations				C
Data created centrally	C			C
Data created locally	L	L	L	l
Needs sophisticated DBMS				c
Data integrated with other locations	l		c	C
Generates data to be used centrally	C			
Is logically complex	c	c		
Requires fast response		l		
Requires high availability			l	
Is entrepreneurial in nature			l	
Is highly critical for the org. unit			L	
Freq. changes due to external factors	C			
Freq. changes due to local factors			l	l
Is responsibility of local managers		l	L	
Needs high level of security	c	c	c	c
Requires high catastrophe protection	C	C	C	C
Needs high accuracy of input data	l	l	L	c
Is highly specialised	c			
Has variants at different locations	L	L	L	L

Figure 15.16 Distribution Factor Table – James Martin Style.

C strong reason for centralization
c weak reason for centralization
L strong reason for distribution
l weak reason for distribution.

Nowadays there are so many shades of distribution (as we have seen in Chapter 8) that a simple 'centralize' versus 'distribute' decision does not address all the options.

15.4.3 *Level of data-sharing analysis*

A somewhat more sophisticated variant of this is to use 'Level of Data-Sharing' analysis, which is addressed in more detail in Chapter 17. This analysis is based on the User Group Access Pattern matrix (introduced earlier in Figure 15.3, here reproduced as Figure 15.17).

Natural System	User Group	Feed Suppliers	Dealers	Dealing Managers	Financial Managers	Support Staff
On-line Feeds		CU L	AB L	BS LT	BS T	S T
Dealing Support			CUA LT	ABS LT	BS T	
Exposure Control			A L	CUABS L	BS LT	S T
Limit Maintenance				UAB L	CU T	
Management Reporting and Query				ABS L	BS T	
Transaction Accounting				BS L	BS T	CUABS T

Key:

C=Create U=Update/Delete (as in CRUD)
A=Ad hoc (retrieve 1 at a time)
B=Browse (retrieve a set of occurrences in some sequence)
S = Summarise (retrieve summaries over a set of occurrences)

L=Local (each user to own site)
F=Foreign (other sites as well as user's own)
T=Total (access any site's data)

Figure 15.17 Example User Group Access Pattern Matrix.

A fuller definition of the letter coding system is as follows.
Top half of cells (type of usage):

C   these users Create new data through this system
U   these users Update (or delete) data through this system
A   these users access single items of data in an *ad hoc* fashion using this system
B   these users Browse data using this system
S   these users extract Summaries of data using this system.

Bottom half of cells (locality of usage):

L   these users only use this system for local data
F   these users mainly use this system for local data, but a certain percentage (say <20%) of the transactions are on data belonging to Foreign sites
T   these users are equally likely to want access to any of the data in this system.

ARCHITECTURE STYLE / DISTRIBUTION FACTOR	Centralised	OLTP on Intermediate Servers	Data Warehouse on Intermediate Servers	Distributed Database stored near Source	Distributed Database stored near Users	Cooperative Message Passing
Data created centrally	++	+	-	--	--	--
Needs sophisticated DBMS	+	+	-	--	-	--
Local use needs 20%+ foreign data	+	+		++		++
Generates data to be used centrally	+	+	-	-	--	-
Data integrated with other locations	+	+	-	-	-	-
Data created locally	--	--	-	++	-	+
Local use is of 90%+ local data	--	--	-	++	++	+
Requires fast user response	-	-		--	++	--
Requires high user availability	--	+		--	++	
Needs high accuracy of input data	-	-		++	--	--
Data consistency is important	++	+	+	--	-	+
Needs high level of access control	+	+		-	--	+
Requires good catastrophe protection	--	+		-	+	
Freq. changes due to local factors	--	--	-	++	++	++
Is responsibility of local managers	--	--	-	++	++	++
System varies at different locations	--	-	+	+	+	++
Usage has high ad hoc element	-	-	+	--	++	
High level of statistical analysis	+	+	++	--	++	

Figure 15.18 Distribution Factor Table – 'LFT' Style.

One possible complication here is that the same user group may need two separate code patterns in the same system, e.g. 70% of the transaction volume is CUA/L in one role, 30% is ABS/T in another.

A Level of Data-Sharing Analysis can then be considered in conjunction with a factor table such as that shown in Figure 15.18 to suggest the level and type of distribution.

15.4.4 *James Martin's distribution analysis technique*

James Martin's Information Engineering methodology (Martin, 1982) uses a letter code to indicate one of a number of standard distribution options for each Natural Database against each Location (User Group) in a chosen architecture:

M   use single master copy only
T   data is not here, get it on demand (Teleprocessing)
D   duplicate data (DS = immediate, DD = deferred updating)
S   sub-set of a database held somewhere else (SS, SD)
R   reorganized sub-set of a database held somewhere else (RS,RD)
P   partitioned (rows stored only at their 'home' site)
V   variant (or 'separate schema' – tables in different systems)
I   incompatible, i.e. only interworking through messages.

This form of analysis is useful as it allows variations to the overall Technical Architecture for individual Natural Databases. The codes can be compared both with the overall architecture and with the performance and security requirements for each database.

The method seems strongly data-oriented, and could also be considered as a tool for documenting shared data designs in more detail, as decribed in Chapter 17.

15.4.5 *Weighted evaluation spreadsheets*

This represents the standard 'Consultant's Approach'. By the tenets of our general methodology, our evaluation must be multi-objective based. So a good approach is to identify the top five or so objectives, in order of priority or criticality as discovered in earlier ISP stages. One can be cleverer and attach weights to each factor, but this may create more confusion than clarity.

As with all such evaluations, it is difficult to find a homogeneous marking system which enables scores to be added up. Three possible measuring scales are:

Evaluation Factor (Solution Style)	Weight	Centralised		OLTP on Int. Servers		Data W'house on Int. S'vers		Distrib. DB near Source		Distrib. DB near User		Coop Message Passing	
		Score	Weighted	Score	Weighted	Score	Weighted	Score	Weighted	Score	Weighted	Score	Weighted
User Response	15	5	75	7	105	8	120	4	60	9	135	8	120
Throughput	10	8	80	7	70	7	70	7	70	6	60	7	70
Availability	10	5	50	7	70	7	70	8	80	9	90	9	90
Accuracy	15	8	120	7	105	6	90	8	120	5	75	4	60
Security	15	8	120	7	105	6	90	6	90	4	60	3	45
Development Time	10	6	60	7	70	8	80	5	50	8	80	8	80
Development Risk	10	6	60	5	50	5	50	4	40	4	40	4	40
Maintenance	8	7	56	6	48	7	56	6	48	5	40	6	48
Enhanceability	7	5	35	6	42	5	35	7	49	7	49	6	42
TOTAL WEIGHTED	100		656		665		661		607		629		595

Figure 15.19 Weighted Evaluation Spreadsheet.

- 'yes/no'   Does the solution meet a requirement or not?

- 'relative score'   How well or badly does the solution meet this criterion, in comparison with other solutions (e.g. 1–5 or 1–10 scale)?

- 'absolute value'   What is the estimate of a key parameter, e.g. response in seconds, cost in $)?

In the example in Figure 15.19, 1–10 scores and weighted evaluation factors have been used.

15.4.6 *Query performance evaluation*

Where user response and throughput are of primary importance, evaluation of alternative architectures can also be assisted by applying some of the techniques of Query Optimization, which is a well-developed topic in single-node databases.

This approach necessarily works by taking one type of query at a time. Each type of query that is critical to the operation of the group of systems should be evaluated. Optimization only becomes an issue in that there could be alternative execution plans for any given query, and in our timing calculations we should assume that the best plan will be used.

In order to evaluate response time or throughput, some assumptions have to be made about the likely hardware and network performance, e.g.:

- data transmission rates
- data transmission delays/breakdowns
- processing times per transaction
- processor delays/breakdowns.

For individual queries we need some statistics on:

- the split of partitioned or sub-set databases
- average hit rate on SELECT and JOIN operations
- locality (F factor) of queries requiring local data.

For throughput calculations we also need:

- transaction inter-arrival times (mean and distribution)
- transaction data volumes.

Evaluation of average performance can be done by relatively simple 'back of an envelope' calculations. This is covered in more detail in Chapter 17.

If some of the utility measures are statistical in form, we may need to use queueing theory or simulation. This is discussed in more detail under Network Design in Chapter 16.

Query performance may also need to be considered in other ways than pure speed. Figure 15.20 shows how one might evaluate the same queries under three different architectures.

15.4.7 *Overall security review*

The Technical Architecture is a good stage at which to ensure that security design is established as an important angle, rather than as a sideline which can be patched up later. Some organizations, of course, may be less security-sensitive than others.

The overall security review technique is based on evaluation by questionnaire. A full questionnaire may be lengthy, and would include many questions unrelated to the distribution angle. The following questions highlight the distribution elements of the Technical Architecture.

1. If 'open access' databases and systems are included, what access control strategy has been proposed?
2. If replication is proposed, what guarantee will there be of data consistency?
3. If EDI is proposed, what guarantees are there of authentication and non-repudiation?
4. What are the planned routes by which users in the 'outside world' could access the 'internal' Technical Architecture?
5. If dial-up is proposed, can the calling number be traced and verified?
6. If internal networks are linked to external ones, what control is proposed for the internetwork traffic?
7. Can security (e.g. encryption, firewalls, etc.) be applied to the networks easily?

If evaluation of a short-listed Technical Architecture exhibits too many uncertain responses to these questions, more resources may be needed than were originally envisaged to make this architecture work.

15.4.8 *Algorithmic optimization*

Operations Research practitioners have considered the possibility of optimizing the distribution of computing resources to meet a given set of Inputs and Outputs at a series of Locations. It is theoretically possible to express the problem as a Linear Program in which, for example, one wishes to minimize a Cost Function while meeting constraints on Response Time and Throughput.

The problem can be considered as somewhat similar to a depot siting problem where intermediate depots have to handle goods arriving from one set of sites and then pass them on either to other depots or to destination sites. Fertuck

TASK	Performance Factor		Distributed Database Stored near Source	Centralized	Distributed Database Stored near Users
Update 2000 bytes of database, for access by 3 user groups		Speed:	all local or LAN, so fast	transmission to centre	multiple transmissions to workgroup servers
		Availability:	local processor & LAN, so high	local & central processors and WAN, so less high	WAN, local & 3 workgroup processors, so yet lower
		Security:	can be made secure by limiting network access to read-only	WAN & central processor may be less secure	less management control over 3 workgroup servers
Retrieve 1000 bytes of data originating at each of 3 sources and combine into a result for a user		Speed:	transmit 3 lots of requests & replies, join etc on workgroup proc, so less good	transmit single request & reply, joining at centre, so moderate	all within user group LAN, so fast
		Availability:	3 source processors, LANs, WAN, user processor, so many points of failure	user group LAN, WAN, and user & central processors, so still vulnerable	LAN, workgroup server and user processor only, so high
		Security:	depends heavily on WAN, but at least it's read-only	depends heavily on WAN, but at least it's read-only	can be enforced at workgroup server, so high

Figure 15.20 Query Comparisons for Different Architectures.

(1992) gives an example based on locating Processing Centres to meet a given set of transaction volumes arising from Canadian cities. The cost function used by Fertuck is:

$$\Sigma D_{ij}V_i \quad \text{where } D_{ij} = \text{distance between location } i \text{ and location } j$$
$$V_i = \text{number of transactions generated at location } i.$$

He also introduces a constraint $D_{ij} < MAX_i$, where MAX_i is the maximum distance that location i can be from a server node (for line quality or whatever other reason).

The distances are taken as a measure of cost, based on the assumption of using leased lines charged by the kilometer. However, if this were so, the client would not be paying per transaction, so the cost function above may not be appropriate. If PSS or Frame Relay were used instead, one would not be paying by distance anyhow!

James Martin (Martin, 1982) also shows a simple algebraic calculation of the break-even point between distribution and centralization, using a cost function of 'Traffic Units'. No localization of access is assumed, i.e. the Data Sharing codes are all 'T'. Both immediate and deferred updating are considered.

The general comment on Optimization methods is that their model of cost, and of other evaluation factors, is very simplistic. Also, the dificulties in modeling options like partial replication, communications cost structures (which may include some combination of distance, volume and speed) as well as containing step functions (e.g. Frame Relay) make things very complex.

15.5 TECHNICAL ARCHITECTURE IN THE CASE STUDIES

15.5.1 *Mr A*

At some time in the future, there may be a choice between a server and simple peer-to-peer messaging. Also, if both Mr A and a clerical assistant could be accessing the same data in the office, there is also a choice between master/slave and peer-to-peer architectures.

15.5.2 *Bay Organic Produce Cooperative*

The choice between server technology and peer-to-peer for the main office has already been discussed, full centralization apparently having been ruled out. Links to markets and major buyers also need to be considered. Potential growth could be an evaluation factor.

15.5.3 *Detox Pharmaceuticals*

There is a choice to be made between centralization and distribution, especially for the Sales system. The issue will be the balance of use of the data between Sales Offices and Head Office. The availability of skills may favor a centralized approach. The high priority of managing overall market share and cost-competitiveness could add to this.

15.5.4 *Electric House*

Keeping multiple computer sites, other than PCs, in Latin America may pose maintenance problems. On the other hand, communication links, with possible restrictions on trans-national data transmission, may also be a factor. The US operation may already be covered by a leased line network. The choice between centralization and geographical distribution is an interesting one.

15.5.5 *Commonwealth Open Polytechnic*

There are arguments for both centralization and distribution of student records – a hybrid solution will probably have to be considered. High-capacity links would be part of an 'ambitious' architecture.

15.5.6 *National Environmental Protection Board*

Both centralized and distributed databases will need to co-exist and there may be a limited number of architectural options for this. The architectural choices for linking to companies and other government departments may be wider.

15.6 EXERCISES

1. Why is it important to have a Performance Checklist before developing a Technical Architecture?

2. What are the two aspects of User Access Patterns?

3. Explain the CUABS LFT coding system.

4. What are the dangers of being driven solely by Technical Opportunism?

5. What are the three columns in O'Brien's view of Technical Opportunism?

6. Is there any fundamental difference between 'Data Warehouse' and 'Centralized' architectures?

7. Suggest five criteria by which a possible Technical Architecture might be ruled out of the Shortlist.

8. What sort of Technical Architecture alternatives might risk considerations rule out? Use Electric House, or a case known to you personally, as an example.

9. Under what conditions is 'store near source' a good policy? Is the NEPB a good example?

10. Why might a fully centralized option be economically desirable yet impossible to achieve?

11. Discuss the difficulties in considering Technical Architecture alternatives when the organization is currently an 'IBM shop'.

12. Does the stipulation of 'special technical needs' run the danger of prejudging the choice of best Technical Architecture?

13. How might user expectations limit the technical alternatives that can seriously be considered?

14. What are the meanings of (a) the columns and (b) the rows on a Technical Architecture diagram?

15. Discuss the value of Factor Tables as a means of evaluating Technical Architecture alternatives.

16. Contrast the factor tables in Figures 15.16 and 15.18. Are they likely to produce conflicting conclusions?

17. Why is an early security review worth attempting?

18. What are the reasons for the lack of success of algorithmic optimization models for evaluating Technical Architectures?

ASSIGNMENT TASK

As with the previous chapter, this task can be treated as a longer-term assignment.

A1. For your chosen case study, draw up an O'Brien three-column table showing the potential benefits of five up-to-date technologies that you have read about in recent magazines or newspapers.

A2. What are the main performance objectives for a Technical Architecture for your case study?

A3. Draw up a User Access Pattern Matrix, based on the Natural Systems you derived in the previous chapter's assignment.

A4. Do any of the Natural Systems have special technical needs?

A5. Draw up at least two alternative Technical Architecture diagrams.

A6. Show example calculations which could be used to evaluate the preference between the two options you created above.

A7. What 'Gilb Goals' might the calculations you have just done fail to take into account?

FURTHER READING

Burch, J. (1992) *Systems Analysis, Design and Implementation*, Boyd and Fraser, Boston, MA, Chapter 14.

Fertuck, L. (1992) *Systems Analysis and Design with CASE Tools*, Brown, Dubuque, IA, Chapter 11.

JMA (1987) *ISP Handbook*, James Martin Associates.

JMA (1988) *BAA Handbook*, James Martin Associates.

Loosley, C. (1994) Performance design: going for gold. *Database Programming & Design*, Nov. 1994.

Martin, J. (1982) *Strategic Data Planning Methodologies*, Prentice Hall, Englewood Cliffs, NJ, Chapter 10.

Martin, J. (1990) *Information Engineering III*, Prentice Hall, Englewood Cliffs, NJ, Chapter 16.

Tozer, E. (1988) *Planning for Effective Business Information Systems*, Pergamon Press, Oxford.

16 Network design

16.1 RATIONALE FOR THIS DESIGN STAGE

Part Two of this book introduced the principle that business needs should determine the data communications network facilities chosen. The technology – through the data communications marketplace – offers many alternatives. These alternatives, as described in Part Two, vary in many ways such as initial and recurring costs, usage charging systems, capacity, behavior under peak loads, security and so forth.

The design task is, given a set of expected system requirements, a general technical architecture and the current situation, to engineer a combination of solutions covering:

- the type, speed and other characteristics of communications lines or services
- the network topology
- the switching and routing equipment
- the software needed to support the network

which will meet the business needs efficiently and effectively.

In this book, Network Design is placed immediately following Information Strategy Planning (ISP) and the choice of a Technical Architecture. This implies that it should be carried out prior to Shared Data Design and Individual Subsystem Design. The rationale is that:

- network costs are high and may require a long financial approval period
- because costs are high, networks have to be shared by the whole organization and not implemented system-by-system
- implementing the results of Network Design often takes longer than with the other design stages, because ordering hardware, wiring buildings, etc., can take longer than purely developing software
- optimizing the distribution of data and processes, which is required in the other design stages, depends on having chosen network speeds and availabilities.

Network design is also placed before any detailed Analysis of the data or functional requirements, with one exception, namely an analysis of overall traffic volumes. Within the overall methodology of this book, Analysis is performed on one system (or a group of systems in a Business Area Cluster), to break down the requirement into enough detail for Database or System Software design. For this reason, Analysis is deferred until the beginning of the next chapter.

By its nature, Network Design is rarely suitable for elegant logical optimization. An engineering approach, in which factors such as risk and growth in demand are built in, has always been the norm.

Designing a data communications network is seen as just one stage in the design of the whole information system. In this chapter we look at a number criteria for design decision making. We will then introduce a pattern of sub-tasks which should be followed. Finally we examine some of the individual techniques which can be used to evaluate different designs.

16.2 INPUTS TO THIS DESIGN STAGE

16.2.1 *Starting points*

The need for Network Design can arise either within a formal methodology, or informally. When using a formal methodology driven from IS Strategy Planning, the Technical Architecture, as described in the previous chapter, is one starting point. Network Design, or Redesign, is also often triggered in a less formal manner. An example of a triggering event could be a predicted, or actual, crisis in the existing infrastructure for moving data. In either case, there are two further starting points for Design: the requirements of the systems (and databases) that will use the network; and the status of the existing comunications network.

Technical architecture

When used formally following IS Strategy Planning, Network Design follows on naturally from the Technical Architecture. This architecture incorporates the decisions that have been made about where natural systems and databases should be located, and what connectivity is required. Generic communications links will have been shown in the Technical Architecture Diagram, but their specification will be limited to terms such as WAN, MAN, LAN, 'Factory', 'High-speed', etc.

Requirements of systems and data stores

In an IS Strategy Planning approach, the critical performance patterns of the natural systems will have been established in the final 'Systems Architecture' stage of Strategy Planning (see Chapter 14). Sub-clustering may have been used to identify areas with different performance characteristics.

In an informal approach, existing systems and databases may not change when a new network is designed. This means that their requirements should already be well established through experience and volume statistics. However, if a Strategy Plan does exist, the designer may want to check whether there are enhancements to these systems that ought to be considered at the same time as the immediate network crisis is fixed.

The required performance (either in units of some measure or as statements of required functionality) of each planned or actual system to be included in the network design or redesign exercise should be summarized in a table (Figure 16.1).

The example shows a variety of requirements from a range of systems. Note that peaks are shown with a percentage figure. This means that in 90 (or 98)% of cases the actual figure should not exceed the figure shown. The requirements in this example are relatively 'cool' – more extreme response times would be shown if applications such as real-time process control were involved.

The existing data communications network

We can assume that there is always an existing set of facilities that is being used to move data about. This can vary from a 'previous-generation' Data Communications network to the use of Fax, Telex, Telephone and Post ('snailmail'). Evaluating the performance of whatever system is in place, both in terms of measures of satisfaction and pure traffic statistics, is useful both as a check on requirements generated from the needs of the systems and as a benchmark in evaluating proposed solutions.

System -> Perf. Measure	Contract Support	Purch-asing	Finance	Product Devt	Sales	Pricing	PR Support	Market Research	Prod Des Support	Des Proj Control
Thruput av	30/day	100/day	200/day	50/day	10/day	5/day/sls	20/day	100/month	100/day/hd	200/week
90% peak	40	120	500	65	15	8	35	200	120	250
98% peak	50	150	1000	80	20	10	50	300	150	300
growth pa	10%	5%	5%	10%	10%	5%	8%	2%	8%	5%
Response av	2 sec	2 sec	2 sec	2 sec	2 sec	5 sec	10 sec	10 sec	2 sec	5 sec
90% peak	5 sec	5 sec	5 sec	5 sec	5 sec	10 sec	20 sec	20 sec	3 sec	10 sec
98% peak	10 sec	10 sec	10 sec	10 sec	10 sec	30 sec	30 sec	30 sec	5 sec	20 sec
Regular cycle	daily	daily	day,month, qtr,year	weekly	daily	-	-	monthly	-	weekly
Batch turn'rnd	3 hour	12 hour	24 hour	12 hour	3 hour	-	-	12 hour	-	3 hour
Availability (hrs/day)	10	8	8	7	10	12	8	8	10	7
Error rate	1%	0.1%	0.1%	1%	0.5%	0.1%	2%	2%	0.1%	1%
Security level	medium	high	very high	high	high	very high	high	high	medium	high
New retrieval request action	1 day	5 days	1 month	2 days	3 hours	-	1 hour	1 hour	1 hour	1 day

Figure 16.1 Multi-dimensional Performance Requirements of Natural Systems.

16.2.2 *Nature of the alternatives*

WANs and MANs

Except in a very few special cases the choice to be made is not so much one of technology but of service. The trend is for the precise technology, e.g. analog/digital, wire/satellite/fiber, etc., to be hidden from the customer. The common carrier or VAN supplier will offer a range of service packages which themselves use various technologies transparently.

The types of services form a spectrum ranging from those appropriate to very casual usage to those supporting very intense, exclusive usage, as shown in the following table:

Usage type	Service	Example charging basis
Very casual	Dial-up lines	Subscription, connect time
Casual	ISDN	Subscription, connect time
	Packet switching	Local calls, subscription, kB sent
Heavy bursts	Frame Relay	Access speed, virtual circuit rental
	SMDS	as Frame Relay
	ATM	as Frame Relay
Intensive use	Software-defined circuits	Virtual circuit rental
(>2–3	Fractional T-1 (or equivalent)	Virtual circuit rental
hours/day)	Leased circuits (Digital/Analog)	Circuit rental (by km)
High-security	Leased circuits	Circuit rental (by km)
	Owned circuits (e.g. Microwave)	Installation & maintenance

In practice, one particular path for the user may require more than one service. Most commonly, the longer-haul parts of the route are more likely to be covered by bulk shared services, with the user's access to gateway nodes using a different, relatively local, service. This can be compared to the problem of traveling from your own home to that of a relation at the other end of the world.

Depending on availability requirements, some links may need backup. This can involve a choice of whether to duplicate the link or to specify a more casual alternative (e.g. degrade to use PSTN).

Sharing of links is provided by most of the VAN services. For leased circuits, however, the organization will have to organize its own sharing. Options like multidrop/polling and multiplexing then come into play.

Within the scope of densely populated metropolitan areas, another alternative is to use MAN facilities such as IEEE802.6 or FDDI, as an alternative to local leased circuits.

If the user groups are mobile and cannot rely on fixed networks, the use of cellular radio links has to be considered. This will have an effect on the speed and quality over part or all of the path.

Further design choices can arise where the terrain is not covered by an existing telecommunications infrastructure (wilderness area, developing country, battle-field, cross-national boundaries where facilities are incompatible), or where the data is so sensitive that the data owners (e.g. military, police, secret services) are not prepared to risk sending it on anyone else's line. Private terrestrial or satellite microwave may be a solution given sufficient encryption, but it would be at considerable cost.

LANs and computer rooms

Most solutions these days are 'off-the-shelf' but there is a range of commercial products from which the user must choose. The danger is of becoming 'supply' rather than 'demand' driven.

Figure 16.2 shows an example table of some typical requirement scenarios and candidate solutions; asterisks represent potentially good solutions, plusses indicate 'possibles', and minuses suggest unsuitable options.

Apart from the above 'standard' options, there are a number of 'variations' to be considered. Ethernet, for example, offers the choice of 10BaseT, 10Base5, 10Base2 and even 100 Mbps super-Ethernet.

There is also a design choice over LAN hierarchy. This involves deciding whether to have, if possible, all workstations or devices connected to a single physical LAN, or to have a backbone LAN bridged to local sub-LANs. With or without such a hierarchy, there may also be options over the layout of hubs, bridges, repeaters, etc. Choices of wiring (i.e. UTP, STP, thin coax, thick coax, fiber, radio) or topology (i.e. star versus ring or bus) may be constrained by the LAN suppliers' commercial offerings and the availability of pre-existing wiring.

Internetworking

This covers the choice of the bridges, routers or gateways which link different networks together, either between LANs or to connect LANs and WANs. The user is not usually concerned with such equipment purely within WANs – unless a private network is being considered – because these are all 'part of the service'.

Typical areas of choice include:

- single large LAN vs interlinked sub-LANs (see LAN hierarchies above)
- standardizing LAN protocols versus using routers to link existing ones
- structure of gateways between LANs and external WANs
- standardizing on common OSI architecture to cut cost of gateways.

Scenario / Solution->	Digital PABX	Appletalk type	Ethernet type	Token Ring	Token Bus / Broadband coax	Wireless LAN	FDDI/ Fast Ethernet	ATM to the Desktop
Office Workgroup	+	++	++	++	-	--	-	+
Multi-workgroup Department	-	+	++	++		--	+	+
Campus-wide Inter-working	--	-	++	++		--	++	++
Factory Floor Machine Group	--	-	+	+	++	++	+	-
Server Cluster or Parallel Processor	--	--	-	-	-	--	++	--
Digital Video Editing	--	--	--	--	--	--	++	++

Figure 16.2 LAN Choice Scenarios and Solutions.

Network software

The type of network software needed is dependent on the style in which the network will be managed, as well as the nature of the natural systems using the network. A primary choice in LANs is between 'server-based' and 'peer-to-peer' Network Operating Systems. The need for different levels of sophistication in Network Management may point to the inclusion of one or more servers specializing in this function, and to different types of Software. This may include support for Data Encryption, but in some applications, e.g. those involving transfers of large sums of money, hardware encryption boxes may be considered.

16.2.3 *Evaluation criteria*

Informally, the criteria of a good Network Design are that it:

- meets the basic pattern of requirements
- can cope with the volumes both now and in the future
- gives adequate message response
- is unlikely to be out of action for too long
- is secure and accurate
- does not cost too much.

To point towards good solutions, a number of general decision factors should be considered. These factors can be used to rule out certain alternatives, or to prefer one alternative style rather than another.

Utilization is a measure indicating the return on investment in line capacity, but high utilization has to be balanced against delays which may be caused by messages having to queue for the heavily loaded facilities.

Traffic concentrations on routes or within areas – traffic may be uneven over the network, and different decisions may be needed for logically similar links.

Stream versus bursty message traffic patterns – transmitting batches of data or transferring files is more continuous than, say, LAN-to-LAN federal processing. Some WAN solutions are better suited for one than the other. The charging algorithm for the different WAN services is often the main determinant of the best solution.

User expectations of message delay – call set-up may be a large element in the response time. User expectations may vary – if he/she knows that dial-up is involved, it may be tolerable if the sounds of the connection can be heard (as happens on many modems). Acknowledgment that a message has been received, even if not processed, may also help. However, none of this would be acceptable to, say, a customer at an airline desk.

Cost of delay if a message cannot be delivered immediately – this may vary enormously, depending for example on whether the distributed system being supported is 'hot' or 'cool'.

Different traffic which could share the same network lines – if the organization spends large sums on Fax or Telephone to the same locations, or is considering Videoconferencing, then as well as the extra line capacity needed to allow this other traffic to share the lines, there needs to be provision for multiplexing between the different message types.

Support for mobile users – if some users (e.g. salespeople) do not operate at a single location, then the network design should support them adequately is ensuring that data is captured in an efficient and timely fashion.

Technical risk involved – some solutions may be risky because the technology is new, qualified support staff are hard to find, or software is not bug-free. Manufacturers' estimates of MTBF and MTTR may be very optimistic.

Manageability – some solutions may be fine on performance but difficult to control, either from an operational point of view or a strategic one.

Some additional evaluation factors for LANs include:

- behavior pattern under peak loads (e.g. CSMA/CD versus Token Passing)
- ability to use existing or standard (UTP) wiring
- availability of built-in networking on user workstations (e.g. Appletalk)
- likelihood of growth in the number of attached workstations
- distances within the LAN site (may limit use of some options)
- electromagnetic interference and other environment factors.

After considering the general decision factors, solutions then need to be evaluated on more specific, measurable criteria. These may sometimes apply to the network as a whole, sometimes to individual links. Criteria relevant to most cases, whether WAN or LAN, are:

- throughput (bulk data rate)
- message response behavior
- availability
- error rate
- security level

- equipment purchase cost (lines and boxes)
- maintenance or service charges
- performance overhead due to encryption, network management, etc.

Additional measurable criteria specific to WANs are:

- initial connection time
- data rates achievable
- resulting MTBF and MTTR
- ancillary equipment cost (purchase/lease/rental) – PAD, router, etc.
- one-off connection charges
- usage charges (e.g. for connect time)
- data volume charges
- line rental charges (leased circuits).

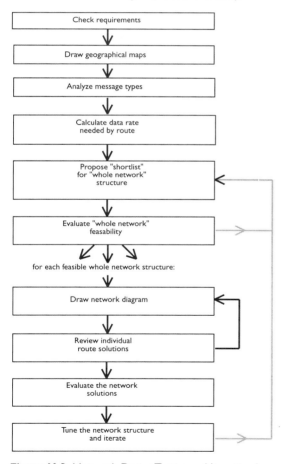

Figure 16.3 Network Design Tactics and Iteration Loops.

16.3 DESIGN TASKS AT THIS STAGE

16.3.1 *Overview of design tactics*

Network Design should follow a recommended series of steps, although the order of these steps is not always vital. Figure 16.3 shows the main tasks in Network Design. These tasks involve two separate loops of iteration. The inner loop consists of specification, evaluation and revision of the choices made for each individual link. The outer loop does the same for the Network as a whole.

16.3.2 *Check requirements*

Check what the real business requirements are, including performance goals and tolerances, and priorities attached to different functions (e.g. mandatory, desirable, 'nice to have'). This may involve aggregating the requirements of several different business units and user groups.

16.3.3 *Draw a geographical map*

Draw up a map (or maps) of the geographical environment, showing the logical routes along which data will need to flow, based on the Technical Architecture. Drawing packages may be used, e.g. GrafNet as described by Fitzgerald (1993). Figure 16.4 shows an example map drawn up in GrafNet style.

Distances may affect cost if leased lines are considered. If so, the actual routes on which lines are proposed can be marked on the map, in contrast to the usual 'cloud' used for a PSS. To provide a measure of distance, Fitzgerald proposes the use of a table of Vertical (V) and Horizontal (H) coordinates of cities in the USA, but not elsewhere. However this technique is of decreasing importance with the trend to Virtual Private Networks (using PSS or Frame Relay) where charges are not dependent on distance.

16.3.4 *Analyze message types*

Each main message type, in each system using the network, should be characterized in terms of message length and occurrence volume, including peaks, growth and possibly the distribution of inter-message times. For an example see the Message Analysis Table in Figure 16.5. The requirement can also be expressed as a Transportation Matrix as in Figure 16.6, which shows the volumes sent from each site to each other site.

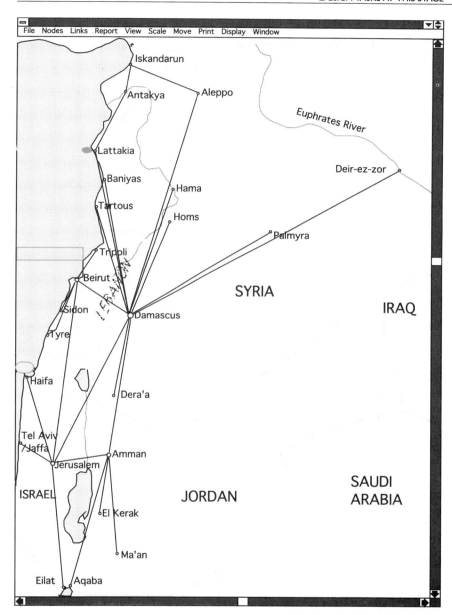

Figure 16.4 Example of a Computer-Drawn Network Map.

Network Link	Message Type	Bytes/Message		Messages/Day		Bytes/Day		Bytes transmitted per hour in each part of the working day							
		Avge	Peak	Avge	Peak	Avge	Peak	7-8	8-11	11-12	12-1	1-3	3-5	5-7	7-9
Damascus to Amman	Currency Exchange	32	34	250	300	8000	10200	400	750	850	300	750	900	350	100
	Account Enquiry	20	20	150	200	3000	4000	50	200	300	250	350	400	100	50
	Funds Transfer	40	60	1200	1500	48000	90000	500	4500	5500	3000	5500	6000	750	500
	Link Totals			1600	2000	59000	104200	950	5450	6650	3550	6600	7300	1200	650

Figure 16.5 Message Analysis Table (after Fitzgerald (1993)).

From \ To	Head Office Mgmt	Department 1	Department 2	Department 3	Sales Office 1	Sales Office 2	Sales Office 3
Head Office Management	-	0.1	0.1	0.1	0.2	0.2	0.2
Department 1	0.5	-	0.01	0.01	20	4	8
Department 2	0.5	0.01	-	0.01	4	25	6
Department 3	0.5	0.01	0.01	-	1	2	10
Sales Office 1	3	10	2	4	-	0.6	0.2
Sales Office 2	8	2	12	3	0.5	-	0.4
Sales Office 3	6	0.5	1	5	0.2	0.3	-

Figures: volumes in Megabytes per day to be transmitted from locations in columns to locations in rows

Figure 16.6 Data Transmission as a Transportation Matrix.

16.3.5 *Calculate data rate needed on each logical route*

We use a two-pronged approach to this calculation, the first part based on response time required, the second on peak throughput. The first has greater weight for on-line systems, the second for batch.

Response time calculation

Select the most critical query or message pair using the route. Add the message lengths in each direction. Divide by the response requirement in seconds. The result gives a minimum data rate that must be supported along the route.

For short messages, the set-up time may be more important than the transmission time. However, this varies according to the physical lines chosen – dial-up is slower than connection over a LAN. We can often rule out some options at this stage.

Peak throughput calculation

The procedure is to: total the message traffic on each logical route, broken down by time of day if very variable; estimate the volumes (average, peak and growth) for each message type from each site; convert these figures to bits per second. Designers often use a 'rule of thumb' approach to ensure that the resulting data rate adequately reflects the peak requirement. We show one such approach in Figure 16.7.

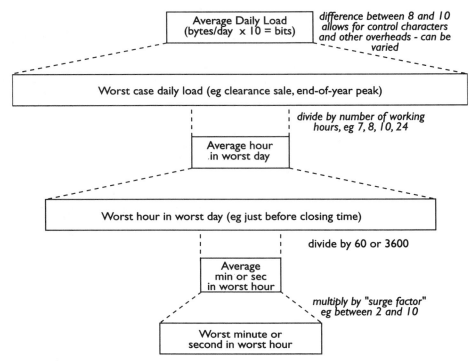

Figure 16.7 Peak Traffic Calculations.

This calculation can be summarized as:

1. divide worst case daily load by 86 400 seconds (peak day average)
2. divide worst case hourly load by 3600 seconds (peak hour average)
3. if surges within a peak hour can occur, multiply the peak hour average in (2) above by a 'surge' factor between two and ten.

If we are designing a WAN, we can mark up these figures on the geographical map as in Figure 16.8.

16.3.6 *Propose shortlist for the whole network structure*

We can now group the routes such that we can propose 'wholesale' solutions for each group. For example, we would separate Local from Long-distance, and Low-volume Casual from Regular and Bursty High-volume. For each group, we will normally consider at least two options – a 'state-of-the-art' solution, where cost is temporarily ignored, and a 'cheaper' option, which would do the job at the least cost. When it comes down to details, the options often have to be selected

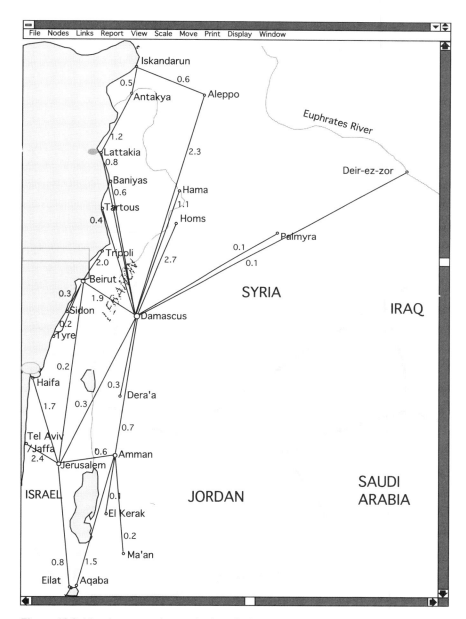

Figure 16.8 Megabytes per day marked on the Network Map.

from a small number of market alternatives e.g. Ethernet, Token Ring or FDDI for LANs; or Leased Lines (Analog/Digital), PSS or Frame Relay for WANs. We must also consider special needs such as mobile users, high-volume multimedia, factory environments, etc.

16.3.7 *Evaluate whole network feasibility*

We now check the shortlisted structures to ensure that the primary overall performance objectives can be achieved. Security can be included at this stage, but it is more commonly left to be evaluated after a full Network Design has been proposed. No detailed calculations are needed at this stage, but some options will typically be ruled out.

From this point we are now into the inner loop of iteration.

16.3.8 *Draw network diagram*

For each feasible Whole Network structure, draw up a Network Diagram (see example in Figure 16.9). For individual routes, we should mark in the solution indicated by the 'wholesale' solution chosen above, but without precise details. We can also include the protocols to be used, and the hardware and software boxes needed for internetworking, and any pre-existing equipment that will continue as part of the configuration.

The example shows a possible layout for a network covering a hospital and its connection to a computer at the local Area Health Board office about 50 kilometers away. The two local LAN segments at the bottom left belong to different departments. There is a pre-existing system in which terminals (some special-purpose) interact with the Hospital Mainframe or its backup. In the solution shown, Terminal Servers have been introduced and attached to the tiered LAN, one to the backbone and one to a sub-LAN. The specialized Minicomputer, which serves a Laboratory, is also pre-existing. The Front-End Processor, which previously handled the mainframe terminals, now provides a switching function for backup for both the mainframe and the AHB WAN connection – the PSS is used as a backup to the leased line.

Note that a Network Diagram is not a Map, and that not all routes need to be shown individually. Areas for which common solutions are proposed can be represented by one 'typical' example, e.g. there may be several 'Specialized Minicomputers' in different Laboratories in the Hospital example.

Many diagramming conventions exist for Network Diagrams, and no particular set is proposed in this book. One of the most complete sets is the one offered in Fitzgerald's book, which is reproduced as Figure 16.10. Fitzgerald's readers are exhorted to copy the page and tape it to the wall!

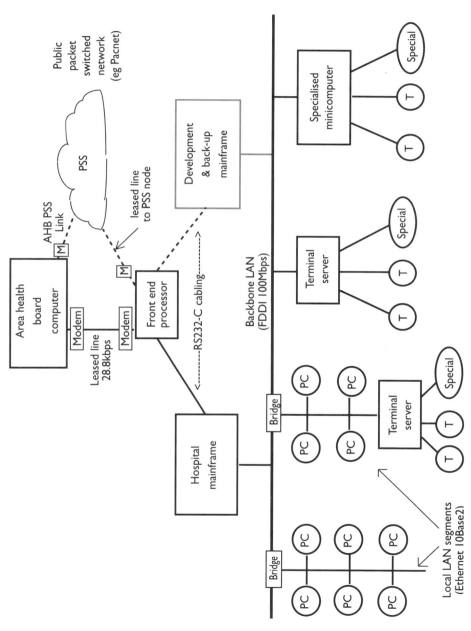

Figure 16.9 Network Diagram Example.

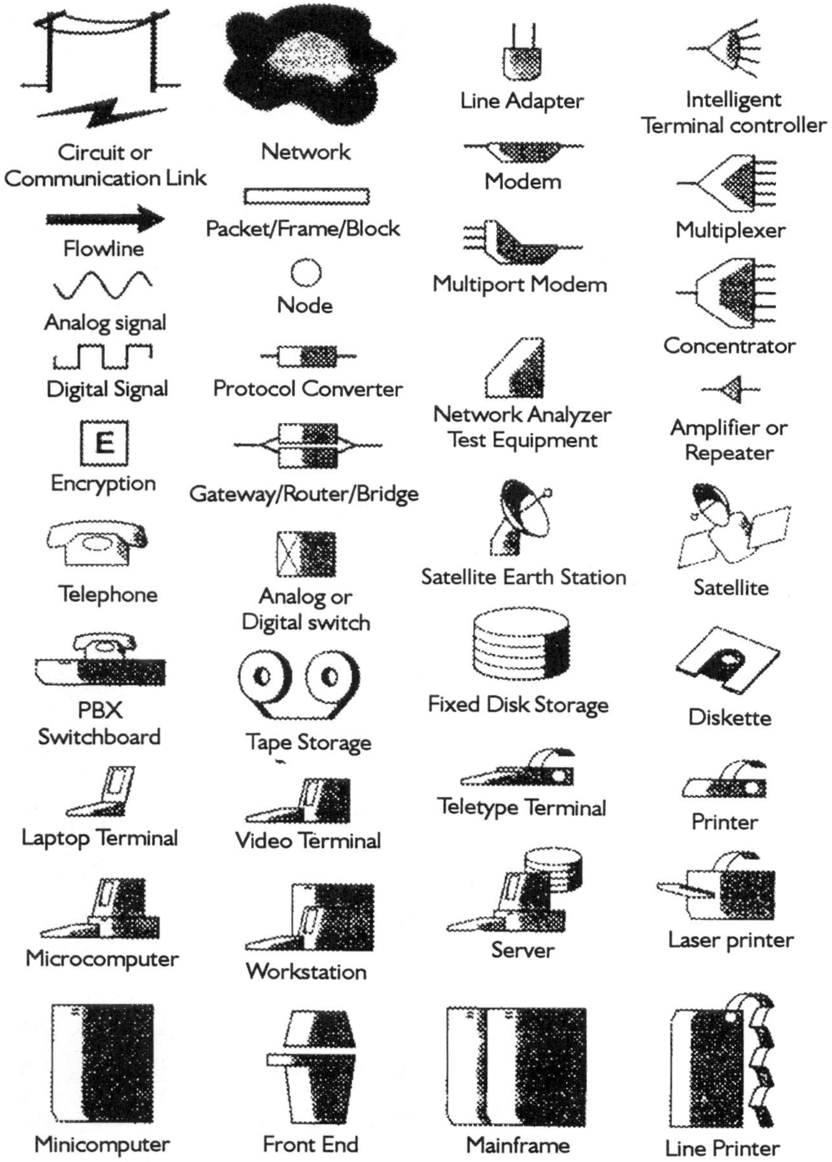

Circuit or
Communication Link

Network

Line Adapter

Intelligent
Terminal controller

Flowline

Packet/Frame/Block

Modem

Multiplexer

Analog signal

Node

Multiport Modem

Concentrator

Digital Signal

Protocol Converter

Encryption

Gateway/Router/Bridge

Network Analyzer
Test Equipment

Amplifier or
Repeater

Telephone

Analog or
Digital switch

Satellite Earth Station

Satellite

PBX
Switchboard

Tape Storage

Fixed Disk Storage

Diskette

Laptop Terminal

Video Terminal

Teletype Terminal

Printer

Microcomputer

Workstation

Server

Laser printer

Minicomputer

Front End

Mainframe

Line Printer

Figure 16.10 Fitzgerald's Network Diagram Icons (from Fitzgerald, J., 'Business data Communications', Wiley, 1973).

16.3.9 *Review individual route solutions*

This stage takes the preliminary calculations in section 16.3.5 above into more detail. Within the 'wholesale' solutions discussed earlier, we choose here the specific data rates to be provided.

Response time considerations

Calculate or simulate average and 'worst' user response times for the main message types. The elements of response time are shown in Figure 16.11 and should include:

- connection set-up
- transmission time
- network delays (e.g. queuing, retransmission due to errors, etc. and the 'turnpike effect' when utilization is high)
- destination processor time
- return message time and delays
- local processing time.

In some cases, response time can be split into 'acknowledgment only' and 'completed transaction' elements.

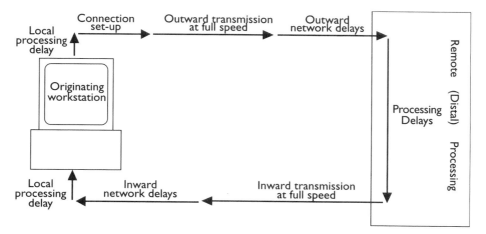

Figure 16.11 Elements of Response Time and Message Delay.

Peak throughput considerations

Consider the bulk data transmission capacity required on individual routes, and check that each route's worst rate can be accommodated without too high utilization. 'Too high' could mean over 70% for a fairly even workload, but over 50% or less if the traffic is bursty. Solution options may form a series of steps in the data rate offered, e.g. a number of PSTN lines, a number of T-1 64 Kbps fractions, or Frame Relay committed rates.

If more than one physical link is being used to support a logical route, then we need to check that the combined solution is adequate for this route.

If changes are made at this stage, we amend the Network Diagram, thus iterating the inner loop.

We then return to the outer loop.

16.3.10   *Evaluate the network solutions*

For each of the shortlisted whole-network solutions, we now calculate or estimate the overall performance factors, e.g.:

- availability (using MTBF and MTTR – and counting boxes as well as lines!)
- error rate
- security
- control features – manageability
- capacity for growth.

Supporting a route by several facilities in series or parallel will affect these performance factors. For instance, availability may be made worse by a series of facilities (stoppages have to be accumulated), but better by parallel facilities which can back each other up. On the other hand, security may be made worse by a parallel structure.

Estimate the total costs (one off and continuing) of the network solution, including lines, hardware and software. A spreadsheet (such as shown in Figure 16.12) can be used as a checklist to ensure all possible cost items are included for each link.

16.3.11   *Tune the network structure and iterate*

We now look to see how we can improve the first set of solutions. A number of different adjustments can be considered. The main area of tuning lies in optimizing the mapping of physical links to logical routes. Our initial Network Design may well have followed the logical routes fairly closely. However, depending on the geography and other factors it may make sense to 're-wire' the

Network Link	Category of Cost ($ p.a.) Leased Circuit	Front Ends & Comms Servers	Modems	Routers	Multi-plexers	Encryption Devices	Software	Test Equipment	Personnel and Facilities	Total Cost for each Link
Damascus to Amman	$1,500		$500	$600	$800	$350	$250	$300	$20,000	$24,300
Damascus to Aleppo	$1,800		$500	$600	$800	$350	$250	$300	$20,000	$24,600
Aleppo to Iskandarun	$700		$500	$600	$800	$350	$250	$300	$20,000	$23,500
Total Cost in each Category	$4,000	$0	$1,500	$1,800	$2,400	$1,050	$750	$900	$60,000	$72,400

Figure 16.12 Link Cost Checklist Table (after Fitzgerald (1993)).

network so that traffic following similar routes or part routes will share a physical link for part of the way, using a router at some intermediate point. This applies especially to 'long and thin' WANs such as might be needed in Canada or New Zealand.

Other possible re-wiring could involve the introduction of tiered LANs or of MANs.

We then return to re-evaluate the whole network feasibility and to redraw and detail the links. This implies an iteration of the outer loop.

16.4 DESCRIPTION OF INDIVIDUAL TECHNIQUES

16.4.1 *Estimating traffic*

The most burdensome task in Network Design is the obtaining and collation of the required set of reliable estimates of the traffic that will use the network – this is sometimes known as the Traffic Mix.

One needs to start planning the data collection well in advance. This is easier if we have an existing network with a Network Management package that collects the statistics. If we have new uses for the network, then there can be a high degree of uncertainty. This is not so bad if the main systems are routine TP, where traffic volumes closely reflect business volumes. But if most of the user work is *ad hoc* query or browsing, then the volumes are very much tied to the level of take-up of the whole application by the users.

Another horror story for traffic estimators at the time of writing (1995) is the growing demand for graphics and multimedia data, culminating in such applications as Videoconferencing and Video On Demand. Introducing such applications can lift traffic estimates by factors of 1000, never mind factors of two or even ten. Figure 16.13 shows some of the data rates that might be needed to cope with these types of traffic. Note that even at ISDN-H rates, little more than a frame per second can be achieved in videoconferencing, hence the jerky 'slow-scan' video often seen. For a Video On Demand (VOD) service, local cabling has to have sufficient bandwidth to multiplex an unpredictable number of subscribers wanting to download the latest box-office hit simultaneously!

As stated earlier, the areas of traffic estimation which are of most interest are the timing and height of **peaks**. Timing is important because different transactions can peak within a day at slightly different times. Many organizations, but not all, show two peaks per day, namely just before lunch and just before going-home time.

Of course peaks occur at many levels, depending on, for example, days of the week, time in the calendar (or accounting) month, quarter ends and climatic seasons. There are also peaks and troughs caused by changes in the level of business activity, which may be tied to growth and recession in economies.

	Example timings (seconds unless stated):		
	ISDN-B @64kbps	ISDN-H @1.5Mbps	ATM @150Mbps
WWW Page: 1 Megabit compressed	15	0.7	0.007
A/V Clip: 10 Megabit chunks compressed	150	7	0.07
Digital video film: 100 Megabit chunks (compressed in MPEG)	4+ hrs	12 mins	7
Videoconference: 1 Megabit per frame	15	0.7	0.007

Figure 16.13 Multimedia Transmission Timings at Different Data Rates.

Growth has to be allowed for, but it is not easy to estimate. Outside the IT field, the planners of Motorways have demonstrated how easy it is to underestimate surges in demand. There are also wider economic trends and cycles to consider, and even the effect of 'Parkinson's Law', whereby work expands to fill the human time available. Also, data-intensive tasks are very often taken on by an organization, but are never discontinued – until of course the 'axe' falls in the next recession!

So, for each type of message or transaction at each location we need to document the estimates of the traffic volume, in messages per second, minute, hour, etc., whichever is appropriate. One can treat locations with similar mixes together, allowing for variability in the total volume. The estimates needed are:

- average, peak and growth – for each message type from each site
- worst daily peak
- worst overall peak (in the lifetime of the network).

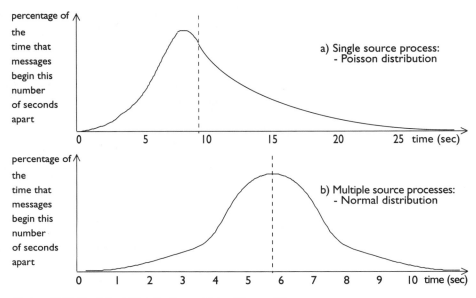

Figure 16.14 Statistical Distributions of Inter-Message Time.

Also, we should decide what is the best assumption about the distribution of inter-arrival times of messages or transactions. For infrequent transactions, a Poisson distribution is simple and reasonably accurate. In very heavy usage situations, different assumptions may be more appropriate (Figure 16.14).

Another problem is that most transactions are not one simple message pair, but a sequence of exchanges between which processing at a node takes place. In these situations traffic estimators normally use message pairs rather than transactions as the units of measurement. Some message pairs are extremely trivial (e.g. ACK/NAK), while others might involve the shipping of a semi-join on distributed relational tables.

16.4.2 *Network evaluation calculations*

There is no magic optimizer (as far as we know) that can take the whole of a requirement (target performance measures and traffic estimates) and, given the parameters of all the technical solutions and services on the market, recommend the one giving the least cost, lowest risk or whatever is left as the Objective Function.

Instead, one has to adopt an approach of proposing solutions and evaluating their behavior by model building. Models come in varying levels of sophistication. Which model we need to use depends on how critical the decision is and how much we are prepared to pay to ensure we make the right decision.

The spectrum of models we can use for evaluating networks is:

- deterministic calculations (discussed below)
- queuing theory (section 16.4.3)
- simulation (section 16.4.4)
- building a pilot network (section 16.4.5).

There are two very rough, deterministic calculations that can be used to see if the basic need can be met. If the design fails these tests, it has to be rejected or improved. Even if things seem satisfactory using a simple calculation, they can still fail in practice because of the unpredictable interactions between different users of a shared facility. This is where the more sophisticated models are needed.

The first calculation is to time an individual transaction, preferably the one that has to ship the most data in the shortest timescale. Assuming no queueing or other delay from anything else going on, can it perform in the timescale specified? We must remember to include set-up times, e.g. dialing-up, connecting to hosts, standard average packet delays, etc.

An example would be in a hotel reservation system trying to operate using dial-up. Our calculations might show:

- response required: 5 seconds in 95% of cases
- 9600 bps modem
- 100 bytes per message $\times$ 2 messages $\times$ 10 bits/byte $= 2000$ bits
- transmission time $2K/10K = 0.2$ seconds – but there is a
- 3 seconds average call set-up delay
- 1 second remote processor delay.

The total here of 4.2 seconds average response might be considered adequate, but perhaps a bit too near the limit to allow for peaks, growth and the possibility of unsuccessful call set-up.

Secondly we choose the worst peak on the busiest link on the network and calculate the utilization in a period, typically a peak hour or day. If it is over 100% or not far short, a higher data rate is needed. This way we can drop really bad solutions very quickly.

Again using the hotel reservation example, if we proposed, instead of the PSTN, a 9600 bps leased line, and the peak hourly load was 100 message pairs, the utilization is 2000×100 divided by 3600×9600, i.e. less than 1%. If the peak hour had 15 000 message pairs, the utilization would be over 80%.

Other calculations may be more appropriate in different processing styles, for instance batch throughput in the case of a large file having to be transmitted (e.g. for backup or end-of-day processing).

These calculations are limited in scope, because they take no account of queuing and contention between message pairs that want to be transmitted at the same time. Therefore the results they give will be very optimistic. If it is important to estimate these effects, a statistical approach is needed. Queuing Theory and Simulation (discussed below) are two possible approaches to this.

16.4.3 *Modelling individual queues in a network*

Where do queues occur in a network? They can occur at any shared component, e.g. a network node or switch, a hub, bridge, router or gateway, and of course a server computer. The medium in an Ethernet LAN also effectively creates a queue, and, with a bigger stretch of the imagination, so does the token in a Token Ring.

If we can identify what will be a critical bottleneck in the network (assuming of course that it is within our control and not the telecommunication company's) we can look at its behavior in isolation using Queuing Theory.

The mathematics of a simple queue depends on three parameters:

- Inter-Arrival-Time Distribution (the time difference between the arrival of one job wanting the shared service and the arrival of the next such job)
- Service Time Distribution (the times it takes to perform the shared service)
- Queue Discipline (the order in which the competing jobs are dealt with).

Figure 16.15 highlights some of the potential differences in queue disciplines, arrival distributions and service time distributions.

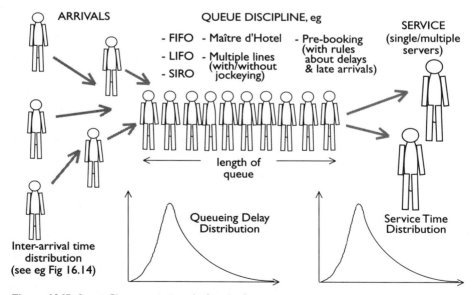

Figure 16.15 Some Characteristics of a Simple Queue.

Queuing theory can often show errors of as much as 20% either way on absolute timings, but it usually gives reliable comparisons of two different solutions.

What we can calculate using such models is the effect of adjustments such as:

- improving the service speed of a facility where there is a queue
- providing parallel facilities (such as in a supermarket with multiple checkouts or a bank with multiple tellers)
- changing the queue discipline to allow priorities

Results are measured in terms such as queue length and waiting time, expressed both as averages and as confidence limits, e.g. 'wait less than 3 seconds 95% of the time'.

16.4.4 *Modeling network performance through simulation*

Packages are available (e.g. COMNET III) which allow designers to test the behavior of a network design. Such packages include the behavior specifications of all the most widely used technologies on the market. The designer has to draw up the topology of the proposed solution using a graphical tool, annotate the traffic estimates and press the button. Figures 16.16 is an example of a screen in COMNET III, showing the network model for a company with operations based in five US cities.

The displays are animated so as to show messages being generated and transported through the network, and the simulation speed can be slowed down for closer observation before being turned back up to full speed.

Output will include measures such as the average and 'worst' response times and the throughput. Response will include connection set-up, transmission time, network delays, destination processor time and return message time. Also other performance factors can be displayed, e.g. availability, error rate and some measure of cost.

Any simulation is only as good as the model it adopts of the 'real' network. It will often be simplified and, for example, may not allow for such possibilities as retransmissions due to errors. As with the simpler techniques, it is still better regarded as a tool for evaluating relative differences between alternative designs rather than as an absolute prediction of response or throughput.

16.4.5 *Pilot or prototype network experimentation*

However good the simulation may be, some organizations prefer to build up a live test bed with a pilot network which includes many of the features of the eventual design, and then to apply generated test transactions to that network. This can be done with equipment 'on approval', or it may be used to fine-tune some decisions once the basic design has been settled.

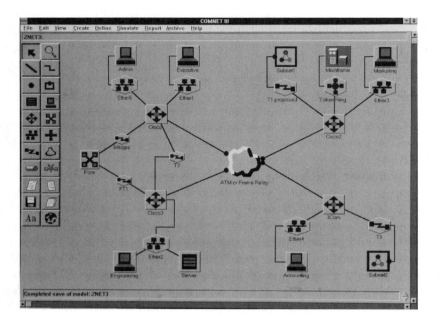

Figure 16.16 Comnet III Screen Showing a Trans-USA network.

16.4.6 *Evaluation for adequacy of security*

If security has a high level of importance for the Natural Systems using a Network, then a formal security assessment of any proposed solution is required. Examples of questions that should be asked in Security Assessment of a Network include the following:

1. What are the business costs of security breaches?
2. What are the potential motivations of attackers?
3. What methods might attackers use?
    *   physical line-tapping
    *   deliberate cutting of links
    *   masquerading as valid users
    *   running programs to record users' keystrokes
    *   worms and viruses.
4. What are the weak points in the Network?
    *   gateways between the 'internal' and 'external' users
    *   inbound dial-up or PSS access

- 'open' remote access, e.g. Telnet, rlogin, ftp, WWW
- trusted processors (is their security adequate?).
5. How is user identity authenticated?
   - overall password
   - application-specific passwords
   - separate read and update rights
6. Where is the user authentication processing done?
7. How are security breaches detected?
   - hardware probes
   - inbound call tracing
   - audit trails of all connections.
8. What counter-measures are proposed?
   - optical rather than electrical signaling (i.e. use optical fiber cables)
   - hardware or software encryption (end-to-end and/or individual links)
   - sophisticated or standard encryption algorithms, e.g. public key, DES
   - screening bridges, routers and gateways
   - firewalls between different sides of internetwork gateways
   - secure distribution and regular change of passwords and keys
   - dial-back of dial-up users
   - secure terminals (locks, electronic shielding, etc.).

Measures of security such as 'breaches per period' are not particularly useful. An alternative is to estimate the cost to an attacker of overcoming the counter-measures. Examples are the processor time needed on a supercomputer to crack encryption keys, or the technology to tap lines or terminals.

Estimates of the costs and the performance overhead of the security measures themselves should also be evaluated.

16.5 APPLICATION TO THE CASE STUDIES

16.5.1 *Mr A*

Volumes are very small but bursty. He will probably prefer to pay by usage. Some connection is needed at his home between his portable and the clerical assitant's PC. Failures are not usually critical, since they can be easily circumvented (e.g. by carrying and converting diskettes).

16.5.2 *Bay Organic Produce Cooperative*

The office needs a LAN that can handle peaks and growth, and that is not subject to breakdowns – some fail-soft arrangement seems desirable. Externally, dial-up or PSS may be adequate for most purposes, unless the Farmers go electronic in a big way, in which case the cooperative could consider installing its own PADs for each local calling area.

16.5.3 *Detox Pharmaceuticals*

Internally, they need LANs for Process Control, Head Office Departments and Regional Offices/Warehouses. Externally they need usage-charged WANs for EDI and various casual links. Some of the EDI (e.g. with Hospital Boards) may justify use of a VAN network if one is available. The Process Control LANs are probably already installed, and as they are in a factory may have special environmental needs, so may justify Token Bus or Wireless LANs. The Head Office LANs will probably need to be multi-tier. The traffic patterns between Regions and Head Office are very bursty, carrying summaries and messages rather than regular transactions unless a centralized architecture is chosen.

16.5.4 *Electric House*

Similar considerations to those for Detox apply for Electric House's Stores, Warehouses and Head Office, although there is no need for Process Control. For communication with Far East producers, international PSS may be sufficient. Alternatives are Internet or a commercial network like CompuServe. A virtual private network may be justified between major US centres of population.

The Casa Electrica situation is somewhat different. Third-world telecommunications may still be the norm outside big population centers like Mexico City, Caracas, Rio, Sao Paulo, Montevideo, Santiago and Buenos Aires. Dial-up, PSS and local Leased Line services, where they exist, may not be totally reliable. A backup fax or even post system may need to be included in the design.

16.5.5 *Commonwealth Open Polytechnic*

LAN needs at the Broken Hill campus and regional centers are relatively simple, though the peaks are extremely skewed. The COP operates on an annual (or semester) cycle of enquiries, enrolment, assignments, assessments, examinations, marking and results. *Ad hoc* messaging between students, tutors and course controllers may provide a more stable base load for the WANs, but only in term-time. Management will try to even out the peaks but traffic volumes will be hard to predict, especially if remote video gets under way. A private arrangement with Telstra or Optus seems to be necessary if this is to succeed.

16.5.6 *National Environmental Protection Board*

Message traffic associated with the inspection and questionnaire processes are fairly even over a year, but could grow to double the initial traffic. The Head Office may need a multi-tiered LAN system with gateways to other government departments. There is also a need for links between Head Office and Regions – PSS or Frame Relay might be appropriate. A usage-charged service would be required for EDI and Email with Subject Organizations. Remote monitoring might bring special needs, e.g. Leased Lines or Frame Relay to large factories. If the paperless goal is to be achieved, then traveling staff need to be equipped with mobiles – these will need to communicate through dial-up (or dial-back from a server computer to the staff PCs which would need to be left switched on overnight).

16.6 EXERCISES

What are the justifications for designing Networks before Analysis and Design of Shared Data? Can you suggest any exceptions to this rule?

What are the main evaluation factors for Network design other than average response time?

What are the constituent parts of response time (a) to give the user an acknowledgment of request only and (b) to complete a transaction?

With choices of WAN service, give examples of options where the costs are (a) distance dependent/independent; (b) volume dependent/independent; and (c) connect-time dependent/independent.

Describe what is meant by 'bursty' traffic.

Why is there no single best choice for a LAN?

What effect might it have on Network Design choice if a mixture of data, voice and fax needs to share the network?

In what respect are the cost evaluations for LAN and WAN fundamentally different?

Why does network traffic vary so much with the hour of the day?

0. How can an estimate of messages per hour be converted into a 'worst case' number of bits per second?

11. How many 100 kilobit 'frames per second' could be transmitted in videoconferencing over a 64 kbps ISDN-B service?

12. Discuss the criteria for choosing between Poisson and Normal distributions of message inter-arrival times.

13. Under what circumstances might the use of a Network Simulation package such as CACI's COMNET III be justified?

14. If he wishes to link two PCs, should Mr A consider putting Ethernet in his home? If not, what should he do instead?

15. Discuss the special Network Design problems that are likely to arise both for Detox in Poland or for Casa Electrica in Latin America.

16. In what way could an organization set a Network policy that inherently caters for growth?

ASSIGNMENT TASK

For your chosen case study, complete the following sub-tasks.

A1. Draw a geographical map of sites, marking in the estimated traffic volumes.

A2. Take one route on your map from sub-task 1 above. What is the mix of different traffic? Contrast the characteristics of the main constituent transactions or messages.

A3. Propose two network solutions and draw up a network diagram for each.

A4. Make an evaluation of the two solutions and nominate your preferred network design.

A5. Suggest any possible tuning improvements to your solution.

FURTHER READING

Burch, J. (1992) *Systems Analysis, Design and Implementation*, Boyd and Fraser, Boston, MA, Chapter 13.

Davis, C. (1991) Systems analysis for data communications networks at an electric utility. *Journal of Systems Management*, Jul.

Fitzgerald, J. (1993) *Business Data Communications – Basic Concepts, Security and Design*, 4th edition, Wiley, New York, Chapter 8.

Kosiur, D. (1991) Building a better network. *Macworld*, Nov.

Law, A. and McComas, M. (1994) Simulation software for communications networks: the state of the art. *IEEE Communications Magazine*, Mar.

Whitten, J. *et al.* (1994) *Systems Analysis and Design Methods*, Irwin, Burr Ridge, IL, Chapter 10.

17 | Designing shared data

17.1 RATIONALE FOR THIS DESIGN STAGE

A prime argument of the 'database-driven' methodology school is that one should design the database early because it is a more slowly changing resource in the organization than the processes. In the methodology followed in this book, design of shared data is addressed relatively late, though still before process design. We have already taken a preliminary look at data structures by building a global conceptual data model within the ISP stage (Chapter 14). This model describes THE database, i.e. all the data of interest to the organization. One of the outputs of clustering is the 'shared data' clusters, sometimes referred to as 'natural databases' or 'data stores'. What we are left with now is the task of optimizing the design of each natural database, which may still need to be distributed.

So the general purpose of this chapter is to describe methods for designing individual collections of data which need to be shared over a network. One particular feature is the design for **replication** of shared data. The design techniques will be based on query performance evaluation and optimization, which require estimates of transmission data rates. These in turn depend on assumptions about the network, which is one good reason for having designed the network before we start designing individual databases.

17.2 INPUTS TO THIS DESIGN STAGE

17.2.1 *Starting points*

The starting points for Shared Data Design will all have been prepared if previous stages of this methodology, namely ISP, Technical Architecture and Network Design, have been followed. If this is not the case, then some preliminary analysis or assumption-making needs to be done in order to fill in the details described below.

Results of clustering

Clustering within the ISP will have suggested the scope of individual databases. We have already observed that the 'shared data' clusters are derived from the two-dimensional 'analysis' clusters. Figure 17.1 shows an example from the ABC Software Co., based on the Texas Instruments (TI) Information Engineering approach. The groupings along the *y*-axis represent the Entity Types which should be included in each cluster.

As discussed already in Chapter 14, there is often a need to adjust or refine the clustering to identify 'shared data' clusters. Different parts of one 'analysis' cluster's data may be very different in nature, e.g. text, multimedia or 'diary' data, and may justify different types of DBMS, File Structure or Groupware. Further, different parts of a cluster's data may require totally different approaches to management of the shared data (e.g. strict database administration versus 'open' contributions).

We may also give some weight to the location dimension in clustering and split databases where the location patterns are different.

Global conceptual data model

This is a broad, preliminary view of the logical structure of the data that is required. Such Conceptual data models arise either from a widely-scoped ISP exercise or from Data Structure analysis on a particular function within an organization. We now have to take the sub-set of this model that corresponds to the entity types in our shared data cluster.

In most Global Conceptual models, the data is regarded as logically stored at a single site. In our methodology, we have, however, also collected some details of the potential localization of use of the data.

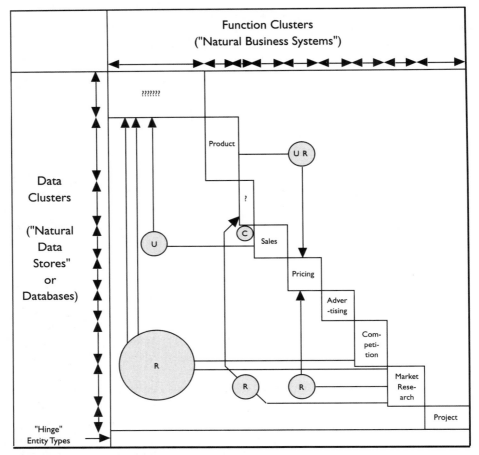

Figure 17.1 Natural Data Stores in a Clustered 'CRUD' Matrix (after TI Methodology).

Technical architecture

The Technical Architecture shows the broad patterns of local and remote use of data, and defines the structure of processing nodes and links. It will indicate where the possible data storage locations lie.

Network design

The Network Design puts specific technology solutions on the links. The design decisions here have been based on the total traffic and mode of use between locations, so they are optimized for more than just the current shared data collection. The network link specifications (capacities etc.) will play a large part in determining the performance of queries, since one must expect many of the queries to make use of the network.

Usage statistics by user group

Finally, a Strategy Planning or Analysis exercise will have collected some usage data, ideally detailing volumes by transaction or query types, as well as batch activities. These details are needed so that we can properly evaluate the various designs for the shared data.

17.2.2 *Nature of the alternatives*

Most established database design techniques are geared to the single-site case. The initial approach is to map, using a set of default rules, the conceptual model to the DBMS in question. The scope of alternatives is in effect limited to applying variations to this default design, in particular by de-normalization. Normalized tables can be split and merged, indexes added or dropped, and underlying file organizations optimized.

In the distributed situation, we also need to resolve the question of where data should be located. This decision obviously depends on the patterns of updating and access of the different data, by users and processes from the various locations.

In Technical Architecture design (Chapter 15) we have already looked at a number of general design alternatives for data, e.g. 'store near sources' or 'store near recipients'. We now look at the alternatives under the following five headings:

- grouping
- partitioning
- replication
- archiving
- software structure.

Grouping alternatives

Grouping (Figure 17.2) means deciding that related data, which might appear in different tables and hence be potentially distributed, should be stored near each other because joint access to them is frequent. Grouping is especially important when starting from a Conceptual Model which results in a large number of small data groupings. An example of this is NIAM (Nijssen, 1989) which models Data Structure as Elementary Facts, i.e. binary (or irreducible *n*-ary) tables in Relational terms.

If starting from an Entity–Relationship model, grouping is less common, but can occur if two entity types are very strongly correlated in their usage patterns

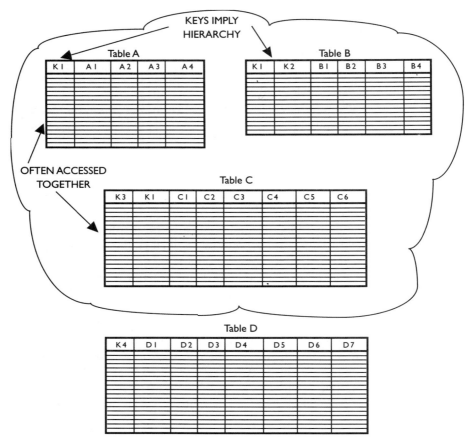

Figure 17.2 Data Grouping.

(e.g. Orders and Order Items). Data placement clustering, as offered in some Relational and Network DBMS, is one way of supporting this in single-site databases.

The spectrum of alternatives lies between:

- doing as much grouping as possible to optimize performance on known queries and transactions and
- retaining flexibility for variable patterns of access by retaining the normalized or canonical data structure.

The criteria for grouping should be the frequency and timescale in which the data items need to be brought together.

Partitioning alternatives

Very often a collection of shared data will be partitioned across several sites to improve performance, within, of course, the constraints of database maintainability and administration. The main partitioning schemes (Figure 17.3) are as follows.

- Partition whole Entity Types, Tables or Object Classes – this applies when a whole table or class is location-specific. Choice of data storage location is based on the source – or the usage – of each table.
- Partition within Table or Class by Occurrence ('horizontal') – this is done on the basis that certain groups of occurrences ('rows' in tables) are particular to different locations – usually the source of the data – and hence have an affinity with particular computers in the architecture.
- Partition within Class by Attribute/Method - 'vertical') – this is done when certain groups of attributes ('columns' in tables) have a particular affinity (in source or usage) at particular sites only.

In Figure 17.3, the codes A1, B2, etc., represent Attribute names, and an asterisk (*) indicates the Primary Key of a table. Partitions may be allocated to individual computers located at data sources, source group servers, user group servers or individual user workstations.

Replication alternatives

By Replication we mean deliberate storage of more than one copy of the data, either in terms of exact copies or modified sub-sets. The business objective is to make user access faster and more resilient to breakdowns. The price of doing this is that the replication process has to be managed so that different sites do not get out of synchronization.

Figure 17.4 shows some of the design options in using Replication. The simplest form of Replication is to keep simple copies of a whole database at a number of different sites. If more is known about patterns of usage, then it can be more cost-effective to limit copies to sub-sets of the data that are relevant to each copy site. There may also be arguments for modifying the structure of some of the sub-sets to better meet user needs.

A special case of modified sub-set Replication is Data Warehousing (Figure 17.5).

Data Warehousing involves copying data from a number of possibly heterogeneous databases and modifying them into an integrated whole. Some transformation, filtering, merging and clean-up may be applied *en route*. Historical and superseded data may be kept for some time in a Data Warehouse, in order to allow for time-based querying. However, the Data Warehouse may then have to take on responsibility for Archiving (see below).

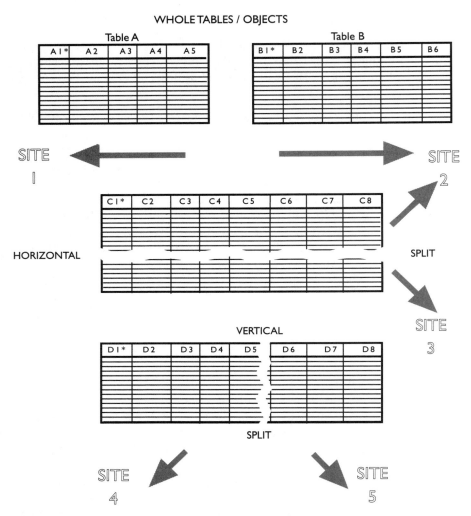

Figure 17.3 Partitioning.

A primary design decision with Replication is whether to immediately propagate changes to the primary source database, or to defer updating to a more convenient time (e.g. in an overnight batch run). The decision will depend on the 'up-to-dateness' requirement which applies to the user Information Need. One interim solution would be to send asynchronous messages about changes to a suspense file. This file could be scanned by users who wished to check for recent changes. Another solution is to allow 'propagation on demand' from a recipient user, either for an individual row, or for the whole table as a mini-batch operation.

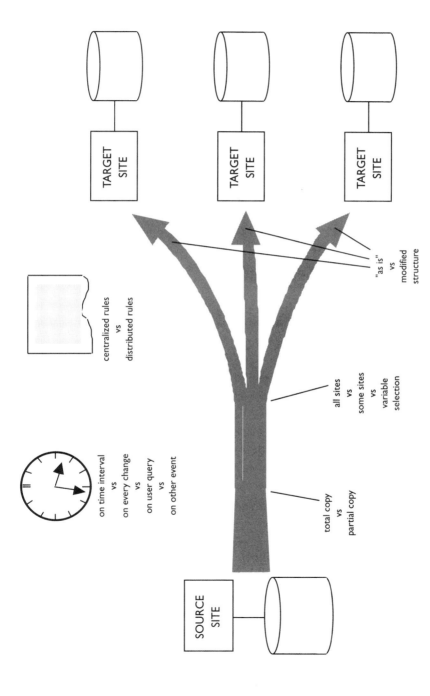

Figure 17.4 Options in Data Replication.

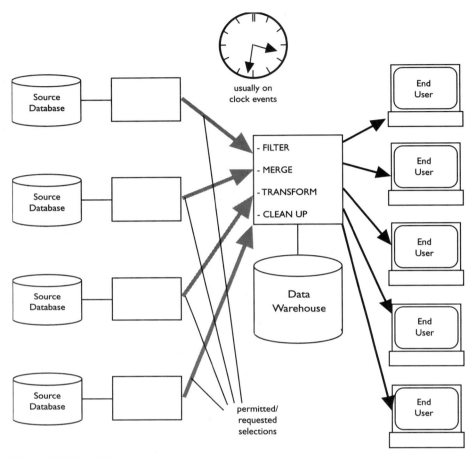

Figure 17.5 Data Warehousing.

Another design decision, suggested by Hansen and von Halle (1995), is whether replication should be 'provider-driven' or 'subscriber-driven' (Figure 17.6). In the provider-driven approach, information is held for each provider processor on where copies of its data are kept, and when and how it should send updates. In the subscriber-driven style, the information is held for each site which will hold copies of data, and lists which providers' data it holds copies on, and how it should get hold of changes.

These approaches can be operated either with centralized or distributed replication control. In the centralized approach one site keeps all the tables and rules for data providing or subscribing; in the distributed form all the information is kept at the providing or subscribing site.

PROVIDER REPLICATION

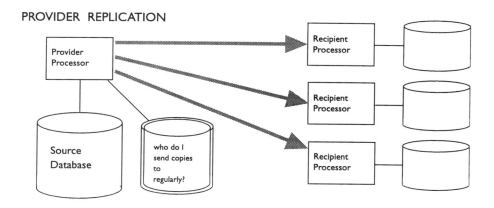

SUBSCRIBER REPLICATION

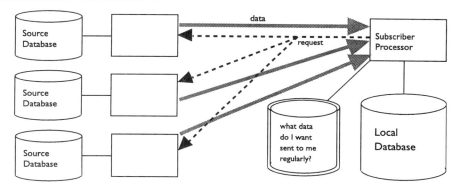

Figure 17.6 Provider versus Subscriber Replication.

Replication is often combined with partitioning – the options can be expressed in a 3 × 4 matrix as in Figure 17.7.

Recently, software package support for Replication has started to become available in the form of 'Replication Servers'. This may encourage more use of this design option in the future.

Archiving alternatives

In a distributed system there are additional choices over how historical or superseded data should be stored. With Centralized databases, some data has to be taken off-line at regular intervals so that the disk requirement does not expand indefinitely. In Distributed and Cooperative systems, especially with Replication, one site may be the originator of the data and may wish to decide its own Archiving policy.

Replicated -> | V Partitioned	to each user workstation	to several workgroup servers	to one central site	no replication
by source processor	rare	very common	possible	unlikely
by source group server	possible	common	very common	possible
single primary database	possible	common	N/A	N/A

Figure 17.7 Replication with Partitioning – Matrix of Options.

A common approach taken by organizations today is to regard Archiving as part of the function of a Data Warehouse.

Software structure alternatives

The final range of data-related design alternatives lies in the location of the software which manages the shared data.

The main decision here is the approach to DBMS, where the choice lies in the following spectrum:

- a full-function Distributed DBMS, where the data is logically centralized
- a Client/Server approach, where one DBMS acts as a server to another
- a Federated DBMS where formal descriptions of global or import/ export data structures are included
- agreement between autonomous DBMSs to pass certain message types.

These alternatives have already been discussed in Chapter 11.

As well as the DBMS, we have to consider the placement of

- the Data Dictionaries
- the Data Communication or components of the DBMSs
- the Archiving functions.

The restrictions of the software packages may tie the location of these components closely to that of the DBMS itself. However, some variation may be possible. The Data Communication component may be moved to a separate 'Transaction Control' server. The Data Dictionary can be regarded as a special part of the database where the primary user is the DataBase Administrator (DBA). The DBA's own access needs can then be balanced against those of the programmers and query users who will access the Data Dictionary tables.

There may also be other data-related software for which design choices exist as to which computer(s) to locate them on. Examples are:

- Constraints and database procedures
- Extract/Download for Data Warehousing
- Inventory and navigation support for a Data Warehouse
- Archive Management.

17.2.3 *Evaluation criteria*

The primary criterion for evaluating designs is the expected performance of queries and transactions. If most of the usage patterns on the data are well-defined and relatively stable, then the design can be optimized to reflect the different priorities and frequencies. Things are more difficult when a lot of the access is *ad hoc*, or where the business needs are very fluid. In this case a decision has to be based on a mix of 'sample' queries and transactions.

The factors to be considered in query performance are similar to other design stages, but there is a greater weight on the processing time and cost. Transmission of data across links in the network may or may not be dominant.

Availability and Security may also be important criteria. Replication schemes can vary widely in these aspects.

An important criterion which is peculiar to this design stage is **ease of Database Administration**. A theoretically optimal partitioning may turn out to be a nightmare for a DBA.

17.3 DESIGN TASKS AT THIS STAGE

17.3.1 *Overview of design tactics*

Apart from the additional analysis needed to establish a more detailed and quantified requirement, the overall tactics are little changed from the single-site situation. There are few, if any, real success stories of using one method to find 'the best' data design.

The design process is essentially an iterative one, in which the stages are:

- generate a first-cut design
- evaluate the first-cut design
- identify profitable directions of improvement
- re-evaluate and iterate.

In shared data design, however good one's assumptions are, they are only a limited guide to what will happen in practical use – if only because the volume of user query activity can be so fickle. A recommended approach is to design for 'built-in tuneability', i.e. to leave some adjustments that can be 'tweaked' even after the data has been loaded, and when users are making full use of the system.

17.3.2   *Further analysis of a shared data area*

For each 'Analysis Project' cluster identified in the ISP (possibly with further 'Database' and 'System' sub-clusters), it is normal at this stage to take a more detailed look at the 'business requirement' in terms of the precise data items needed and the exact processing functions which are to take place. Such analysis can either follow a traditional 'dualistic' Data/Function philosophy, or take an Object Oriented approach.

Data structure analysis

In the well-known modeling methods such as Entity-Relationship Modeling or Object-Role Modeling (NIAM), we are looking for a canonical view of the data that has to be stored in the database. But for potentially distributed databases we also need to capture the Location dimension. We want to be able to document, for any data item, the following factors:

- which user group is the source?
- what is the split of this user group by geographic location?
- by which user groups does the item need to be accessed?
- what is the split of these user groups by geographic location?
- what is the localization pattern (i.e. how many recipient users are at the same geographic location as the source users, and what is the split of the others by position in the Technical Architecture, or by network distance)?

Note that we have already looked at localization patterns of entity types and shared data clusters, in order to suggest a good Technical Architecture.

Functional analysis

Traditional Structured Analysis, using such methods as hierarchical DFDs, is based on a paradigm of interacting processes which can be complex. From the data design point of view, analysis of functions tells us which data items are needed together or in defined sequences.

Recent trends in Analysis have seen an increasing reallocation of what would have been independent processes into database-related declarative statements such as rules and constraints.

We can use Functional Analysis to provide some information about Location, via the User Groups that perform each function.

Object oriented analysis (OOA)

This phrase is somewhat self-contradictory: 'Object Oriented' is essentially a type of solution, whereas 'Analysis' should be concerned with solution-independent requirements. More to the point, current OOA methods are relatively primitive, and do not offer the immediate prospect for analysis which incorporates the Location Dimension.

17.3.3 *Generate first-cut design*

The aim of this stage is to create a feasible, but not necessarily optimal, allocation of fragments and copies to sites. The method is to use a set of 'first-cut design rules' which lead to a starting design quickly without attempting to be too clever.

Some first-cut design rules are very crude. For example, one set of rules is:

1. resolve all many-to-many relationships with intersection entity types
2. map each entity type to one table stored at a central site.

However, this may not be compatible with the Technical Architecture.

A different set of rules, more suitable for a distributed environment, is the 'store near data source' system. On the basis of retaining maximum flexibility, each entity type is placed or partitioned on those processors in the Technical Architecture which are nearest to where the data is collected. All subsequent access is 'on demand' to those processors.

A more sophisticated first-cut can be built up using a 'User Group Access Pattern' Matrix incorporating the 'LFT' analysis introduced in Chapter 15. We look at the usage (C and U as well as A, B and S) by User Groups of the various Entity Types (or Object Classes which relate closely to Real-World Entities).

In this method, the first-cut design is arrived at by siting on the processor nearest to that user group all Entity Types or Object Classes that are specific to an individual user or robot group (i.e. coded L) or those whose likely use is more than 80% by one user or robot (i.e. coded F). For Entities or Objects which do not have a high affinity towards one user or robot site, or where user interest covers all occurrences of the type (coded T), we use a processor nearer to the users. This could be a User Group Server or a computer at an Intermediate Node, depending on the Technical Architecture.

17.3.4 *Evaluate first-cut design*

Usually, a fairly coarse evaluation against key indicators will indicate what the shortcomings of the first cut are.

The key indicators that need to be evaluated are:

- response time on the highest-volume user transactions (possibly several)
- the elapsed-time feasibility of any batch operations
- the probability of the system being unavailable to the users for more than some given time.

Normally, back-of-an-envelope calculations will be enough for the first evaluation, though Simulation or Test Prototypes could be used if available.

17.3.5 *Identify profitable directions of improvement*

A search for improvements depends on the choice of first cut.

From a central starting point, some strategies are:

- fragment tables based on location analysis of different attributes
- fragment tables based on locality of use of groups of rows
- create a Data Warehouse and store near the 'recipient' user groups.

From a 'store near data source' starting point:

- 'warehouse' the data by aggregating it based on an approximate idea of user access needs and transferring it to nodes nearer the users of the data
- move the 'F' objects away from the source nodes
- replicate data on several nodes.

The selection of a useful strategy will need to take account of the frequencies of use of data, and processor and communications capacities and costs.

17.3.6 *Re-evaluate and iterate*

Later cuts of the Data Design should be evaluated against a more extensive set of criteria. We need to be sure that there are no transactions which are too slow, or other potential infeasibilities.

As with Network Design, we use both coarse evaluation – to see if the design is vaguely feasible – and a finer evaluation to give more confidence that it really will work.

Iteration to produce another, better design should be continued until the designer feels confident that he or she can defend the design, not only to his/her manager, but to the Consultant that might be brought in!

17.4 DESCRIPTION OF INDIVIDUAL TECHNIQUES

Given the design procedure described above, there is less emphasis on formal design methods, but more on evaluation of alternatives.

The generation of first-cut designs involves following a set of rules, which vary according to the Technical Architecture direction chosen earlier.

A number of authors have considered the possibility of using algorithms to optimize the placement of data in a distributed system. However, most of these seem to rely on a relatively crude model of the problem. Bell and Grimson (1992) conclude that the models show that data placement does have a very significant impact on response times, but that many of the associated optimization problems are mathematically intractable or 'NP-complete'.

17.4.1 *Performance estimation for individual queries*

This involves a simple deterministic calculation of the processing time, and possibly also space, requirements of each type of query. Not all possible queries need to be evaluated; a few high-frequency ones, plus a sample query representing complex queries, are usually sufficient. In this stage of design, we are concerned with individual queries or 'units of work', but not multi-stage transactions.

The procedure for these deterministic calculations is described in the sub-sections (a) to (d) below. The capitalized words refer to Relational Table operations using 'Relational Algebra', with which the reader is assumed to be familiar.

(a) Data needed

The basic data needed to estimate query performance are:

- table volumes (number of rows, columns, bytes per tuple, length of keys)
- hit rates (what % of the rows might be 'hit' by likely SELECT functions)
- estimates of numbers of rows in JOIN results
- speed of data communications over the lines in the Network Design
- speed characteristics of SELECT, PROJECT, JOIN, etc., operations at the various nodes.

Not all this data is easy to come by. Estimating hit rates and JOIN result sizes depends on making informed assumptions about the likely distribution of attribute values. For example, in Figure 17.8, what proportion of the Patients in the survey have been hospitalized? Some degree of 'guesstimation' is inevitable.

The speed of relational operations can also be difficult to estimate. Simple assumptions, like X microseconds per table row processed, may lead to reasonable comparisons but may bear little relation to reality. Both SELECT and JOIN times will depend on whether appropriate indexes or hash keys will exist. JOIN times will also depend on the JOIN method, e.g. 'nested loop' or 'sort-merge'.

(b) Relational algebra and 'query trees'

The principle is to reduce the query to Relational Algebra sequences, for each of the alternative execution plans that are possible. For each execution plan one can draw a 'query tree' (see below).

Figures 17.8 and 17.9 are examples from Bell and Grimson (1992) which show two execution plans for a simple case with three tables at three different sites. These are evaluated using formulae which take account of both Processing and Data Transmission times. Bell and Grimson (1992) refer to a study where the calculated response times for different execution plans for the same query ranged from 20 seconds to 6 days.

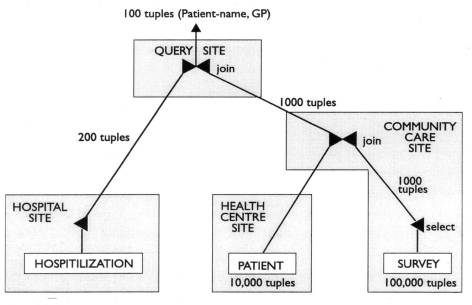

Figure 17.8 Example of a Query Tree (by permission, D. Bell and J. Grimson, 'Distributed Database Systems', 1992 © Addison-Wesley Publishing Co. Inc.).

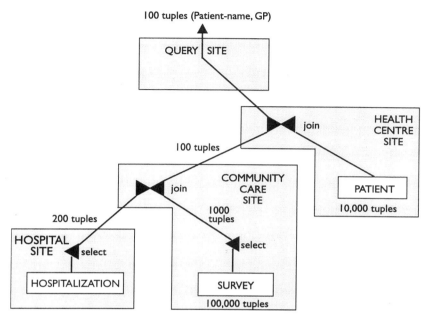

Figure 17.9 Alternative Query Tree for Previous Example (by permission, D. Bell and J. Grimson, 'Distributed Database Systems', 1992 © Addison-Wesley Publishing Co. Inc.).

(c) Calculating a response time estimate

We now time each task on the execution plan. In the distributed case, some of the tasks can be performed in parallel, so the situation is analagous to Critical Path Analysis where the **longest** path has to be considered.

Figure 17.10 shows how the query tree can be timed according to a set of basic assumptions.

In this particular example, data transmission time outweighs processing time. In practice we would PROJECT out early any attributes which are needed neither for the result nor for later JOINs. We could also consider 'semi-joins', as described in section 17.4.3 below.

(d) Comparing response times for different data placement designs

Having calculated response times for sample queries for each alternative data placement design, we can then make a choice or look for further improvements.

Operation	Method (a)	Method (b)
	1 second per	1 microsecond per row input (for joins,
Select 200,000 Hospitalizations down to 200 tuples	200 rows out x 1000 bytes = 0.2 sec	200k microsec = 0.2 sec
Select 100,000 Surveys down to 1000 tuples	1000 rows out x 1000 bytes = 1 sec	100k microsec = 0.1 sec
Join 200 Hosps x1000 Surveys resulting in 100 tuples @ 1500 bytes	100 rows out x 1500 bytes = 0.15 sec	200 x 1000 microsec - = 0.2 sec
Join 100 tuples from above with 100,000 Patients	100 rows out x 2000 bytes = 0.2 sec	100 x 10,000 microsec = 1 sec
TOTAL NON-DISTRIBUTED	1.35 sec	1.4 sec

Transmit 200 Hosps to Community Care site @ 64 kbps	200 x 1000 x 10 bits @ 64 kbps ~= 30 sec	
Transmit 100 joins to Health Centre site @ 64 kbps	100 x 1500 x 10 bits @ 64 kbps ~= 22.5 sec	
Transmit 100 results to Query site @ 14.4 kbps	100 x 2000 x 10 bits @ 14.4 kbps	

Figure 17.10 Rough Timing Calculation for the Previous Query Tree (using alternative methods for processor timing).

17.4.2 *Some guidelines for query optimization*

The term 'Query Optimization', as used here, does not mean that we are directly optimizing the data placement design. Instead, for each data design, we choose the best strategies for executing the sample queries. This enables us to make fair comparisons between the alternative designs.

Query optimization methods may help us to identify possible directions of improvement in the design of the shared data. For example, if a relational JOIN between two remote tables is very slow in the current design, we could consider replicating one of the tables so that the transmission time is reduced.

Well-established heuristic rules for drawing up good query plans are:

- perform SELECTs early – eliminate as many rows as possible as soon as possible
- resolve conditions with ANDs even if in different tables
- then do PROJECTs – this helps save on intermediate-result table size
- leave JOINs until later
- don't evaluate the same sub-expression twice.

Optimization for distributed data is similar to that for single-site databases but with a number of extra factors:

- communications cost is significant
- if data is replicated, one can use the potential parallelism
- if data is fragmented geographically, additional estimates need to be made of the proportion of the data in a table which involves access to remote sites
- remote data access can be done either by bulk transfer of whole (or extract) tables, or by *ad-hoc* sub-queries – both methods have pros and cons
- communication timing must include transmission of request messages as well as actual data transmission – this may be significant if call set-up time is significant (e.g. if using dial-up).

17.4.3 *Semi-joins*

One technique which has had some popularity in distributed query optimization is the use of SEMI-JOINs. A SEMI-JOIN is a JOIN result PROJECTed on to the columns of just one of the two tables being JOINed (Figure 17.11). We can have a LEFT SEMI-JOIN and a RIGHT SEMI-JOIN, depending on whether we PROJECT on to the columns of Table A or Table B.

The technique as used in distributed query optimization is to transmit a cut-down version of Table A, containing only the values of the attribute(s) which will be used for the JOIN. We can further cut down the volume sent by applying any SELECTS to remove unwanted rows before transmitting the keys (Figure 17.12).

This single-column table is then JOINed with Table B at the receiving site, and the result is a SEMI-JOIN, since matching has been applied but only the columns from Table B appear in the result. Such SEMI-JOINs can be sent back, subsequently processed and relayed to further sites. Their advantage lies in reducing the volumes transmitted, which will in most cases outweigh the extra transmissions. Figure 17.13 shows an example calculation of the pay-off of using this method.

17.4.4 *Simulation of a query mix*

Simulation can be used to evaluate a fuller mix of queries, which could include an allowance for contention for processors and communication lines. It may be possible to do this as an extension to the Network Simulation mentioned in the previous chapter. Purpose-built models, using a simulation language or toolkit, could be justified if the design decision is very critical to the mix of query types.

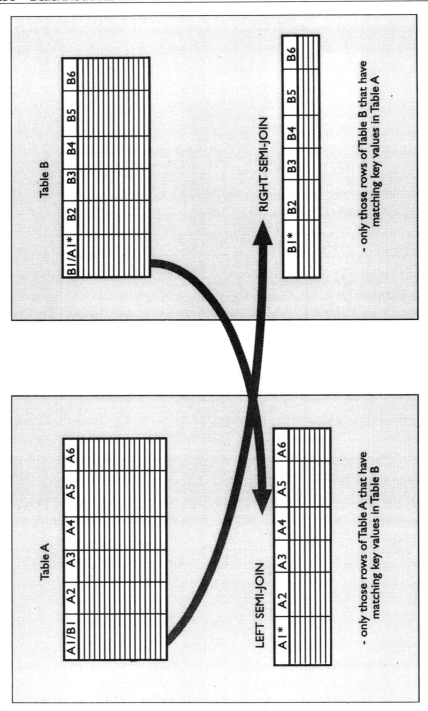

Figure 17.11 Left and Right Semi-Joins.

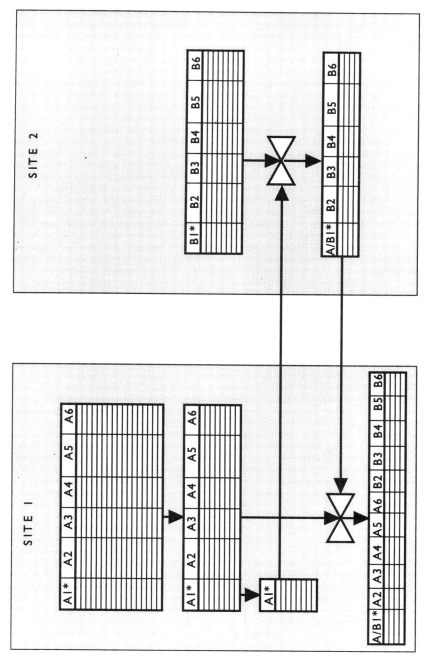

Figure 17.12 Semi-Join Method with Pre-SELECT.

WITHOUT SEMI-JOINS

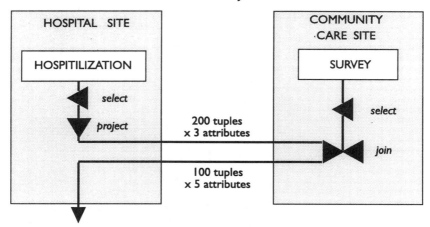

1100 attributes transmitted + 1 join, 2 selects, 1 project

WITH SEMI-JOINS

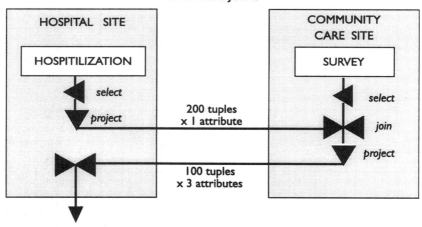

500 tuples transmitted + 2 joins, 2 selects, 2 projects

Figure 17.13 Pay-off of the Semi-Join Method (based on example by permission, D. Bell and J. Grimson, 'Distributed Database Systems', 1992© Addison-Wesley Publishing Co. Inc.).

17.4.5 *Data security evaluation*

This is an area where distributed systems are frequently challenged. With sophisticated use of fragmentation and replication, security (against both intentional and unintentional loss or corruption of the data) is harder to

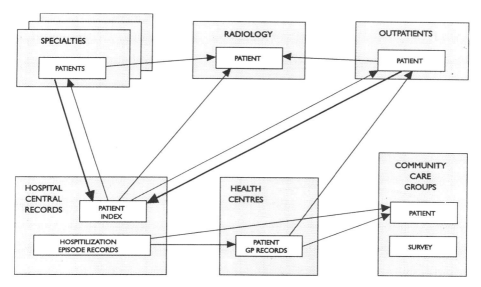

Figure 17.14 Example Replication Flow Diagram for Checking Security.

control. To help satisfy auditors, as well as managers, two approaches can be proposed.

The first involves drawing up a diagram showing the means by which different copies, and different fragments of data, flow through the system as designed. An example is shown in Figure 17.14, which shows the flow of Patient information between different processors in and around a Hospital. Thick lines represent automatic bulk replication; thin arrows show the passing of copies of sub-sets of Patient details to sites needing data on specific Patients.

The second technique is to design (into the system) processes by which multiple copies are periodically reconciled, and different fragments checked for consistency. This could involve a periodic upload of the copy from each distributed sites followed by a batch comparison with an agreed 'accurate' version.

17.5 CASE STUDIES IN SHARED DATA DESIGN

17.5.1 *Mr A*

For the time being, Mr A is unlikely to have other than a single-site database. With Associates, he is likely to have a Federal Database (or loose cooperation).

Fragmentation will be based on the individual responsible. Administration data would still be genuinely shared, and there would be some sharing of Supplier and Customer information (e.g. have we/they paid their bills?).

17.5.2 *Bay Organic Produce Cooperative*

Even if peer-to-peer architecture is chosen, there has to be a consistent logical view of a single database for most purposes. The main entity types concern Farmers, Produce Lots, Produce Types, Price Events, Buyers and Warehouse Stocks. If some staff specialize, certain entity types might be split, and replication of the data needed by the general (non-specializing) staff would be required. Replication of most updates could be propagated nightly, but some transactions should be broadcast immediately.

17.5.3 *Detox Pharmaceuticals*

The main entity types are Products/Raw Materials, Product Movements, Customers, Orders, Deliveries, Warehouse Stocks and Total Markets. A lot of the key information about market share is derived and summarized, while a lot of Customer and Warehouse data could be distributed. If so, there will be a need for daily or hourly propagation of some changes, e.g. Prices. Data Warehousing may be a possibility for Head Office decision support, with daily propagation of updates.

17.5.4 *Electric House*

Stores and Warehouses, both inside and outside the USA, will probably operate their databases and systems autonomously. Apart from these areas, entity types will include Suppliers, Product Purchase Prices, Product Movements (planned/actual), and Transport Operations (planned/actual). Some of these affect Warehouse operations (e.g. planned Movements) so will need to be replicated. Data Warehousing is again a possibility for Head Office Decision Support, not just for Head Office but for each Latin American country as well.

17.5.5 *Commonwealth Open Polytechnic*

Student records may be centralized, but Regional Offices will need to have either fast access or replicated copies, especially at peak activity times in the annual cycle of Registration, Assessment and Examination. The choice will depend on the network economics. Other data is probably centralized, and decision support can operate directly from the central database.

17.5.6 *National Environmental Protection Board*

The Research and Intelligence databases will be a mixture of Centralized and loose Federal. Inspection and Questionnaire result data will probably be geographically distributed, with summarized extracts being replicated to the Head Office. Remote Monitoring data will probably remain local, the results being summarized into the Inspection database.

17.6 EXERCISES

1. How might a 'shared data' cluster differ from an 'analysis' cluster?

2. What are the advantages and disadvantages of starting Shared Data Design from a location-independent Global Conceptual Data Model?

3. What is the argument for leaving Shared Data Design until after Network Design?

4. How can one determine whether splitting an entity type by attributes (i.e. vertically) is justified?

5. When might 'grouping' of conceptual data elements into larger collections be appropriate?

6. Distinguish the three types of partitioning.

7. Identify five areas of choice in replication design.

8. How does one determine whether replication is justified or not, and if so, what speed of propagation of changes should be used?

9. What is 'Data Warehousing'? How does if differ from the concept of an 'Information Center'?

10. Which items of software would you expect to locate with copies of the DBMS, and which might be moved to separate servers?

11. If we find that a 'store near source' first-cut design has performance unacceptable to some remote users, what aspects of the design can we consider changing?

12. What is the problem about estimating the size of interim results when timing a query tree?

13. Does the use of very simplistic models of processing time for relational operations mean that comparisons are unreliable?

14. How do you think the same query could take 20 seconds using one query execution plan and six days using another?

15. What are the basic heuristic rules for query optimization?

16. Describe how a 'semi-join' works, and why it may help in distributed queries.

17. Describe two approaches to satisfying auditor concerns about the security of a replicated distributed database.

18. Discuss in more detail the potential partitioning of Mr A and his Associates' Customer data between what is shared and what is local to each Associate.

19. Supposing staff in BOPC specialize and a peer-to-peer architecture with locally-stored data is preferred. How might a suitable replication plan operate?

20. For Electric House's Product Movements and Transport Operations, draw up a User Group Access Pattern matrix of data types against user groups. Does this help suggest how this data should be located?

21. Explain the likely life-cycle of Inspection data in the NEPB, and discuss the implications for Distribution and Replication.

22. A staff member in NEPB wishes to analyze some Inspection and Questionnaire results (1000 rows of 2000 bytes at each of ten Regional Offices) against a table of average figures that he has assembled from 50 other Countries, and that he has now stored in a database on a Head Office server computer. Describe two possible query paths and compare their likely timing, given an internal LAN speed of 10M bps and links to the Regional Offices of 64 kbps.

ASSIGNMENT TASK

For your chosen case study, complete the following sub-tasks.

    A1. Propose two 'first-cut' data placement plans, possibly using your Technical Architecture alternatives as a guideline.

    A2. Identify a sample query involving at least two JOINs and access to data at two separate sites, and make estimates of initial and intermediate result volumes.

A3. Propose optimized queries and draw up their query trees.

A4. Time the query responses using one of the rough methods shown in Figure 17.10.

A5. Suggest what possible improved data placement might be considered.

A6. Outline an appropriate security policy to satisfy the auditors.

FURTHER READING

Bell, D. and Grimson, J. (1992) *Distributed Database Systems*, Addison-Wesley, Reading, MA, Chapter 5.

Ferguson, M. (1994) Parallel database – the shape of things to come. *Database Programming and Design*, Oct.

Ferguson, M. (1994) Breaking up is hard to do (article on parallel databases). *Database Programming and Design*, Nov.

Fertuck, L. (1992) *Systems Analysis and Design with CASE Tools*, Brown, Dubuque, IA, Chapter 11.

Hansen, M. and Halle, B. von (1995) Breaking boundaries through worldwide data replication. *Database Programming and Design*, Jan.

Inmon, W. and Caplan, J. (1992) *Information Systems Architecture: Development in the 90s*, QED, Boston, MA, Chapters 9 and 12.

Poe, V. (1995) *Building a Data Warehouse for Decision Support*, Prentice Hall, Englewood Cliffs, NJ.

Poe, V. (1995) Data warehouse: architecture is not infrastructure. *Database Programming and Design*, Jul.

Zornes, A. *et al.* (1995) Shedding light on data warehousing. *Computing (UK)*, Mar.

18 Design within an individual system or sub-system

18.1 RATIONALE FOR THIS DESIGN STAGE

After all the preceding stages of design, what is left is the 'rump' of systems design within an individual system (or sub-system) that has been identified by clustering and other refinements. The Technical Architecture has been settled, a Network designed and the data positioning established. The major remaining distribution task is to decide what sort of software will be required, and where to place the various modules. Besides this there is still a lot of detailed work to do to complete IS design, but little of that work is specifically to do with distribution.

In this chapter we will concentrate primarily on this software distribution task, but will also place it in the context of the general sub-systems design methodology. However, we stop short of getting into the design of programs or individual modules of software.

18.2 INPUTS TO THIS DESIGN STAGE

18.2.1 *Starting points*

Statement of requirements

We need to refer back now to a set of functional requirements, whether we are designing a large system or an 'incremental' sub-system. The primary sources for these are the Information Needs Lists and Process Models that have been drawn up within ISP or some other Analysis exercise.

ISP clustering results

The clustering process in IS Strategy Planning, which has already been built on in order to arrive at the Technical Architecture, the Network and the 'natural' Databases, also suggests natural boundaries for systems which make suitable units for design work.

These 'Natural Systems' may in practice need to be subdivided further because different scopes of management or of decision timescale may require information systems with quite different characteristics. For example, it does not make sense to try to merge, say, Process Control and Decision Support within the same system, even if they have a large overlap of data access. Other splitting could be suggested by differences in the dominant response speed, e.g.:

- sub-second real-time
- *ad hoc* queries allowing 5–30 seconds
- overnight batch.

We have already discussed other rationales for splitting clusters in Chapters 14, 15 and 17. Examples of these sub-clustering schemes (Figure 18.1) are:

- decision support systems (suggested by off-diagonal 'R' clusters)
- database storage and retrieval systems (suggested by tall thin clusters)
- message-oriented systems (suggested by short fat clusters)
- groupware and workflow systems (suggested by 'hinge' Entity Types).

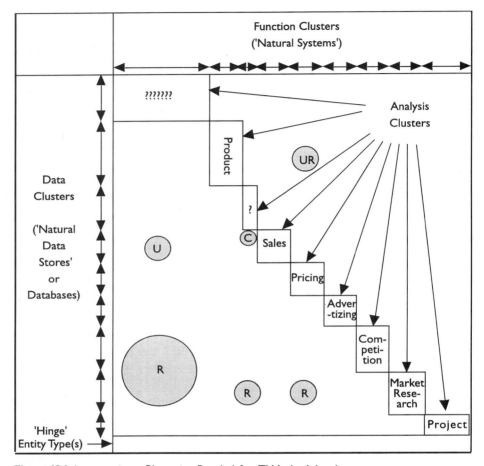

Figure 18.1 Interpreting a Clustering Result (after TI Methodology).

Business systems architecture

In Information Engineering, the usual way of presenting a recommended set of IS to an organization's management is the Natural Systems Architecture diagram. The example in Figure 18.2 comes from the Texas Instruments book *A Guide to Information Engineering Using the IEF* (1991). The grid of this diagram is the same as for the Information Needs Map (see Chapter 14), so it serves to show how the Information Needs will be covered. The recommended Natural Systems, based on the clusters but possibly further subdivided, are shown as sausages. Systems supporting 'hinge' Entity Types appear as long flat jumbo sausages, usually near the middle horizontal boundaries. Arrowed lines between the sausages represent flows of data between systems.

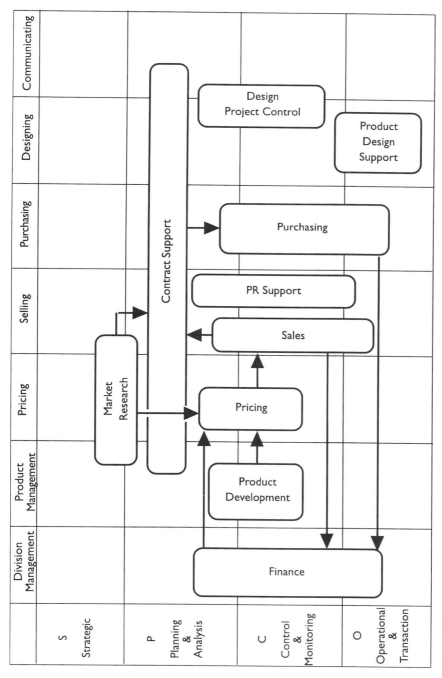

Figure 18.2 Natural Systems Architecture Diagram for ABC Software Co. (after TI Methodology).

Identification of project-sized chunks

Identification of actual sub-systems also depends on how the organization can get from where it is now to where it should be to meet its Business and IS Strategy. In practical terms, development has to be done in **projects**. Example types of projects might be:

- develop a brand-new system (if the current system is manual, provides poor support of needs, or is unmaintainable)
- re-engineer the current system for the new technical architecture (with minor functional changes)
- develop an add-on sub-system to the current system (to provide desired extra functionality)
- fix the current system (replace certain modules only).

Timing and synchronization requirements

By this we mean establishing constraints which say that certain processing tasks must happen in a certain order. In traditional structured methodologies, these can be captured through Control Flows, when used in Data Flow Diagrams.

Event-based and Object Oriented methodologies provide methods of ensuring that these requirements are incorporated. Examples are Timing diagrams (Booch, 1991), Event Trace diagrams (Rumbaugh, 1991) and Interaction diagrams (Jacobson, 1992). In Jacobson's approach 'Control Object Classes' are also identified. An example of an Interaction Diagram as used in Jacobson's approach is shown in Figure 18.3.

This example describes a Warehouse Management system, in which the Use Case being focused on concerns redistribution of inventory from warehouse to warehouse. The diagram represents the Planning aspect of this Use Case. The leftmost object class, Manual Redistribution Window, is an interface object, while the next class, Planning, is a control object. The remainder are entity object classes.

In a distributed system, some of these objects may reside on different processors, which makes synchronization of yet higher importance. This can be still further complicated if some of the entity objects have been replicated in the design of the shared data.

Usability requirements

The form of the required user interfaces should also be included as a starting point. It may be a design **solution**, rather than a basic requirement, that dialogues should follow an exact pattern, but there may be genuine requirements saying that users should be offered options in a certain way or order. Jacobson's approach includes identifying Interface Objects at an early stage of Analysis and Design.

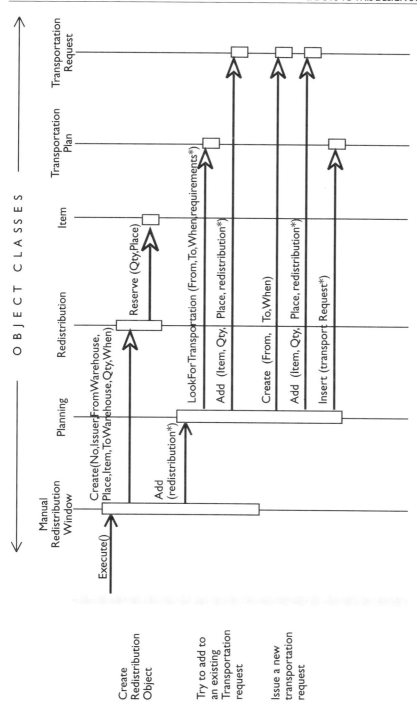

Figure 18.3 Example of an Interaction Diagram (I. Jacobson, M. Christerson, P. Jonsson & G. Övergaard, 'Object-Oriented Software Engineering – A Use Case Driven Approach', 1992 © 1992 ACM Press. A division of the Association for Computing Machinery Inc. (ACM). With permission from the publishers, Addison-Wesley Publishing Company Inc.).

Usability is also geared to what groups of users have come to expect. Thus the starting point for design of Interface Objects will normally be to tailor the use of a standard set of components, as shown in Figure 18.4.

18.2.2 *Nature of the alternatives*

The primary question in this chapter is how to break down a Natural System into smaller units for the following purposes:

- to align with available application packages (full or tailorable skeletons)
- to align with re-usable software modules or objects
- to allocate as tasks for software designers and programmers
- to distribute to different clients or servers for cost-efficient processing
- to be acceptable as manageable projects (see section 18.2.1).

Any partitioning of applications may therefore be geared to a number of different objectives.

One good way of partitioning follows Jacobson's Object Oriented approach introduced earlier. Three possible categories can be created for functional elements of the system:

Data oriented:
> this includes, as well as support for the basic CRUD operations, data analysis and summarization, database constraint enforcement, and access control routines.

Control oriented:
> this includes enforcement of synchronization, event sequencing, state transitions, process dependencies and may include some TP monitor functions.

User interface oriented:
> this includes user dialogue handling, support for graphics input and output devices, language parsing, and sophisticated features such as image matching.

18.2.3 *Evaluation criteria*

Most of the evaluation criteria at this stage are much the same as in earlier stages, namely response, throughput, availability, security and cost.

The main additions are development cost together with the risk of failed development, since we are now talking about specific projects.

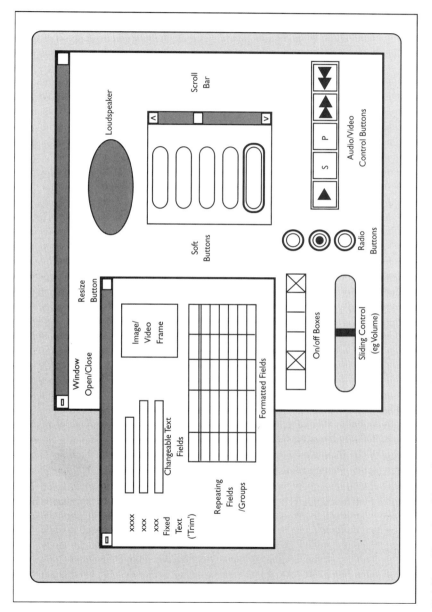

Figure 18.4 Typical Interface Object Components in a GUI.

18.3   DESIGN TASKS AT THIS STAGE

18.3.1 *Overview of design tactics*

Some degree of Feasibility Review and Detailed Requirements Analysis is normally required for individual projects. Following this no one pattern of systems design is appropriate for all situations. What we propose in this chapter is a 'pick and mix' approach from of four styles:

- Top-down
- Bottom-up
- Component engineering
- Cooperative agreement.

These styles are described in sections 18.3.4–18.3.7 below.

18.3.2 *Feasibility review*

The purpose of a review at this stage is to check that the project can still succeed, while some but not all of the design decisions have been made, before committing the major expenditure of resources. We need to review what the criteria for success or failure are, and talk to the sponsor of the projects, to avoid later recriminations when expectations are not realized.

Figure 18.5 shows the overall task structure of such a Feasibility study.

A number of areas of Feasibility should be considered:

- Statement of Objectives Review
- Cost-Benefit Review
- Operational Performance Review
- Maintainability Review
- Implementation Program Review.

The Operational Performance Review should include Archiving – a matter which is often forgotten, resulting in unchecked growth in database volumes.

Figure 18.6 shows an example from Gilb (1988), in which the objectives of the system have been expressed in measurable terms.

18.3.3 *Detailed requirements analysis*

Our approach for Requirements Analysis in an individual Natural System closely follows what we do in the wider Information Strategy stage, but in more detail.

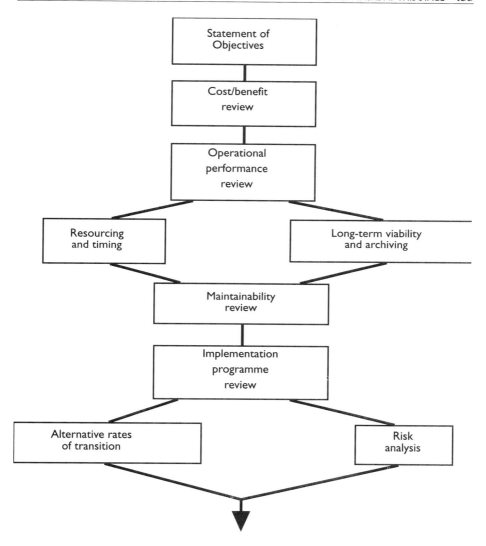

Figure 18.5 Feasibility Task Structure.

For Distribution Analysis purposes, we can use the User Group Access Pattern matrix using the same CUABS and LFT notation discussed in earlier chapters. Figure 18.7 shows an example from a Financial Trading company.

Note that we have been stricter at this stage about identifying several different usage patterns for the same system by one User Group. This split coding may suggest that the two component parts of the System could be separated.

Criteria	Scale	Worst Acceptable	Plan	Best	Current Situation
10-year operating cost	$ compared with current +6% pa growth	85-95%	65-85%	40-60%	100%
Interactive response speed	seconds from 'enter' to full response	10->20 sec	3->7 sec	0->1 sec	3->40 sec
Data integrity	% errors	.5->1.5%	.3->.8%	0->.1%	
Availability	% uptime	93->97%	96->100%	98->100%	
Security	corruptions per year	10->20	2->6	0->2	
Ease of use	days training	15->25	4->6	0->2	
Ease of enhancement	% of software impacted by average change	2->3%	0	0	
User report & analysis	problems per year per system	6->18	0->4	0->1	
Data completeness	problems per year per system	5->10	0->1	0	
External interface	requests per day	3->5	0->1	0	

Figure 18.6 Feasibility – Statement of Objectives (by permision, T. Gilb 'Principles of Software Enginering Management', Addison-Weslely, 1988 © Tom Gilb and Susannah Finzi).

Natural System / User Group ->	Dealers	Dealing Managers	Financial Managers	Support Staff
On-line Feed Handling	ABL	BSLT	BST	
On-line Dealing	CUAL	ABSL	BST	
Exposure Control	AL	CUABSL -80% ABF - 20%	CUABST	
Trading Partners	CUL - 40% AF - 60%	UABL	CUABT	UT
Dealing Statistics & Accounts	AL	ABSL	BST	CUST

Key:

C=Create U=Update/Delete
A=Ad hoc read   B=Browse S = Summarise

L=Local   F=Foreign as well as local   T=Total access to any site

Figure 18.7 Different User Access Patterns within one System.

18.3.4 *Top-down design*

Top-down design follows the traditional structured approach of successive refinement of detail, typified by the leveling of Data Flow Diagrams. In an Object Oriented Design approach, the approach is only slightly different, proceeding from 'normal' cases into the detail of exceptions and ancillary housekeeping tasks. The prime advantage of the top-down approach is that individual procedures, when turned into software or manual instructions, are always maintained in their place within the higher-level objectives.

However, a disadvantage is that the components identified by a pure top-down approach are not necessarily suitable for component-style re-use. Also, if one does not consider the location dimension of where the data is required and is captured, there is no information on which to base software distribution optimization decisions.

For the distributed situation that we are addressing in this book, the procedure for allocating processing components to computers is an iterative one, with a 'first-cut', evaluation and iteration, much as in the previous chapter. The first-cut solution may be based on the LFT analysis – more details of this are given in section 18.4.1 below.

In any partitioning of applications, an object oriented (OO) approach is useful, since it is geared to creating naturally separate units of software that are linked by message passing. However, existing OO methodologies are not always strong in the modeling of the dynamic aspects of a system. A fuller discussion of allocating software components to processors in an OO Design (OOD) methodology can be found in Booch's 1991 book (Booch, 1991).

18.3.5 *Bottom-up design*

An approach almost diametrically opposed to the above is favored by many Object Oriented Programming (OOP) experts. The method proceeds by designing the system or sub-system in terms of logical objects, which are then implemented as software objects. These objects are all potentially distributed by default, since objects are encapsulated and all inter-object communication is through message passing. What can be a software object is based on the designer's previous expertise, or on the availability of Libraries of previously coded Object Classes.

The approach is bottom-up in the sense that the programmers often start with code that they already have, usually in the form of Object Classes. These Classes are then specialized to meet the more particular requirements of the system being designed.

As is normal with OOD, programmer/designers usually prototype a small central part of the requirement first, without taking account of details like data storage, exceptions, or future enhancements. This results in the ability to demonstrate the basic functionality early, and to worry about fine details later.

Because OO techniques are still relatively immature, the success or otherwise of this approach is still very dependent on the competence and flair of the individual programmers. A large design could be very difficult to share or to transfer between programmers.

18.3.6 *Component engineering*

The third major design alternative is what we call the 'Component Engineering' approach. It falls somewhere in between the top-down and bottom-up approaches. The idea is to try to match parts of the system being designed against elements of a 'standard' structure of application types. This standard structure actually combines two hierarchies:

- the **is-a** hierarchy where application elements are 'sub-types' of others (Figure 18.8)
- the **part-of** hierarchy where application elements are combined to form a composite element (Figure 18.9)

This structure will be immediately recognisable to OO devotees – all we are doing here is to apply the OO approach to units of 'software requirement'. In fact one

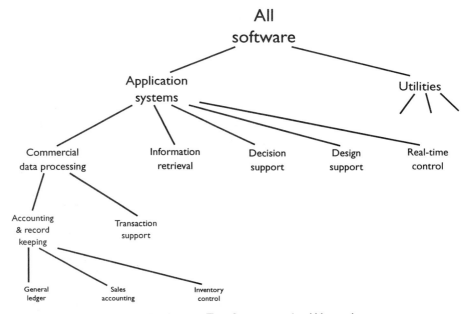

Figure 18.8 Example of an Application-Type Structure – 'is-a' Hierarchy.

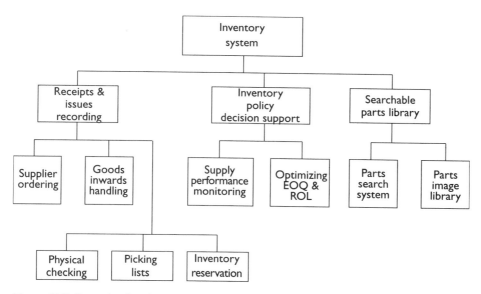

Figure 18.9 Example of an Application-Type Structure – 'part-of' Hierarchy.

way of using Component Engineering is to have an OO Class Library which is itself structured in this fashion.

As observed earlier, however, most Class Libraries are still at too low a level to meet the bottom of our 'component model', i.e. the structure we build for our own organization's requirements. For the time being, the user organization will have to keep a 'shopping list' of where it can go to acquire a packaged component that does something similar to what is wanted.

The 'User Interface' components of a sub-system requirement can also be matched with type hierarchies of generic components, e.g. a 'mouse/window/ button GUI' or an 'SQL-compliant RDBMS'.

In the Component Engineering approach, the emphasis shifts from 'green field' coding to 'gluing' components together. Products which can be used as glue to help link components are now readily available in the commercial market-place. Examples are Software Agents, Middleware, Fourth-Generation Languages (4GLs), Scripting Languages and Visual Basic etc.

18.3.7 *Cooperative agreement*

Increasingly often, a sub-system project does not involve developing new software components for specific application needs. The project may rather be to introduce new functionality by merging 'islands' of currently isolated systems in the organization (or between different organizations). This introduces the need for a fourth design approach.

Ceri (1990) has suggested the use of a design technique where each node starts by optimizing its design individually, and is then involved in negotiation of joint cooperative design decisions with other nodes.

The main stages in this approach are:

- agreeing the overall objectives of the combined system
- establishing 'contracts and responsibilities' for each member of the federation, as discussed in Wirfs-Brock (1990) and Gradwell (1992)
- getting cooperative agreement on interfaces
- tailoring member-sub-system components using some 'glue' facility
- building federal controls

and these will of course be complemented by appropriate and progressive prototyping and testing plans.

Agreeing the overall objectives of the combined system

This is largely a political task. Meetings should be held to decide on the priorities and CSFs of the combined system. It is almost certain that each constituent sub-system will have differing views of what they wish to get out of the system, so there has to be some horse-trading. However, someone sufficiently high up in the organization should be able to answer the question 'what is the bottom-line business need being met by this integration?' or the project should not be underway in the first place.

Establishing contracts and responsibilities

Figure 18.9 shows some of the information-related contracts that might have to be struck between a Government Regulatory Organization (e.g. the NEPB in Case Study 6) and the external organizations it deals with.

The NEPB occupies the middle of the diagram in Figure 18.10, the companies who have to comply with the legislation are on the left, and the researchers under contract to the NEPB are on the right. The four ellipses represent four information areas which are 'traded'. The remarks on the ends of the 'spokes' represent the contract terms that the party has to meet.

The tasks involved are rather like those of a lawyer after a main agreement has been signed. It means dotting 'i's and crossing 't's. Most of the work will be deciding what happens when the exceptions occur. Some requirements may involve statistical measures, e.g. response time or availability percentiles.

Cooperative agreement on interfaces

The central design task is to decide on the interfaces, i.e. what each federation member will send to each other, when, and how. This task follows largely from

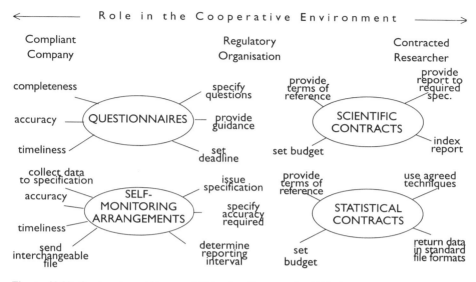

Figure 18.10 Contracts and Responsibilities in a Cooperative IS Environment.

the previous stage, but involves the problems of coping with heterogeneous hardware and software platforms and possibly also data communication protocols. A new application-layer protocol may have to be built on the top of others, unless agreement to use a standard can be arranged.

Tailoring member subsystem components

Consequent on the above, pre-existing member systems will probably have to be tailored to meet the contractual requirements and to conform to the agreed interfaces. This is normally a task delegated to the individuals responsible for the individual sub-systems. However, they may not have the skill to perform the task, and a specification may have to be prepared for a software specialist. The individual sub-systems will often not be built using a procedural programming language, but may either be generated from 4GL or Menu definitions, or may even be run interpretively (e.g. some 4GLs, RPG, old Basic).

Building federal controls

The final design task is to ensure that there are adequate controls on the federal system to meet the overall objectives such as privacy and security. A designated controller node will probably be used for some functions such as statistics, but it is likely that all nodes will need to contain a 'client' version of federation software, which will link with the 'federation server' function on the controller node.

18.4   DESCRIPTION OF INDIVIDUAL TECHNIQUES

18.4.1   *Using LFT analysis for process location*

The Technical Architecture (see Chapter 15 above) will have defined a structure of computers and network links which will efficiently support the expected combined needs of users and robots. Some guidance will have been included regarding placement of data and functions.

Assuming that a Location Analysis has already been done as described in section 18.2.1 above, the first-cut design is arrived at by siting all processes that are specific to a group of users or robots (coded **L**), or those whose likely use is more than 80% by a User Group (coded **F**), on the processor nearest to the user. For processes which are not weighted heavily towards one user or robot site, shared data and overall control processes (coded **T**), we use a processor nearer to the users. This could be a User Group or an intermediate node server, depending on the Technical Architecture.

From the first cut, design improvement proceeds by trying improvements in order to meet the performance requirements or improve the evaluation criterion which represents the 'highest priority objective function', e.g. cost. Figure 18.11 shows some possible direction of improvement, but the procedure is inevitably relatively informal.

18.4.2   *Class library matching*

The art of effective engineering for object re-use is still in its infancy. Figure 18.12 shows an idealized way in which re-use could work, which involves a mixture of bottom-up and top-down design.

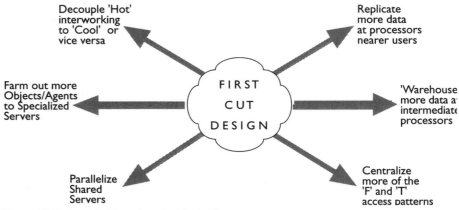

Decouple 'Hot' interworking to 'Cool' or vice versa

Replicate more data at processors nearer users

Farm out more Objects/Agents to Specialized Servers

'Warehouse more data a intermediate processors

FIRST CUT DESIGN

Parallelize Shared Servers

Centralize more of the 'F' and 'T' access patterns

Figure 18.11 Possible Directions for Design Improvement.

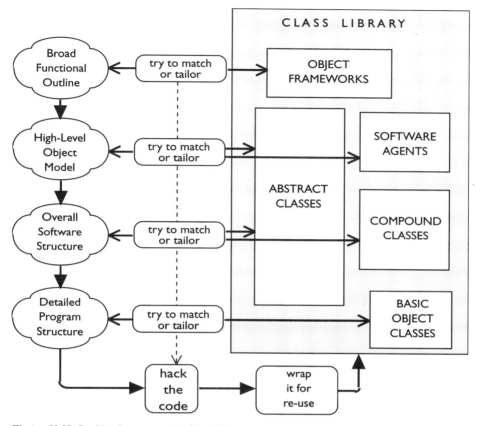

Figure 18.12 Re-Use Strategy with Class Libraries.

An efficient matching system for the contents of Class Libraries has yet to become established. Many of the classes in such Libraries are themselves built 'bottom up', i.e. by generalizing or aggregating smaller functionality, rather than supporting a given business function.

To stand a realistic chance of wider adoption, some form of indexing of Class Libraries is necessary. Since there is no guarantee that any two people will use the same names for anything, such indexing has to be on the semantics rather than simply the text of data or procedure names. Indexing of a description of the purpose as well as just the interface of the class is also desirable. Figure 18.13 shows a suggested scheme for searching on Class Library indexes.

As Object Classes are added to a system being developed using this approach, it will become clear to the expert OO Programmer where the natural breaks fall, i.e. which sets of Objects have close coupling and which

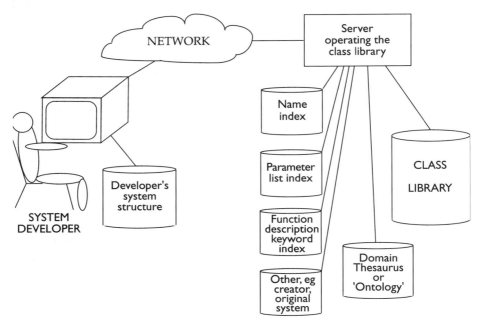

Figure 18.13 Searching Class Libraries through Indexes.

ṣets communicate more rarely. Using the assumption made earlier, that User (or Robot) Interface object classes will sit near the physical interfaces, some sort of clustering could theoretically be used to determine how to split objects between nodes. However, it is more likely that different designs will be tested by trial and error.

18.4.3 *Application-type matching in component engineering*

The principles of Component Engineering and the Application-Type Structure were discussed in section 18.3.6 above. A metamodel for the Application-Type Structure and possible matching is shown in Entity-Relationship diagram form in Figure 18.14. The dotted boxes at the bottom represent available components, and the grey double-headed arrows the possible areas in which requirements could be matched to existing software.

As with Class Libraries, we are once again talking about re-use – but this time at the level of design requirements, and without the strict Object Oriented Programming connotations.

The first stage is to match our sub-system requirement with a generic system type on a standard Application-Type Structure. As an example, we could describe our project requirement as being for a 'Membership' system or a 'Sales

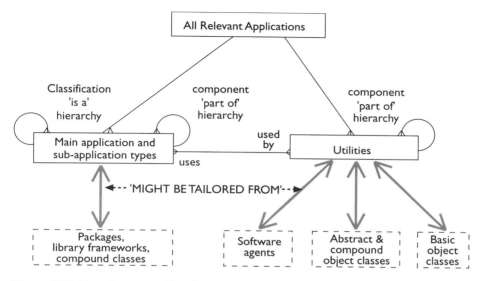

Figure 18.14 Meta Application-Type Structure.

Accounting' system. Clearly the number of potential Application Types is quite large, but there is considerable overlap in what different organizations require.

Figure 18.15 shows a possible standard Application-Type Structure for a Manufacturing organization, showing only the 'part-of' relationships.

It would be theoretically possible to build up a universal Application-Type Structure in which any re-usable software component, from any source, could be classified. In practice, each organization may choose to keep its own individual Structure.

What needs to be going on at the other side of the matching is for a 'software component librarian' to index all the available re-usable software modules, as they are created or are announced in the press, in the context of the Application-Type Structure. This is not currently a common role in organizations' IT departments, but may be so in a few years time.

Possible sources of re-usable software include the following:

- object frameworks and complex classes
- software agents
- shareware
- in-house or sister organization re-usable modules
- skeleton packages offering tailorable module toolkits
- complete packages.

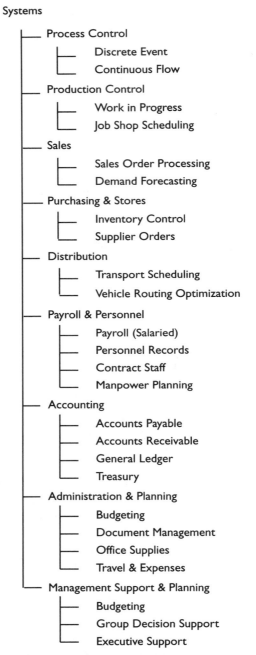

Figure 18.15 Example of an Application-Type Structure: Required Systems for a Manufacturing Organization.

If complete packages are to be considered, they should have standard (or well-published) enough interfaces so that different modules from other sources can be plugged in and out.

The actual matching process would be similar to that used for Object Class Libraries. Since the available software may come from a variety of sources, names cannot be expected to match, and intelligent searching of descriptions, together with the ability to browse up and down the hierarchies, are needed.

18.4.4 *Software agents*

Software Agents (McKie, 1995) form a new approach which offers a way of building systems by assembling generalized components, using of course considerable amounts of tailoring and 'glue'. Software Agents are collections of re-usable chunks of code which react intelligently to defined events. They form a natural outgrowth of the development of the Object Oriented approach to systems and data. Their advent can also be related to that of Middleware, which was discussed in Chapter 10 as a primary underpinning of the Client/Server style.

The main classes of Software Agents that can be used are:

- Filtering Agents (searching a database – DBMS-independent)
- Focusing Agents (looking for events on a database)
- Brokering Agents (searching object repositories, class libraries, etc.)
- Workflow Agents (automating routing of decision-making or document flow)
- Cataloging Agents (performing CRUD on a database)
- Construction Agents (intelligent data mining)
- Enforcement Agents (enforcing a set of integrity and/or security rules).

The method of making use of these Agents is to purpose-design a simple control module, or a structure of such modules, which will set the script for the overall system objective and which will create some of the events to which the Agents will respond.

With this approach, the designer can create his or her modules around what is provided by the Software Agents.

18.5 CASE STUDIES IN INDIVIDUAL SUB-SYSTEM DESIGN

18.5.1 *Mr A*

No significant application projects are foreseen while Mr A is working without Associates. After this, development of a cooperative system of working between the Associates is likely to be the top priority. Such a system will probably not be in the 'hot' category – asynchronous Message Passing is enough. The two main tasks will be to agree interfaces and to amend existing sub-systems which will interface to the cooperative data exchange system.

18.5.2 *Bay Organic Produce Cooperative*

The major project here will be the Produce Movement Planning system which will support the work of the ten staff. This system combines Lots to be received from Farmers, Sales to Buyers and Movements to and from the Warehouse. This is an operational system with a response requirement of up to five seconds. It is probably not an application for which existing components are plentiful. If using Client/Server, a top-down design approach seems most appropriate.

18.5.3 *Detox Pharmaceuticals*

The highest priority is replacement of the centralized legacy system which collects the basic data on Sales. This needs to work on an immediate data collection, but daily reporting, cycle. The Production Control system has a response requirement of about one hour, and tailoring of existing packaged components seems a possibility. Similar systems are needed for Sales Support in each region, with possible variations as some regions may be largely rural, as opposed to metropolitan Warsaw or Upper Silesia.

18.5.4 *Electric House*

In Electric House proper, the main project is Transport Fleet Management, which is an interesting distributed system. Scheduled movements need to be exchanged with Store and Warehouse systems within five minutes. Tailorable package software may be available, but if not, a combination of top-down and bottom-up design will be required.

With the merger, the priority is to equip Latin American Stores and Warehouses with systems compatible with the Electric House ones. Long-term replacement by software similar to the US systems is desirable, so hopefully in-house component matching could be used. Shorter-term tailoring of existing software in order to provide a reasonable data exchange is more likely.

18.5.5 *Commonwealth Open Polytechnic*

The COP needs to develop a number of systems which should be similar to those in other academic institutions, but with variations because of the 'distance' style of COP's operations. This suggests a Component Engineering or Class Library approach. Some of the other projects are 'infrastructure', for example a Student Video On Demand service, which depends on students having fast network links to their homes.

Setting up the student Email service may require considerable project planning as well as some software tailoring. Mailbox storage, authentication and accounting procedures are likely to be the main issues.

18.5.6 *National Environmental Protection Board*

The NEPB is effectively in a start-up situation, so a good choice of feasible projects is important. A lot of the key applications revolve around message passing. The Inspection report and Questionnaire handling applications could be developed using application generators. The Statistical Database applications could use tailorable statistical packages such as SAS or SPSS, etc.

18.6 EXERCISES

1. Why may analysis clusters need to be split when identifying sub-systems?

2. How does a Natural Systems Architecture diagram help management to understand the collection of sub-system projects that has been proposed?

3. What are the four different types of sub-system project that might be required to get an organization from its present IS state to a better one?

4. How can timing and synchronization requirements in a sub-system be analyzed?

5. What division of a sub-system's processes is suggested by Jacobson's Object-Oriented software engineering method?

6. 'Feasibility appears to be another case of considering physical design before completing analysis.' Is this a valid criticism?

7. In what way does Archiving present a Feasibility problem?

8. What does a 'split' LFT coding in a User Group Access Pattern matrix suggest to the designer?

9. What are the risks of using bottom-up design with Object Classes?

10. What types of software product could be used as the 'glue' in a Component Engineering approach?

11. Why might individual sub-system components have to be tailored in a Cooperative Agreement design approach?

12. What are the arguments for a sub-system coded as F for a user group (in a User Group Access Pattern matrix) running (a) on each user's workstation; (b) on the user group server; and (c) at a central site?

13. In an Object Class Library approach, what control can be applied to ensure that, when new code needs to be hacked, it is wrapped properly for re-use?

14. What are the differences between Object Class Library and Application-Type matching?

15. Application-Type matching appears to depend heavily on the effectiveness of the Software Component Librarian. Discuss the qualifications needed to fill this role.

16. How could a designer possibly make use of Software Agents?

17. Give examples of the likely interfaces that would need to be standardized for Mr A's Associate Cooperation system.

18. The BOPC has decided that it needs a new high-priority Market Intelligence System. What characteristics does this have? What are the critical feasibility checks? How might it be designed in detail?

19. The Detox Production Control system will capture summary data from the Process Control systems' processors every 15 minutes (more often on demand). What style of sub-system would be used to feed back Sales information into Production Control?

20. Assume Casa Electrica's existing Inventory systems are not driven by goods sold at the checkouts, but are based on daily physical counting of what is on the shelves. What would be the nature of the project to make them able to interwork with Electric House systems?

21. Discuss the design program for developing the COP's student email service. Do you think that tailorable components are likely to be available?

22. What development approach would be appropriate for the NEPB system to upload Inspectors' reports and to download the Inspection Schedule and messages for the next day?

ASSIGNMENT TASK

For your chosen case study, pick one system or sub-system which involves frequent user interfacing and data from multiple sites.

A1. Describe how the system's feasibility could be checked.

A2. Decide on the LFT entries for each User Group involved in the system.

A3. Choose a detailed design approach and justify your choice.

A4. Write a short summary report indicating how the software for each part of the system should be acquired and implemented.

FURTHER READING

Gradwell, D. (1992) *Objected-Oriented Requirements Capture and Analysis*, British National Conference on Databases (BNCOD), Aberdeen.

Goodwin, C. (1993) Divine distribution (article on electronic software distribution). *Computing (UK)*, 23 Sep.

Jacobson, I. *et al.* (1992) *Object-Oriented Software Engineering: A Use Case Driven Approach*, Addison-Wesley, Wokingham, pp 215–230.

McKie, S. (1995) Software agents: application intelligence goes undercover. *DBMS Magazine*, Apr.

Newing, R. (1995) Open sesame (article on object-oriented client/server systems). *Management Consultancy (UK)*, Mar.

Rumbaugh, J. *et al.* (1991) *Object-Oriented Modelling and Design*, Prentice Hall, Englewood Cliffs, NJ.

19 Outsourcing the design

19.1 WHY CONTRACT-OUT DESIGN TASKS?

The main rationale for outsourcing design is that, with the increasing breadth of knowledge required to develop distributed systems, only the very biggest organizations and groups can afford to maintain an in-house team with all the skills needed. Furthermore, the need for any one skill is going to show very violent peaks and troughs. Figure 19.1 presents a series of graphs showing how the demand for staff with a particular skill could peak at different times within a series of development tasks. The hope of being able to smooth demand to avoid such peaks is a very faint one.

With a centralized architecture, once the hardware and software platform has been acquired, an organization is often able to 'do the rest themselves'. With distributed architectures, and with more 'incremental' projects, the balance of the development work which has to be done shows a significant change. New tasks include:

- more frequent changes to the data communications infrastructure
- more interfacing with existing systems (internal or external).

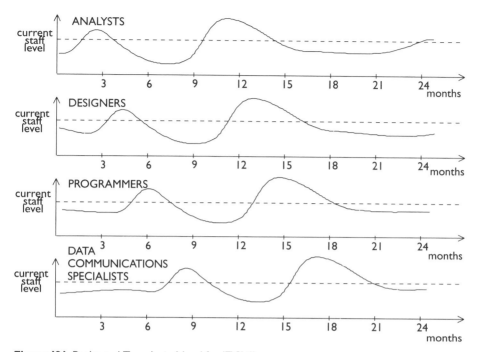

Figure 19.1 Peaks and Troughs in Need for IT Skills.

A frequent problem with outsourcing is that many suppliers or contractors are wedded – emotionally if not commercially – to a particular architectural approach or to a specific manufacturer's solution. This is true not just of the suppliers themselves: even independent consultancies are looking for implementation work for their junior staff, and they want the client to choose a design which leads to implementation which can use the skills of their own staff.

19.1.1 *The use of 'design by call for tender'*

Because of this last problem, an approach has grown up of using the tendering process itself to assist with design tasks. In this approach, the statement of requirements is deliberately kept open enough not to presuppose any particular architectural solution. The tenderers must propose their own architecture and design so as to best meet the requirement (Figure 19.2).

The motivation for the purchasing organization is that, if they prepare well and set up good evaluation criteria, they can get someone else to do the hard work of proposing design alternatives and evaluating their performance and cost.

The motivation for the tenderer is the prospect of lucrative implementation contracts using their own preferred approach. Tenderers who find themselves

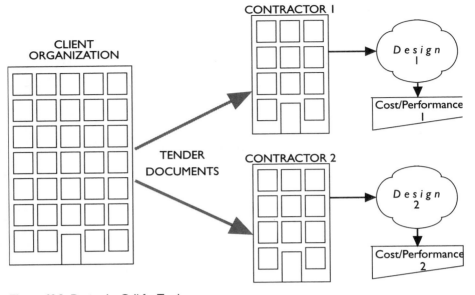

Figure 19.2 Design by Call for Tender.

losing too many of such tendering situations may need to reposition themselves for future competition.

The problem in the past is that clients have not been smart enough to play this game, or it has been a seller's market – too many clients chasing too few contractors meant that the contractors sometimes got away with murder!

19.2 EXAMPLES OF CONTRACTS THAT MIGHT BE PLACED

Both simple outsourcing of design and 'design by call for tender' can be considered at any of the stages described in the foregoing chapters:

- IS strategic planning
- technical architecture design
- network design
- shared data design
- individual system/sub-system design.

19.2.1 *IS strategic planning contracts*

Many organizations hope to buy a 'no obligation' ISP study, but contractors are often keen to use an ISP study as an opener to a long run of contracts. Some contractors have a business objective of selling software, in particular CASE tools. This software may require a particular architecture (e.g. centralized) or even a particular hardware/software supplier (e.g. IBM), thus limiting the options further into the development cycle.

Organizations often use a contractor where they already have good relations with the leading consultants or partners – so at least they have some comeback in the case of problems. This probably explains the high market share held by the Accountancy-oriented consultancies in this market!

Design by call for tender is not really appropriate at this stage, except to evaluate different tenderers' approaches to overall development methodology.

19.2.2 *Technical architecture design contracts*

Many ISP methodologies are relatively weak on Technical Architecture, and may stop short once they have identified the potential areas for future IS. If this is the case, then Technical Architecture planning can be separately outsourced.

This is also an ideal area for design by tendering, since the results of ISP work can be included in the tender specification. Given sufficient incentive, potential contractors may be willing to show their ability to appreciate the different architectural alternatives which could support the ISP requirements.

19.2.3 *Network design contracts*

In the area of Networks, the main profit that can be made by many contractors is in the actual provision of equipment, perhaps using traditional OEM discounts and re-badging mark-ups. If the purchaser is up-to-date enough on communications equipment and usage prices, the organization can get a yardstick on how much the contractors stand to gain in this way!

There is therefore a good incentive for the supplier to offer a network design as part of his or her tender. The tender typically includes three main sub-stages:

- network configuration, design and management consultancy
- network provision and installation
- network facilities management.

Use of an independent consultant may also be an option for Network Design, but such individuals sometimes have their own irrational- or even outdated- preferences.

19.2.4 *Shared data design contracts*

Within user organizations, skills in Distributed Database, Client/Server and Replication are in very short supply at the time of writing. The supplier has to be sure that prospective contractors are competent to do the work, and the purchaser should ask for references or samples of the prospective contractors' previous relevant work.

The incentive for the contractor to propose design ideas here depends on the prospect of a 'bread and butter' implementation contract. Large contractors with analysts and programmers to 'sell' may be keener than the independents with the specialist knowledge.

19.2.5 *Individual system/sub-system design contracts*

Very similar comments apply to those for Shared Data Design. The danger with the large contractors is that they may need to sell their programmers, rather than to engineer your system at the cheapest cost by gluing re-usable components together with a 4GL.

19.3 TYPES OF SUPPLIER OR CONTRACTOR

The effectiveness of outsourcing Design will depend on the type of supplier or contractor. The most likely possibilities are:

- Management Consultancy Companies
- Information Technology Consultancy Companies
- Hardware/Software Suppliers
- Network Suppliers
- Systems Contractors
- Facilities Management Contractors
- Independent Consultants.

A few comments on the suitability of each of these types appear below.

19.3.1 *Management consultancy companies*

This means the 'Big Six' – or whatever the number is after the latest merger – plus a number of smaller, but possibly more specialist, companies. The Big Six includes groups like Coopers & Lybrand, Arthur Andersen, Price Waterhouse, Ernst & Young, Peat Marwick, Deloittes, who operate in most countries. Most of their national offices will have IT teams, and some will have data communications specialists. These companies have an incentive to charge out their staff's time to customers at high rates. They may not be keen to provide free design advice in tenders unless there is a good prospect of follow-on business.

These firms employ a lot of bright, work-motivated young graduates. They follow formal methodologies which they keep up-to-date by having worldwide research centers. They often work with CASE tools, either their own or ones they have licensed.

An advantage of using these companies is that if there is some unforeseen difficulty, an expert can usually be flown in to sort the problem out and the company will put in a lot of effort to ensure that no 'bad smells' are left behind.

19.3.2 *Information technology consultancy companies*

This is a large class of companies which are not quite such 'household names' as the Big Six above or the suppliers below. Often they overlap with the System Contractors, but these are addressed later since they can have different objectives. Examples of firms specializing as consultants are TI Software, James Martin & Co, Learmonth & Burchett, BIS and Computer Consultants Australia.

These firms are like Management Consultancies in that billable hours are a large element in their revenue. They also have house methodologies, CASE tools and other package software which they may be interested in selling. They do not have the ties with big Accountancy, Auditing and General Management Consultancy practices though.

Their technical knowledge in the area of Distributed Systems is often more up-to-date than that of Management Consultancies. Some companies may specialize as 'System Integrators' which may be the most suitable for Cooperative Systems and Component Engineering. The problem is that firms come and go, and some newer companies may not have acquired the same level of stability as others. However, they may be very keen to propose designs in tenders if this can help them win new business.

19.3.3 *Established hardware and software suppliers*

The time has passed when IBM, Digital and other hardware suppliers were the only font of all wisdom, but user organizations still often turn to these companies for reliable design consultancy. Nowadays software suppliers such as Oracle also offer consultancy help. So far the giants of the PC end of the market, such as Microsoft, do not appear to have entered the design outsourcing market.

Most of these companies now make money by selling software. Hardware is largely a commodity that can be swapped in or out – there are 'plug compatibles' for everything from IBM mainframes through Unix machines to PCs and even Apples. Services are an increasing part of revenue but are usually subordinate. Therefore these companies may be prepared to offer a certain amount of design in a tender if there are prospects of selling software or some other product.

As design contractors these firms may be of less value, since they are probably geared to optimizing for their own flagship products.

19.3.4 *Network suppliers*

This group covers several heterogeneous sub-types:

- common carriers (e.g. national 'Telecom' companies and competitors)
- communications box and cable vendors (e.g. Cisco, Wellfleet, Newbridge, Bay Networks)
- LAN system suppliers (e.g. Novell, Banyan)
- VAN suppliers (e.g. Frame Relay specialists, Tymnet, GEIS, Compuserve).

All of these are in business to sell specific products or services. As with the vendors above, they are less useful as design contractors before the Network Design stage, but are ideal once you have already decided to use their products.

As potential 'designers by tender' they can be used strategically by picking candidates who can represent the different technical architectures. Some telecommunication companies are so large and dispersed that they may even provide you with different architectures depending on who you speak to.

19.3.5 *Systems contractors*

These are large outfits who make money by delivering IT solutions. They sometimes work on a billable hours basis, but more often they work to a fixed-price contract – somewhat like a house builder. The price may include a big original equipment manufacturer (OEM) element as their task is to integrate as well as just build. Some of these companies also offer 'System Integrator' services as mentioned above in section 19.3.2.

Like the Management Consultancies, they have to keep a horde of junior staff busy. They also have central groups of experts, but are often structured along 'industry' lines. Good examples are EDS, Logica, SEMA and Computer Sciences Corporation.

These firms can often be used for fairly unbiased design advice, since the only prejudice towards technical solutions is often the size of the OEM discounts they get from suppliers. Staff are also technically competent and up-to-date. What they do always have half an eye on is follow-on work, whether it is for more consulting or an implementation contract. This makes them a good choice for design by tender.

19.3.6 *Facilities management contractors*

Often overlapping with the above, these are firms which will take the whole risk away from you and run your IS for a fee. If you don't mind paying this high fee, you need not be so bothered about the actual design. Your only use of tendering is to see who can do the whole job cheaper. A possible disadvantage is that once you have chosen a Facilities Management contractor, it is not so easy to dismiss them and appoint another contractor in their place.

19.3.7 *Independent consultants*

This covers small firms and individuals, ranging from management consultancy to product-specific technical work. The problem is to identify suitable consultants that have adequate up-to-date skills to actually contribute to your needs. Sometimes using consultants who belong to 'cooperatives' is worthwhile, since if they don't know the answers personally, they can bring in one of their associates.

By character many of these consultants do tend to be genuinely disinterested in who gets the follow-on business, but many are none the less stuck in time-warps about what Technical Architecture should be like for all situations.

Adequately qualified consultants are ideal for contracted design studies, and may be prepared to do some design at the tender stage, but they cannot usually afford to do too much design for free.

19.4 THE CONTRACTING PROCESS

19.4.1 *Deciding on the bidding list*

The main things to ensure are competence (by references and demonstrations of previous work) and a good appreciation of alternative approaches. For example, it is not sound to ask only Management Consultancies to bid for an ISP study – a Purchaser should try an IT Consultancy and a Systems Contractor as well. Many organizations are constrained in their bidding lists, these having been preset by some bureaucrats who make general rules for all situations.

For architectures and network designs, the Purchaser may need to check potential bidders beforehand to see who is likely to cover the different alternatives.

19.4.2 *Form and contents of tender documents*

The main additional task, when calling for tenders to do a design contract, is to ensure that it is clear what will be considered an acceptable design. A full list of the parameters should be given, and benchmarks for evaluation should be stated. Since we are talking about distributed systems, the 'boundary conditions', i.e. the need to interface with surrounding hardware, software or systems, are a vital part of the contract terms, so is adherence to common standards.

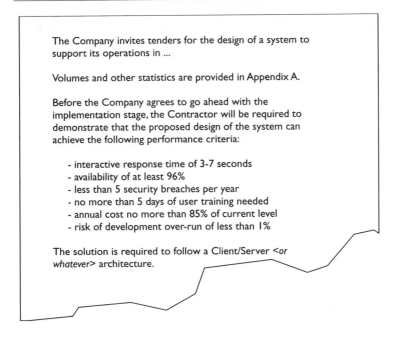

The Company invites tenders for the design of a system to support its operations in ...

Volumes and other statistics are provided in Appendix A.

Before the Company agrees to go ahead with the implementation stage, the Contractor will be required to demonstrate that the proposed design of the system can achieve the following performance criteria:

- interactive response time of 3-7 seconds
- availability of at least 96%
- less than 5 security breaches per year
- no more than 5 days of user training needed
- annual cost no more than 85% of current level
- risk of development over-run of less than 1%

The solution is required to follow a Client/Server <*or whatever*> architecture.

Figure 19.3 Example Wording for a 'Fixed Architecture' Tender Invitation.

If the Purchaser is looking for 'design by tender' then it is always best to come clean, and to say that the contract will be awarded based on evaluation of the architectural approach (or network design, or whatever) that is proposed.

Example wording for two typical cases is shown in Figures 19.3 and 19.4.

19.4.3 *Procedure to be observed*

This may be determined by the purchasing company's rules, but it is the norm for computer-related contracts to have some form of bidders' conference. However, if you are going for design by tender, this may not be appropriate, as bidders may compare notes and be influenced by what other people say at the conference.

Additional procedures may involve appointing a second bidder as quality controller for the work done by the winner, or appointing parallel contracts (obviously this should be stated up front). This could also apply to the possibility of an in-house alternative based on ideas gained in the tendering – also using one tenderer's ideas but with another bidder doing the job.

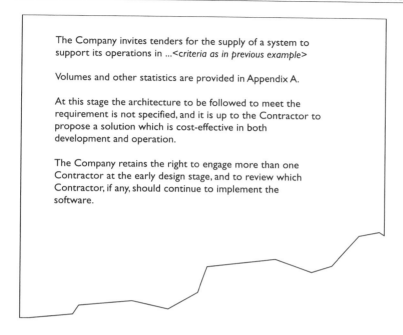

The Company invites tenders for the supply of a system to support its operations in ...*<criteria as in previous example>*

Volumes and other statistics are provided in Appendix A.

At this stage the architecture to be followed to meet the requirement is not specified, and it is up to the Contractor to propose a solution which is cost-effective in both development and operation.

The Company retains the right to engage more than one Contractor at the early design stage, and to review which Contractor, if any, should continue to implement the software.

Figure 19.4 Example Wording for a 'Design by Tender' Invitation.

Another right the Purchaser may want to exercise is to appoint a main contractor and to require that others contractors, whose knowledge and experience are valuable but could not for other reasons be awarded the main contract, should be included as sub-contractors in addition to those nominated by the winning main contractor.

19.4.4 *Evaluating tenders*

As well as weighting the stated parameters in each submission, the Purchaser should also make a further subjective assessment of each bid, for overall technical competence, likely ability to conduct the current and possible subsequent projects, and risk of problems on contract.

Where the technical design is beyond the level of competence of any staff in the Purchasing organization, the Purchaser may also appoint a further contractor to help evaluate the tenders – 'set a thief to catch a thief' as one organization described it.

19.5 WORKING WITH SUPPLIERS OR CONTRACTORS

This is an almost inescapable part of developing any Distributed or Cooperative IS nowadays, but not one where much wisdom is available. Contractors' styles vary so much, from the 'always on site and sometimes in your hair' to the 'doing it mostly at their place: hardly ever see them – who knows what they'll deliver and when' style.

In our experience it works best if you insist on regular progress meetings at which milestones are set, results are clearly measured and objectives for the next period are clearly stated.

19.5.1 *Goals and measurable objectives*

The goals and objectives used, apart from those concerned simply with adhering to the project plan, should be closely tied to those of the overall IS project, of which the contractors' role should be counted as just a part. The temptation to refer to the project as 'The XXXX Project', where XXXX is the name of your main contractor, should be resisted!

19.5.2 *Reviewing and terminating*

A suggested cycle of activities is illustrated in Figure 19.5. A full review should be allowed for under certain eventualities, for example if people feel that things are getting off track, taking too long or costing too much. There will also be major check points built into the project plan.

Towards the end a major 'pre-acceptance review' is desirable, to clarify what acceptance tests will be executed and how integration with other systems will be established. This review will include planning the termination of the project.

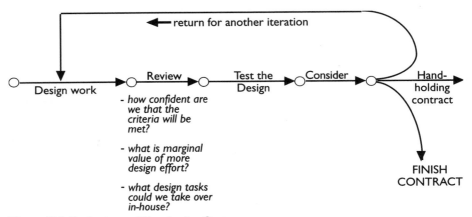

Figure 19.5 Reviewing and Terminating Contracts.

User organizations are often very reluctant to terminate supplier or contractor contracts – hand-holding is often felt necessary. However, this should be discussed up front as part of the 'maintenance cost' parameter. Of course contractors are equally keen to maintain the umbilical cord as it is so much easier for them to get 'return business'.

19.6 OPPORTUNITIES FOR CONTRACTING OUT IN THE CASE STUDIES

19.6.1 Mr A

Mr A certainly has no resources for in-house developments. He is likely to look for an Independent Consultant to check general plans and to deliver the Associate Cooperation system.

19.6.2 Bay Organic Produce Cooperative

The cooperative will have to engage a Contractor to design its Network and build its Database and Systems. A small local software house would seem best.

19.6.3 Detox Pharmaceuticals

Detox clearly has internal IT staff, but their knowledge is possibly out of date. It should do its best to 'up-skill', but it will still need outside experts. Design of the Network could be helped by competitive tender, with the carrot of further work guiding project development for the winner. Unless Detox has very rich sponsors, however, it may not be able to afford the 'Big Six'. Local consultants may have limited experience, so it should look for joint proposals between Western European contractors and local firms. Another possibility is to bring in appropriately skilled Independent Consultants into a scratch team but with an experienced Project Leader. There is a risk of not being able to get rid of the contractors, so definite end-points need to be set.

19.6.4 Electric House

There will be a strong internal team in the US, but skills in Casa Electrica may be very variable between countries. It seems likely that a team of Electric House IT experts will need to travel as internal contractors to oversee the changes. However, management may wish to counter-balance this with an Independent

Consultant to ensure that the current Electric House architecture does not become inappropriately 'set in concrete'. There is likely to be a round of tendering for new configurations in the most important Latin American countries.

19.6.5 *Commonwealth Open Polytechnic*

The internal teams developing the registration and timetabling systems may not have sufficient skills to design an effective network. Competitive tendering for the Email system may be worthwhile. The VOD and Multimedia work may also need specialist design contracts.

19.6.6 *National Environmental Protection Board*

There seems a good case for bringing in contractors early to work from Information Strategy Planning (ISP) onwards. If the country's finances are good, a reputable practice (Big Six or ISP specialists) would be appropriate. The Board might consider requiring the inclusion of additional sub-contractors for Network Design. The need for in-house IT staff is not likely to be high once the initial developments are completed, so most of the once-off design work might justifiably be contracted out.

19.7 EXERCISES

1. What are the main risks in outsourcing design work?

2. Why does so much more work get contracted out in distributed systems development, compared with single-site systems?

3. Describe a situation in which 'design by call for tender' could be a worthwhile policy.

4. Discuss the motivation for a contracting firm to be involved in 'design by call for tender'.

5. 'Consultants specializing in ISP and BPR charge into organizations with a fixed mindset and trample roughshod over the carefully evolved interworking practices.' Is this fair comment, and if so, is it good or bad?

6. How would you suggest managing a contractor of the 'hardly ever see them' variety?

7. Do you think that the Bay Organic Produce Cooperative should consider a Facilities Management contract?

8. In the Casa Electrica interfacing and conversion projects, discuss the relative merits of using (a) Electric House internal consultants; (b) local IT staff; and (c) local contractors.

9. Assuming you are the Computer Support Director at the COP, how would you cope with the risks involved in the VOD and 'Remote Tutorials via Video-conferencing' projects?

10. If the NEPC were to go for a Facilities Management contract, what people from its own staff should be involved and in what roles?

Assignment task

Select a design area from your chosen case study where you feel that the organization's in-house staff levels and skills may be insufficient to achieve an effective design within the desired timescale. How would you word the key parts of your invitation to tender?

Further reading

Massey, J. (1995) Telecommunications (article on skills and contract opportunities). *Computer Contractor (UK)*, 3 Feb.

Glossary of terms

ACID
Atomicity, Consistency, Isolation, Durability – the four basic requirements of a correct TP system.

ACK
Positive acknowledgment. In Data Communications, generally a single-character code sent by the receiver of a message to the sender to indicate a successful transmission.

AD
Application Development – an acronym used in longer acronyms and names – *see* AD/Cycle.

AD/Cycle
An IS development methodology initiative started in the late 1980s by IBM and its chosen partners, in which the 'toolbox' to be used for development was given a certain structure, interfaces were defined, and conformant products nominated.

Agent
In a distributed system, an autonomous software component. The implication is that an agent provides a service or facility for some other components. Often an agent is an intermediary in a communication, taking some well-defined action such as passing a message on, but someTimes an agent simply responds to queries.

Allocation Schema
In a distributed database, a description of how fragments are allocated to sites for storage.

Alphabet
An agreed collection of **symbols**.

Analog Transmission (someTimes Analogue)
Passing a signal from sender to receiver by means of continuous waves, similar to sound. The implication is that, in order to communicate digital data, the waves have to be **modulated** so as to signify 1s and 0s. With the exception of the public telephone network, most data communications can now be regarded as **digital transmission** (even though analog transmission may be hidden underneath) and so the term is now used less frequently.

Anisochronous
Another term for **Asynchronous**.

ANSI
American National Standards Institute – a standards setting body in the USA.

API
Application Program(ming) Interface – set of program calls which are made available with a piece of software acting in a **server** role, for the use of requestor programs (**clients**) wishing to invoke services.

APPC
Advanced Program-to-Program Communication – an IBM protocol for peer-to-peer communication between programs. *See also* LU6.2.

Appletalk
In this book, a term to describe the built-in **LAN** features of Apple Macintosh computers, which are now offered under a variety of names such as LocalTalk, LocalNet, etc. Physically operates over **UTP** at speeds up to 384 Kbps.

Application Generator
A piece of software that converts formal design specifications and/or **4GL** into an executable program.

Application Type Structure
A hybrid structure of generic software elements, which form a pattern against which the availability of re-usable software components or sub-systems can be evaluated.

ARA
Appletalk Remote Access. A commercial product from Apple allowing a user to dial into a LAN and operate as if part of that LAN.

Architecture
In information systems generally, a specification of overall style aimed at ensuring consistency, inter-operability, and potential for growth.
   In data communications, a **network architecture** identifies all relevant standards and the circumstances under which they might be used, and often includes specific products or familes of products. Generally void of implementation specifics, such as proper names or physical layout.

In distributed systems, a **technical architecture** incorporates both a network architecture and identification of application products, a pattern of supply; a **requirements** or **business systems architecture** identifies a pattern of demand.

ARQ
Automatic Repeat Request. In Data Communications, a frame sent by the recipient of a message to the sender to request a repeat of a transmission.

ASCII
The *de facto* standard code for text in data communications, each character being represented by seven bits (but often packed out to eight so as to be an **octet**).

Asynchronous
Strictly, not aligned in time. Contrasted with **Synchronous**.
(1) traditionally used to describe data communication where each character is framed and transmitted separately, hence **asynchronous transmission**.
(2) can also be used to describe a process performed outside the main line of control of a computer program, e.g. printing or **message passing**.

ATM
Asynchronous Transfer Mode – high-speed (typically 2 Mbps and upwards) version of packet switching which employs fixed length frames of 53 octets. It is suitable for long-distance **LAN–LAN** interconnection, amongst other things.

Attentuation
Loss of amplitude (i.e. signal strength) as a signal passes through a **medium**. If the attentuation is too great then a receiver will not be able to distinguish the signal from background noise.

Bandwidth
Strictly speaking, the range of frequencies which can be carried successfully on a channel. For example 300–3400 Hz is the bandwidth of a typical voice telephone channel. Bandwidth is detemined by the physical properties of the medium and the design of transmitter and receiver; and, in its turn, determines the channel capacity (expressed in bits per second (**bps**)).

Bandwidth Manager
A device which enables the simultaneous operation of multiple connections comprising data, voice and video over a single channel or cable. See also **Multiplexor**.

Baseband
Strictly, direct **digital transmission** such that the entire bandwidth of the medium is used during a transmission. In **LANs**, it is generally associated with the Ethernet/ IEEE802.3 style, where the channel capacity is 10 Mbps.

Batch Processing
A form of computer processing, very common in earlier years, where input data is assembled into batches before being processed. The opposite to **on-line**.

B-ISDN
Broadband **ISDN**, i.e. ISDN providing higher data rates through use of such methods as **ATM**.

Bit rate
See **data rate**.

Block
See **Frame**.

Body
See **Data Body**.

BPR, BPI
Business Process Re-engineering (Redesign) or Business Process Improvement. A theme in management consultancy started in the early 1990s in response to widespread need for business restructuring caused by recession and sharper competition. Involves rethinking the structure of business processes, often resulting in the elimination of unnecessary intermediate steps. Impacts on IS design because it creates a moving target for the IS to support.

bps
Bits per second, a measure of channel capacity. Often scaled as kbps (kilo or thousands of bits per second), Mbps (mega or millions of bits per second), or Gbps (giga or thousand millions of bits per second). N.B. although 1 Mbps is 1 000 000 bits per second, 1 megabyte (**MB**) is 1 048 576 bytes or 8 388 608 bits.

Bridge
In **LANs**, a node that interconnects two sub-networks which share a common data link layer standard. Because they are designed not to transfer frames unnecessarily between sub-networks, bridges are generally used to isolate two busy segments of a LAN from one another, thus improving performance on each segment.

Bridgeware
Software used temporarily to allow two different systems to interwork during a period when the new system has only partly replaced the old one.

Broadband
Strictly, describes a system of multi-channel links using analog transmission, typically using coaxial cable (coax). In **LANs**, most often associated with the token bus style, but someTimes with cabling carrying both LAN and video transmissions simultaneously.

Brouter
Combined **bridge** and **router**.

Browse
To read a computer file by moving forward and backward.

Browser
In the context of Internet, a client program which enables the user to traverse remote data in an *ad hoc* fashion. See also **surfing**.

Bursty
Describes a pattern of traffic on a link where messages come in short, sharp bursts, e.g. on-line transactions or query requests. Opposite to **stream**.

Bus
In **LANs**, a **topology** where a number of nodes share a single **channel**. The implication is that the nodes are, in some sense, peers.

Byte
Normally, a set of eight bits (see **octet**) used to represent one text character or symbol using a code. Commonly used as a unit measure for data storage.

CAD
Computer Aided Design. A class of applications in which the computer maintains a database of design decisions and supports the user in changing and inspecting the design, usually through a GUI.

CAM (CIM)
Computer Automated (or Integrated) Manufacturing. A class of applications in which manufacturing robots and sensors are controlled by a computer program, to meet a manufacturing plan.

Capacity
The maximum **data rate** (measured in **bps**) that can be carried by a channel.

Carrier
The basic waveform which is to be **modulated** in analog transmission.

CASE, CASE Tool
Computer Aided (or Assisted) Software (or Systems) Engineering. A type of software product which supports part or all of a development methodology. Typically, a CASE tool provides electronic workbenches for developing models of processes, data or objects, and for linking and cross-checking the different models.

CBT
Computer Based Training. A class of applications in which the user's learning process is mediated by the computer system.

CCITT

Comité Consultatif International des Telephones et Telegraphes – an international standards-setting body for transnational telecommunications. Now part of the International Telecommunications Union (ITU).

CD-ROM

Compact Disk – Read Only Memory. A widespread data storage medium, used for large collections of data which are not subject to frequent change.

Cell

A **frame** where the total size is fixed, typically at 48 octets data body + 5 octets header as in ATM.

Cellular Data

A low-speed wireless public data network service, analogous to cellular telephone services.

Cell Relay

See **ATM**. Not to be confused with data transmission over **cellular** links.

Channel

Strictly, a single path through a **medium**. In this book, the term encompasses transmitter, path and receiver, as these must be matched.

Checkpoint

A point in the execution of a computer program when all details of the state of the system that are held in computer memory are copied to some non-volatile data storage for recovery purposes. A checkpoint should be at a 'quiet point', i.e. when no transactions are in process.

CICS

Customer Information and Control System – a **TP Monitor** marketed by **IBM**.

CIO

Chief Information Officer. More generally, the most senior person in an organization with responsibility for information, IS and computers.

Circuit

Strictly, a contiguous arrangement of wires and switches though which an electric current can be passed. Little used now, but see also **line**, **circuit-switching**.

Circuit-switching

Traditionally, a process whereby a switch such as a telephone exchange is used to establish a connection between two stations for a period of time. Although most modern switches do not allow physical **circuits** to be established, circuit-switching is still used to describe any system which requires dialing to establish a connection.

Class, Classes

See **Object Class**.

Class Library
A collection of previously coded and re-usable **Object Classes**.

Client
The processor or software program or object which takes the 'requestor' role at a given level of a **Client/Server** hierarchy.

Client/Server
An architecture where the elements form a hierarchy of 'requestor'-to-'server' relationships. The elements may be processors, or alternatively software programs or objects. In **LANs**, it typically implies a relationship between stations on a network whereby (many) client stations use (a few) server stations to extend their capabilities.

Close-Coupled, Tightly-Coupled
Two or more computer processors that behave to the user as if they constituted a single processor.

Cluster, Clustering
(1) A group of processors in a tight (**close-coupled**) **processor-pool** architecture.
(2) A grouping of processes and **entity types** (or **object types**) which have similar behavior patterns.

Codasyl
Conference On Data SYstems Languages – a joint industry group set up to propose computer language standards, and whose major product is COBOL. In this book, the term is used to describe a class of DBMS which conform to this group's proposals for a network-structured Data Description Language (DDL).

Code
In data communications, representation of each letter of the common alphabet (A–Z, 0–9,..., etc.) together with various special characters, by a sequence of more basic symbols, generally a sequence of bits. Often the sequences are of constant length. See also **ASCII**.

Commit
Recognition that a transaction has completed successfully, generally initiating the writing of a log record to allow recovery to a consistent state.

Common Carrier
A supplier of long-distance data communications services, generally a public telecommunications company.

Compression
Filtering of redundant symbols from a message prior to its being sent, so as to reduce the overall length of the message and thus the time taken for transmission.

Conceptual Schema
An analysis-level description of data that could be stored in a database, providing a potential consensus for different user views.

Concurrency
Simultaneous similar activity, especially when a number of users perform transactions at the same time in a **TP** system.

Connection
A logical path through which data can be passed. Often a connection may pass through many agents, nodes and channels.

Connectionless
Of a service (data transfer, **protocol**, or **standard**), implies that each envelope sent stands on its own and the sender and recipient operate asynchronously. Opposite of connection-oriented (where the route, actual switched circuit, or session number carries forward from one envelope to the next).

Connection-oriented
Of **packet switching** systems and **LAN** protocols, implies that once a message transmission has been requested, a routing is decided on and all frames/packets follow this route. Also called **virtual circuit**.

Convergence
In data communications, the trend whereby data, voice and video will be integrated into a common form of digital transmission.

Cool Processing
Computer processing where a requesting sub-process is prepared to accept delays in queuing for resources. The opposite to **Hot** processing.

Cooperative System, Cooperative Information System
An information system comprising a number of autonomous elements which each do certain tasks which contribute to the whole system, and which pass requests and data between each other according to some agreed pattern.

CORBA
Common Object Request Broker Architecture, a software approach proposed by the Object Management Group, a jointly funded corporation. The purpose is to allow linking between separate **object oriented** (and non-object oriented) systems so that one object can send messages invoking the operations of another object, regardless of the fact that the objects may be distributed and heterogeneous. It uses a system of software stubs similar to **DCE**. It sets a standard for commercial implementations, one of which is **OpenDoc**.

CRUD
Create Read Update Delete – an acronym for the four basic operations on data. Used in matrices of **entity types** against processes (functions) in **Information Engineering** methodologies.

CSF
Critical Success Factor – something such that, if it does not go well, will cause a person or organization to fall short of their objectives.

CSMA/CD
Carrier Sense Multiple Access/Collision Detection. A MAC protocol for sharing a medium, used in Ethernet LANs.

CUABS (LFT)
A variant of **CRUD** used in this book. Delete is merged with Update, and Read is divided into *ad hoc*, Browse and Summarize. LFT indicates a Local, Foreign or Total access pattern. This variant gives more clues to distribution decisions than simple CRUD.

Data Base (Database, DB)
An integrated and managed collection of shareable data, usually held in a computer system.

Data Body
The part of a frame which is not interpreted by the sending or receiving agent; it is simply passed on by them for some other agent or application.

Data Communications Network
See **Network**.

Data Dictionary (DD)
An ancillary **database** which stores details of the structure of the main database. This is often managed by a Data Dictionary System (**DDS**).

Datagram
See **connectionless**.

Data Rate
A number of **bps**, either what a channel needs to carry to support the **traffic**, or that represents the **capacity** of the channel.

Data Warehouse (Data Warehousing)
A collection of data, derived and extracted from the primary **databases** used by one or more **TP** systems, which is re-packaged for the benefit of groups of users.

DBA
Database Administrator. A role in the organization with the responsibility of managing a shared database.

DBMS
DataBase Management System – the piece of software which facilitates the operation of a **database**.

DC

Data Communications.

(1) The technical foundation for distributed computer systems, being concerned with data transmission media, hardware, software and protocols. Alternatively, the use of any electronic communication system to transmit digital data rather than analog signals or voice.

(2) That part of a **DBMS** which provides **TP Monitor** facilities, e.g. **IMS/DC**.

DCE

(1) Data Circuit-terminating Equipment. In modern practice, it is a term used in standards for a device or agent through which a user may interface with a network or data communications service. Generally, the term is applied to the node of a public data network to which one might directly connect.

(2) Distributed Computing Environment – a Technical **Architecture** proposed by the Open Software Foundation (**OSF**).

DDBMS

Distributed **DBMS**.

DDE

Dynamic Data Exchange – a mechanism for allowing different applications to work cooperatively within a Microsoft Windows environment.

DDS

Data Dictionary System – piece of software which manages data structure definitions, and possibly other information, that is held in a **Data Dictionary**.

DEC

Digital Equipment Corporation – a major supplier of minicomputers, PCs, networks and software.

Dedicated

In data communications, a medium or channel permanently connecting just two stations. Otherwise, a processor which performs a single process or a restricted range of processes.

DES

Data Encryption Standard – a standard advocated by the US Government and other groups.

Destination, Destination Address

That portion of a **frame** which the receiver uses to recognize that it is the intended recipient. Generally, agents in each different layer of the **OSI** framework can and will use different addressing systems. For example, a station on an **Ethernet LAN** would have a unique Ethernet address used by the data link layer, a unique **IP** address used by the network layer, and a unique **SMTP** (mail) address used by the application layer.

DFD
Data Flow Diagram – a convention used in **structured** methodologies to show the interaction between processes and the data which they use as input and output.

DIA
Document Interchange Architecture – a standard for preserving document content and layout under transmission between heterogeneous computer systems.

Dial-up
Accessing a service by **circuit-switching**, involving the setting up of a circuit by dialing the number (usually a telephone number) of the target station.

Digital Transmission
Conveying discrete signals directly on a medium. Generally, the alphabet would consist of 0 and 1, with each signified by the presence of a particular voltage, current or level of light. See also **Analog Transmission**.

Distributed System, Distributed Information System
An information system which is located on more than one station. The implication is that the stations themselves are not in the one room, although this is not essential.

DOS
Disk Operating System. Unless otherwise stated, this refers to Microsoft MS-DOS or its derivatives.

Download
The copying of data from a processor into the storage area of another processor nearer to the user. The source processor is typically 'higher' in a hierarchy, e.g. a **server** or **mainframe**.

Downsizing
Replacement of large (and usually expensive) processors, such as **mainframes**, by one or more smaller and cheaper processors which can do the same job.

DSOM
Distributed Systems Object Model, IBM's **CORBA**-compliant object-linking approach.

DTE
Data Terminal Equipment – a user's physical device that is to be connected to the network or data communications service. See also **DCE**.

DTU
See **NTU**.

Dumb
Describes a DTE that is not programmable, typically a terminal that is totally under the control of a **mainframe**. Opposite to **intelligent**.

Duplex
A connection capable of simultaneous bi-directional communication, generally by employing two channels through one medium.

EBCDIC
IBM's standard eight-bit code for text.

EDI
Electronic Data Interchange.

EFTPOS
Electronic Funds Transfer at Point of Sale. Used to describe any terminal device with this capability.

Electronic Conferencing
A message-passing application where unstructured text messages are posted from originating user site to a shared site which stores a structured collection of the messages received (e.g. into topics and threads). Other users can then read and comment on earlier messages.

Email, Electronic Mail
A message-passing application where unstructured text messages are posted from a sending user site to a computer-stored mailbox at a site accessible to the recipient user.

Embedding
See Encapsulation.

Encapsulation
In data communications, placing an **envelope** around a message to create a **frame**.

Encryption
Disguising the content of a message by transforming its bit patterns, but in such a way that the transformation can be reversed by an authorized recipient.

Entity/Relationship model
A convention for describing a **conceptual schema**, in which **entity types** and **relationships** between them are recognized.

Entity type
A modeling construct used to group 'things' of interest to an organization (which are to be represented in a **conceptual schema**) which have similar data structure and behavior.

Envelope
A sequence of bits placed around a message that will enable a series of agents or devices to reliably forward the message to its intended destination. Often includes attention-gaining bit patterns, such as a destination address, and error detection and correction bit patterns.

ESD
Electronic Software Distribution – an approach to delivering new software – and new versions of existing software – to multiple users on a network.

Ethernet
A type of **LAN** which uses a logical bus topology and the CSMA/CD protocol for sharing the communications medium. Similar to the IEEE802.3 standard.

Export Schema
In a distributed database, a description of the structure of data that one site is prepared to let other sites have access to.

Factor Table
A heuristic (rule of thumb) approach, derived from management consultancy, to evaluate a decision when several different factors have to be taken into account, without any clear overall measure to be optimized.

Fail-soft
The design principle of ensuring that the failure of one component in a system does not prevent other components from continuing to perform at least part of the system's function.

FDDI
Fiber Distributed Data Interface – a LAN standard making use of **optical fibre** in a dual-ring topology and operating at 100 Mbps.

FDM
Frequency Division Multiplexing, i.e. sharing of channel capacity by dividing the frequency range into separate bands, each band then forming an independent sub-channel.

Federal
An architecture in which autonomous units join together in providing a single information system to a group of users.

FEP
Front End Processor. A computer, separate from a main computer, which acts as a 'receptionist' for messages to and from the main computer, which is then left with more capacity to carry out its primary functions.

Firewall
A mechanism involving hardware and/or software, to control message flow between interconnected networks, primarily for the purpose of security.

First Cut
A design solution which is worked out by transforming the model of the requirement according to a set of standard 'default' rules, and which is then improved upon iteratively.

Fragmentation Schema
In a distributed database, a description of the ways in which data could be partitioned, e.g. by occurrences (horizontal) or by attributes (vertical).

Frame
A sequence of bits incorporating both **envelope** and message **body**. If the sequence is always the same length then it is generally called a **cell**; if the message body has a defined maximum length then it is generally called a **packet**. Traditionally, byte-oriented frames used in synchronous transmission were called **blocks** or **messages**.

Frame Relay
A form of fast **packet switching** based on the use of **PVCs**. In the protocol the size of the envelope is minimized to reduce overheads, leaving error checking to the sending and receiving applications.

FTAM
File Transfer Access and Management. An OSI standard for File Transfer.

FTP
File Transfer Protocol – a standard for making files available for **downloading** by remote users, typically over the Internet. Uploading may also be supported, depending on the user's local software.

Full-duplex
See **Duplex**.

Functional Distribution
Distribution of processing and/or data to multiple processors on the basis of the type of processing.

Gateway
In data communications, an agent, station, or node that links two comparable but dissimilar network services so as to allow interoperability. A Gateway could connect two networks with dissimilar architectures, or two application support services from differing vendors (e.g. electronic mail). Generally belongs to the higher layers of the **OSI** framework, i.e. Transport and above.

In more general terms, any means of linking two heterogeneous computer systems, e.g. different **DBMS**.

Gbps
See **bps**.

Geographical Distribution
Distribution of processing and/or data to multiple processors on the basis of the geographic area or site to which the data pertains.

Global Schema
A single description of the structure of all the data held in a distributed or federal database.

Gopher
A public-domain distributed system running over the Internet, which allows users to make selections from remote menus and hence access remote data.

Groupware
Software which supports cooperative work on a shared set of files or databases.

GSM
Group Système Mobile. A standard, originating in Europe, for digital cellular mobile telephones.

GUI
Graphical User Interface – a form of **presentation** in which users interact with graphical objects displayed on a screen, rather than typing in text commands.

Half-duplex
A connection capable of bi-directional communication, but where only one direction can be used at a time, i.e. the flow of data will alternate (in direction) through a single channel. SomeTimes called **two-way alternate**. See also **duplex**.

Header
That portion of the envelope or frame which precedes the message body.

Hierarchical
Any architecture or structure in which some elements are subordinate to, or controlled by, other elements. Opposite to **peer-to-peer**.

Hinge Entity Type
An **entity type** which is accessed by a high proportion of the processes in a matrix, as used in **Information Engineering**.

Hot Processing
Computer processing where a requesting sub-process wishes to get a response as instantaneously as possible, and wants to minimize delays involved in queuing for resources. The opposite of **Cool processing**.

HTC
Hybrid Transmission Circuit – a combination of fiber-optic and coaxial-cable technologies used to provide very high data rates to private homes.

HTML (and HTTP)
Hypertext Markup Language. A language used to format text with embedded graphics and cross-references, as used on the World Wide Web. HTTP (Hypertext Transfer Protocol) is the associated protocol.

Hub
The central or common node in a star topology. The implication is that the node is passive and is simply there as a junction.

Hybrid
Made up of mixed topologies. Most networks are hybrid.

IBM
International Business Machines Corporation, the largest vendor of computer products and services.

IEEE
Institute of Electrical and Electronic Engineers – a standards-setting body.

IGES
Initial Graphics Exchange Standard. An OSI protocol for Graphical Data Transfer.

IMS
Information Management System – a **DBMS** marketed by **IBM** since the mid-1970s.

Inference Engine
A software server which combines defined rules and known facts in order to output their logical conclusion.

Information Provider
A company or organization that makes data available for public access, either commercially or in the public domain.

Ingres (CA-Ingres)
A commercially-marketed relational DBMS.

Intelligent
Describes a **DTE** that is programmable. It can operate as either a limited or a totally autonomous processor. Opposite to **dumb**.

Internal Schema
A description of the structure of the data in a database as defined in a **DBMS**, including physical optimization such as indexing.

Internetworking
The process of connecting two dissimilar networks, generally two whose ownership is different.

Interface
The common boundary between two systems. In data communications, the boundary between two components such as a device or a cable.

Internet
A worldwide federation of networks that agree to exchange messages using the **IP** standard.

Information Engineering (IE)

A school of methodologies proposed by James Martin in a series of textbooks. The methodologies grew out of a diverse collection of earlier techniques. They were developed through James Martin associated companies such as DDI, DMW, JMA and Knowledgeware, and through **CASE** tools such as IEF, IEW and ADW. Many other companies also use methodologies which are largely IE-based.

Information Need

A statement of what one or several users need in the way of information to do their job.

IP

Internet Protocol – the **datagram switching protocol** used between networks on the Internet.

IRDS

Information Resource Directory Standards. An international standards programme geared to allowing interchange of Data Dictionary and other information repository or directory data.

IS

Information Systems. Systems where the chief commodity being handled is information. Alternatively, computer and clerical systems where the data processed is used to provide information to human users.

ISDN

Integrated Services Digital Network, a public **circuit-switched** communications network based on digital technology, as opposed to the analog approach used in the **PSTN**.

ISDN-H

A high-speed ISDN channel, such as is needed to carry **videoconferencing** traffic, which is faster than the standard B channel of 64 kbps.

ISO

International Standards Organization – a standards-setting body.

Isochronous

See **Synchronous**.

ISP (ISSP, SISP)

Information Strategy Plan(ning), IS Strategic Planning, Strategic IS Planning – a preliminary phase in **Information Engineering** and other methodologies, where business needs and directions are studied to set priorities for IS developments.

IT

Information Technology. The collection of equipment, tools and methods, often connected with electronic computers, that can provide the infrastructure for Information Systems.

JAD
Joint Application Development. An IS development methodology which allows for formal user staff involvement in the development process.

JAVA
A portable interpreted programming language for distributed applications. JAVA is used to enhance WWW pages, allowing the addition of dynamic features such as animation.

JIT
Production and distribution systems in which work-in-progress and inventory are kept to a minimum, by manufacturing products as late as possible but still in time to reach the customer as requested.

kbps
See **bps**.

LAN
Local Area Network – a network confined to a single location of an organization. Generally high speed, greater than1 Mbps.

LAP, LAP-B, LAP-D
Link Access Protocol (Balanced, D-channel). Alternative protocols at the Data Link Layer.

Layer
One of seven strata of the **ISO OSI** framework. See **OSI Framework**.

Level
See **Layer**.

Leased Line, Leased Circuit
A permanent physical circuit between two sites, leased from a telecommunications provider.

LFT Analysis
In this book, used to denote the use of the coding system for access patterns described under **CUABS**.

Line
Traditionally, a single circuit which connects one or more outlying stations to a hub. Now, that which connects one or more distant stations to a hub, whether a true circuit or not.

Link
(1) In hardware, the physical data communications connection between two stations.
(2) In software, a reference in a program indicating the need for a request for services from another program, possibly running on a remote processor.

LLC
Logical Link Control. The upper (link control) half of the Data Link Layer (layer 2) of the OSI profile.

Lock, Locking
A mechanism that prevents two transactions interacting incorrectly, by allowing only one transaction at a time to use certain resources, usually items or groups of data.

Lotus
A software company, the first to gain a large market in PC spreadsheet software with its 1-2-3 package. More recently successful with its Notes groupware/workflow package, where it has recently become allied with **IBM**.

LP
Linear Programming. A form of computer algorithm used to optimize large-scale allocation problems.

LU6.2
Logical Unit 6.2. A protocol proposed by **IBM** for **peer-to-peer RPC**.

Mainframe
A large, shared computer, typically with hundreds or thousands of terminals connected to it.

MAC
Media Access Control. The lower half of the Data Link Layer (layer 2) of the OSI profile, concerned with the method of sharing the communications medium.

MAN
Metropolitan Area Network – a public data network within a metropolitan area.

MAP
Manufacturing Automation Profile – a family of standards for open systems interconnection in manufacturing operations.

Mbps
See **bps**.

Medium, Media
In distributed systems, the physical material through which a disturbance or signal can be propagated at near-light speeds. Typical media are twisted-pair cable, coaxial cable, fiber-optic cable and air/free space.

Mesh
Topology where there is more than one route between any two nodes. Generally used to increase reliability.

Message
A piece of data, consisting of a sequence of bits or octets, sent by one element in a computer system to another element in the same or a different system.

Messaging
A subset of computer applications in which the major element is the sending of messages between different stations, and where the task of interpreting and acting on messages is left to the autonomous control of the receiving stations.

Message Passing
A style of distributed or cooperative processing where requests are expressed as asynchronous messages, rather than synchronous calls to programs, as with **RPCs**.

Microsoft
The largest-selling computer software vendor at the time of writing, marketing such packages as MS-DOS, Word, Excel, Works, Access.

Microwave
A transmission system using certain frequency ranges across air or space. May be **terrestrial** (i.e. directly between tower or rooftop receivers/transmitters) or via **satellite**.

Middleware
Software which assists in the interworking of two different hardware/software environments, typically between **clients** and **servers**.

MIPS
Millions of instructions per second, a common measure of computer processing power.

MMS
Manufacturing Message Specification. A protocol used for messages in a CAM (or CIM) system; part of the MAP standards profile.

Mode
In Data Communications, strictly, the physical manner in which a signal propagates through a medium. In this book, the matched set of **transmitter, medium, channel**, and **receiver** needed to transfer data between two devices.

Modem
MOdulator/DEModulator – an **NIU** used to connect a station to other computer systems over analog, voice-grade (telephone) lines. Typically offers channel speeds of up to 28 800 bps.

Modulation
In data communications, the process by which a digital pattern is carried on an analog transmission. Generally this is accomplished by varying the carrier waveform in frequency, amplitude, phase, or a combination of these.

MOMA
Message Oriented Middleware Association. An organization seeking to advance, and propose standards for, the use of a Message Passing approach to communication between different programs.

MOSC
Mission, Objectives, Strategies, Critical Success Factors – an acronym used in this book to indicate use of a formal statement of business strategy in these terms (also Goals and Action Plans) as a driver of the need for IS. Based on **Information Engineering** methodologies.

MPEG
Motion Picture Experts Group. Denotes a set of standards for compression and multiplexing of digitally-encoded video, audio and other data.

MTA
Message Transfer Agent. Generally, a server that handles electronic mailboxes for a number of users. In the X.400 standards, the units between which the main protocol applies.

MTBF
Mean Time Between Failures – a widely used measure of system reliability.

MTTR
Mean Time To Repair – another widely used measure used in calculating system availability.

Multi-drop, Multi-point
A channel connecting more than two devices. Examples are a **bus**, or a **leased line** which branches to multiple terminals.

Multiplexing, Multiplexor
Simultaneous operation of multiple independent data connections on a single channel or cable, often as a means of reducing costs. Not often used over short distances.

Multi-tasking
Sharing of a single processor by two or more concurrent tasks.

NAK
Negative Acknowledgement. In Data Communications, a single-character code sent by the receiver of a message to the sender to indicate an unsuccessful transmission.

Natural (Business) System, Natural Data Store
Groupings of processes and/or **entity types** identified by **clustering** in an **Information Engineering** methodology.

Network
That part, or sub-system, of a distributed information system which is concerned purely with the movement of data between stations. Includes both hardware and software but, in this book, applications software is specifically excluded.

Network Application
Applications software which is specifically designed to work in a distributed fashion. Typical examples are **distributed DBMS, email** systems and **groupware**.

Network-aware
Describes an application package which will operate satisfactorily over a network. Such an application will be tolerant of partial or total network outages.

Network Operating System
An Operating System which resides on a computer which acts as a server on a network, and which controls shared use of resources on that computer.

NIAM
Natural language (or Nijssen's) Information Analysis Method – a type of model for a **Conceptual Schema** in which all data is represented as elementary facts.

NIU
Network interface unit – the physical device (containing transmitter and receiver) that connects a station to a data communications **medium**, such as cabling. An NIU may be located inside the station ('inboard', e.g. a **LAN** card in a PC) or alongside ('outboard', e.g. a **modem**).

Normal Distribution
One of the standard statistical distributions, commonly exhibited when the measured events arise from a combination of a number of independent processes.

Novell
Currently the largest vendor of **LAN** software, in particular the NetWare server-based LAN **OS**, and NetWare Lite for **peer-to-peer**.

NT
Network Termination. A term used particularly with ISDN, to describe the device at a user's station. See also NTU.

NTU
A network interface unit (**NIU**) installed on the customer's premises by a common carrier, often forming a port to a public data network operated by that common carrier. A packet-switched network might be an example of such a service.

Object
A software element which reacts only to a set of defined service requests. The current status of an object is held in a data structure which is kept private, and which is not accessible to other objects except through the defined services.

Object Class, Object Type
A group of **objects** with the same structure and behavior. The **Class** denotes the collection; the **Type** defines the rules for belonging to the Class.

Object Oriented (OO)
Development of a system in terms of **Objects** (see above). Can apply at any or all of the Analysis, Design or Programming stages.

OCR
Optical Character Recognition. The process of analyzing image data and recognizing text and other characters; a type of software that performs this function.

Octet
A sequence of eight bits.

ODA
Office Document Architecture. An OSI protocol for exchanging document content and layout between heterogeneous computer systems.

ODAPI
Open DataBase **API** – a **protocol** proposed by Apple, Borland and others to allow **SQL**-based requests from **clients** to relational database **servers**.

ODBC
Open DataBase Connectivity – a protocol proposed by Microsoft to allow **SQL**-based requests from **clients** to relational database **servers**.

OEM
Original Equipment Manufacturer – traditionally, a company that buys hardware from manufacturers at a discount and sells-on to clients packaged configurations at a marked-up price.

OLE
Object Linking and Embedding – a software mechanism proposed by Microsoft to allow better linkage between different software products, based on an **object oriented** approach. Several non-Microsoft vendors have announced OLE-compliant products.

OLTP
On-line Transaction Processing.

On-line Processing
A form of computer processing in which input data is processed as soon as it is available. The opposite to **batch** processing.

OO
Object-Oriented. Describes any software or method in which all structure and procedure is modelled in terms of autonomous objects that interact.

OOA
Object-Oriented Analysis.

OOD
Object-Oriented Design.

OOP
Objected-Oriented Programming. Computer programming that follows the OO model.

OOPL
Object-Oriented Programming Language.

OPAC
On-line Public Access Catalog. A database representing the catalog of material held by one or more libraries, available for public searching by dial-up or other networking.

OpenDoc
A consortium of software suppliers who have proposed **CORBA**-compliant object linking facilities.

Oracle
A widely used, commercially marketed relational **DBMS**. Also the name of the company selling the DBMS and related software products.

OS, Operating System
The underlying software controlling all communication with a computer.

OSF
Open Software Foundation, an industry group working towards improved interconnectivity of Unix-based software. Proposers of **DCE** (2).

OSI
Open Systems Interconnection – the process of interconnecting, or the ability to interconnect, hardware and software systems from differing vendors. Often used to refer to the architecture and family of standards defined by **ISO**.

OSI Architecture, OSI Framework, OSI Model
A generic design for Open Systems Interconnection, in which desirable network/ data communications functionality is categorized into seven **layers**. Each layer provides services to the layer above, with physical transmission in the bottom layer and applications support in the top layer.

PABX, PBX
Use of an automated, internal telephone exchange to provide a **LAN** service. Modems are required and data rates may be limited compared with true LANs.

Packet
A sophisticated type of **frame** in which the message body has a defined maximum length, with comprehensive routing and error-checking data in the **envelope**.

Packet Switching, Packet-switched
Use of a mesh network to transmit messages in **packets**.

PAD
Packet Assembler/Disassembler – a facility for connecting simple, character-oriented terminals to a packet-switched network. Characters from a terminal are assembled into packets to be sent through the network; packets arriving for a terminal are disassembled into characters before being passed to the terminal.

Parallel
In data communications, the use of several channels simultaneously to transmit a group of symbols (generally bits) so as to increase the effective capacity of the connection. For example, eight channels are used to transmit an octet in one eighth of the time it would take to transmit the octet over a single channel.

In distributed processing, parallel refers to the subdivision of a task between a number of individual processors, each of which will carry out its part of the work simultaneously.

Partitioning
In data distribution, the combination of **fragmentation** and allocation of fragments to processors.

PC
Personal Computer. An autonomous computer generally used by a single user.

PCTE
Portable Common Tools Environment. A protocol for exchanging design and Data Dictionary information.

Peer-to-peer
An architecture or structure in which no one element is subordinate to, or controlled by, another element. Opposite to **hierarchical**.

Plug-in
A modular approach to design of hardware or software where certain components can be removed and replaced by improved components which can utilize the same hardware connections or software links.

Point-to-point
A connection comprising exactly two nodes and a channel or line connecting them.

PPP
Point-to-point protocol. See SLIP.

Poisson Distribution
One of the standard statistical distributions, commonly exhibited by infrequently occurring events of a single type.

Port
That part of a **hub** or active device to which a line might be connected.

Posix
An industry group working towards better Unix standards and improved interconnectivity of Unix-based software.

Presentation
The interface to a system as seen by human users.

Primary Value Chain
That **value chain** in an organization which represents the main line of business in serving the organization's customers.

Profile
A family of interrelated standards which provide services across several layers of the **OSI Framework**.

Process Control
A type of computer application in which the system monitors and adjusts an automatic real-world process, using sensors, switches and robots. Normally operates in **real-time**.

Processor Pool
A **technical architecture** in which several, usually similar, processors are organized to process a single workload.

Protocol
An agreement which determines the procedure for establishing inter-operation between two parts of a computer system. In data communications, a protocol specifies the types of message structure or frames which may be sent in either direction, and the sequence in which these may occur.

PSS
Packet Switching Service – a common example of a **VAN** service: provided by most national telecommunications companies and available to users on a national or international basis.

PSTN
Public Switched Telephone Network, i.e. the traditional telephone system.

PVC
Permanent Virtual Circuit – a **virtual circuit** which is available to the user 24 hours a day.

Queue Discipline
The rules governing the behavior of objects forced to wait in a queue, which may affect the distribution of delay Times.

RAD
Rapid Application Development – a modification to **Information Engineering** and other methodologies in which the multiple stages are fast-tracked, typically by involving user group staff directly and using prototyping techniques.

RAEW
Responsibility, Authority, Expertise, Work – a coding system used in matrices showing organizational aspects of IS strategy plans in **Information Engineering** and other methodologies.

RDA
Remote Data (or Database) Access. An OSI standard for access to remote databases.

RDBMS
See **Relational DBMS**.

Real-time
A form of computer processing in which responses to data inputs are produced in the same Timescale as the real-world events being described. Real-time will always be **on-line**, but some applications (e.g. process control) have much more stringent response requirements than others.

Receiver
In data communications, a device that recovers sequences of bits from disturbances in the medium. A **transmitter** is a device that generates disturbances in the medium corresponding to sequences of bits. A **transceiver** combines both functions.

Redundancy, Redundant
The use of excess resources to improve performance or reliability. Redundant bits in a frame are used to detect and correct errors; redundant connections are used to maintain service when a single connection fails. In databases, redundant data can be used to give faster local query response and to provide backup in case part of the database goes down.

Relational DBMS
A **DBMS** following the Relational Model, in which all data resides in simple tables and tables are related only by matching designated columns.

Relationship
In an **entity/relationship model** a relationship is a construct used to describe a pattern of association between **entity types**.

Remote Access
In distributed systems, this refers to using a switched network to access a local service from a distant location. An example might be using a **dial-up** connection to participate in **LAN** activity.

Remote Procedure Call (RPC)
A style of distributed or cooperative processing where requests are expressed as invocations of the target process, rather than by sending asynchronous messages.

Repeater
A node which replicates an incoming transmission onto all other ports, bit by bit. Generally, such a device would be regarded as passive at all **OSI layers** above the Physical Layer. However, modern repeaters are also capable of active participation in a network management system.

Replication
A design option in which more than one processor holds the same data or performs the same processing. Similar to **Redundancy** in a data design context.

Ring
In **LANs**, a ring is a **topology** where a number of nodes are each connected to just two neighboring nodes by point-to-point channels, so as to form a loop. The implication is that the nodes are, in some sense, peers. Often associated with **token-passing** as in, for example, a **token ring**.

Router
A node capable of deciding, for a frame received on one port, which other port and destination address should be used for onward transmission. Often, routers are used to improve reliability because of their ability to manage redundant paths and their ability to screen out unwanted traffic. Distinguished from a **switch** primarily by its ability to rewrite destination addresses.

RPC
See **Remote Procedure Call**.

RPG
Report Program Generator. A programming language, still widely used on some ranges of medium-sized computers, that follows a standard processing pattern.

Schema
A description of the structure of data held in a **database**.

Semi-join
A technique for optimizing query performance in a distributed system, by splitting relational joins into two stages to minimize the volume of data transmitted.

Serial
In data communications, a connection where a single channel is used to send a sequence of symbols (generally bits) one after another.

Server

An element in a computer system, either a computer processor or software program/object, which performs a specified service at the request of other elements.

Shannon–Hartley Law

A formula which, in theory, relates the physical properties of a channel to its maximum data-carrying capacity. Frequently used to show the positive relationship between bandwidth and capacity, and the negative effect of noise.

Shared Line

A line shared by multiple stations. The implication is that some protocol, such as token passing, is necessary to ensure the efficient use of the line. See also Multi-drop.

Simplex

A connection in which data flows in only one direction. Generally, a single channel.

Site

A geographic location at which computer processors may operate.

SLIP/PPP

Serial Line Internet Protocol/Point-to-Point Protocol. Two standards for the transmission of IP datagrams over dial-up or leased lines (SLIP is obsolete and is being replaced by PPP). Often used to extend the Internet to a remote workstation which is **TCP/IP** capable through the **PSTN**.

SMDS

Switched Multimegabit Data Service, a type of fast **packet switching** service.

SMTP

Simple Mail Transfer Protocol. A mail transfer protocol used in the TCP/IP profile.

SNA

Systems Network Architecture, an **architecture** designed by **IBM** to improve the interoperability of IBM products on a network.

SNMP

Simple Network Management Protocol. A protocol for passing network management information, used in the TCP/IP profile.

Software Agents

Intelligent pieces of software which offer generic services that are commonly required in applications.

Source, Source Address

The name of the sender of a frame.

SQL
Structured Query Language, a widely-used standard data language for **relational databases**.

SSM
Soft Systems Methodology, an approach proposed by Checkland and others, which moves the emphasis of Analysis more towards user needs and expectations, generally in qualitative terms and less in 'hard' formats and procedures.

Standard
A formal specification which is intended to facilitate interoperability. In the context of this book, can apply to data communications at many levels, program–program interworking, and human–computer interfaces.

Star
A **topology** in which a central node, the **hub**, is connected point-to-point to a number of other nodes. The implication is that the central node is either dominant, e.g. a computer of some kind, or that it is a passive repeater.

Station
An active node in a network. This means active at the application level in ISO-OSI terms.

STDM
Statistical Time Division Multiplexing, i.e. TDM (see below) in which the length of the time slices is adjusted dynamically to optimize overall throughput.

STP
Shielded Twisted Pair – an upgraded form of 'telephone' cable used in **Token Ring LANs**.

Stream
Describes a pattern of traffic where data is transmitted continuously over a period of time, e.g. file transfer. Opposite to **bursty**.

Structured Methodology
Broadly, any method for developing a computer system that involves creation of formal models of processes and data structures in advance of coding or other implementation. Originally applied more strictly to process modeling in which all processing is grouped into sub-processes which are invoked by – and return control to – higher-level processes (rather than using random transfer of control typified by the GO TO programming construct).

Stub
A piece of program code which enables one application program to run as if the remote programs it wishes to call (or respond to) were in fact running locally.

Surfing
In the context of Internet, serendipitously browsing remote data through a service such as **WWW** or **Gopher**, without any clear idea of what data one might come across or where one will look next after finding it.

Switch
A multi-port node capable of connecting two ports together. Can refer to a private or public telephone exchange or similar line switching device, or to nodes in a **packet switching** network.

Switched
A line or circuit which passes through one or more **switches**, in contrast to a permanent physical circuit.

SWOT
Strengths, Weaknesses, Opportunities and Threats – an acronym used in management consultancy, often adopted in **Information Engineering** and other methodologies.

Sybase
A commercially marketed relational **DBMS**, based on a **client/server** architecture.

Symbol
Basic unit of significance in communication, the unit that is understood by transmitter and receiver. In data communications, generally a '1' or a '0' representing the value of a single bit; but someTimes equivalent to a short sequence of bits.

Synchronous
Strictly, this means 'aligned in time'. Traditionally, synchronous transmission is where both transmitter and receiver agree on a time at which the value of a bit can be read from the channel, and long sequences of bytes can be sent as a continuous stream.

Tandem
Tandem Corporation, a computer supplier specializing in high-availability systems.

TCP/IP
Transmission Control Protocol/Internet Protocol – a multi-layer data communications architecture historically developed through the Unix-using community.

TDM
Time Division Multiplexing, i.e. sharing of channel capacity by dividing the channel time into slices to be used in rotation by each message source that shares the channel.

Telnet
Strictly, a virtual terminal protocol widely used in the Unix world. Also, a program offered publicly by NCSA (National Center for Supercomputing Applications) in USA to allow remote logging in to Unix-based processors from **clients** which may not be Unix-based. Familiarly, as a verb, to log in to a remote computer.

Terminal
A node which interfaces with a human or robotic user, connected to a single channel. Traditionally comprises a simple keyboard and VDU or hard-copy device, incapable of running application programs locally.

Thesaurus
A hierarchy, or more complex structure, of groups of words or phrases with similar meanings.

Thread
(1) In **OLTP**, the execution of a program or sub-program for one particular transaction. Multiple threads may be supported either by multiple program copies or by sharing re-entrant program code. In either case separate storage is needed for each transaction.
(2) In **electronic conferencing**, a set of linked messages within a topic that form a logical sequence, e.g. a series of comments on a previous user's submission.

Token Bus
A **LAN** standard based on **token passing**, bus topology, coaxial cable and frequency-multiplexed analog data transmission, much as used for cable TV.

Token passing
A type of protocol for multiple stations sharing a connection, or multiple nodes sharing a channel where a single frame is continuously passed around in a circular fashion. This frame, the token, is the only vehicle for moving data from one node to another.

Token Ring
A **LAN** standard proposed by IBM based on **token passing**, ring topology and **STP** wiring.

TOP
Technical and Office Protocol. A standards profile often used in conjunction with MAP to integrate office functions with manufacturing.

Topology
A distinctive arrangement of nodes and the channels connecting them. Commonly recognized topologies are the **ring**, **star**, **bus** and **tree**; although most networks comprise a mixture of these.

TP
Transaction Processing (q.v.) or Teleprocessing.

TP Monitor
A piece of software which controls the sharing of computing resources in a high-concurrency multi-user TP system, typically on a **multi-tasking** computer.

TQM
Total Quality Management, a modern management principle developed from methods used in Japanese companies following consultancy by Deming after World War II.

Traffic
The load of data that a link has to carry.

Trailer
Sequence of bits which follows the data body of an envelope or frame, often containing redundant bits which are used to detect and correct errors in the envelope.

Transaction Processing (TP)
An area of computer application in which processing is expressed as simple or complex transactions, each of which may cause a change in the status of the data in the system.

Transfer
A software link under a TP Monitor where the requesting program hands over control to the server program, with no expectation of a return.

Transmission
A pattern of disturbance on a channel as a frame passes from one node to another.

Transmitter, Transceiver
See **receiver**.

Transponder
In data communications, a **transceiver** located on a satellite.

Tree
A topology in which a central node, generally a host computer of some kind, is connected to other nodes by radiating **multi-drop** lines.

Trunk
A circuit or channel which forms part of the backbone of a switched network.

Tunneling
Making a connection through some other, incompatible, connection mechanism by encapsulating the messages so as to disguise their significance. Generally refers to two mechanisms in the same OSI layer.

Turnpike effect
Degradation of network performance as the **traffic data rate** approaches **capacity**, by analogy with the slow crawl experienced on a busy road.

Twisted Pair
A medium comprising two insulated copper wires twisted together throughout their length. Inexpensive and easily installed, but frequently affected by noise from electric motors and the like. Often used for telephone systems.

Unix
A loose, but widely adopted, standard for Operating Systems.

Upload
The copying of data from a processor near to the user into the storage area of another processor, typically one 'higher' in a hierarchy, e.g. from a **client** to a **server** or **mainframe**.

UPS
Uninterruptable Power Supply – a device to ensure computers can continue to run in spite of a temporary loss of the normal electrical power supply.

URL
Universal Resource Locator. The unique name of a 'page' on the World Wide Web, incorporating system name, file name and file transfer protocol.

UTP
Unshielded Twisted Pair – the simplest type of 'telephone' cable.

Value Chain
A management consultancy term used to indicate a sequence of activities carried out by an organization, each of which adds value to the product of a previous activity in the chain.

VAN
Value-Added Network – a public network which offers services over and above simple connections between client stations. An example might be a **packet-switched** network operated by a telephone company.

VAX
A very successful range of minicomputers marketed by DEC.

Videoconferencing
An application where video of each participant in a two (or more) way telephone conversation is transmitted and displayed to the other participant(s).

Virtual circuit
A switched circuit which gives the user the impression of a constant connection for a given period of time. See also **connection-oriented**.

VOD
Video on Demand – a digital video service whereby films are **downloaded** from a remote film library database and decoded to run on video/TV equipment in the home or at the desk top.

VSAM
A file organization marketed by IBM which allows several basic structures, i.e. entry-sequenced, hashed random and indexed (with one or more indexes).

WAIS
A public-domain distributed system running over the Internet, which allows users to make bibliographic searches across multiple remote databases as long as these use the Z39.50 protocol.

WAN
Wide Area Network – a network connecting several remote locations, both within an organization and beyond its boundaries.

Wideband
A medium capable of carrying multiple channels. Typically corresponds to certain types of coaxial cable.

Wireless LAN
A **LAN** which uses air/free space as the medium. Generally uses radio or infrared transmission over short distances.

Workflow
A type of application in which office tasks have to be routed from one user to another to conform to a defined procedure.

World Wide Web (WWW)
A public-domain distributed system running over the Internet, which allows users to follow paths from one document to another using Hypertext links regardless of location.

X.12
A family of **protocols** proposed by **ANSI** for **EDI**.

X.25
The most common **protocol** for connecting to a **PSS**.

X.400
A family of **protocols** proposed by **CCITT** for **message-passing**.

X/Open
A group of Unix suppliers who have proposed a standard **RPC** protocol.

2PC (two-phase commit)
A recovery protocol in which all processors first vote whether a transaction should be committed or aborted. Then if all votes are to commit, all processors are instructed to do so, otherwise they are instructed to abort.

2PL (two-phase locking)
An isolation protocol in which all acquisition of locks needed for a transaction is completed before any locks are released.

4GL

Fourth Generation Language – a language used to specify processing on a computer which offers its user a significantly higher-level interface than a programming language.

10BaseT

A **LAN** cabling and transmission system using star-wired **UTP**.

10Base2

A **LAN** cabling and transmission system using bus-wired thin coaxial cable.

10Base5

A **LAN** cabling and transmission system using bus-wired thick coaxial cable.

100BaseT

A faster form of **LAN** cabling using star-wired **UTP**.

Bibliography

Apple Corporation (1994a) *Apple Open Collaborative Environment*, training manual.

Apple Corporation (1994b) *OpenDoc*, introductory brochure.

Apple Corporation (1994c) *VITAL*, introductory manual.

Atre, S. (1992) *Distributed Databases, Cooperative Processing, & Networks*. McGraw-Hill, New York.

Atre S. and Storer, P. (1995) Weaving your client/server security blanket. *DBMS Magazine*, Feb.

Avison, D. E. and Fitzgerald, G. (1988) *Information Systems Development* Alfred Waller, UK.

Barr, J. (1994) Developing large-scale cross-platform applications, *Cross-Platform Strategies* 1 No 1.

Barry, W. F. (1994) Moving to client/server application development: caveat emptor for management. *NZCS Journal*, Sep.

Barker, R. (1994) Managing open systems now that the glass-house has gone. In *Directions in Databases* (ed. D. Bowers), Springer Verlag, Berlin.

Bartholomew, D. and Caldwell, B. (1995) Top priority loses its lustre (article on BPR). *The Dominion (NZ)*, Mar 27.

Baum, D. (1993) Apple Open Collaboration Environment. *Infoworld*, May.

Bell, D. and Grimson, J. (1992) *Distributed Database Systems*, Addison-Wesley, Reading, MA.

Bennett, K. (1991) OSI tries to shake off 'boring' tag. *Communications News (UK)*, May.

Betz, M. (1994) Inter-operable objects – laying the foundation for distributed object computing. *Dr Dobb's Journal*, Oct.

Black, U. (1993) *Data Communications and Distributed Networks*, 3rd edn. Prentice-Hall, Englewood Cliffs, NJ.

Boehm, B. W. (1988) A spiral model of software development and enhancement. *IEEE Computer*, May.

Booch, G. (1991) *Object Oriented Design with Applications*, Benjamin/Cummings, Redwood City, CA.

British Telecom (1990) *Business Information Services on Telecom Gold*.

Brodie, M. L. (1993) *Interoperable Information Systems*, tutorial notes, VLDB Conference, Dublin, Ireland.

Brodie, M. L. (1994) *Distributed Object Management – a Core Technology for Future Computing*, tutorial notes, EDBT Conference, Cambridge, UK.

Burch, J. G. (1992) *Systems Analysis, Design & Implementation*, Boyd & Fraser, Boston, MA.

Bux, W. (1981) Local Area Networks: A Performance comparison. *IEEE Transactions on Communications*, 29(Oct.), 1465–73.

Byte Magazine (1990) Multiuser Databases, feature, May.

CACI (1994a) *A Quick Look at Comnet III*, introductory brochure.

CACI (1994b) *Modsim III*, advertisement.

Cashin, J. (1993) *Client/Server Technology – The New Direction in Computer Networking*, Computer Technology Research Corporation, South Carolina, USA.

Chappell, C. (1994) The missing link (article on Middleware). *Computing (UK)*, Dec.

Cheswick, W. and Bellovin, S. (1994) *Firewalls and Internet Security: Repelling the Wily Hacker*, Addison-Wesley, Reading, MA.

Chorafas, D. N. (1994) *Beyond LANs – Client/Server Computing*, McGraw-Hill, New York.

Coulouris, G. F. and Dollimore, J. (1988) *Distributed Systems – Concepts and Design*, Addison-Wesley, Reading, MA.

CompuServe (1994) *Introductory Membership*, sales brochure.

Computing (UK) (1994a) Focus on Network Management, magazine supplement, 24 Feb.

Computing (UK) (1994b) Focus on mobile computing, magazine supplement, 31 Mar.

Computing (UK) (1994c) Novell reaffirms faith in OpenDoc, short article, 13 Oct.

Computing (UK) (1995) Focus on electronic data interchange, magazine supplement, 26 Jan.

Constantinidis, V. (1995) *A Critical Analysis of Distributed Database Recovery Protocols*. Proc. 6th Australasian Database Conference, Jan.

Cronin, M. (1993) *Doing Business on the Internet*, Van Nostrand–Reinhold, Princeton, NJ.

Croucher, P. (1990) *Communications and Networks – A Handbook for the First-Time User*, Sigma Press, Wilmslow, UK.

Crowell, D. A. (1994) An introduction to the client/server environment. *IS Audit & Control Journal*, Vol III.

Cullinet Corporation (1983) *IDMS-DC User Manual*.

Darabi and Howard-Healy (1992) *Virtual Private Networks: Market Strategies*, Ovum, London, UK, Jan.

Datamation (1991) Microsoft's client/server challenger.

Date, C. J. (1990) *An Introduction to Database Systems*, Vol 1, 5th edn. Addison-Wesley, Reading, MA.

Dauber, S. M. (1991) Finding fault. *Byte Magazine*, Mar.

Davis, C. K. (1991) Systems analysis for data communications networks at an electric utility. *Journal of Systems Management*, Jul.

Davis, R. (1989) Sharing the wealth. *Byte Magazine*, Sep.

Derfler, F. J., Jnr. (1994) Betting on the dream (article on ISDN). *PC Magazine*, 25 Oct.

Dettmer, R. (1995) Anyhow, anywhere – the rise of open distributed processing. *IEE Review*, Jan.

Digital Equipment Corporation (1992) *Networks Buyer's Guide*, 1992–3 edn, Digital Equipment Corporation, Maynard, MA.

Dordick, H. S. (1989) Telecommunications deregulation in New Zealand: testing the limits of non-regulation. *Columbia Journal of World Business*, **24** No 1.

Dowty Communications Ltd (1991a) *The Pocket Book of Computer Communications*, UK.

Dowty Communications Ltd (1991b) *The CASE Pocket Book*, OSI introductory booklet.

Dudman, J. (1992) Valued client. *Computing (UK)*, 7 May.

Dykman, C. A., Davis, C. K. and Smith, A. W. (1991) Turf wars: managing the implementation of an international electronic mail system. *Journal of Systems Management*, Jul.

Edelstein, H. (1993) Replicating Data. *DBMS Magazine*, Jun.

Edelstein, H. (1994) Unravelling client/server architectures. *DBMS Magazine*, May.

Ferguson, M. (1994a) Parallel database – the shape of things to come. *Database Programming and Design*, Oct.

Ferguson, M. (1994b) Breaking up is hard to do. *Database Programming and Design*, Nov.

Fertuck, L. (1992) *Systems Analysis and Design with CASE Tools*, Brown, Dubuque, IA.

Finkelstein, R. (1995) The new middleware. *DBMS Magazine*, Feb.

Fitzgerald, J. (1993) *Business Data Communications – Basic Concepts, Security and Design*, Wiley, New York, 4th edn.

Gellersen, H.-W. (1993) Graphical design support for DCE applications. *Proc. International DCE Workshop* (ed. A. Schill), Springer-Verlag, Berlin, Oct.

Gilb, T. (1988) *Principles of Software Engineering Management*, Addison-Wesley, Reading, MA.

Glass, L. B. (1990) Building heterogeneous networks. *Byte LAN Supplement*.

Goodwin, C. (1993) Divine distribution (article on electronic software distribution). *Computing (UK)*, 23 Sep.

Goodwin, C. (1995) Standard life (article on open systems standards). *Computing (UK)*, 26 Jan.

Gradwell, D. (1992) *Object-Oriented Requirements Capture and Analysis*, British National Conference on Databases (BNCOD), Aberdeen, UK.

Gray, J. and Reuter, A. (1993) *Transaction Processing*, Morgan Kaufmann, Cambridge, MA.

Gullo, K. (1989) McDonald's ISDN troubled. *Information Week*, 23 Jan.

Hall, J. *Distributed Systems – a European Perspective*. Proc. BCS DMSG Conference, Cambridge, UK.

Halsall, F. (1992) *Data Communications, Computer Networks and Open Systems*, 3rd edn. Addison-Wesley, Reading, MA.

Hammer, M. and Mangurian, G. E. (1987) The changing value of communications technology. *Sloan Management Review*, winter pp 65–71.

Haney, C. (1994a) Client-Server Hype Faces Users' Doubts. *Computing (UK)*, 22 Sep.

Haney, C. (1994b) Database strategies overlook DCE doubts. *Computing (UK)*, 3 Nov.

Hansen, M. and von Halle, B. (1995) Breaking boundaries through worldwide data replication. *Database Programming & Design*, Jan.

Harding, C. and Frangon, G. (1989) Worldwide interchange (article about EDI over X.400). *Connexion (UK)*, 5 Jul.

Hayward, D. (1994) Desktop faces the downside of its own success. *Computing (UK)*, 10 Nov.

Hsiao, D. K. (1990) *Federal Databases and Systems*, tutorial notes, VLDB Conference, Brisbane, Australia.

Hugo, I. (1991) An architecture still open to interpretation. *Computing (UK)*, 31 Oct.

Hugo, I. (1993) Division of labour. *Computing (UK)*, 7 Oct.

Hugo, I. (1994) Breaking the speed limit (article on rapid application development). *Computing (UK)*, 6 Oct.

IBM (1985) *Planning for Distributed Information Systems*, Publication no. GE20-0655-1.

IBM (1988a) *Concepts of Distributed Data*, Publication no. SC26-4417-0, Dec.

IBM (1988b) *Introduction to Distributed Relational Data*, Publication no. GG24-3200-00, Sep.

IBM (1989) Milestones on the way to fully distributed data (sponsored supplement). *DBMS Magazine*.

IBM (1992) *A Guide to Open Enterprise Computing*, publicity poster and simple introduction.

IBM (1993a) *Application Development for Client/Server*, seminar notes.

IBM (1993b) *Managing a World of Difference*, notes from network management seminar.

IBM (1993c) *NetFinity Remote Personal Systems Management*, seminar notes.

IBM (1993d) *Network Computing Today*, seminar notes.

IBM (1993e) *Networking Systems ATM Strategy*, seminar notes, 13 Jul.

IBM (1993f) *Networking Systems Multi-Protocol Extensions*, seminar notes.

IBM (1994) *A Guide to Open Client/Server*, publicity poster, May.

IBM Systems Journal (1988) Special Issue on SAA.

IBM Systems Journal (1992) Special issue on network management.

Inmon, W. H. (1993) *Developing Client/Server Applications*, Wiley, New York.

Jacobson, I., et al. (1992) *Object-Oriented Software Engineering: A Use Case Driven Approach*, Addison-Wesley, Wokingham, UK.

Jacobson I, Ericsson, M. and Jacobson, A. (1994) *The Object Advantage – Business Process Reengineering with Object Methodology*, Addison-Wesley, Reading, MA.

James Martin Associates (1987) *ISP Handbook*, training notes, Ashford, Middx, UK, Apr.

James Martin Associates (1988) *BAA Handbook*, training notes, Ashford, Middx, UK, Jan.

James Martin Associates (1991) *RAD Handbook*, training notes, Ashford, Middx, UK, Jul.

Jones, R. (1995) Challenging the real cost of client-server. *Computing (UK)*, 16 Feb.

Kaiser, J. (1991) Let's get physical, *Byte Magazine*, Mar.

Kanugo, S. (1994) Identity authentication in heterogeneous computer environments: a comparative study for an integrated framework. *Computers and Security*, 13(3), 231–53.

King, J. (1994) Conferences seek to raise EDI awareness. *Computing (UK)*, Mar 31.

King, J. (1994) IBM joins the rate to launch EDI service. *Computing (UK)*.

Kling, R. (1991) Multivalent social relationships in computer supported workplaces. Longer version of paper in *CACM* **34**, Dec.

Knight, J. (1990) *EDI – an Overview*. 2nd Australian Computer Abuse Research Bureau Conference, Gold Coast, Australia, Nov.

König, W. (1994) Distributed information systems in business and management (guest editorial for special issue). *Information Systems* **19** No 8.

Korpi, N. and Taylor, S. (1991) Frame relay goes public. *Datamation*, Nov.

Kosiur, D. (1991) Building a better network. *Macworld*, Nov.

Korzeniowski, P. (1993) Make way for data (article on middleware). *Byte Magazine*, Jun.

Kroenke, D. & Dolan, K. (1988) *Database Processing*, 3rd edn. Science Research Associates, Chicago, IL.

Krol, E. (1992) *The Whole Internet*, O'Reilly & Associates, Sebastopol, CA.

Lam, R. (1992) Four steps to choosing your LAN route. *Computerworld NZ*, Apr.

Langsford, A. and Moffett, J. (1992) *Distributed Systems Management*, Addison-Wesley, Reading, MA.

Laughlan, S. (1994) Vendors take sides on replication issue. *Computing (UK)*, 24 Nov.

Law, A. M. and McComas, M. G. (1994) Simulation software for communications networks: the state of the art. *IEEE Communications Magazine*, Mar.

Layne, R. and Medford, C. J. (1988) McDonald's serves up global ISDN strategy. *Information Week*, 15 Feb.

Lee, D. L. and Lochovsky, F. H. (1985) Text Retrieval Machines, Chapter 14 of *Office Automation* (ed. D. Tsichritzis), Springer Verlag, Berlin.

Lewis, E. G. (1994) Where is computing headed?, *IEEE Journal*, Aug.

Liebenau, J. and Backhouse, J. (1990) *Understanding Information*, Macmillan, London.

Linthicum, D. (1995) Reconsidering message middleware. *DBMS Magazine*, Mar.

Loosley, C. (1994) Performance design: going for gold. *Database Programming & Design*, Nov.

Lübich, H. (1995) *Towards a CSCW Framework for Scientific Cooperation in Europe*, Springer Verlag, Berlin.

Lynch, M. (1994a) Government review represents serious threat to EDI funding. *Computing (UK)*, Aug.

Lynch, M. (1994b) Code crackers publish formula for encryption key on Internet. *Computing (UK)*, 22 Sep.

Lynch, M. (1994c) Electronic shopping to be offered on Internet. *Computing (UK)*, 22 Sep.

Lynch, M. (1994d) Client-server problems fail to discourage users. *Computing (UK)*, 3 Nov.

Lynch, M. (1994e) Safety nets (article on IS security). *Computing (UK)*, 3 Nov.

Lynch, M. (1995) SuperJANET puts ATM service in five colleges. *Computing (UK)*, 16 Feb.

MacMillan, G. (1993) Royal Mail sets the seal on its EDI services range. *Computing (UK)*, 7 Oct.

Manchester, P. (1994) Where's the plumbing? (article on middleware). *iText Magazine (UK)*, 1 No 1.

Mansell-Lewis, E. (1995) Open house (article on data warehousing). *Computing (UK)*, 30 Mar.

Manson, C. and Haugdahl, J. S. (1991) Dynamic and distributed. *Byte Magazine*, Mar.

Marney-Petix, V. (1994) *Business Strategies for the 1990s and ATM (B-ISDN)*, NZ Center for Educational Research, Wellington, Nov.

Marney-Petix, V. and Parker, C. (1995) Who needs 100VGAnyLAN? and Maybe Cat3 UTP? *Network News and Views*, Numidia Press, Jun.

Martin, J. (1990a) *Information Engineering*, Vol. I, Prentice Hall, Englewood Cliffs, NJ.

Martin, J. (1990b) *Information Engineering*, Vol. III, Prentice Hall, Englewood Cliffs, NJ.

Martin, J. (1992) *Strategic Data Planning Methodologies*, Prentice Hall, Englewood Cliffs, NJ.

Massey, J. (1994) Spotlight on Novell. *Computer Contractor (UK)*, 4 Feb.

Massey, J. (1995) Telecommunications (article on skills and contract opportunities). *Computer Contractor (UK)*, 3 Feb.

McClanahan, D. (1992) Preparing your LAN for client/server. *DBMS Magazine*, Nov.

McCusker, T. (1991) The latest in high-speed protocols. *Datamation*, 15 Jan.

McKie, S. (1995) Software agents: application intelligence goes undercover. *DBMS Magazine*, Apr.

Mohan, C. (1993) *High Performance Transaction Processing*, tutorial notes, VLDB Conference.

Morton, M. S. (ed.) (1991) The Corporation of the 1990s, Oxford University Press, Oxford.

Newing, R. (1995) Open sesame (article on object oriented client/server systems). *Management Consultancy (UK)*, Mar.

New Zealand Telecom (1992) *Your Guide to Data Communications* (introductory booklet), Wellington, NZ.

Nijssen, G. and Halpin, T. (1989) *Conceptual Schema and Relational Database Design*, Prentice-Hall, Englewood Cliffs, NJ.

North, K. (1994) Multidatabase development. *DBMS Magazine*, Oct.

Oberweis, A., Scherrer, G. and Stucky, W. (1994) Income/Star: methodology and tools for the development of distributed information systems. *Information Systems* **19**, No 8.

O'Brien, J. (1993) *Management Information Systems: a Managerial End User Perspective*, 2nd Edn, Irwin, Burr Ridge, IL.

Ogdin, C. (1994) *What's significant about Groupware?*, paper at Groupware '94 Conference, Boston, Mar.

Oxborrow, E. A. (1989) *Databases and Database Systems*, 2nd edn, Chartwell-Bratt, UK, Chapter 6.

Özsu, T. (1991) *Distributed Data Management: Unsolved Problems and New Issues*, tutorial notes, VLDB Conference.

Panko, R. (1988) *End User Computing*, Wiley, New York.

Parry, D. (1993) Middle management. *Computing (UK)*, 30 Sep.

Pearson, D. (1994) *State of the Art Client-Server Systems*, Proc. BCS DMSG Conference, Cambridge, UK.

Quinlan, T. (1995) The second generation of client/server. *Database Programming & Design*, May.

Ranum, M. (1995) *Thinking About Firewalls*, Trusted Information Systems Inc. Glenwood, MD.

Retix Corp (1988) *ISO OSI and CCITT Data Communication Standards*, wall poster.

Ricardo, C. (1990) *Database Systems – Principles, Design and Implementation*, Macmillan, New York.

Ricciuti, M. (1991) Universal database access! *Datamation*, 1 Nov.

Riehl, J. (1991) *Data Communication Education – Who Needs It?*, Virginia Commonwealth University School of Business.

Roche, E. (1991) *Telecommunications and Business Strategy*, Dryden Press.

Rumbaugh, J., et al. (1991) Object-Oriented Modelling and Design, Prentice Hall, Englewood Cliffs, NJ.

Sawitzki, G. (1992) The NetWork project: distributed computing on the Macintosh, Parts I and II. *Apple Technical Journal*.

Scales, I. (1995) ATM is dead – long live ATM. *iText Magazine (UK)*, **1** No 1.

Schatz, W. (1988) EDI: putting the muscle in commerce and industry. *Datamation*, 15 Mar.

Schill, A. (ed.) (1993) *DCE – The OSF Distributed Computing Environment*, Springer Verlag, Berlin.

Scott, K. (1991) Parlez-vous TCP/IP?. *Infoworld*, 7 Oct.

Seer Technologies (1993) *Systems Development with Seer·HPS*, publicity brochure.

Sheth, A. (1991) *Federal Database Systems*, tutorial notes, VLDB Conference.

Sheth, A. and Larson, J. (1990) Federated database systems for distributed, heterogeneous and autonomous databases, *ACM Computing Surveys*, 22(3).

Silver, G. and Silver, M. (1991) *Data Communications for Business*, 2nd edn. Boyd and Fraser, Boston, MA.

Sloane, A. (1994) *Computer Communications – Principles and Business Applications*, McGraw-Hill, New York.

Sprague, R. and McNurlin, B. (1993) *Information Systems Management in Practice*, 3rd edn, Prentice-Hall, Englewood Cliffs, NJ.

Spurr, K. *et al.* (eds) (1994) *Software Assistance for Business Re-Engineering*, Wiley, Chichester.

Stallings, W. and van Slyke, R. (1994) *Business Data Communications*, 2nd edn, Macmillan, New York.

Stamper, D. (1994) *Business Data Communications*, 4th edn. Benjamin/Cummings, New York.

Standards Australia and Standards New Zealand (1995) *Interim Exposure Report of the Digital Video Services Task Group*, draft report, Wellington, NZ, Jun.

Stephenson, P. (1991) Mixing and matching LANs, *Byte Magazine*, Mar.

Stevenson, I. and Almeida, A. (1994) *Strategies for LAN Interconnect*, Ovum (UK), Jun.

Stoll, C. (1995) *Silicon Snake Oil*, Doubleday, New York.

Tagg, R. M. (1994) *Distribution of Data and Processing*, BCS DMSG Conference, Cambridge, UK.

Tagg, R. M. (1994) *The Network IS the Database*, internal seminar, Massey University, NZ.

Tandem Inc. (1987) *Introduction to NonStop SQL*, introductory manual, Cupertino, CA.

Tandem (UK) Ltd (1992a) EDI is dead – long live electronic commerce. *Trends* (Tandem UK Magazine), London, UK, Oct.

Tandem (UK) Ltd (1992b) Electronic mail delivered to your laptop (article on EMBARC (Electronic Mail Broadcast to a Roaming Computer)). *Trends* (Tandem UK Magazine), London, UK, Oct.

Tasker, D. (1994) It's how you say it (article on object message passing versus subroutine calling). *Database Programming and Design*, Nov.

Texas Instruments (1991) *A Guide to Information Engineering Using the IEF*, Dallas, TX.

Tozer, E. E. (1987) *Network Management*, public seminar overheads, Pergamon Infotech, Oxford.

Trusted Information Systems Inc (1993) *Internet Firewall Toolkit – An Overview*, seminar notes.

Ullman, E. (1993) Client/server frees data. *Byte Magazine*, Jun.

Unicom Seminars Ltd (1993) *Securing your Information Network: Technical and Legal Issues*, Jun.

Valduriez, P. (1990) *Distributed and Parallel Database Systems*, Tutorial Notes, VLDB Conference.

Van Name, M. L. and Catchings, W. (1989) Serving up data. *Byte Magazine*, Sep.

Vicom Technology Ltd (1993) *Communication and Connection Solutions for the Macintosh*, product literature, Vancouver, BC.

Viehland, D. (1994) *The Growth of Information Services: A Vision of the Future of the Internet in New Zealand*, public seminar notes, Massey University, NZ, Oct.

Viehland, D. (1995) E-mail bonding (article on mail reflectors). *CIO Magazine*, Jun.

Vogler, J. (1994) Networking with DECnet, *Computer Contractor (UK)*, 4 Mar.

Ward, M. (1994) IBM turns spotlight on client-server strategy. *Computing (UK)*, Nov.

Waters, G. and Read, B. (ed.) (1992) *Distributed Databases*, IEE (UK) colloquium, 11 Dec.

White, C. (1995) The key to a data warehouse. *Database Programming and Design*, Feb.

Whitten, J., Bentley, L. and Barlow, V. (1994) *Systems Analysis and Design Methods*, 3rd edn, Irwin, Burr Ridge, IL.

Wigley, J. (1993) Networking for complete beginners (and other articles). *Bits & Bytes (NZ)*, Apr.

Wild, G. A. (1993) Getting a line on telecomms. *Management Consultancy (UK)*, Oct.

Wing Kai Cheng (1993) Distributed object database management systems. *Journal of Object Programming*, Mar–Apr.

Wirfs-Brock, R., Wilkerson, B. and Wiener, L. (1990) *Designing Object-Oriented Software*, Prentice-Hall, Englewood Cliffs, NJ.

Xephon Consultancy Report (1994) *Beyond Client/Server: Cooperative Processing for TP Systems*, London, UK, May.

Youett, C. (1995) Muddleware or middleware? *Computer Contractor (UK)*, 11 Jan.

Zornes, A., Inmon, W., White, C., Hackney, D. and Parker, R. (1995) *Shedding Light on Data Warehousing*, special advertising supplement to unspecified UK magazines, Mar.

Index

Note: page numbers in bold type indicate the main mention, or definition; page numbers prefixed by the letter 'g' indicate glossary page references.